THE VIKING BOOK OF
Poetry
OF THE ENGLISH-SPEAKING WORLD

VOLUME ONE

'Tis with our judgments as our watches, none
Go just alike, yet each believes his own.
In poets as true genius is but rare,
True taste as seldom is the critic's share.

ALEXANDER POPE

REVISED, MID-CENTURY EDITION

THE VIKING BOOK OF

Poetry

OF THE

ENGLISH-SPEAKING WORLD

Edited by Richard Aldington

VOLUME ONE

New York · The Viking Press

The Viking Book of Poetry of the English-Speaking World
Revised, Mid-Century Edition

PUBLISHED IN 1958 BY THE VIKING PRESS, INC.
625 MADISON AVENUE, NEW YORK 22, N. Y.

ORIGINAL ONE-VOLUME EDITION PUBLISHED IN 1941

Note to the Revised, Mid-Century Edition

The additions and revisions in this edition were most kindly
undertaken for me by the editorial staff of The Viking Press,
assisted by Malcolm Cowley, since pressure of work made it
impossible for me to give the time for an adequate revision.
Since no two persons ever think alike or choose alike in
anthology-making, I leave to them all the responsibility and
praise for the alterations and additions from page 1122 on.

RICHARD ALDINGTON

INTRODUCTION

THIS anthology is "general" rather than "personal." By "general" I mean such works as *The Oxford Book of English Verse* and *The Oxford Anthology of English Poetry*. By "personal" I mean anthologies where the compiler puts in only what appeals to his own special taste and ignores popular poems. Aldous Huxley's *Texts and Pretexts* and *The Spirit of Man* by the late Dr. Bridges will at once occur to everybody as examples of the "personal" anthology. The difference between these two types of anthologist is that the "personal" anthologist is on the lookout for unusual or neglected poetry, whereas the "general" anthologist tries to give the best of a period—which in the present case is poetry in the English language. But then the most personal of anthologists, even Mr. Huxley, cannot avoid quoting some poems which other people have heard of; and the most conventional of general anthologists does display a personal taste, even if that taste turns out to be merely timid, academic, and correct.

This book is not a re-shuffling of anthology pieces, but is based on a re-reading of the complete works of the poets quoted and of a good many which were not quoted. Of course, collections have been used, such as *The Oxford Book of Ballads*, Sidgwick and Chambers's useful little selection of medieval lyrics, and Bullen's *Lyrics from the Elizabethan Song-Books*. Other anthologies were used only as a check, and the number of poems added as a result has been surprisingly small.

In a very few cases, a poem is given solely on the authority of an anthologist. There is, for example, Mr. Gilfillan, a mid-Victorian gentleman who, among other activities, published three volumes of *Lesser-Known British Poets*. There I found the anonymous eighteenth-century poem supposed to have been written with a diamond on the window of a London lodginghouse. Mr. Gilfillan doesn't say where he found it, and I have never found anyone who could tell me.

Every "general" anthology must be built round a self-selecting nucleus of universally admired poems. Even if he wanted to do anything so absurd, the "general" anthologist could not omit Spenser's "Epithalamion," Shakespeare's songs

v

and sonnets, "Lycidas," the "Ode to a Nightingale," and scores of other poems which must be included in such a book. Around that nucleus I have collected the less obvious poems, in choosing which there is room for the play of personal taste. This has been done on liberal lines, reaching far back into the past and coming down to include numerous living writers. "English" poetry has been interpreted as "poetry written in the English language" and not poetry written by Englishmen.

Among the advantages resulting from a re-survey of poetry is that even in standard poets the reader may find work that is new to him. Two examples from many—the "Epithalamium" of Richard Crashaw was first printed from MS. in 1924, and the last four lines which now complete Clough's well-known satirical poem "The Latest Decalogue" were not made public until 1936.

This book contains over 1200 poems by about 300 known poets and a considerable number of anonymous writers. But no matter how voluminous an anthology is, it cannot possibly claim to be complete in the sense of being beyond the elementary criticism which is invariably applied to all anthologies: "If A is included, why is B omitted?" All that criticism means is that an anthology is a selection, that selection is a matter of taste, and that people differ in their tastes. The most the anthologist may hope for is that readers will not find too many of their pet aversions included or too many of their favourite pieces omitted.

There is a difference of some importance between an anthology which is academic and historical and one, such as this, which is popular and aesthetic—in the sense that the poems are chosen in the hope of giving pleasure to all people who enjoy poetry for its own sake. The popular anthologist must take into account certain human limitations which his more austere confrere of the academic world very properly disregards. The most important is the fact that for the modern reader without some little specialist training real pleasure in English poetry begins about the early Tudor period, for the simple reason that the poets then began writing an English which is still substantially ours—at any rate, it can be modernized fairly easily, with no particular damage to sense and rhythm.

That takes us back four centuries or more, which is a long

time. And yet such is the antiquity of English poetry that
when Skelton was writing in the days of Henry VIII and
Cardinal Wolsey there was then nearly a thousand years of
it behind him. Among the literatures which succeeded classi-
cal Latin none has greater antiquity than the English. Un-
fortunately, in the course of thirteen or fourteen centuries a
language is apt to change, and Old English poetry (or Anglo-
Saxon poetry) was written at a stage of the language so remote from our own that to all intents and purposes it is a
foreign tongue. If you found somebody who had never read
anything but modern English and put before him a page of
Beowulf or of Caedmon, he would probably strenuously deny
that it is the same language.

Here, for example, are three lines which are said to be
"perhaps among the oldest our language has to show":

> *Hal wes thu, folde, fira modor,*
> *beo thu growende on godes faethme;*
> *fodre gefylled firum to nytte.*

They are a pre-Christian invocation to the Earth goddess, and
are translated by Stopford Brooke:

> *Hale be thou, Earth, Mother of men!*
> *Fruitful be thou in the arms of the god.*
> *Be filled with thy fruit for the fare-need of man!*

But when we come to the Early Transitional English of the
period following the Conquest, the similarity to our own
tongue is at once apparent. These lines from the "Luve Ron"
(Love Rune) of Thomas de Hales were written before 1240:

> *Hwer is Paris and Heleyne*
>   *That weren so bryht and feyre of bleo:*
> *Amadas, Tristram, and Dideyne,*
>   *Yseude and alle theo;*
> *Ector with scharpe meyne*
>   *And Cesar riche of worldes feo?*
> *Heo beoth iglyden ut of the reyne,*
>   *So the schef is of the cleo.*

I have substituted the modern "th" for the obsolete letter,
but even our imaginary person who had never read anything
except modern English would have to admit there were some

words he recognized. And if we jump on about a century and a half to the Middle English of *Piers the Plowman,* the identity is obvious:

> *Pore peple, thi prisoneres, Lord, in the put of myschief,*
> *Comforte tho creatures that moche care suffren,*
> *Thorw derth, thorw drouth, alle her dayes here,*
> *Wo in wynter tymes for wanting of clothes,*
> *And in somer tyme selde soupen to the fulle;*
> *Comforte thi careful, Cryst, in thy ryche!*

If it is explained that "put" means "pit," "moche" "much," "thorw" "through," "her" "their," "selde" "seldom," and "ryche" "kingdom," anyone can understand that passage.

If this early poetry were to be properly illustrated in an anthology, we should have at least to quote from *Beowulf,* "Widsith," "The Wanderer," "The Seafarer," "Deor," and the Christian Saxon poets, Caedmon and Cynewulf. From the post-Conquest epochs of Transitional and Middle English we should have to put in something from Layamon's *Brut,* "The Owl and the Nightingale," "Ormulum," the metrical romances such as *Sir Gawayne and the Grene Knight, Havelok,* and *Guy of Warwick,* the anonymous poem "The Pearl," Robert Mannyng of Brunne, Langland, Lydgate, Occleve, Gower, and of course Chaucer. And we should have to quote from the poets of medieval Scotland, who were quite as gifted as their rivals south of the border but wrote an even more crabbed "Ynglis."

Now, an academic and historical anthology would very properly include specimens of all these and more. But it would be absurd to burden a popular anthology with pages of Old English which most of its readers wouldn't want, or with translations. So I have contented myself with quoting the opening lines of *Beowulf* in the modern version by C. K. Scott-Moncrieff. This "token" extract is given merely as a reminder that there was a flourishing English poetry between the sixth century and the Norman Conquest.

For the Middle English period preceding Chaucer a similar token representation has been adopted. The English school is shown by three exquisite and very well-known anonymous lyrics, and the Scottish school by the equally famous lines on freedom from John Barbour's lengthy poem, *The Bruce.*

There is one Middle English poet who is too important from his humanity, his humour, his mastery of the art, to be passed over with a merely token representation; and he of course is Chaucer. Even though his lines must be accompanied by a glossary I think most readers would not have wished him left out. Yet if there is one negative truth about Chaucer which hardly admits of dispute, it is that we do not value him chiefly or even very highly as a purely lyric poet. He is a great narrative poet, a teller of stories and a brilliant recorder of human character, who gives the first real indication of coming triumphs in the drama and the novel, and one of the most attractive personalities of the Middle Ages. Of course, Chaucer cannot be equalled to Dante in depth, passion, power of intellect, and beauty of expression, but then he had a something the virulent Italian lacked. I think it will be obvious why I have specially emphasized the character sketches in the Prologue to *The Canterbury Tales*.

For the period between Chaucer and Skelton I have gone back to token representation with a handful of lyrics by anonymous authors—a couple of carols, a love song, a mock aubade, and two drinking songs. After Skelton, Dunbar, and Hawes, I give my selection from the ballads and a small group of carols.

There has been controversy about both the date and the possible authorship of the ballads, but it seems to me that they ought to come before the great and expanding achievement of Tudor-Stuart poetry. Obviously many of the texts as we have them come from that and even later periods, but practically no genuine ballads were composed after the end of the fifteenth century. Why not, therefore, quote them at about the time of their fullest expansion, even if the texts are not exactly of that time and in spite of the fact that later and spurious work may be mixed in?

I have never been able to go along with those who think that ballads were written by "the people." Just how do "the people" set about writing a poem? Such a collective enterprise either in a village or in a town seems highly improbable. But I do think the ballads were popular, in the sense that they were composed *for* the people by forgotten poets who most probably were *of* the people. I would also agree that the people made alterations to them, but quite unintentionally,

as they passed by oral tradition from generation to generation. But I doubt whether this collaboration was always an
improvement. For instance, in the early version of "Chevy
Chase" (given here) we find this quatrain:

> For Witherington my heart was woe
> That ever he slain should be:
> For when both his legs were hewn in two
> Yet he kneeled and fought on his knee.

which in the later version becomes:

> For Witherington needs must I wail
> As one in doleful dumps,
> For when his legs were smitten off
> He fought upon the stumps.

I should have liked to give more specimens of the early
Scottish poets. There are passages in their work which I feel
would be greatly appreciated by those who believe that poetry is spoiled by being made too clear. It would be gratifying to be able to include something to please everybody and
I fear that most of this book errs on the side of clarity. But
how about this by William Dunbar?

> Bot fowll, jow-jowrdane-hedit jevellis,
> Cowkin-kenseis, and culroun kewellis;
> Stuffettis, strekouris, and stafische strummellis;
> Wyld haschbaldis, dysouris, dyvouris, drewellis;
> Misgydit memberis of the dewellis . . .

It would be unfair to Gavin Douglas to say that his translation of Vergil is written in the same style, but it is near
enough to make one see why Douglas has been taken up as
the "only translator" of Vergil—I can't say in English, but
in the British Isles.

From the time of Henry VIII onwards the language difficulty disappears, and the anthology becomes comparatively
full. Of course, if you read yourself into any period or into
one of the major poets, it is possible to go on almost indefi-
nitely adding more and more examples. A halt has to be called
somewhere if any proportion is to be kept. But naturally
every anthologist tends to emphasize his own tastes, and I
find that in my case the Tudor-Stuart period comes first.

During the Middle Ages a good deal of English poetry was written by ecclesiastics; some, if not written by the people, came out of the people; and there was a certain amount of Court poetry. The great enemy of all culture is prolonged war and its miseries. At the time of Edward III and Chaucer, English poetry stood high and seemed to have a brilliant future. But when, after the Hundred Years War and the Wars of the Roses, Henry VII found leisure to look around for a poet laureate, he had to pick a Frenchman, as there were apparently no Englishmen available. This gives some idea of the destruction that took place, and the situation was not improved by Henry VIII's suppression of the monasteries.

When English poetry really revived again, in the reign of Elizabeth, it had much to assimilate—the New Learning, the poetry of Renaissance Italy, the French Pléiade, and the Spaniards. As was natural, the assimilation occurred first with Court poets—fine gentlemen who were rich enough to travel and to buy expensive books. Henry VIII's laureate, Skelton, was no doubt a more vigorous poet than either Wyatt or Surrey, yet he seems uncouth and old-fashioned in comparison with them. A generation or so later they were followed by other Court poets—Dyer, Raleigh, Sidney, Brooke.

The greatest, though perhaps not the most read, of these poets is Spenser. His pastorals suffer from a theory of rusticity which makes them sometimes clumsy, and he went archaizing in *The Faery Queen* when he should have done just the opposite. If that enormous suite of tapestry designs in words has grown faded and perhaps a little tedious, few poems have had such lasting and happy effects on later poets. It is surely an achievement to have inspired *The Castle of Indolence* and *Childe Harold's Pilgrimage*. And, although Spenser's sonnets are too closely modelled after French and Italian originals, he made a unique contribution with his two odes, the "Prothalamion" and the "Epithalamion." Everybody drank of that Pierian source, from Shakespeare and Milton to Dryden, to Coleridge, Wordsworth, and Keats, to Arnold and Swinburne.

If Elizabethan poetry had gone no farther than these poets —and we may throw in with them such happy lyrics as Lyly and Lodge, Greene and Peele—the achievement would have been gratifying but not remarkable. After all, much of what they did had already been done on the Continent. Boiardo, Ariosto, and Tasso showed the way for *The Faery Queen*; and one can never be quite sure of any sonnet and lyric of the period that it will not turn out to have an Italian or French original. Spenser translated du Bellay, and Ronsard and his Pléiade were very popular. There is a lyric of Greene's, for instance, which has a French refrain, very much in the manner of the Pléiade:

> *N'oserez-vous, mon bel, mon bel,*
> *N'oserez-vous, mon bel ami?*

There was a learned movement in England—Ascham, Gabriel Harvey, the Countess of Pembroke's efforts to uplift British drama on the lines of Robert Garnier's synthetic Roman tragedies—but luckily it didn't amount to much. The most learned of the Stuart poets, Milton, Donne, and Ben Jonson, managed to hammer their learning into poetry.

The emancipation of Elizabethan poetry came through the stage, as we all know. Here the poet was given that most precious of opportunities, a general and not a specialist audience. When Voltaire came to England he was amazed to see a peer take off his coat and fight ten rounds with a Covent Garden porter to settle a point in dispute. And Voltaire's sixteenth-century predecessor would have been equally amazed to see young nobles from the Court in the same theatre with citizens, prentices, and punks. It was also an advantage for the actors that they were rogues and vagabonds before they were noblemen's servants, so they were spared the upper-class amateur. And though they had to pray for the queen at every performance, that mattered very little, since their poets seldom had to write for her.

All these valuable advantages would have been wasted if there had been nobody to make use of them. Lyly and Peele and Greene and the earlier, forgotten dramatists were all very well, but the man who changed everything and in turn gave Shakespeare his stimulus was Christopher Marlowe. This lewd, atheistic, overweening, bombastic genius worked on the grand scale. He endowed the English stage with his "drumming decasillabons" and showed it how to treat great themes in terms of great poetry.

All Marlowe's greatest writing is in his plays, and it seems

absurd to represent him only by the pretty pastoral, "Come
live with me and be my love." Marlowe's plays are quotable
because they contain passages of splendid rhetoric and lyrical
quality. The same is true of other Tudor-Stuart dramatists,
and while I don't pretend to have given a complete set of
extracts, something like a cross-section will be found. The
one exception is Shakespeare. On the one hand, his songs and
sonnets are sufficient to show his commanding position in
English literature; and, on the other, I found that to quote
the plays adequately I should need an impossibly large number of pages. *Venus and Adonis* and *The Rape of Lucrece* are
passed over for similar reasons.

Among the glories of Tudor-Stuart poetry are its songs.
Many of these were written to be sung on the stage; a few
may be found in the novels of the time; but a large number,
including some of the finest, come from the song books.
After Shakespeare, the most successful of the song-writing
dramatists is John Fletcher; and among the purely lyrical
writers Campion and Herrick are deservedly very popular.
But there are so many great poets in this epoch! Rather apart
from the rest is Donne. He is the inventor of what Johnson
attacked as the "metaphysical school," and from time to time
he is taken up as an exclusive fad by the cliques. Yet Ben
Jonson had more insight than Sam Johnson when he said
Donne was the first poet in the world for some things.

After the death of Shakespeare and the slow decline of the
great poets of the theatre, the Tudor-Stuart period ends as
it began with a covey of Court poets. Herrick is that and
something more, but it applies to the Carews and Lovelaces
and Sucklings and the rest of them. But what grace and elegance and command of subtle rhythm these careless fashion-
ables possessed! In search of these virtues I have gone through
George Saintsbury's valuable collection of minor Caroline
poets.

On the other side from the king's poets we have the great
figure of Milton, the lesser figure of Marvell, and the still
lesser figure of Wither. Milton, the Milton of "Arcades" and
Comus and "Lycidas" and "L'Allegro" and "Il Penseroso,"
is one of those supreme artists who close an epoch by giving
the last polish of consummate style to themes and methods
inherited from their predecessors. It is quite true that Milton

is filled with reminiscences, but without him we should have lost some of the most beautiful poetry in English. The fact that he also possessed and used all the scholarship of the late Renaissance should not be held against him. It was, I think, Mark Pattison who pointed out that a real appreciation of Milton is one of the rewards of a liberal education.

It is not possible to fix any hard and fast date for the end of this epoch any more than for its beginning. The names of Crashaw, Cowley, Marvell, Herbert, Vaughan, and even Cotton still suggest links with the age of Shakespeare. But Dryden, Swift, Gay, Pope, Thomson, Gray, Collins at once suggest a totally different epoch with quite different views of poetry.

Samuel Johnson was a great man and in his day a great critic, but from our point of view his taste in poetry seems wrong. I know of course that he did not select the poets in the collected edition for which he wrote his critical *Lives*—that was the work of the booksellers. But Johnson did arrange for four poets to be added to the list, and if anything they seem more perverse than the original choice. I have gone through the *Lives* again, and find some curious statistics. If Dr. Johnson and his bookseller friends had compiled this anthology, they would have omitted everything before Milton and Cowley—a little more than the first third of the book. There would have been thirty-two poets whose work I have omitted, and only nineteen in common.

It is interesting to consider Johnson's list, which I give here, printing in italics those names which are found in this anthology: *Cowley, Denham, Milton, Butler, Rochester,* Roscommon, *Dryden, Waller,* Pomfret, Dorset, Stepney, J. Philips, *Walsh, Otway,* Smith, Duke, King, Sprat, Halifax, Parnell, Garth, Rowe, *Addison,* Hughes, Buckingham, *Prior, Congreve,* Blackmore, Fenton, *Gay,* Granville, Yalden, Tickell, Somervile, Savage, *Swift,* Broome, *Pope,* Pitt, *Thomson,* Watts, A. Philips, West, *Collins,* Dyer, *Shenstone, Young,* Mallet, Akenside, *Gray,* Lyttleton.

Period specialists can of course say that all this only goes to show that I don't properly appreciate Augustan poetry. To which I should reply that the majority of poetry readers today are less interested in Augustan poetry than in the poetry which preceded and followed it. The dominant poets of the epoch are Dryden and of course Pope, and their taste on the

whole was that of the French in the age of Louis XIV, with
Dryden inclining more to Corneille and Pope to Boileau. But
even in France, where it produced great work, this taste was
essentially narrow and arrogant, concentrating on a few
selected models and rejecting much that now seems to us
more valuable than those very models.

Each country had its critical clichés which were thought
to dispose of whole generations of poets without more ado.
"*Enfin Malherbe vint.*" But to a modern reader of French
poetry the coming of Malherbe seems no great happiness,
since he succeeded merely in quenching for a long period
a lyric beauty which had existed in France for centuries.
(Amusingly enough, his most admired and quoted fragment
has been proved to owe its charm to a printer's error.) The
equivalent in England is: "Waller was smooth." But who
now cares about Waller's smoothness, and who would dream
of ranking him with the Tudor-Stuart poets he was supposed
to have superseded for ever?

One of the greatest glories of England is that its poetry
counts twice in the history of world literature: that after
producing the age of Spenser, Shakespeare, and Milton there
were still enough energy and imagination to produce the
secondary but still splendid epoch of Blake, Wordsworth,
and Shelley. It is due to the Romantic poets that we now rate
the poetry of the eighteenth century below its own complacent
estimate of itself, and it is also due to them that we value so
highly the Tudor-Stuart poets, whom the Augustans wanted
to throw on the scrap-heap as obsolescent. An epoch of great
poetry will always sympathize with the others, but an age of
little poets will have little critics. "*Cosa bella mortal passa,
ma non d'arte,*" said Leonardo da Vinci. It is the little criticism which passes, and not the great poetry.

There is an often-quoted line from Elizabethan drama:

Cover her face; mine eyes dazzle; she died young.

It seems the appropriate epitaph for English Romantic poetry
partly because two of its two brightest Occidental stars,
Shelley and Keats, died young, and partly because the period
itself was brief. We cannot put it much before the publication
of the Kilmarnock Burns in 1786, and it died at Missolonghi
with Byron in 1824. Romantic poetry is the poetry of young

men, who either died into immortality or survived like hoary
Tithonuses incapable of the Muse's bed.

The poets of England and America who succeeded the
Romantics and tried to carry on their tradition succeeded in
giving the impression of fabulous respectability. I will not go
so far as to say that poetry and respectability are incompat-
ible, but it is hard to think of respectable poets in any other
epoch. Even Vergil wrote on dubious themes, and neither
Sophocles nor Racine was a member of the Anglican Church
or even a Quaker. Of course the Victorians were not so respectable as people thought they were. Tennyson used to
get drunk on port, but it was all hushed up, and neither the
queen nor the British public ever heard of it. And the same
is true of that little scandal of Wordsworth's youth in France,
the discovery of which triumphantly restored Wordsworth to
the human race. If I am told that Wordsworth ranks among
the Romantics, I shall point out that while he was enthusi-
astically cooperating with the French Revolution he certainly
was a great Romantic poet, but by the time he had qualified
to be the good and great queen's poet laureate and a piece of
indispensable furniture in every home, he was reduced to the
mental indigence of writing "Ecclesiastical Sonnets."

These views have naturally influenced the building up of
this anthology. I have not given as much attention to the
Augustans and their successors as would be expected from a
contemporary of Boswell or from a modern critic who tries to
persuade us that "The Hind and the Panther" is greater
poetry than "Prometheus Unbound." Yet it will be found that
I have allowed both Dryden and Pope to have their say, and
have included some of those whom Dodsley the publisher
used to call "eminent hands." But at the same time I have
used the eighteenth century also to bring out those occasional
foretastes of the coming Romantics which show what the
more sensitive poets were vaguely and perhaps unconsciously
trying to express. Kit Smart (so renowned for trying to make
Dr. Johnson say his prayers in Fleet Street) may have been
mad when he wrote his "Song to David" and sane when he
wrote his frightful odes, but for us his madness was more
fruitful than his sanity. I have ventured to give more of this
interesting poem than is included in many anthologies because it is the gradual working up which brings out the full
effect of the grand finale.

The feebleness of English poetry in the latter part of the eighteenth century is well described by an early poem, "To the Muses," by a then totally unknown poet, William Blake, who now ranks very high indeed:

> *How have you left the ancient love*
> *That bards of old enjoy'd in you!*
> *The languid strings do scarcely move!*
> *The sound is forc'd, the notes are few!*

The last two lines could very appropriately be used to describe the poetical labours of Blake's unsatisfactory patron, William Hayley, who enjoyed a greater reputation than Blake ever did in his lifetime, and who (I blush to say) was actually praised by Gibbon. Among the more preposterous creations of eighteenth-century poetry I would recommend to the curious in such things the incredible "epic" of "Leonidas" by Richard Glover, and Grainger's didactic poem on the sugar cane. There is even one on hop gardens, which contains a superb passage on manure.

I have now accounted for most of the main groups of poets, however superficially. There remain the American poets, the Victorians proper, the poets of the nineties, and the moderns. I don't think the Victorians are under-represented, although I admit they do not stir me as the Romantics do, except perhaps Browning and Swinburne. Browning seems to me the most important of the post-Romantic poets of England. Indeed, I am inclined to think he was the last really major poet England produced. I think it indisputable that there is a decline in the second half of the nineteenth century, in spite of such interesting figures as Hardy, Blunt, Hopkins, Bridges, and Henley.

While standard American poetry gave me anxious moments and I realized that my taste might not always be acceptable, all that was nothing compared with the difficulties of the modern section, American, British, and Dominions.

It is impossible to include everybody who might be held to deserve the attention of posterity, so the partisans of somebody—and probably of many poetical somebodies and nobodies—are going to be offended. On the other hand, by including even a little new and experimental work which has not yet acquired a trace of patina or prestige, the anthologist exposes himself to the charge of gross incompetence by including trash in a volume which contains Shakespeare and Milton. Moreover, by allotting only one or two poems to as many poets as possible, the effect may be given that they are all of equal importance or unimportance. Thus, the treatment of the moderns is a return to the "token" system used at the beginning of this book, though the difficulty here is the mass of material. This is especially true of Dominions poetry, of which I have been able to give only a very few "token" examples.

There remain two or three points which I should like to make clear to avoid any misapprehensions about the scope and limits of this book. I have given examples of light verse from "I Have a Gentil Cok" in the fifteenth century to G. K. Chesterton in the twentieth, but I hope I have succeeded in keeping out the facetious and the whimsy-whamsy. I have tried to limit translations to such universally admired works as Fitzgerald's Omar and William Cory's "Heraclitus," which are poems in their own right, and I have tried to track down and to eliminate the unacknowledged translation or paraphrase. Thus Drummond of Hawthornden's "Sweet Spring, Thou Turn'st" and "Alexis, Here She Stay'd" and "The Beauty and the Life" were all rejected because they are translated respectively from Petrarch, Ronsard, and Guarini.

A standard anthology of the English-speaking world should limit itself to poems in standard English, and therefore I have rejected dialect poets, even the pleasant Dorset poet Barnes. Scots is not a dialect but that branch of Middle "Ynglis" which has been spoken and written for centuries in the ancient Kingdom of Scotland. Anybody who doubts this statement is requested to take up the matter with the first Scotsman he meets. I felt some doubt about two of the Kipling poems, but on discovering that not a word needs to be glossed I thought they might scrape by as standard English. The same prohibition applies to poems in thieves' jargon and in jabberwocky, neither of which can be called standard English. Parody and nonsense verses were also barred as being outside the book's logical scheme and because if you admit one you must admit a host. If you admit the Lewis Carroll parodies which delighted our childhood (when we didn't know they were parodies) then you must admit *Rejected Addresses* and "Quoth the Raven: Nelly Moore,"

and "Butter and Eggs and a Pound of Cheese" and the
brilliant parodies by Chesterton and Sir John Squire and
Swinburne's parody of himself and A. E. Housman's parody
of a Greek tragedy and more and more. Though usually light-
hearted, parody can be cruel. For instance, Byron's two
parodies of Cowper's "Stanzas to Mary" rather mercilessly
killed the original.

In the case of all standard and early writers I have tried to
use a good text, by which I mean a text edited by a reputable
scholar or published by a university press or by one of the
large publishing houses which specialize in producing accu-
rate texts of standard authors. In the case of some rare poets I
have had to be content with the editions of Grosart, who, I
discover, is not very highly esteemed by more recent and
exact scholars.

The spelling of modern poets has of course been left un-
changed—English spelling for the British, American for the
Americans. But I must point out that some American poets
seem to prefer English spelling or a style closer to it than to
modern American standards. I have tried to respect these
individual preferences. For Middle English and Scots I have
made a glossary at the foot of each page. For that long period
in England when spelling differed from modern usage, I
have modernized. There are objections to this, I know, in
the cases of Spenser and Milton and even of Dryden, but
I justify these liberties (which some readers will certainly
dislike) on the ground that the object is to make as much
poetry as possible accessible to as many readers as possible.

There was evidently a period when a past participle such
as "looked" could be pronounced either "lookéd" or "look'd."
Poets continued to write "look'd" and similar words long after
the necessity for the usage had gone. Where I thought it
desirable an improvement, I have ventured to write "looked"
instead of "look'd," and where in reading I found a "lookéd"
word unmarked and it held me up in scanning the line I have
also ventured to accent the "e." But I have *not* tried to make
this a uniform "style." I have simply trusted my eye and ear
in the individual poem or line, so that there may be variations
on the same page. My reason for this liberty is once again the
convenience of the modern reader.

As far as I could, I have freed the poems in this book of

the fancy titles imposed on untitled poems by editors or anthologists. These are often confusing and a positive hindrance in search, because different people give different titles to the same poem. The obvious method of identifying an untitled poem is by part or the whole of the first line. If any invented titles are used here, the reason is that some editor has misled me.

A worse deception on the reader than this is to print an extract from a poem as if it were actually a whole short poem, or to drop one or more stanzas from a poem without warning the reader. This objectionable practice is very common. In this book whenever there is an extract from a longer poem, or if any line or stanzas has been omitted from a short poem, the reader is always warned that what he is about to read is not a complete work by the fact that the title is preceded by "FROM." Thus under Milton the description of Athens in *Paradise Regained* is not printed as if it were a separate complete poem under some invented title; it is marked "FROM *Paradise Regained*." And so throughout the book.

Since many songs and lyrics originally appeared as part of a longer work such as a play or novel, I thought it might be worth noting the fact at the foot of the poem by giving the title of the play or novel from which it is quoted. This does not mean that the song or lyric is incomplete; it is complete in itself but taken from a play or novel and not from a collection of lyrics. I have also given the names of Elizabethan and Jacobean song books and collections, such as *England's Helicon*, followed by their dates. The dates of plays are of the first performance, whenever that is known; in other cases, the dates are of the earliest known publication.

RICHARD ALDINGTON

1956

CONTENTS OF VOLUME ONE

Sonnets

THE VIKING BOOK OF
Poetry
OF THE ENGLISH-SPEAKING WORLD

VOLUME ONE

ANONYMOUS

FROM *Beowulf*

What! We of Spear-Danes in spent days,
Of the Folk-Kings' force have heard,
How the Athelings excelled in fight.
Oft Shield of the Sheaf from scathing hordes,
From many meinies their mead-stools tore.
Affrighted them the Earl, since erst he was
Found, unwealthy; then friendship he awaited,
Waxed under the welkin, in worship throve,
Until each one of those out-dwelling
Over the whale-road, must hearken to him,
Gold must give him. That was a good King.
His offspring was afterwards known,
Young in the yards, whom God sent
The folk to befriend; the fierce dearth He knew
They had ere then endured, lacking elders
A long while. To him the Life-Lord
Glory's Wielder, world-honour gave.
Noble was Beowulf (bloomed wide his name)
Shielde's son in the Scede-lands.
So shall a young groom work his own good,
By full fees given to friends of his father,
That with him in his age they may ever abide,
Willing comrades, whenas war cometh,
To serve the people; by praised deeds shall
One man thrive among all man-kind.
Turned aside then Shield in the time shaped for him,
Full-ripe, to fare in Frea's keeping.
Him then out they bare to the brink of ocean,
His sweet companions, so himself had bidden,
While his words had weight, welcome friend of Shieldings;
A beloved land-chief, long had he reigned.
There in the roads ring-stemmed she stood,
Icy, out-faring, an atheling's craft:
Laid they down then the lovely Prince,
Bestower of bracelets, in the breast of the ship,
Their man by the mast. There was a mass of wealth,
Fretted gold ferried from far away.

1

Nor heard I of a keel more comely-wise garnished
With brave weapons and battle-weeds,
With bills and byrnies; on his breast lay
Many treasures that must with him
In the flood's keeping fare afar.
Nothing less of gifts they allowed him,
Of their possessions than had those
Who at his first faring forth had sent him
Alone over ocean, an infant indeed.
Still more, they stood up for him a golden standard
High over head; they let the holm bear him,
Sent him to the Spear-Man; sad was their soul,
Mournful their mood. For men knew not
How soothly to say, men seely in council,
Of their hero under heaven who that lading received.

Translated from Old English by C. K. Scott-Moncrieff

ANONYMOUS

(13TH CENTURY)

"Sing Cuccu..."

Sing cuccu nu! Sing cuccu!
Sing cuccu! Sing cuccu nu!

Sumer is icumen in,
   Lhudë sing cuccu;
Groweth sed and bloweth med
   And springeth the wdë nu.
      Sing cuccu!
Awë bleteth after lomb,
   Lhouth after calvë cu;
Bulluc sterteth, buckë verteth;
   Murie sing cuccu.
      Cuccu, cuccu,
   Well singës thu, cuccu,
   Ne swik thu naver nu.

Nu, *now.* Lhudë, *loud.* Sed, med, *seed, mead.* Wdë, *wood.* Awë, *ewe.*
Lhouth, *loweth.* Cu, *cow.* Verteth, *hides in the green wood.* Murie,
merry. Swik, *cease.*

ANONYMOUS

(14TH CENTURY)

"Bytuenë Mersh and Averil"

Bytuenë Mersh and Averil,
　　When spray biginneth to springe,
The lutel foul hath hire wyl
　　On hyre lud to synge.
　　Ich libbe in love-longinge
　　For semlokest of allë thinge;
　　He may me blissë bringe;
Icham in hire baundoun.
　　　　An hendy hap ichabbe yhent;
　　　　Ichot from hevene it is me sent;
　　　　From allë wymmen mi love is lent
　　　　Ant lyht on Alysoun.

On heu hire her is fayr ynoh,
　　Hire browë broune, hire eyë blake;
With lossum chere he on me loh,
　　With middel smal ant wel ymake.
　　Bote he me wollë to hire take,
　　Fortë buen hire owen make,
　　Longe to lyven ichulle forsake,
Ant feye fallen adoun.

Nihtës when I wende ant wake,
　　Forthi myn wongës waxeth won.
Levedi, al for thinë sake
　　Longinge is ylent me on.
　　In world nis non so wytermon,
　　That al hire bountë tellë con.
　　Hire swyre is whittore then the swon
Ant feyrest may in toune.

Lutel foul, *little bird.* Hire, *her.* Lud, *voice.* Ich libbe, *I live.* Semlokest, *seemliest.* He, *she.* Icham, *I am.* Baundoun, *lordship.* Hendy,
fair. Hap, *fortune.* Ichabbe, *I have.* Yhent, *gained.* Ichot, *I wot.* Lyht,
lights. Heu, *hue.* Hire her, *her hair.* Lossum, *lovesome.* He, *she.* Loh,
laughed. Bote, *unless.* Fortë buen, *for to be.* Make, *mate.* Ichulle, *I shall.*
Feye, *lifeless.* Wende, *turn.* Forthi, *therefore.* Wongës, *cheeks.* Won, *wan.*
Levedi, *lady.* Nis, *is not.* Wytermon, *wise man.* Swyre, *neck.* May, *maid.*

Icham for wowing al forwake,
  Wery so water in wore.
Lest eny revë me my make,
  Ichabbe y-yernéd yore.
  Betere is tholien whylë sore,
  Then mournen evermore.
  Geynest under gore,
Herknë to my roun.
    An hendy hap ichabbe yhent;
    Ichot from hevene it is me sent;
    From allë wymmen mi love is lent
  Ant lyht on Alysoun.

ANONYMOUS

(14TH CENTURY)

"Lenten Is Come..."

Lenten is come with love to toune,
With blosmen and with briddës roune,
  That al this blissë bringeth,
Dayës-eyës in this dales,
Notës suete of nytëgales;
  Uch foul song singeth.
The threstelcoc him threteth oo;
Away is huere wynter woo,
  When wodërovë springeth.
This foulës singeth ferly fele
And wlyteth on huere wynter wele,
  That al the wodë ryngeth.

The rosë rayleth hire rode;
The levës on the lyhtëwode
  Wexen all with wille.

Wowing, wooing. Wore, weir. Revë, rob. Yore, long. Tholien, to endure.
Geynest, most graceful. Gore, skirt. Roun, song.

Lenten, Lent. Briddës, birds. Roune, song. Uch, each. Foul, bird.
Threstelcoc, blackbird. Threteth oo, ever chides. Huere, their. Woo, woe.
Wodërovë, wood-ruff. Ferly fele, wondrous many. Wlyteth, whistle. Wele,
joy. Rayleth, sends forth. Rode, red. Wille, desire.

The monë mandeth hire bleo;
The lilie is lossom to seo,
    The fenyl ant the fille.
Wowës thisë wildë drakes;
Milës murgeth huere makes,
    Ase strem that striketh stille.
Mody meneth, so doth mo.
Ichot ycham on of tho
    For love that likës ille.

The monë mandeth hire lyht;
So doth semly sonnë bryht,
    When briddës singeth breme.
Deawës donketh the dounes,
Deores with huere dernë rounes,
    Domës fortë deme.
Wormës woweth under cloude;
Wymmen waxeth wounder proude,
    So wel hit wol hem seme.
Yef me shal wontë wille of on,
This wunnë weole I wole forgon,
    Ant wyht in wode be fleme.

JOHN BARBOUR

(1320?–1395)

FROM *The Bruce*

A! fredome is a noble thing!
Fredome mayss man to haiff liking;
Fredome all solace to man giffis:
He levys at ess that frely levys!

Mandeth hire bleo, *sends out her light.* Lossom to seo, *lovesome to see.*
Fenyl, *fennel.* Fille, *thyme.* Wowës, *woos.* Milës murgeth huere makes,
Wild things make merry (with) their mates. Ase, *as.* Striketh, *flows.* Mody
meneth, so doth mo, *The passionate man complains, and so do others.*
Ichot ycham, *I wot I am.* On of tho, *one of those.* Breme, *valiantly.*
Deawës, *dews.* Donketh, *moisten.* Dounes, *downs.* Deores, *animals.* Dernë,
secret. Domës fortë deme, *whereby they converse.* Wormës woweth under
cloude, *Worms woo under clod.* Hit, *it.* Yef, *if.* Wontë, *want.* Wunnë
weole, *wealth of delight.* Fleme, *fugitive.*

Mayss, *makes.* Haiff, *have.* Liking, *happiness.* Giffis, *gives.* Levys, *lives.*

A noble hart may haiff nane ess
Na elles nocht that may him pless,
Gyff fredome failhe; for fre liking
Is yharnyt our all othir thing.
Na he, that aye hass levyt fre
May nocht knaw weill the propyrte,
The angyr, na the wrechyt dome,
That is cowplyt to foule thyrldome;
Bot gyff he had assayit it
Than all perquer he suld it wyt,
And suld think fredome mar to pryss
Than all the gold in warld that is.

GEOFFREY CHAUCER

(1340?–1400)

FROM *The Prologue to the Canterbury Tales*

1.

Whan that Aprille with his shoures soote
The droghte of March hath perced to the roote,
And bathed every veyne in swich licour
Of which vertu engendered is the flour;
Whan Zephyrus eek with his sweete breeth
Inspired hath in every holt and heeth
The tendre croppes, and the yonge sonne
Hath in the Ram his halve cours yronne,
And smale fowles maken melodye,
That slepen al the nyght with open ye
(So priketh hem nature in hir corages);
Thanne longen folk to goon on pilgrimages,
And palmeres for to seken straunge strondes,
To ferne halwes, kowthe in sondry londes;

Ess, *ease.* Nane, *no.* Na elles nocht, *nor aught else.* Pless, *please.* Gyff, *if.*
Failhe, *fail.* Yharnyt, *desired.* Our, *above.* Na, *nor.* Nocht knaw, *not know.*
Dome, *fate.* Cowplyt, *coupled.* Thyrldome, *thralldom.* Bot, *but.* Assayit,
experienced. Perquer, *thoroughly.* Suld, *should.* Mar, *more.* Pryss, *prize.*

Whan, *when.* Shoures, *showers.* Soote, *sweet.* Droghte, *drought.* Veyne,
sap-vessel. Swich, *such.* Licour, *moisture.* Flour, *flower.* Inspired, *breathed.*
Holt, *cultivated land.* Heeth, *heath, wild land.* Yonge, *young.* His halve
cours yronne, *has run half his course.* Fowles, *birds.* Ye, *eye.* Priketh, *stirs.*
Hem, *them.* Corages, *desires.* Thanne, *then.* Strondes, *strands.* Ferne
halwes, *distant saints.* Kowthe, *known.* Londes, *lands.*

And specially from every shires ende
Of Engelonde to Caunterbury they wende,
The hooly blisful martir for to seke,
That hem hath holpen whan that they were seeke.

2.

There was also a Nonne, a Prioresse,
That of hir smylyng was full symple and coy;
Hire gretteste ooth was but by Seinte Loy;
And she was cleped madame Eglentyne.
Ful weel she soong the service dyvyne,
Entuned in hir nose ful semely,
And Frenssh she spak ful faire and fetisly,
After the scole of Stratford atte Bowe,
For Frenssh of Paris was to hire unknowe.
At mete wel ytaught was she with alle:
She leet no morsel from her lippes falle,
Ne wette hir fyngres in hir sauce depe;
Wel koude she carie a morsel and wel kepe
That no drope ne fille upon hire brest.
In curteisie was set ful muchel hir lest.
Hir over-lippe wyped she so clene
That in her coppe there was no ferthyng sene
Of grece, whan she dronken hadde hir draughte.
Ful semely after hir mete she raughte.
And sikerly she was of greet desport,
And ful plesaunt, and amyable of port,
And peyned hire to countrefete cheere
Of court, and to been estatlich of manere,
And to ben holden digne of reverence.
But, for to speken of hire conscience,
She was so charitable and so pitous
She wolde wepe, if that she saugh a mous
Kaught in a trappe, if it were deed or bledde.
Of smale houndes hadde she that she fedde

Seeke, *sick.*

Nonne, nun. Hir, hire, *her.* Ooth, oath. Seinte Loy, *Saint Eligius.* Cleped,
named. Semely, *pleasantly.* Fetisly, *gracefully.* Mete, *meat.* Ne, *nor.*
Koude, *could.* Fille, *fell.* Lest, *desire.* Ferthyng, *farthing, bit.* Grece, *grease.*
Raughte, *reached.* Sikerly, *certainly.* Desport, *mirth.* Port, *behaviour.*
Peyned, *took pains.* Estatlich, *dignified.* Digne, *worthy.* Pitous, *full of pity.*

With rosted flessh, or milk and wastel-breed.
But soore wepte she if oon of hem were deed,
Or if men smoot it with a yerde smerte;
And al was conscience and tendre herte.
Ful semyly hir wympul pynched was;
Hir nose tretys, hir eyen greye as glas,
Hir mouth ful smal, and thereto softe and reed;
But sikerly she hadde a fair forheed;
It was almoost a spanne brood, I trowe;
For, hardily, she was nat undergrowe.
Ful fetys was hir cloke, as I was war.
Of smal coral aboute hire arm she bar
A peire of bedes, gauded al with grene,
And theron heng a brooch of gold ful sheene,
On which ther was first write a crowned A,
And after *Amor vincit omnia.*

3.

A Marchant was ther with a forked berd,
In mottelee, and hye on horse he sat;
Upon his heed a Flaundryssh bever hat,
His bootes clasped faire and fetisly.
His resons he spak ful solempnely,
Sownynge alwey th' encrees of his wynnyng.
He wolde the see were kept for any thyng
Betwixe Middelburgh and Orewelle.
Wel koude he in eschaunge sheeldes selle.
This worthy man ful wel his wit bisette:
Ther wiste no wight that he was in dette,
So estatly was he of his governaunce
With his bargaynes and with his chevyssaunce.
For sothe he was a worthy man with alle,
But, sooth to seyn, I noot how men hym calle.

Wastel-breed, *fine white bread.* Yerde, *stick.* Tretys, *well-shaped.* Hardily,
certainly. Fetys, *graceful.* War, *aware.* Peire, *pair.* Gauded, *trimmed.*
Sheene, *bright.*

Berd, *beard.* Mottelee, *parti-coloured cloth.* Flaundryssh, *Flanders.* Resons,
opinions. Sownynge, *proclaiming.* Encrees, *increase.* Wynnyng, *gains.* He
wolde the see were kept, *he wanted the sea held.* Middelburgh, *Mid-
delburg, Holland.* Orewelle, *the river Orwell, England.* Sheeldes, *French
money.* His wit bisette, *applied his mind.* Wiste, *knew.* Wight, *person.*
Estatly, *dignified.* Governaunce, *demeanour.* Chevyssaunce, *dealing in
money.* Noot, *know not.*

4.

A Clerk ther was of Oxenford also,
That unto logyk hadde longe ygo.
As leene was his hors as is a rake,
And he nas nat right fat, I undertake,
But looked holwe, and therto sobrely.
Ful thredbare was his overeste courtpey;
For he hadde geten hym yet no benefice,
Ne was so worldly for to have office.
For hym was levere have at his beddes heed
Twenty bookes, clad in blak or reed,
Of Aristotle and his philosophie,
Than robes riche, or fithele, or gay sautrie.
But al be that he was a philosophre,
Yet hadde he but litel golde in coffre;
But al that he myghte of his freendes hente,
On bookes and on lernynge he it spente,
And bisily gan for the soules preye
On hem that yaf hym wherwith to scoleye.
Of studie took he moost cure and moost heede.
Noght o word spak he moore than was neede,
And that was seyd in forme and reverence,
And short and quyk and ful of hy sentence;
Sownynge in moral vertu was his speche,
And gladly wolde he lerne and gladly teche.

5.

A Frankeleyn was in his compaignye.
Whit was his berd as is the dayesye;
Of his complexioun he was sangwyn.
Wel loved he by the morwe a sop in wyn;
To lyven in delit was evere his wone,
For he was Epicurus owene sone,
That heeld opinioun that pleyn delit

Hadde longe ygo, *had long been studying.* Nas nat, *was not.* Holwe, *hollow.* Overeste courtpey, *short overcoat.* Geten, *gotten.* Office, *secular employment.* Hym was levere, *he would rather.* Fithele, *fiddle.* Sautrie, *psaltery.* Hente, *obtain.* Preye, *pray.* Yaf, *gave.* Scoleye, *study.* Cure, *care.* Noght o, *not one.* Sentence, *significance.* Sownynge in, *making for.*

Frankeleyn, *a franklin, a wealthy land-owner.* Dayesye, *daisy.* Morwe, *morning.* Sop in wyn, *bread dipped in wine.* Wone, *custom.* Pleyn, *complete.*

Was verraily felicitee parfit.
An householdere, and that a greet, was he;
Seint Julian he was in his contree.
His breed, his ale, was always after oon;
A bettre envyned man was nowher noon.
Withoute bake mete was nevere his hous
Of fissh and flessh, and that so plentevous,
It snewed in his hous of mete and drynke,
Of all deyntees that men koude thynke.
After the sondry sesons of the yeer,
So chaunged he his mete and his soper.
Ful many a fat partrich hadde he in muwe,
And many a breem and many a luce in stuwe.
Wo was his cook but if his sauce were
Poynaunt and sharp, and redy al his geere.
His table dormant in his halle alway
Stood redy covered al the longe day.
At sessiouns ther was he lord and sire;
Ful ofte tyme he was knyght of the shire.
An anlaas and a gipser all of silk
Heeng at his girdel, whit as morne milk.
A shirreve hadde he been, and a countour.
Was nowher such a worthy vavasour.

6.

A good Wif was ther of biside Bathe,
But she was somdele deef, and that was scathe.
Of clooth-makyng she had swich an haunt,
She passed hem of Ypres and of Gaunt.
In al the parisshe wif ne was ther noon
That to the offrynge bifore hire sholde goon;
And if ther dide, certayn so wrooth was she,

Seint Julian, *saint of hospitality.* Breed, *bread.* After oon, *uniformly good.* Envyned, *stocked with wine.* Noon, *none.* Snewed, *snowed.* Deyntees, *dainties.* Koude, *could.* Soper, *supper.* Muwe, *coop.* Breem, *bream.* Luce, *pike.* Stuwe, *stew.* Geere, *utensils.* Table dormant, *a permanently fixed table.* Anlaas, *anlace, a dagger.* Gipser, *purse.* Heeng, *hung.* Morne, *morning.* Shirreve, *sheriff.* Countour, *accountant or non-professional pleader in the law courts.* Vavasour, *a minor feudal land-holder.*

Somdele, *somewhat.* Deef, *deaf.* Scathe, *a pity.* Swich an haunt, *so much skill.* Ne was ther noon, *there was none.* Offrynge, *offering in church.* Wrooth, *angry.*

That she was out of alle charitee.
Hir coverchiefs ful fyne weren of ground;
I dorste swere they weyeden ten pound
That on a Sonday weren upon hir heed.
Hir hosen weren of fyn scarlet reed,
Ful streite yteyd, and shoes ful moyste and newe.
Boold was hir face, and fair, and reed of hewe.
She was a worthy womman al hir lyve:
Housbondes at chirche dore she hadde fyve,
Withouten oother compaignye in youthe,
But thereof nedeth nat to speke as nowthe.
And thries hadde she been at Jerusalem;
She hadde passed many a straunge strem;
At Rome she hadde been, and at Boloigne,
In Galice at Seint Jame, and at Coloigne.
She koude muchel of wandrynge by the weye.
Gat-tothed was she, soothly for to seye.
Upon an amblere esily she sat,
Ywympled wel, and on hir heed an hat
As brood as is a bokeler or a targe;
A foot-mantel about her hipes large,
And on hir feet a paire of spores sharpe.
In felaweshipe wel koude she laughe and carpe.
Of remedies of love she knew per chaunce,
For she koude of that art the olde daunce.

7.

The Millere was a stout carl for the nones;
Ful byg he was of brawn, and eek of bones.
That proved wel, for over al ther he cam,
At wrastlynge he wolde have alwey the ram.

Coverchiefs, head-dress. Ground, texture. Dorste, durst. Weyeden, weighed. Hosen, stockings. Reed, red. Streite yteyd, tightly tied. Moyste, soft. Hewe, hue. As nowthe, now. Thries, thrice. Boloigne, Boulogne sur Mer. Galice at Seint Jame, Sant' Iago de Compostela in Galicia. Coloigne, Cologne. Koude, knew. Gat-tothed, teeth set wide apart. Amblere, an ambling horse. Ywympled, wrapped in a wimple. Bokeler, buckler. Targe, shield. Foot-mantel, a cloth covering worn over the skirt in riding. Hipes, hips. Spores, spurs. Felaweshipe, fellowship. Koude, could. Carpe, talk. Koude, knew.

Carl, fellow. For the nones, indeed, exceedingly. Over al ther he cam, above all others in the place from which he came. The ram, the prize.

He was short-sholdred, brood, a thikke knarre;
Ther was no dore that he nolde heve of harre,
Or breke it at a rennyng with his heed.
His berd as any sowe or fox was reed,
And thereto brood, as though it were a spade.
Upon the cop right of his nose he hade
A werte, and theron stood a toft of herys,
Reed as the brustles of a sowes erys;
His nosethirles blake were and wyde.
A swerd and bokeler bar he by his syde.
His mouth as greet was as a greet forneys.
He was a janglere and a goliardeys,
And that was moost of synne and harlotries.
Wel koude he stelen corn and tollen thries;
And yet he hadde a thombe of gold, pardee.
A whit cote and blew hood wered he.
A baggepipe wel koude he blowe and sowne,
And therwithal he broghte us out of towne.

FROM *The Reeve's Tale*

At Trumpyngtoun nat fer from Cantebrigge,
Ther gooth a brook, and over that a brigge,
Upon the whiche brook ther stant a melle;
And this is verray sooth that I yow telle:
A millere was ther dwellynge many a day.
As any pecok he was proud and gay.
Pipen he koude and fisshe, and nettes beete,
And turne coppes, and wel wrastle and sheete;
Ay by his belt he baar a long panade,
And of a swerd ful trenchant was the blade.

Brood, broad. Thikke knarre, *thickset heavy man.* Nolde heve of harre, *could not lift off its hinge.* Rennyng, *running.* Heed, *head.* Berd, *beard.* Reed, *red.* Cop, *tip.* Werte, *wart.* Toft of herys, *tuft of hairs.* Brustles, *bristles.* Erys, *ears.* Nosethirles, *nostrils.* Bokeler, *buckler.* Bar, *carried.* Greet, *great.* Forneys, *furnace.* Janglere, *chatterer.* Goliardeys, *coarse buffoon.* Tollen thries, *charge people three times over.* A thombe of gold, *a thumb of gold; i.e., honest for a miller.* Pardee, *truly.* Koude, *could.*

Cantebrigge, *Cambridge.* Brigge, *bridge.* Melle, *mill.* Koude, *could.* Nettes beete, *weave nets.* Turne coppes, *make wooden cups.* Sheete, *shoot.* Baar, *carried.* Panade, *cutlass.*

A joly poppere baar he in his pouche;
Ther was no man, for peril, dorste hym touche.
A Sheffeld thwitel baar he in his hose.
Round was his face, and camus was his nose;
As piled as an ape was his skulle.
He was a market-betere atte fulle.
Ther dorste no wight hand upon hym legge,
That he ne swoor he sholde anon abegge.
A theefe he was for sothe of corn and mele,
And that a sly, and usant for to stele.
His name was hoote deynous Symkyn.

A wyf he hadde, ycomen of noble kyn;
The person of the toun hir fader was.
With hire he yaf ful many a panne of bras,
For that Symkyn sholde in his blood allye.
She was yfostred in a nonnerye.
And she was proud, and peert as is a pye.
A ful fair sight was it upon hem two;
On halydayes biforn hire wolde he go
With his typet bounden aboute his heed,
And she cam after in a gyte of reed;
And Symkyn hadde hosen of the same.
Ther dorste no wight clepen hire but "dame";
Was noon so hardy that wente by the weye
That with hire dorste rage or ones pleye,
But if he wolde be slayn of Symkyn
With panade, or with knyf, or boidekyn.
For jalous folk ben perilous everemo;
Algate they wolde hire wyves wenden so.
And eek, for she was somdel smoterlich,

Joly poppere, *neat dagger*. For peril, *because of the risk*. Dorste, *durst*.
Sheffeld thwitel, *large Sheffield knife*. Camus, *snub-nosed*. Piled, *usually*
"*bald*," *but here probably* "*hairy*." Market-betere, *swaggerer at market*
places. Wight, *person*. Swoor, *swore*. Abegge, *pay dearly for it*. For sothe,
forsooth. Usant, *accustomed*. Stele, *steal*. Hoote, *called*. Deynous, *scornful*.
Ycomen, *come*. Person, *parson*. Hire, *her*. Yaf, *gave*. Panne, *pan*. Bras,
brass. Allye, *ally*. Yfostred, *reared*. Nonnerye, *nunnery*. Peert, *saucy*. Pye,
magpie. Halydayes, *holidays*. Biforn, *before*. Typet, *tippet*. Heed, *head*.
Gyte of reed, *red garment*. Clepen, *call*. Noon, *none*. Hardy, *bold*. Rage,
flirt. Ones, *once*. Pleye, *make jokes*. But if he wolde, *unless he wanted to*
be. Boidekyn, *bodkin*. Perilous, *dangerous*. Everemo, *evermore*. Algate,
nevertheless. Hire, *their*. Wenden so, *go in this way*. Somdel smoterlich,
somewhat besmirched (i.e., *as illegitimate daughter of a priest*).

She was as digne as water in a dich,
And ful of hoker and of bisemare.
Hir thoughte that a lady sholde hire spare,
What for her kynrede and hir nortelrie
That she had lerned in the nonnerie.

FROM *The Wife of Bath's Tale*

In th'olde dayes of the Kyng Arthour,
Of which the Britons speken greet honour,
Al was this land fulfild of fayerye.
The elf-queene, with hir joly compaignye,
Daunced ful ofte in many a grene mede.
This was the olde opinion, as I rede;
I speke of manye hundred yeres ago.
But now kan no man se none elves mo,
For now the greet charitee and prayeres
Of lymytours and othere hooly freres,
That serchen every lond and every streem,
As thikke as motes in the sonne-beem,
Blessynge halles, chambres, kichenes, boures,
Citees, burghes, castels, hye toures,
Thropes, bernes, shipnes, dayeryes—
This maketh that ther been no fayeryes.
For ther as wont to walken was an elf,
Ther walketh now the lymytour hymself
In undermeles and in morwenynges,
And seyth his matyns and his hooly thynges
As he gooth in his lymytacioun.
Wommen may go now saufly up and doun
In every bussh or under every tree;
Ther is noon oother incubus but he,
And he ne wol doon hem but dishonour.

Digne, *haughty.* Dich, *ditch.* Hoker, *disdain.* Bisemare, *scorn* Spare, *be reserved.* Kynrede, *kindred.* Nortelrie, *education.*

Greet, *great.* Fulfild, *full.* Fayerye, *fairy-folk.* Joly, *merry.* Grene mede, *green meadow.* Rede, *think.* None elves mo, *no more elves.* Lymytours, *begging friars.* Hooly freres, *holy friars.* Serchen, *visit.* Lond, *land.* Thikke, *thick.* Sonne-beem, *sunbeam.* Boures, *women's rooms.* Hye, *high.* Thropes, *villages.* Bernes, *barns.* Shipnes, *stables.* Dayeryes, *dairies.* Undermeles, *afternoons.* Morwenynges, *mornings.* Matyns, *matins.* Lymytacioun, *friar's limit.* Saufly, *safely.* Noon, *none.*

FROM *The Parliament of Fowls*

The lyf so short, the craft so long to lerne,
Th'assay so hard, so sharp the conquerynge,
The dredful joye, alwey that slit so yerne:
Al this mene I by Love, that my felynge
Astonyeth with his wonderful werkynge
So sore iwis, that whan I on hym thynke,
Nat wot I wel wher that I flete or synke.

Of usage—what for lust and what for lore—
On bokes rede I ofte, as I yow tolde.
But wherfore that I speke al this? Not yoore
Agon, it happede me for to beholde
Upon a bok, was write with lettres olde,
And therupon, a certeyn thing to lerne,
The longe day ful faste I redde and yerne.

For out of olde feldes, as men seyth,
Cometh all this newe corn from yer to yere,
And out of olde bokes, in good feyth,
Cometh al this newe science that men lere.
But now to purpos as of this matere
To rede forth hit gan me so delite,
That al that day me thoughte but a lyte.

FROM *Troilus and Criseyde*

Go, litel bok, go, litel myn tragedye,
Ther God thi makere yet, er that he dye,
So sende myght to make in some comedye!

Assay, *trial.* Dredful, *timid.* Slit so yerne, *passes so quickly.* Astonyeth, *confounds.* Iwis, *assuredly.* Whan, *when.* Nat wot I, *I know not.* Wher, *whether.* Flete, *float.* Lust, *pleasure.* Lore, *learning.* Yow, *you.* Yoore, *long.* Ful faste, *eagerly.* Redde, *read.* Yerne, *desired.* Feldes, *fields.* Seyth, *say.* Yer, yere, *year.* Feyth, *faith.* Lere, *learn.* Gan, *did.* A lyte, *a little, i.e., short.*

Bok, *book.* Ther God &c., *and so may God grant that thy poet may write comedy before he dies.* Makere, *poet.* Make, *write poetry.*

But litel book, no makyng thow n'envie,
But subgit be to alle poesye;
And kis the steppes, where as thow seest pace
Virgil, Ovide, Omer, Lucan, and Stace.

And for ther is so gret diversitie
In Englissh and in writyng of oure tonge,
So prey I God that non myswrite the,
Ne the mysmetre for defaute of tonge.
And red wherso thow be, or elles songe,
That thow be understonde, God I beseche!
But yet to purpos of my rather speche.

O yonge, fresshe folkes, he or she,
In which that love up groweth with youre age,
Repeyreth hom fro worldly vanyte,
And of youre herte up casteth the visage
To thilke God that after his ymage
Yow made, and thynketh al nys but a faire
This world, that passeth soon as floures faire.

And loveth hym, the which that right for love
Upon a crois, oure soules for to beye,
First starf, and roos, and sit in hevene above;
For he nyl falsen no wight, dar I seye,
That wol his herte al holly on hym leye.
And syn he best to love is, and most meke,
What nedeth feyned loves for to seke?

Lo here, of payens corsed olde rites,
Lo here, what alle hire goddes may availle;
Lo here, this wrecched worldes appetites;
Lo here, the fyn and guerdoun for travaille

No makyng thow n'envie, do thou envy no other writing. Subgit, subject.
Omer, Homer. Stace, Statius. Tonge, tongue. Non, none. The, thee. Mysmetre, falsify the metre. Red, read. Elles songe, or else sung. Repeyreth
hom, return home. Fro, from. Thilke, that. Al nys, all is—negative. Floures,
flowers. Loveth, love—imperative. The which, who. Crois, cross. Beye,
redeem. Starf, died. Roos, rose. Sit, sits. Nyl falsen, will not betray. Wight,
person. Holly, wholly. Leye, recline. Syn, since. Meke, meek. Feyned, pretended. Seke, seek. Payens, pagans. Corsed, accursed. Hire, their. Fyn, end.
Guerdoun, reward.

Of Jove, Appollo, of Mars, of swich rascaille!
Lo here, the forme of olde clerkis speche
In poetrie, if ye hire bokes seche.

O moral Gower, this book I directe
To the and to the, philosophical Strode,
To vouchen safe, ther nede is, to correcte,
Of your benignities and zeles goode.
And to that sothefast Crist, that starf on rode,
With al myn herte of mercy evere I preye,
And to the Lord right thus I speke and seye:

Thow oon, and two, and thre, eterne on lyve,
That regnest ay in thre, and two, and oon,
Uncircumscript, and al maist circumscrive,
Us from visible and invisible foon
Defende, and to thy mercy, everichon,
So make us, Jesus, for thi mercy digne,
For love of mayde and moder thyn benigne.
          Amen.

FROM *The Legend of Good Women*

And as for me, though that my wit be lite,
On bokes for to rede I me delyte,
And in myn herte have hem in reverence,
And to hem yeve swich lust and swich credence
That there is wel unethe game non
That fro my bokes make me to gon,
But be it other upon the halyday,
Or ellis in the joly tyme of May,
What that I here the smale foules synge,

Swich rascaille, such a mob. Seche, seek. Gower, *English poet.* The, thee.
Strode, probably *Ralph Strode, the scholar.* Ther, where. Benignities, gra-
ciousness. Sothefast, true. Rode, rood. Oon, one. Eterne on lyve, eternally
living. Maist, mayest. Foon, foes. Everichon, every one. Digne, worthy.
Benigne, gracious.

Lite, slight. Rede, read. Hem, them. Yeve, give. Swich lust, such pleasure.
Wel unethe game non, scarcely any amusement. Fro, from. Gon, go. Halyday, holiday. Ellis, else. Here, hear. Foules, birds.

And that the floures gynne for to sprynge.
Farwel my stodye, as lastynge that sesoun!
Now have I therto this condicioun,
That of alle the floures in the mede,
Thanne love I most these floures white and rede,
Swyche as men calle dayesyes in oure toun.
To hem have I so gret affeccioun,
As I seyde erst, whan comen is the May,
That in my bed there daweth me no day
That I n'am up and walkynge in the mede
To sen these floures agen the sonne sprede,
The longe day thus walkynge in the grene.

Balade de Bon Conseil

Flee fro the prees, and dwelle with sothfastnesse,
Suffyce unto thy good, though it be smal;
For hord hath hate, and climbing tikelnesse,
Prees hath envye, and wele blent overal;
Savour no more than thee bihove shal;
Reule wel thyself, that other folk canst rede;
And trouth thee shal delivere, it is no drede.

Tempest thee noght al croked to redresse,
In trust of hir that turneth as a bal:
Gret reste stant in litel besinesse;
Be war also to sporne ayeyns an al;
Stryve not, as doth the crokke with the wal.
Daunte thyself, that dauntest otheres dede;
And trouthe thee shal delivere, it is no drede.

Floures, *flowers.* Gynne, *begin.* Stodye, *study.* As lastynge, *during.* Condicioun, *state of mind.* Mede, *meadow.* Thanne, *then.* Rede, *red.* Dayesyes, *daisies.* Erst, *at first.* Whan, *when.* Daweth, *dawneth.* N'am, *am not.* Agen, *towards.*

Fro, *from.* Prees, *throng.* Sothfastnesse, *truth.* Hord, *avarice.* Tikelnesse, *instability.* Wele blent, *success blinds.* Bihove, *behove.* Rede, *advise.* Drede, *doubt.* Tempest, *distress.* Noght, *not.* Al croked, *all crooked things.* Hir, *here, i.e., Fortune.* Reste, *repose.* Be war, *beware.* Sporne, *kick.* Ayeyns, *against.* Al, *awl.* Crokke, *crock.* Daunte, *control.*

That thee is sent, receyve in buxumnesse,
The wrastling for this world axeth a fal.
Her is non hoom, her nis but wildernesse:
Forth, pilgrim, forth! Forth, beste, out of thy stall
Know thy contree, look up, thank God of al;
Hold the heye way, and lat thy gost thee lede;
And trouthe thee shal delivere, it is no drede.

ENVOY

Therfore, thou Vache, leve thyn old wrecchednesse
Unto the world; leve now to be thral;
Crye him mercy, that of his hy goodnesse
Made thee of noght, and in especial
Draw unto him, and pray in general
For thee, and eek for other, hevenlich mede;
And trouthe thee shal delivere, it is no drede.

The Complaint of Chaucer to His Purse

To yow, my purse, and to noon other wight
Complayne I, for ye be my lady dere!
I am so sory, now that ye been lyght;
For certes, but ye make me hevy chere,
Me were as leef be layd upon my bere;
For which unto your mercy thus I crye:
Beth hevy ageyn, or elles mot I dye!

Now voucheth sauf this day, or yt be nyght,
That I of yow this blissful soun may here,
Or see your colour lyk the sonne bryght,
That of yelownesse hadde never pere.
Ye be my lyf, ye be myn hertes stere,
Quene of comfort and of good companye:
Beth hevy ageyn, or elles moote I dye!

Buxumnesse, submission. Axeth, asketh. Her is non hoom, here is no home.
Contree, country. Gost, spirit. Lede, lead. Vache, cow. Hevenlich mede,
heavenly reward.

Stere, pilot.

Now purse, that ben to me my lyves lyght
And saveour, as doun in this world here,
Out of this toune help me thurgh your myght,
Syn that ye wole nat ben my tresorere;
For I am shave as nye as any frere.
But yet I pray unto your curtesye:
Beth hevy agen, or elles moote I dye!

LENVOY DE CHAUCER

O conqueror of Brutes Albyon,
Which that by lyne and free eleccion
Been verray king, this song to yow I send;
And ye, that mowen alle oure harmes amende,
Have mind upon my supplicacion!

ANONYMOUS
(15TH CENTURY)
"I Sing of a Maiden"

I sing of a maiden
   That is makëles,
King of all kinges
   To her sone sche ches.

He cam also stille
   There his moder was,
As dew in Aprille
   That falleth on the grass.

He cam also stille
   To his moderës bour,
As dew in Aprille
   That falleth on the flour.

Nye, *close.* Frere, *friar.* Lyne, *descent.* Mowen, *have power to.* Harmes,
misfortunes.

Makëles, *mateless.* Sche, *she.* Ches, *chose.* Moder, *mother.* Bour, *bower.*

He came also stille
  There his moder lay,
As dew in Aprille
  That falleth on the spray.

Moder and maiden
  Was never non but sche;
Well may swich a lady
  Godës moder be.

ANONYMOUS
(15TH CENTURY)
"Can I Not Sing..."

Can I not sing but "Hoy,"
Whan the joly shepard made so much joy?

The shepard upon a hill he satt;
He had on him his tabard and his hat,
His tarbox, his pipe, and his flagat;
His name was called Joly Joly Wat,
    For he was a gud herdës boy.
          Ut hoy!
For in his pipe he made so much joy.

The shepard upon a hill was laid;
His dog to his girdell was taid;
He had not slept but a litill braid,
But "Gloria in excelsis" was to him said.
          Ut hoy!
For in his pipe he made so much joy.

The shepard on a hill he stode;
Round about him his shepe they yode;
He put his hond under his hode,
He saw a star as rede as blode.
          Ut hoy!
For in his pipe he made so much joy.

Swich, such.

Tabard, short coat. Flagat, flagon. Taid, tied. Braid, time. Yode, went.
Hond, hand. Hode, hood. Blode, blood.

The shepard said anon right,
"I will go see yon farly sight,
Where as the angel singeth on hight,
And the star that shineth so bright."
        Ut hoy!
    For in his pipe he made so much joy.

"Now farewell, Mall, and also Will!
For my love go ye all still,
Unto I cum again you till,
And evermore, Will, ring well thy bell."
        Ut hoy!
    For in his pipe he made so much joy.

"Now must I go there Crist was born;
Farewell! I cum again to morn.
Dog, keep well my shepe from ye corn,
And warn well 'Warroke' when I blow my horn!"
        Ut hoy!
    For in his pipe he made so much joy.

Whan Wat to Bedlem cum was,
He swet, he had gone faster than a pace;
He found Jesu in a simpell place,
Between an ox and an ass.
        Ut hoy!
    For in his pipe he made so much joy.

"Jesu, I offer to thee here my pipe,
My skirt, my tar-box, and my scripe;
Home to my felowes now will I skipe,
And also look unto my shepe."
        Ut hoy!
    For in his pipe he made so much joy.

"Now farewell, mine owne herdes man Wat!"
"Yea, for God, lady, even so I hat;
Lull well Jesu in thy lape,
And farewell, Joseph, with thy round cape!"
        Ut hoy!
    For in his pipe he made so much joy.

Farly, *marvellous.* Scripe, *scrip.* Hat, *am called.*

"Now may I well both hope and sing,
For I have bene at Cristes bering;
Home to my felowes now will I fling.
Crist of heven to his bliss us bring!"
                    Ut hoy!
        For in his pipe he made so much joy.

ANONYMOUS

(15TH CENTURY)

"I Am as Light as Any Roe"

I am as light as any roe
To preise womene where that I go.

To onpreise womene it were a shame,
    For a woman was thy dame.
Our blessëd lady bereth the name
    Of all womene where that they go.

A woman is a worthy thing;
    They do the washe and do the wringe;
"Lullay, lullay!" she dothe thee singe;
    And yet she hath but care and wo.

A woman is a worthy wight;
    She serveth a man both day and night;
Thereto she putteth alle her might;
    And yet she hath but care and wo.

ANONYMOUS

(15TH CENTURY)

"I Have a Gentil Cok"

I have a gentil cok
    Croweth me day;
He doth me risen erly
    My matines for to say.

Bering, birth.

I have a gentil cok;
    Comen he is of grete;
His comb is of red corel,
    His tail is of get.

I have a gentil cok;
    Comen he is of kinde;
His comb is of red corel,
    His tail is of inde.

His leggës ben of asour,
    So gentil and so smale;
His sporës arn of silver white
    Into the wortëwale.

His eyen arn of cristal,
    Loken all in aumber;
And every night he percheth him
    In mine ladyes chaumber.

ANONYMOUS

(15TH CENTURY)
"Bring Us in Good Ale..."

Bring us in good ale, and bring us in good ale;
For our blessëd Lady sake bring us in good ale!

Bring us in no browne bred, for that is made of brane,
Nor bring us in no white bred, for therein is no gane.
    But bring us in good ale!

Bring us in no befe, for there is many bones,
But bring us in good ale, for that goth downe at ones,
    And bring us in good ale!

Bring us in no bacon, for that is passing fate,
But bring us in good ale, and gife us enough of that;
    And bring us in good ale!

Get, jet. Inde, indigo. Asour, azure. Sporës, spurs. Wortëwale, the skin
of the claws. Loken, set.

Bring us in no mutton, for that is often lene,
Nor bring us in no tripes, for they be seldom clene,
      But bring us in good ale!

Bring us in no eggs, for there are many schelles,
But bring us in good ale, and gife us nothing elles;
      And bring us in good ale!

Bring us in no butter, for therein are many heres,
Nor bring us in no pigges flesch, for that will make us bores,
      But bring us in good ale!

Bring us in no podinges, for therein is all Godes good,
Nor bring us in no venesen, for that is not for our blod;
      But bring us in good ale!

Bring us in no capons flesch, for that is oftë dere,
Nor bring us in no dokes flesch, for they slober in the mere,
      But bring us in good ale!

ANONYMOUS

(15TH CENTURY)

"How, Butler, How!"

How, butler, how!
   Bevis a tout!
O fill the boll, jentill butler,
  And let the cup rout!

Jentill butler, bellamy,
Fill the boll by the eye,
That we may drink by and by,
  With "How, butler, how!"
    Bevis a tout!
  Fill the boll, butler,
    And let the cup rout!

Brane, bran. Heres, hairs. Bores, boars. Podinges, puddings. Dokes, ducks.
Slober, slobber.

Bevis a tout, drink to all (Fr.). Rout, move. Bellamy, fair friend (Fr.).
Boll, bowl.

Here is metë for us all,
Both for grete and for small,
I trow we must the butler call,
   With "How, butler, how!"

I am so dry I cannot speke;
I am nigh chokëd with my mete;
I trow the butler be aslepe.
   With "How, butler, how!"

Butler, butler, fill the boll,
Or elles I beshrewe thy noll.
I trow we must the bell toll,
   With, "How, butler, how!"

If the butler's name be Water,
I would he were a galow claper;
But if he bring us drink, the rather
   With "How, butler, how!"

JOHN SKELTON

(1460?–1529)

FROM *Philip Sparrow*

How shall I report
All the goodly sort
Of her features clear,
That hath none earthly peer?
The favour of her face
Ennewed all with grace,
Comfort, pleasure and solace.
Mine heart doth so embrace,
And so hath ravished me
Her to behold and see,
That in wordës plain
I cannot me refrain
To look on her again:

Noll, *noddle*. Galow claper, *Gallows clapper*. But if, *unless*.

Alas, what should I feign?
It were a pleasant pain
With her aye to remain.

Her eyen gray and steep
Causeth mine heart to leap;
With her brows bent
She may well represent
Fair Lucrece, as I ween,
Or else fair Polexene,
Or else Calliope,
Or else Penelope;
For this most goodly flower,
This blossom of fresh colour,
So Jupiter me succour,
She flourisheth new and new
In beauty and virtue.

The Indy sapphire blue
Her veins doth ennew;
The orient pearl so clear,
The whiteness of her lere;
Her lusty ruby ruddies
Resemble the rose buddës;
Her lips soft and merry
Enblooméd like the cherry:
It were an heavenly bliss
Her sugar'd mouth to kiss.

FROM *Elinor Rumming*

And this comely dame,
I understand, her name
Is Elinor Rumming,
At home in her wonning;
And as men say

Lere, complexion.

Wonning, dwelling.

She dwelt in Surrey,
In a certain stead
Beside Leatherhead.
She is a tonnish gib,
The devil and she be sib.

But to make up my tale,
She breweth nappy ale,
And maketh thereof pot-sale
To travellers, to tinkers,
To sweaters, to swinkers,
And all good ale-drinkers,
That will nothing spare
But drink till they stare
And bring themselves bare,
With *"Now away the mare!*
And let us slay care."
As wise as an hare!

Come who so will
To Elinor on the hill
With "Fill the cup, fill!"
And sit there by still,
Early and late.
Thither cometh Kate,
Cisly, and Sare,
With their legs bare,
And also their feet
Hardely full unsweet;
With their heelës daggéd,
Their kirtles all to-jaggéd,
Their smockës all to-raggéd,
With titters and tatters,
Bring dishes and platters,
With all their might running
To Elinor Rumming
To have of her tunning:
She lendeth them on the same,
And thus beginneth the game.

Tonnish gib, *stylish cat.* Sib, *kin.* Swinkers, *labourers.* Hardely, *hardly.*
Daggéd, *bemired.*

FROM *Against Garnesche*

What, have ye kithéd you a knight, Sir Douglas the Doughty,
  So currishly to beknave me in the king's palace?
Ye sturdy strong stallion, so stern and stouty,
    Ye bear ye bold as Barrabas, or Sir Terry of Thrace;
    Ye grin grimly with your gummës and with your grisly face!
But say me yet, Sir Satrapas, what authority ye have
In your challenge, Sir Chesten, to call me a knave?

Your wind-shaken shanks, your long loathly legs,
  Crooked as a camock, and as a cow calfless,
Brings you out of favour with all female tegs:
    That Mistress Punt put you off, it was not all causeless;
    At Orwell her haven your anger was lawless.
But say me yet, Sir Satrapas, what authority ye have
In your challenge, Sir Chesten, to call me a knave?

I say, ye solemn Saracen, all black is your ble;
  As a glede glowing, your eyen glister as glass,
Rolling in your hollow head, ugly to see;
    Your teeth tainted with tawny; your snivelly snout doth pass
    Hookéd as an hawkës beak, like Sir Thopas.
Boldly bend you to battle, and busk yourself to save:
Challenge yourself for a fool, call me no more knave!

FROM *Speak, Parrot*

So many moral matters, and so little used;
  So much new making, and so mad time spent;
So much translation into English confused;
    So much noble preaching, and so little amendment;
    So much consultation, almost to none intent;
So much provision, and so little wit at need—
Since Deucalion's flood there can no clerkës read.

Camock, *hockey stick.* Tegs, *sheep.* Ble, *visage.* Glede, *ember.*

So little discretion, and so much reasoning;
   So much hardy dardy, and so little manliness;
So prodigal expence, and so shameful reckoning;
   So gorgeous garments, and so much wretchedness;
   So much portly pride, with purses penniless;
So much spent before, and so much unpaid behind—
Since Deucalion's flood there can no clerkës find.

So much forecasting, and so far an after deal;
   So much politic prating, and so little standeth in stead;
So little secretness, and so much great council;
   So many bold barons, their hearts as dull as lead;
   So many noble bodies under a daw's head;
So royal a king as reigneth upon us all—
Since Deucalion's flood was never seen nor shall.

To Mistress Margery Wentworth

With margerain gentle,
   The flower of goodlihead,
Embroidered the mantle
   Is of your maidenhead.
Plainly I cannot glose;
   Ye be, as I divine,
The pretty primrose,
   The goodly columbine.
With margerain gentle,
   The flower of goodlihead,
Embroidered the mantle
   Is of your maidenhead.
Benign, courteous, and meek,
   With wordës well devised;
In you, who list to seek,
   Be virtues well comprised.
With margerain gentle,
   The flower of goodlihead,
Embroidered the mantle
   Is of your maidenhead.

To Mistress Isabel Pennell

By Saint Mary, my lady,
Your mammy and your daddy,
Brought forth a goodly baby!

  My maiden Isabel,
Reflaring rosabel,
The fragrant camomel;
  The ruddy rosary,
The sovereign rosemary,
The pretty strawberry;
  The columbine, the nept,
The gillyflower well set,
The proper violet:
  Ennewéd your colour
Is like the daisy flower
After the April shower;
  Star of the morrow gray,
The blossom on the spray,
The freshest flower of May;
  Maidenly demure,
Of womanhood the lure;
Wherefore I make you sure
  It were an heavenly health,
It were an endless wealth,
A life for God himself,
  To hear this nightingale
Among the birdës smale
Warbling in the vale,
  Dug, dug,
  Jug, jug,
    Good year and good luck,
    With chuck, chuck, chuck, chuck!

To Mistress Margaret Hussey

  Merry Margaret,
    As midsummer flower,
  Gentle as falcon
  Or hawk of the tower:

With solace and gladness,
Much mirth and no madness,
All good and no badness;
So joyously,
So maidenly,
So womanly
Her demeaning
In every thing,
Far, far passing
That I can indite,
Or suffice to write
Of Merry Margaret
As midsummer flower
Gentle as falcon
Or hawk of the tower.
As patient and still
And as full of good will
As fair Isaphill,
Coliander,
Sweet pomander,
Good Cassander,
Steadfast of thought,
Well made, well wrought,
Far may be sought
Ere that he can find
So courteous, so kind
As Merry Margaret,
This midsummer flower,
Gentle as falcon
Or hawk of the tower.

WILLIAM DUNBAR

(1460–1520?)

FROM *The Lament for the Makaris*

I that in heill was and gladness
Am trublit now with great sickness
And feblit with infirmitie;
Timor Mortis conturbat me.

Makaris, poets. Heill, *health.* Trublit, *troubled.* Feblit, *enfeebled.* Timor
Mortis conturbat me, *fear of death troubles me.*

Our plesance here is all vain glory,
This fals world is but transitory,
The flesh is bruckle, the Feynd is slee;
    Timor Mortis conturbat me.

The state of man does change and vary,
Now sound, now sick, now blyth, now sary,
Now dansand mirry, now like to die;
    Timor Mortis conturbat me.

No state in Erd here standis sicker,
As with the wynd wavis the wicker,
So wannis this world's vanitie;
    Timor Mortis conturbat me.

Unto the ded gois all Estatis,
Princes, Prelatis, and Potestatis,
Baith rich and poor of all degree;
    Timor Mortis conturbat me.

He takis the knichtis in to the field
Enarmit under helm and scheild,
Victor he is at all mellie;
    Timor Mortis conturbat me.

That strong unmerciful tyrand
Takis, on the motheris breast sowkand,
The babe full of benignitie;
    Timor Mortis conturbat me.

He takis the campion in the stour,
The captain closit in the tour,
The lady in bour full of bewtie;
    Timor Mortis conturbat me.

He spairis no lord for his piscence,
Na clerk for his intelligence,
His awful straik may no man flee;
    Timor Mortis conturbat me.

Bruckle, *brittle.* Feynd, *fiend.* Slee, *sly.* Sary, *sorry.* Mirry, *merry.* Erd, *earth.*
Sicker, *sure.* Wicker, *willow.* Wannis, *wanes.* Mellie, *battle.* Sowkand,
sucking. Campion, *champion.* Stour, *battle.* Tour, *tower.* Piscence, *puis-
sance.* Straik, *stroke.*

Art-magicianis and astrologgis,
Rethoris, logicianis, and theologgis,
Them helpis no conclusionis slee;
> *Timor Mortis conturbat me.*

In medicine the most practicianis,
Leechis, surrigianis, and physicianis,
Themself fra ded may not supplee;
> *Timor Mortis conturbat me.*

I see that makaris amang the lave
Playis here their padyanis, syne gois to grave,
Sparit is nocht their facultie;
> *Timor Mortis conturbat me.*

Sen he has all my brethren tane,
He will naught let me live alane,
Of force I man his next prey be;
> *Timor Mortis conturbat me.*

Since for the Death remeid is none,
Best is that we for Death dispone,
After our death that live may we;
> *Timor Mortis conturbat me.*

STEPHEN HAWES

(1475?–1523?)

FROM *The Passetyme*

O mortal folk, you may behold and see
How I lie here, sometime a mighty knight;
The end of joy and all prosperity
Is death at last, thorough his course and might:
After the day there cometh the dark night,
For though the day be never so long,
At last the bells ringeth to evensong.

Fra, from. Supplee, save. Makaris, poets. The lave, the rest. Padyanis,
pageants. Syne, soon. Sparit, spared. Sen, since. Tane, taken. Alane, alone.
Man, must. Remeid, remedy. Dispone, make ready.

BALLADS

ANONYMOUS

(PERIODS UNCERTAIN)

Sir Patrick Spens

The king sits in Dumferling toune,
　　Drinking the blude-reid wine:
O quhar will I get guid sailór,
　　To sail this schip of mine?

Up and spak an eldern knicht,
　　Sat at the king's richt knee:
Sir Patrick Spens is the best sailór,
　　That sails upon the sea.

The king has written a braid letter,
　　And signed it wi' his hand;
And sent it to Sir Patrick Spens,
　　Was walking on the sand.

The first line that Sir Patrick red,
　　A loud lauch lauched he:
The next line that Sir Patrick red,
　　The teir blinded his ee.

O quhar is this has don this deid,
　　This ill deid don to me;
To send me out this time o' the zeir,
　　To sail upon the sea?

Mak haste, mak haste, my mirry men all,
　　Our good schip sails the morn.
O say na sae, my master deir,
　　For I feir a deadlie storme.

85

Late late yestreen I saw the new moone
 Wi' the auld moone in hir arme;
And I feir, I feir, my deir mastér,
 That we will come to harme.

O our Scots nobles wer richt laith
 To weet their cork-heild schoone;
But lang owre a' the play were played,
 Their hats they swam aboone.

O lang, lang, may the ladies stand
 Wi' their fans into their hand,
Or e'er they see Sir Patrick Spens
 Come sailing to the land.

O lang, lang, may the ladies stand
 Wi' thair gold kems in their hair,
Waiting for their ain deir lords,
 For they'll see them na mair.

Have owre, have owre to Aberdour,
 It's fifty fadom deip:
And thair lies guid Sir Patrick Spens,
 Wi' the Scots lords at his feit.

The Falcon

Lully, lulley! lully, lulley!
The faucon hath borne my make away!

He bare him up, he bare him down,
He bare him into an orchard brown.

In that orchard there was an halle,
That was hangéd with purple and pall.

And in that hall there was a bed,
It was hangéd with gold sa red.

And in that bed there li'th a knight,
His woundés bleeding day and night.

At that bed's foot there li'th a hound,
Licking the blood as it runs down.

By that bed-side kneeleth a may,
And she weepeth both night and day.

And at that bed's head standeth a stone,
Corpus Christi written thereon.

Lully, lulley! lully, lulley!
The faucon hath borne my make away.

FROM *The Birth of Robin Hood*

And mony ane sings o' grass, o' grass,
    And mony ane sings o' corn,
And mony ane sings o' Robin Hood
    Kens little whare he was born.

It wasna in the ha', the ha',
    Nor in the painted bower;
But it was in the gude green-wood,
    Amang the lily-flower.

FROM *Robin Hood and the Monk*

In somer, when the shawes be sheyne,
    And leves be large and long,
Hit is full mery in feyre foreste
    To here the foulys song:

To se the dere draw to the dale,
    And leve the hillés hee,
And shadow hem in the levés grene,
    Under the grene-wode tre.

Hit befel on Whitsontide,
  Erly in a May mornyng,
The Son up feyre can shyne,
  And the briddis mery can syng.

"This is a mery mornyng," said Litull John,
  "Be Hym that dyed on tre;
A more mery man then I am one
  Lyves not in Christianté.

"Pluck up thi hert, my dere mayster,"
  Litull John can sey,
"And think hit is a full fayre tyme
  In a mornyng of May."

FROM *The Death of Robin Hood*

"I never hurt maid in all my time,
  Nor at mine end shall it be;
But give me my bent bow in my hand,
  And a broad arrow I'll let flee;
And where this arrow is taken up
  There shall my grave digged be.

"But lay me a green sod under my head,
  And another at my feet;
And lay my bent bow at my side,
  Which was my music sweet;
And make my grave of gravel and green,
  Which is most right and meet.

"Let me have length and breadth enough,
  And under my head a sod;
That they may say when I am dead,
  Here lies bold Robin Hood."

The Three Ravens

There were three ravens sat on a tree,
They were as black as they might be.

The one of them said to his make,
"Where shall we our breakfast take?"

"Down in yonder greené field
There lies a knight slain under his shield;

"His hounds they lie down at his feet,
So well they their master keep;

"His hawks they flie so eagerly,
There's no fowl dare him come nigh."

Down there comes a fallow doe
As great with young as she might go.

She lift up his bloudy head
And kist his wounds that were so red.

She got him up upon her back
And carried him to earthen lake.

She buried him before the prime,
She was dead herself ere evensong time.

God send every gentleman
Such hounds, such hawks, and such a leman.

The Unquiet Grave

"The wind doth blow to-day, my love,
    And a few small drops of rain;
I never had but one true-love;
    In cold grave she was lain.

"I'll do as much for my true-love
  As any young man may;
I'll sit and mourn all at her grave
  For a twelvemonth and a day."

The twelvemonth and a day being up,
  The dead began to speak:
"Oh who sits weeping on my grave,
  And will not let me sleep?"

" 'Tis I, my love, sits on your grave,
  And will not let you sleep;
For I crave one kiss of your clay-cold lips,
  And that is all I seek."

"You crave one kiss of my clay-cold lips;
  But my breath smells earthy strong;
If you have one kiss of my clay-cold lips,
  Your time will not be long.

" 'Tis down in yonder garden green,
  Love, where we used to walk,
The finest flower that e'er was seen
  Is withered to a stalk.

"The stalk is withered dry, my love,
  So will our hearts decay;
So make yourself content, my love,
  Till God calls you away."

Thomas the Rhymer

True Thomas lay on Huntlie bank;
  A ferlie he spied wi' his e'e;
And there he saw a ladye bright
  Come riding down by Eildon Tree.

Ferlie, wonder.

Her skirt was o' the grass-green silk,
　　Her mantle o' the velvet fyne;
At ilka tett o' her horse's mane
　　Hung fifty siller bells and nine.

True Thomas he pu'd aff his cap,
　　And louted low down on his knee:
"Hail to thee, Mary, Queen of Heaven!
　　For thy peer on earth could never be."

"O no, O no, Thomas," she said,
　　"That name does not belang to me;
I'm but the Queen o' fair Elfland,
　　That am hither come to visit thee.

"Harp and carp, Thomas," she said;
　　"Harp and carp along wi' me;
And if ye dare to kiss my lips,
　　Sure of your bodie I will be."

"Betide me weal, betide me woe,
　　That weird shall never daunten me."
Syne he has kissed her rosy lips,
　　All underneath the Eildon Tree.

"Now ye maun go wi' me," she said,
　　"True Thomas, ye maun go wi' me;
And ye maun serve me seven years,
　　Thro' weal or woe as may chance to be."

She's mounted on her milk-white steed,
　　She's ta'en true Thomas up behind;
And aye, whene'er her bridle rang,
　　The steed gaed swifter than the wind.

O they rade on, and farther on,
　　The steed gaed swifter than the wind;
Until they reached a desert wide,
　　And living land was left behind.

Tett, *tuft.* Siller, *silver.* Harp and carp, *play and recite.*

"Light down, light down now, true Thomas,
    And lean your head upon my knee;
Abide ye there a little space,
    And I will show you ferlies three.

"O see ye not yon narrow road,
    So thick beset wi' thorns and briars?
That is the Path of Righteousness,
    Though after it but few inquires.

"And see ye not yon braid, braid road,
    That lies across the lily leven?
That is the Path of Wickedness,
    Though some call it the Road to Heaven.

"And see ye not yon bonny road
    That winds about the fernie brae?
That is the Road to fair Elfland,
    Where thou and I this night maun gae.

"But, Thomas, ye sall haud your tongue,
    Whatever ye may hear or see;
For speak ye word in Elfyn-land,
    Ye'll ne'er win back to your ain countrie."

O they rade on, and farther on,
    And they waded rivers abune the knee;
And they saw neither sun nor moon,
    But they heard the roaring of the sea.

It was mirk, mirk night, there was nae starlight,
    They waded thro' red blude to the knee;
For a' the blude that's shed on the earth
    Rins through the springs o' that countrie.

Syne they came to a garden green,
    And she pu'd an apple frae a tree:
"Take this for thy wages, true Thomas;
    It will give thee the tongue that can never lee."

Weird, doom, fate. Braid, broad. Leven, ? level or lawn. Abune, above.

"My tongue is my ain," true Thomas he said;
  "A gudely gift ye wad gie to me!
I neither dought to buy or sell
  At fair or tryst where I might be.

"I dought neither speak to prince or peer,
  Nor ask of grace from fair ladye!"
"Now haud thy peace, Thomas," she said,
  "For as I say, so must it be."

He has gotten a coat of the even cloth,
  And a pair o' shoon of the velvet green;
And till seven years were gane and past,
  True Thomas on earth was never seen.

Chevy Chase

FYTTE I

The Percy out of Northumberland,
  An avow to God made he
That he would hunt in the mountains
  Of Cheviot within days three,
In the maugre of doughty Douglas,
  And all that e'er with him be.

The fattest harts in all Cheviot
  He would kill and carry away.
"By my faith," said the doughty Douglas again,
  "I will let that hunting if I may!"

Then the Percy out of Banborowe came,
  With him a mighty meinye,
With fifteen hundred archers bold
  Chosen out of shirés three.

This began on a Monday at morn,
  In Cheviot the hills so hye;
The child may rue that is unborn,
  It was the more pitye.

Dought, could.

Fytte, canto. In the maugre, despite. Let, hinder. Meinye, train.

The drivers through the woodés went
    All for to raise the deer,
Bowmen bicker'd upon the bent
    With their broad arrows clear.

Then the wild thoro' the woodés went
    On every sidé shear;
Greyhounds thoro' the grevés glent
    For to kill their deer.

This began on Cheviot the hills abune
    Early on a Monenday;
By that it drew to the hour of noon
    A hundred fat harts dead there lay.

They blew a mort upon the bent,
    They 'sembled on sidés shear;
To the quarry then the Percy went
    To the brittling of the deer.

He said, "It was the Douglas' promise
    This day to meet me here;
But I wist he would fail, verament!"
    A great oath the Percy sware.

At the last a squire of Northumberland
    Lookéd at his hand full nigh;
He was ware o' the doughty Douglas coming,
    With him a great meinye.

Both with speär, bill and brand,
    'Twas a mighty sight to see;
Hardier men both of heart nor hand
    Were not in Christianté.

They were twenty hundred spearmen good,
    Withouten any fail:
They were born along by the water o' Tweed
    I' the boun's o' Teviotdale.

Bicker'd, *skirmished.* Bent, *heath.* Shear, *sheer.* Grevés, *?.* Glent, *glitter or move swiftly.* Abune, *above.* Mort, *bugle call at the kill.* Brittling, *cutting up.* Wist, *thought.* Verament, *truly.* Bill, *halberd.*

"Leave off the brittling of deer," he said;
  "To your bows look ye take good heed,
For sith ye were on your mothers born
  Had ye never so mickle need."

The doughty Douglas on a steed
  Rode all his men beforn;
His armour glitter'd as did a gleed,
  Bolder bairn was never born.

"Tell me whose men ye are," he says,
  "Or whose men that ye be;
Who gave you leave in this Cheviot chase
  In the spite of mine and of me?"

The first man that him answer made
  It was the good Lord Percye:
"We will not tell whose men we are,
  Nor whose men that we be;
But we will hunt here in this chase
  In spite of thine and of thee.

"The fattest harts in all Cheviot
  We have killed to carry away."
"By my troth," said the doughty Douglas again,
  "The one of us dies this day.

"Yet to kill allé these guiltless men
  Alas, it were great pitye!
But, Percy, thou art a lord of land,
  I an earl in my countrye—
Let all our men on a party stand,
  And do battle of thee and me!"

"Christ's curse on his crown," said the lord Percye,
  "Whosoever thereto says nay!
By my troth, thou doughty Douglas," he says,
  "Thou shalt never see that day,

Gleed, ember.

Neither in England, Scotland nor France,
　Nor for no man of woman born,
But, that and fortune be my chance
　I dare meet him, one man for one."

Then bespake a squire of Northumberland,
　Richard Witherington was his name;
"It shall never be told in South England
　To King Harry the Fourth for shame.

"I wot you bin great lordés two,
　I am a poor squire of land;
Yet I'll ne'er see my captain fight on a field
　And stand myself and look on.
But while that I may my weapon wield
　I'll not fail, both heart and hand."

That day, that day, that dreadful day!
　The first fytte here I find:
An you'll hear any more o' the hunting of Cheviot,
　Yet there is more behind.

FYTTE II

The Englishmen had their bows y-bent,
　Their hearts were good enow;
The first of arrows that they shot off
　Seven score spearmen they slew.

Yet bides the Earl Douglas upon the bent,
　A captain good enoghe;
And that was seené verament,
　For he wrought them both woe and wouche.

The Douglas parted his host in three,
　Like a chief chieftain of pride;
With suré spears of mighty tree
　They came in on every side;

Verament, truly. Wouche, ? pain.

Throughé our English archery
   Gave many a woond full wide;
Many a doughty they gar'd to dye,
   Which gainéd them no pride.

The Englishmen let their bowés be,
   And pull'd out brands that were bright;
It was a heavy sight to see
   Bright swords on basnets light.

Thoro' rich mail and manoplie
   Many stern they struck down straight;
Many a freyké that was full free
   There under foot did light.

At last the Douglas and the Percy met,
   Like to captains of might and of main;
They swapt together till they both swat
   With swordés of fine Milan.

These worthy freykés for to fight
   Thereto they were full fain,
Till the blood out of their basnets sprent
   As ever did hail or rain.

"Yield thee, Percy," said the Douglas,
   "And i' faith I shall thee bring
Where thou shalt have an Earl's wages
   Of Jamie our Scottish king.

"Thou shalté have thy ransom free,
   I hight thee here this thing;
For the manfullest man thou art that e'er
   I conquered in field fighting."

But "Nay," then said the lord Percye,
   "I told it thee beforn
That I would never yielded be
   To man of a woman born."

Basnets, *helmets.* Manoplie, *panoply.* Freyké, *brave man.* Swapt, *fought.*
Swat, *sweated.* Hight, *promise.*

With that an arrow came hastily
   Forth of a mighty wane;
And it hath stricken the Earl Douglas
   In at the breasté-bane.

Thoro' liver and lungés both
   The sharp arrów is gone,
That never after in his life-days
   He spake mo words but one:
'Twas, "Fight ye, my merry men, whilst ye may,
   For my life-days bin gone!"

The Percy leanéd on his brand
   And saw the Douglas dee;
He took the dead man by the hand,
   And said, "Woe is me for thee!

"To have saved thy life I'd have parted with
   My lands for yearés three,
For a better man of heart nor of hand
   Was not in the north countrye."

All this there saw a Scottish knight,
   Sir Hugh the Montgomerye:
When he saw the Douglas to the death was dight,
   Through a hundred archerye
He never stint nor he never blint
   Till he came to the lord Percye.

He set upon the lord Percý
   A dint that was full sore;
With a suré spear of a mighty tree
   Thro' the body him he bore,
O' the t'other side that a man might see
   A large cloth-yard and more.

An archer of Northumberland
   Saw slain was the lord Percye:
He bare a bent bow in his hand,
   Was made of a trusty tree.

Wane, ? bow. Stint, ceased. Blint, stopped. Dint, blow.

An arrow that was a cloth-yard long
　　To the hard steel haléd he,
A dint that was both sad and sair
　　He set on Montgomerye.

The dint it was both sad and sair
　　That he on Montgomerye set;
The swan-feathers that his arrow bare
　　With his heart-blood they were wet.

There was never a freyké one foot would flee,
　　But still in stoure did stand;
Hewing on each other, while they might dree,
　　With many a baleful brand.

This battle began in Cheviot
　　An hour before the noon,
And when the even-song bell was rung
　　The battle was not half done.

They took their stand on either hand
　　By the lee light of the moon;
Many had no strength for to stand
　　In Cheviot the hills abune.

Of fifteen hundred archers of England
　　Went away but seventy-and-three;
Of twenty hundred spearmen of Scotland
　　But even five-and-fiftý.

There was slain with the bold Percye
　　Sir John of Agerstoune,
Sir Roger, the hendé Hartley,
　　Sir William, the bold Herone.

Sir George, the worthy Loumlye,
　　A knight of great renown,
Sir Ralph, the riché Rabye,
　　With dints were beaten down.

Stoure, *battle.* Dree, *endure.* Lee, *dim.* Abune, *above.*

For Witherington my heart was woe
    That ever he slain should be:
For when both his legs were hewn in two
    Yet he kneeled and fought on his knee.

There was slain with the doughty Douglas
    Sir Hugh the Montgomerye,
Sir Davy Lambwell, that worthy was,
    His sister's son was he.

Sir Charles a Murray in that place,
    That never a foot would flee:
Sir Hew Maxwell, a lord he was,
    With the Douglas did he dee.

So on the morrow they made them biers
    Of birch and hazel so gray;
Many widows with weeping tears
    Came to fetch their makes away.

Teviotdale may carp of care,
    Northumberland may make moan,
For two such captains as slain were there
    On the March-parts shall never be none.

Word is come to Edinboro',
    To Jamie the Scottish King,
Earl Douglas, lieutenant of the Marches,
    Lay slain Cheviot within.

His hands the King did weal and wring,
    Said, "Alas! and woe is me!
Such another captain Scotland within
    I' faith shall never be!"

Word is come to lovely London
    To the fourth Harry, our King,
Lord Percy, lieutenant of the Marches,
    Lay slain Cheviot within.

Dee, die. Makes, mates. Carp, tell. Weal, twist.

"God have mercy on his soul," said King Harry,
  "Good Lord, if thy will it be!
I've a hundred captains in England," he said,
  "As good as ever was he:
But Percy, an I brook my life,
  Thy death well quit shall be."

And as our King made his avow
  Like a noble Prince of renown,
For Percy he did it well perform
  After, on Homble-down;

Where six-and-thirty Scottish knights
  On a day were beaten down;
Glendale glittered on their armour bright
  Over castle, tower and town.

This was the hunting of the Cheviot;
  That e'er began this spurn!
Old men, that knowen the ground well,
  Call it of Otterburn.

There was never a time on the Marche-partés
  Since the Douglas and Percy met,
But 'tis marvel an the red blood run not
  As the reane does in the street.

Jesu Christ! our balés bete,
  And to the bliss us bring!
This was the Hunting of the Cheviot:
  God send us all good ending!

Waly, Waly

O waly waly up the bank,
  And waly waly down the brae,
And waly waly yon burn-side
  Where I and my love were wont to gae!

Brook, keep. Quit, revenged. Spurn, ? contest. Reane, rain. Balés bete,
deaths conquer, i.e., redeem us to life.

Waly, exclamation of sorrow. Brae, slope. Burn-side, brook-side.

I leant my back unto an aik,
    I thought it was a trusty tree;
But first it bowed, and syne it brak,
    Sae my true love did lichtly me.

O waly waly gin love be bonny
    A little time while it is new;
But when it's auld it waxeth cauld
    And fades awa' like morning dew.
O wherefore shuld I busk my heid?
    Or wherefore shuld I kame my hair?
For my true love has me forsook,
    And says he'll never loe me mair.

Now Arthur-Seat sall be my bed;
    The sheets shall ne'er be fyl'd by me:
Saint Anton's Well sall be my drink,
    Since my true love has forsaken me.
Marti'mas wind, when wilt thou blaw
    And shake the green leaves aff the tree?
O gentle Death, when wilt thou come?
    For of my life I am wearie.

'Tis not the frost, that freezes fell,
    Nor blawing snaw's inclemencie,
'Tis not sic cauld that makes me cry,
    But my love's heart grown cauld to me.
When we came in by Glasgow town,
    We were a comely sight to see;
My love was clad in the black velvét,
    And I myself in cramasie.

But had I wist, before I kist,
    That love had been sae ill to win;
I had lockt my heart in a case of gowd
    And pinned it with a siller pin.
And O! if my young babe were born,
    And set upon the nurse's knee,
And I myself were dead and gane,
    For a maid again I'se never be.

Aik, *oak*. Syne, *later*. Gin, *if*. Busk, *dress*. Heid, *head*. Kame, *comb*. Fyl'd, *defiled*. Cramasie, *crimson cloth*. Gowd, *gold*. Siller, *silver*.

Fair Helen

I wish I were where Helen lies;
Night and day on me she cries;
O that I were where Helen lies
　　On fair Kirconnell lea!

Curst be the heart that thought the thought,
And curst the hand that fired the shot,
And in my arms burd Helen dropt,
　　And died to succour me!

O think na ye my heart was sair
When my love dropt down and spak nae mair!
There did she swoon wi' meikle care
　　On fair Kirconnell lea.

As I went down the water-side,
None but my foe to be my guide,
None but my foe to be my guide,
　　On fair Kirconnell lea;

I lighted down my sword to draw,
I hackéd him in pieces sma',
I hackéd him in pieces sma',
　　For her sake that died for me.

O Helen fair, beyond compare!
I'll make a garland of thy hair
Shall bind my heart for evermair
　　Until the day I die.

O that I were where Helen lies!
Night and day on me she cries;
Out of my bed she bids me rise,
　　Says, "Haste and come to me!"

O Helen fair! O Helen chaste!
If I were with thee, I were blest,
Where thou lies low and takes thy rest
　　On fair Kirconnell lea.

I wish my grave were growing green,
A winding-sheet drawn ower my een,
And I in Helen's arms lying,
    On fair Kirconnell lea.

I wish I were where Helen lies;
Night and day on me she cries;
And I am weary of the skies,
    For her sake that died for me.

Bonny George Campbell

Hie upon Hielands,
    And laigh upon Tay,
Bonny George Campbell
    Rade out on a day:
Saddled and bridled,
    Sae gallant to see,
Hame cam' his gude horse,
    But never cam' he.

Down ran his auld mither,
    Greetin' fu' sair;
Out ran his bonny bride,
    Reaving her hair;
"My meadow lies green,
    And my corn is unshorn,
My barn is to bigg,
    And my babe is unborn."

Saddled and bridled
    And booted rade he;
A plume in his helmet,
    A sword at his knee;
But toom cam' his saddle
    A' bloody to see,
O hame cam' his gude horse,
    But never cam' he!

Laigh, *low*. Greetin', *weeping*. Bigg, *build*. Toom, *empty*.

Barbara Allen's Cruelty

In Scarlet town, where I was born,
    There was a fair maid dwellin',
Made every youth cry *Well-a-way!*
    Her name was Barbara Allen.

All in the merry month of May,
    When green buds they were swellin',
Young Jemmy Grove on his death-bed lay,
    For love of Barbara Allen.

He sent his man in to her then,
    To the town where she was dwellin';
"O haste and come to my master dear,
    If your name be Barbara Allen."

So slowly, slowly rase she up,
    And slowly she came nigh him,
And when she drew the curtain by,
    "Young man, I think you're dyin'."

"O it's I am sick and very very sick,
    And it's all for Barbara Allen."
"O the better for me ye'se never be,
    Tho' your heart's blood were a-spillin'!"

"O dinna ye mind, young man," says she,
    "When the red wine ye were fillin',
That ye made the healths go round and round,
    And slighted Barbara Allen?"

He turned his face unto the wall,
    And death was with him dealin':
"Adieu, adieu, my dear friends all,
    And be kind to Barbara Allen!"

As she was walking o'er the fields,
    She heard the dead-bell knellin';
And every jow the dead-bell gave
    Cried "Woe to Barbara Allen."

"O mother, mother, make my bed,
    O make it saft and narrow:
My love has died for me to-day,
    I'll die for him to-morrow.

"Farewell," she said, "ye virgins all,
    And shun the fault I fell in:
Henceforth take warning by the fall
    Of cruel Barbara Allen."

Get Up and Bar the Door

It fell about the Martinmas time,
    And a gay time it was then,
When our goodwife got puddings to make,
    And she's boiled them in the pan.

The wind sae cauld blew south and north,
    And blew into the floor;
Quoth our goodman to our goodwife,
    "Gae out and bar the door."

"My hand is in my hussyfskap,
    Goodman, as ye may see;
An' it shou'dna be barred this hundred year,
    It's no be barred for me."

They made a paction 'tween them twa,
    They made it firm and sure,
That the first word whae'er should speak,
    Should rise and bar the door.

Then by there came two gentlemen,
    At twelve o'clock at night,
And they could neither see house nor hall,
    Nor coal nor candle-light.

Martinmas, *Feast of St. Martin, Nov.* 11. Hussytskap, *housewifery.*

"Now whether is this a rich man's house,
   Or whether is it a poor?"
But ne'er a word wad ane o' them speak,
   For barring of the door.

And first they ate the white puddings,
   And then they ate the black.
Tho' muckle thought the goodwife to hersel'
   Yet ne'er a word she spake.

Then said the one unto the other,
   "Here, man, tak ye my knife;
Do ye tak aff the auld man's beard,
   And I'll kiss the goodwife."

"But there's nae water in the house,
   And what shall we do than?"
"What ails ye at the pudding-broo,
   That boils into the pan?"

O up and then started our goodman,
   An angry man was he:
"Will ye kiss my wife before my een,
   And sca'd me wi' pudding-bree?"

Then up and started our goodwife,
   Gied three skips on the floor:
"Goodman, you've spoken the foremost word!
   Get up and bar the door."

Muckle, much. Than, then. Broo, broth. Bree, broth.

ANONYMOUS

(PERIODS UNCERTAIN)

"Joseph Was an Old Man"

Joseph was an old man,
    And an old man was he,
When he wedded Mary
    In the land of Galilee.

Joseph and Mary walked
    Through an orchard good,
Where was cherries and berries
    So red as any blood.

Joseph and Mary walked
    Through an orchard green,
Where was berries and cherries
    As thick as might be seen.

O then bespoke Mary,
    So meek and so mild,
"Pluck me one cherry, Joseph,
    For I am with child."

O then bespoke Joseph
    With words so unkind,
"Let him pluck thee a cherry
    That brought thee with child."

O then bespoke the babe
    Within his mother's womb,
"Bow down then the tallest tree
    For my mother to have some."

Then bowed down the highest tree
Unto his mother's hand:
Then she cried, "See, Joseph,
I have cherries at command!"

O then bespake Joseph—
"I have done Mary wrong;
But cheer up, my dearest,
And be not cast down.

"O eat your cherries, Mary,
O eat your cherries now;
O eat your cherries, Mary,
That grow upon the bough."

Then Mary plucked a cherry
As red as the blood;
Then Mary went home
With her heavy load.

"As Joseph Was A-Walking"

As Joseph was a-walking,
He heard an angel sing:
"This night shall be born
Our heavenly King.

"He neither shall be born
In housen nor in hall,
Nor in the place of Paradise,
But in an ox's stall.

"He neither shall be clothéd
In purple nor in pall,
But all in fair linen,
As were babies all.

Pall, *fine cloth.*

"He neither shall be rocked
In silver nor in gold,
But in a wooden cradle
That rocks on the mould.

"He neither shall be christened
In white wine nor red,
But with fair spring water
With which we were christenéd."

"As I Sat under a Sycamore Tree"

As I sat under a sycamore tree,
A sycamore tree, a sycamore tree,
I looked me out upon the sea
On Christ's Sunday at morn.

I saw three ships a-sailing there,
A-sailing there, a-sailing there,
Jesu, Mary and Joseph they bare
On Christ's Sunday at morn.

Joseph did whistle and Mary did sing,
Mary did sing, Mary did sing,
And all the bells on earth did ring
For joy our Lord was born.

O they sailed into Bethlehem,
To Bethlehem, to Bethlehem;
St. Michael was the sterésman,
St. John sate in the horn.

And all the bells on earth did ring,
On earth did ring, on earth did ring:
"Welcome be thou Heaven's King,
On Christ's Sunday at morn!"

"God Rest You Merry, Gentlemen"

God rest you merry, gentlemen,
  Let nothing you dismay,
For Jesus Christ, our Saviour,
  Was born upon this day,
To save us all from Satan's power
  When we were gone astray.
      O tidings of comfort and joy!
      For Jesus Christ, our Saviour,
      Was born on Christmas Day.

In Bethlehem, in Jewry,
  This blessèd babe was born,
And laid within a manger,
  Upon this blessèd morn;
The which His mother, Mary,
  Nothing did take in scorn.

From God, our Heavenly Father,
  A blessèd angel came;
And unto certain shepherds
  Brought tidings of the same:
How that in Bethlehem was born
  The Son of God by name.

"Fear not," then said the angel,
  "Let nothing you affright,
This day is born a Saviour
  Of virtue, power and might,
So frequently to vanquish all
  The friends of Satan quite."

The shepherds at those tidings
  Rejoicèd much in mind,
And left their flocks a feeding
  In tempest, storm and wind,
And went to Bethlehem straightway,
  This blessèd babe to find.

But when to Bethlehem they came,
 Whereat this infant lay,
They found Him in a manger,
 Where oxen feed on hay,
His mother Mary kneeling
 Unto the Lord did pray.

Now to the Lord sing praises,
 All you within this place,
And with true love and brotherhood
 Each other now embrace;
This holy tide of Christmas
 All others doth deface.
  O tidings of comfort and joy!
  For Jesus Christ, our Saviour,
  Was born on Christmas Day.

"The First Nowell..."

The first Nowell the angels did say
Was to certain poor shepherds in fields as they lay,
In fields where they lay keeping their sheep,
On a cold winter's night that was so deep.
  Nowell, Nowell, Nowell, Nowell,
  Born is the King of Israel.

They lookéd up and saw a star
Shining in the East beyond them far,
And to the earth it gave great light,
And so it continued both day and night.
  Nowell &c.

And by the light of that same star
Three wise men came from country far;
To seek for a King was their intent,
And to follow the star wherever it went.
  Nowell &c.

The star drew nigh to the north-west,
O'er Bethlehem it took its rest,
And then it did both stop and stay
Right over the place where Jesus lay.
      Nowell &c.

Then entered in those wise men three,
Most reverently upon their knee,
And offered there in His presence
Their gold and myrrh and frankincense.
      Nowell &c.

Then let us all with one accord
Sing praises to our heavenly Lord,
That hath made heaven and earth of naught,
And with His blood mankind hath bought.
      Nowell, Nowell, Nowell, Nowell,
      Born is the King of Israel.

ANONYMOUS

(15TH–16TH CENTURY)

FROM "The Maidens Came"

The maidens came
When I was in my mother's bower;
I had all that I would.
   The bailey beareth the bell away;
   The lily, the rose, the rose I lay.
The silver is white, red is the gold;
The robes they lay in fold.
   The bailey beareth the bell away;
   The lily, the rose, the rose I lay.
And through the glass window shines the sun.
How should I love, and I so young?
   The bailey beareth the bell away;
   The lily, the lily, the rose I lay.

ANONYMOUS

(15TH–16TH CENTURY)

"Back and Side Go Bare..."

Back and side go bare, go bare,
   Both hand and foot go cold,
But belly, God sent thee good ale enough
   Whether it be new or old!

But if that I may have truly
   Good ale my belly full,
I shall look like one, by sweet Saint John,
   Were shorn against the wool.
Though I go bare, take ye no care,
   I am nothing cold,
I stuff my skin so full within
   Of jolly good ale and old.

I cannot eat but little meat,
   My stomach is not good;
But sure I think that I could drink
   With him that weareth an hood.

Drink is my life; although my wife
  Some time do chide and scold,
Yet spare I not to ply the pot
  Of jolly good ale and old.

I love no roast but a brown toast,
  Or a crab in the fire;
A little bread shall do me stead;
  Much bread I never desire.
Nor frost, nor snow, nor wind I trow,
  Can hurt me if it wold,
I am so wrapped within and lapped
  With jolly good ale and old.

I care right nought, I take no thought
  For clothes to keep me warm;
Have I good drink, I surely think
  Nothing can do me harm.
For truly than I fear no man,
  Be he never so bold,
When I am armed and thoroughly warmed
  With jolly good ale and old.

But now and than I curse and ban,
  They make their ale so small;
God give them care and evil to fare!
  They stry the malt and all.
Such peevish pew, I tell you true,
  Nor for a crown of gold
There cometh one sip within my lip,
  Whether it be new or old.

Good ale and strong maketh me among
  Full jocund and full light,
That oft I sleep and take no keep
  From morning until night.
Then start I up and flee to the cup;
  The right way on I hold;
My thirst to staunch, I fill my paunch
  With jolly good ale and old.

And Kit, my wife, that as her life
　　Loveth well good ale to seek,
Full oft drinketh she, that ye may see
　　The tears run down her cheek.
Then doth she troll to me the bowl,
　　As a good malt-worm shold,
And say "Sweet-heart, I have take my part
　　Of jolly good ale and old."

They that do drink till they nod and wink,
　　Even as good fellows should do,
They shall not miss to have the bliss
　　That good ale hath brought them to.
And all poor souls that scour black bowls,
　　And them hath lustily trolled,
God save the lives of them and their wives,
　　Whether they be young or old!

ANONYMOUS
(16TH CENTURY)
"Western Wind, When Wilt Thou Blow"

Western wind, when wilt thou blow,
　　The small rain down can rain?
Christ, if my love were in my arms
　　And I in my bed again!

KING HENRY VIII
(1491–1547)
"As the Holly Groweth Green"

As the holly groweth green,
　　And never changeth hue,
So I am, ever hath been
　　Unto my lady true;

As the holly groweth green
　　With ivy all alone,
When flowerës can not be seen
　　And green wood leaves be gone.

Now unto my lady
   Promise to her I make,
From all other only
   To her I me betake.

Adieu, mine own lady,
   Adieu, my special,
Who hath my heart truly,
   Be sure, and ever shall!

ANONYMOUS

Harpalus' Complaint

Phyllida was a fair maid,
   As fresh as any flower;
Whom Harpalus the herdman prayed
   To be his paramour.

Harpalus and eke Corin
   Were herdmen both yfere;
And Phyllida would twist and spin
   And thereto sing full clear.

But Phyllida was all too coy
   For Harpalus to win,
For Corin was her only joy,
   Who forced her not a pin.

How often would she flowers twine,
   How often garlands make
Of cowslips and of columbine?
   And all for Corin's sake.

But Corin, he had hawks to lure,
   And forcéd more the field;
Of lovers' law he took no cure,
   For once he was beguiled.

Yfere, in comradeship. Forcéd, cared for.

Harpalus prevailéd nought,
  His labour all was lost;
For he was farthest from her thought,
  And yet he loved her most.

Therefore waxed he both pale and lean,
  And dry as clod of clay;
His flesh it was consuméd clean,
  His colour gone away.

His beard it had not long be shave,
  His hair hung all unkempt;
A man most fit e'en for the grave,
  Whom spiteful love had shent.

His eyes were red and all forwatched,
  His face besprent with tears;
It seemed unhap had him long hatched,
  In midst of his despairs.

His clothes were black, and also bare;
  As one forlorn was he;
Upon his head always he ware
  A wreath of willow tree.

His beasts he kept upon the hill,
  And he sat in the dale;
And thus with sighs and sorrows shrill
  He gan to tell his tale.

Oh Harpalus! thus would he say,
  Unhappiest under sun,
The cause of thine unhappy day
  By love was first begun.

For thou went'st first by suit to seek
  A tiger to make tame,
That sets not by thy love a leek,
  But makes thy grief her game.

Shent, ruined. Unhap, misfortune.

As easy 'twere for to convert
    The frost into the flame,
As for to turn a froward heart
    Whom thou so fain wouldst frame.

Corin he liveth careless,
    He leaps among the leaves;
He eats the fruits of thy redress;
    Thou reap'st, he takes the sheaves.

My beasts a while your food refrain
    And hark your herdman's sound,
Whom spiteful love alas! hath slain
    Through girt with many a wound.

O happy be ye, beastës wild,
    That here your pasture takes,
I see that ye be not beguiled
    Of these your faithful makes.

The hart he feedeth by the hind;
    The buck hard by the doe;
The turtle dove is not unkind
    To him that loves her so.

The ewe she hath by her the ram;
    The young cow hath the bull;
The calf with many a lusty lamb
    Do feed their hunger full.

But well-away! that nature wrought
    Thee, Phyllida, so fair,
For I may say that I have bought
    Thy beauty all too dear.

What reason is that cruelty
    With beauty should have part?
Or else that such great tyranny
    Should dwell in woman's heart?

I see therefore to shape my death
    She cruelly is pressed,
To th'end that I may want my breath;
    My days be at the best.

O Cupid, grant this my request,
    And do not stop thine ears;
That she may feel within her breast
    The pains of my despairs.

Of Corin that is careless
    That she may crave her fee,
As I have done in great distress
    That loved her faithfully.

But since that I shall die her slave,
    Her slave and eke her thrall,
Write you, my friends, upon the grass
    This chance that is befall:

"Here lieth unhappy Harpalus
    By cruel love now slain;
Whom Phyllida unjustly thus
    Hath murdered with disdain."

Tottel's Miscellany, 1557

ANONYMOUS
(16TH CENTURY)

A Praise of His Lady

Give place, you ladies, and begone,
    Boast not yourselves at all;
For here at hand approacheth one
    Whose face will stain you all.

The virtue of her lively looks
    Excels the precious stone;
I wish to have none other books
    To read or look upon.

In each of her two crystal eyes
    Smileth a naked boy;
It would you all in heart suffice
    To see that lamp of joy.

I think nature hath lost the mould
    Where she her shape did take,
Or else I doubt if nature could
    So fair a creature make.

She may be well compared
    Unto the phoenix kind,
Whose like was never seen nor heard
    That any man can find.

In life she is Diana chaste,
    In truth Penelopey,
In word and eke in deed steadfast;
    What will you more we say?

If all the world were sought so far,
    Who could find such a wight?
Her beauty twinkleth like a star
    Within the frosty night.

Her rosial colour comes and goes
    With such a comely grace,
More ruddier too, than doth the rose,
    Within her lively face.

At Bacchus' feast none shall her meet
    Ne at no wanton play,
Nor gazing in an open street,
    Nor gadding as astray.

The modest mirth that she doth use
    Is mixed with shamefastness,
All vice she doth wholly refuse
    And hateth idleness.

O Lord! it is a world to see
How virtue can repair,
And deck in her such honesty,
Whom nature made so fair.

Truly, she doth as far exceed
Our women nowadays,
As doth the gillyflower a weed;
And more a thousand ways.

How might I do to get a graff
Of this unspotted tree?
For all the rest are plain but chaff
Which seem good corn to be.

This gift alone I shall her give
When death doth what he can,
Her honest fame shall ever live
Within the mouth of man.

Tottel's Miscellany, 1557

ANONYMOUS

(16TH CENTURY)

Against Women either Good or Bad

A man may live thrice Nestor's life,
Thrice wander out Ulysses' race,
Yet never find Ulysses' wife;
Such change hath chancéd in this case.

Less age will serve than Paris had
Small pain (if none be small enough)
To find good store of Helen's trade;
Such sap the root doth yield the bough.

For one good wife Ulysses slew
A worthy knot of gentle blood;

For one ill wife Greece overthrew
The town of Troy. Sith bad and good
Bring mischief, Lord, let be Thy will
To keep me free from either ill.

Tottel's Miscellany, 1557

ANONYMOUS
(16TH CENTURY)

As You Came from the Holy Land

As you came from the holy land
Of Walsinghame,
Met you not with my true love
By the way as you came?

How shall I know your true love,
That have met many a one,
As I went to the holy land,
That have come, that have gone?

She is neither white nor brown,
But as the heavens fair;
There is none hath a form so divine
In the earth or the air.

Such a one did I meet, good sir,
Such an angelic face,
Who like a queen, like a nymph, did appear,
By her gait, by her grace.

She hath left me here all alone,
All alone, as unknown,
Who sometime did me lead with herself,
And me loved as her own.

What's the cause that she leaves you alone,
And a new way doth take,
Who loved you once as her own,
And her joy did you make?

I have loved her all my youth,
  But now old, as you see;
Love likes not the falling fruit
  From the withered tree.

Know that Love is a careless child,
  And forgets promise past;
He is blind, he is deaf when he list,
  And in faith never fast.

His desire is a dureless content,
  And a trustless joy;
He is won with a world of despair,
  And is lost with a toy.

Of womenkind such indeed is the love,
  Or the word love abuséd,
Under which many childish desires
  And conceits are excuséd.

But true love is a durable fire,
  In the mind ever burning,
Never sick, never old, never dead,
  From itself never turning.

ANONYMOUS

(16TH CENTURY)

"Fain Would I Have a Pretty Thing"

Fain would I have a pretty thing
  To give unto my Lady:
I name no thing, nor I mean no thing,
  But as pretty a thing as may be.

Twenty journeys would I make,
  And twenty ways would hie me,
To make adventure for her sake,
  To set some matter by me:
    But fain would I &c.

Some do long for pretty knacks,
  And some for strange devices:
God send me that my lady lacks,
  I care not what the price is.
    Thus fain, &c.

Some go here, and some go there,
  Where gazes be not geason;
And I go gaping everywhere,
  But still come out of season.
    Yet fain &c.

I walk the town and thread the street,
  In every corner seeking:
The pretty thing I cannot meet,
  That's for my lady's liking.
    Fain would &c.

The mercers pull me, going by,
  The silk-wives say, "What lack ye?"
"The thing you have not," then say I,
  "Ye foolish fools, go pack ye!"
    But fain &c.

It is not all the silk in Cheap,
  Nor all the golden treasure,
Nor twenty bushels on a heap
  Can do my lady pleasure.
    But fain &c.

The gravers of the golden shows
  With jewels do beset me;
The sempsters in the shop that sews,
  They do no thing but let me.
    But fain &c.

But were it in the wit of man
  By any means to make it,
I could for money buy it then,
  And say, "Fair Lady, take it."
    Thus fain &c.

O Lady what a lack is this,
   That my good willing misseth
To find what pretty thing it is
   That my good lady wisheth.
Thus fain would I have had this pretty thing
   To give unto my lady:
I said no harm, nor I meant no harm,
   But as pretty a thing as may be.

Clement Robinson's A Handful of Pleasant Delights, 1584

SIR THOMAS WYATT

(1503–1542)

The Lover Sheweth How He Is Forsaken of Such
as He Sometime Enjoyed

They flee from me, that sometime did me seek,
   With naked foot stalking within my chamber:
Once have I seen them gentle, tame and meek,
   That now are wild, and do not once remember,
   That sometime they have put themselves in danger
To take bread at my hand; and now they range
Busily seeking in continual change.

Thankèd be Fortune, it hath been otherwise
   Twenty times better; but once especial,
In thin array, after a pleasant guise,
   When her loose gown did from her shoulders fall,
   And she me caught in her arms long and small,
And therewithal so sweetly did me kiss,
And softly said, "Dear heart, how like you this?"

It was no dream; for I lay broad awaking:
   But all is turn'd now, through my gentleness,
Into a bitter fashion of forsaking;
   And I have leave to go of her goodness;
   And she also to use new fangleness.
But since that I unkindly so am served:
How like you this, what hath she now deserved?

The Lover Beseecheth His Mistress Not to Forget
His Steadfast Faith and True Intent

Forget not yet the tried intent
Of such a truth as I have meant;
My great travail so gladly spent,
　　　Forget not yet!

Forget not yet when first began
The weary life ye know, since whan
The suit, the service, none tell can;
　　　Forget not yet!

Forget not yet the great assays,
The cruel wrong, the scornful ways,
The painful patience in delays,
　　　Forget not yet!

Forget not! oh! forget not this,
How long ago hath been, and is
The mind that never meant amiss,
　　　Forget not yet!

Forget not then thine own approv'd,
The which so long hath thee so lov'd,
Whose steadfast faith yet never mov'd:
　　　Forget not this!

The Lover Complaineth the Unkindness
of His Love

My lute, awake, perform the last
Labour that thou and I shall waste;
And end that now I have begun:
And when this song is sung and past,
My lute, be still, for I have done.

As to be heard where ear is none;
As lead to grave in marble stone;
My song may pierce her heart as soon.
Should we then sigh, or sing, or moan?
No, no, my lute, for I have done.

The rocks do not so cruelly
Repulse the waves continually,
As she my suit and affection:
So that I am past remedy;
Whereby my lute and I have done.

Proud of the spoil that thou hast got
Of simple hearts thorough Love's shot,
By whom unkind thou hast them won:
Think not he hath his bow forgot,
Although my lute and I have done.

Vengeance shall fall on thy disdain,
That makest but game on earnest pain;
Think not alone under the sun
Unquit to cause thy lover's plain;
Although my lute and I have done.

May chance thee lie withered and old
In winter nights, that are so cold,
Plaining in vain unto the moon;
Thy wishes then dare not be told:
Care then who list, for I have done.

And then may chance thee to repent
The time that thou hast lost and spent,
To cause thy lover's sigh and swoon:
Then shalt thou know beauty but lent,
And wish and want as I have done.

Now cease, my lute, this is the last
Labour that thou and I shall waste;
And ended is that we begun:
Now is this song both sung and past;
My lute, be still, for I have done.

HENRY HOWARD, EARL OF SURREY

(1516–1547)

A Vow to Love Faithfully, Howsoever He Be Rewarded

Set me whereas the sun doth parch the green
Or where his beams do not dissolve the ice;
In temperate heat, where he is felt and seen;
In presence prest of people, mad or wise;
Set me in high, or yet in low degree;
In longest night, or in the shortest day;
In clearest sky, or where clouds thickest be;
In lusty youth, or when my hairs are grey:
Set me in heaven, in earth, or else in hell,
In hill, or dale, or in the foaming flood;
Thrall, or at large, alive whereso I dwell,
Sick, or in health, in evil fame or good,
Hers will I be; and only with this thought
Content myself, although my chance be nought.

The Means to Attain Happy Life

Martial, the things that do attain
The happy life, be these, I find:
The riches left, not got with pain;
The fruitful ground, the quiet mind:

The equal friend, no grudge, no strife;
No charge of rule, nor governance;
Without disease, the healthful life;
The household of continuance:

The mean diet, no delicate fare;
True wisdom join'd with simpleness;
The night dischargéd of all care,
Where wine the wit may not oppress:

The faithful wife, without debate;
Such sleeps as may beguile the night;
Contented with thine own estate;
Ne wish for Death, ne fear his might.

FROM *The Fourth Book of Virgil's Aeneid*

Then Mercury 'gan bend him to obey
His father's mighty will; and to his heels
His golden wings he knits, which him transport
With a light wind above the earth and seas.
And then with him his wand he took, whereby
He calls from hell pale ghosts; and other some
Thither also he sendeth comfortless,
Whereby he forceth sleeps, and them bereaves,
And mortal eyes he closeth up in death.
By power whereof he drives the winds away
And passeth eke amid the troubled clouds,
Till in his flight he 'gan descry the top
And the steep flanks of rocky Atlas' hill,
That with his crown sustains the welkin up;
Whose head forgrown with pine, circled alway
With misty clouds, is beaten with wind and storm;
His shoulders spread with snow; and from his chin
The springs descend; his beard frozen with ice.
Here Mercury with equal shining wings
First touched; and with body headling bent
To the water then took he his descent;
Like to the fowl that endlong coasts and strands
Swarming with fish, flies sweeping by the sea;
Cutting betwixt the winds and Libyan lands,
From his grandfather by the mother's side,
Cyllene's child so came, and then alight
Upon the houses with his wingéd feet,
Tofore the towers where he Aeneas saw
Foundations cast, arearing lodges new;
Girt with a sword of jasper starry bright,
A shining 'parel, flamed with stately eye
Of Tyrian purple, hung his shoulders down,
The gift and work of wealthy Dido's hand,
Stripéd throughout with a thin thread of gold.

GEORGE GASCOIGNE
(1525?–1577)

The Praise of Philip Sparrow

Of all the birds that I do know
   Philip my Sparrow hath no peer;
For sit she high or lie she low,
   Be she far off, or be she near,
There is no bird so fair, so fine,
Nor yet so fresh as this of mine.

Come in a morning merrily
   When Philip hath been lately fed,
Or in an evening soberly
   When Philip list to go to bed;
It is a heaven to hear my Phip
How she can chirp with cherry lip.

She never wanders far abroad,
   But is at hand when I do call,
If I command she lays on lode
   With lips, with teeth, with tongue and all;
She chants, she chirps, she makes such cheer,
That I believe she hath no peer.

And yet beside all this good sport
   My Philip both can sing and dance,
With new found toys of sundry sort
   My Philip can both prick and prance;
And if you say but "fend cut Phip"
Lord! how the peat will turn and skip!

Her feathers are so fresh of hue
   And so well provéd every day,
So lacks no oil, I warrant you,
   To trim her tail both trick and gay;
And though her mouth be somewhat wide,
Her tongue is sweet and short beside.

And for the rest I dare compare
   She is both tender, sweet and soft;
She never lacketh dainty fare,
   But is well fed, and feedeth oft;
For if my Phip have best to eat,
I warrant you, Phip lacks no meat.

And then if that her meat be good
   And such as like do love alway,
She will lay lips thereon, by rood!
   And see that none be cast away;
For when she once hath felt a fit,
Philip will cry still, "Yet, yet, yet!"

And to tell truth, he were to blame
   Which had so fine a bird as she,
To make him all this goodly game
   Without suspect or jealousy;
He were a churl and knew no good
Would see her faint for lack of food.

Wherefore I sing, and ever shall,
   To praise as I have often proved,
There is no bird amongst them all
   So worthy for to be beloved.
Let others praise what bird they will,
Sweet Philip shall be my bird still.

NICHOLAS BRETON

(1542–1626)

A Sweet Lullaby

Come little babe, come silly soul,
Thy father's shame, thy mother's grief,
Born as I doubt to all our dole
And to thyself unhappy chief;
   Sing lullaby, and lap it warm,
   Poor soul that thinks no creature harm.

Thou little think'st and less dost know
The cause of this thy mother's moan,
Thou want'st the wit to wail her woe,
And I myself am all alone;
 Why dost thou weep? why dost thou wail?
 And knowest not yet what thou dost ail.

Come, little wretch, ah, silly heart!
Mine only joy, what can I more?
If there be any wrong thy smart,
That may the destinies implore;
 'Twas I, I say, against my will,
 I wail the time, but be thou still.

And dost thou smile, Oh! thy sweet face,
Would God Himself He might thee see,
No doubt thou wouldst soon purchase grace,
I know right well, for thee and me;
 But come to mother, babe, and play,
 For father false is fled away.

Sweet boy, if it by fortune chance
Thy father home again to send,
If death do strike me with his lance,
Yet may'st thou me to him commend;
 If any ask thy mother's name,
 Tell how by love she purchas'd blame.

Then will his gentle heart soon yield,
I know him of a noble mind,
Although a lion in the field,
A lamb in town thou shalt him find;
 Ask blessing, babe, be not afraid,
 His sugared words hath me betrayed.

Then may'st thou joy and be right glad,
Although in woe I seem to moan,
Thy father is no rascal, lad,
A noble youth of blood and bone;
 His glancing looks if he once smile
 Right honest women may beguile.

Come, little boy, and rock asleep,
Sing lullaby, and be thou still,
I that can do nought else but weep,
Will sit by thee, and wail my fill;
  God bless my babe, and lullaby,
  From this thy father's quality.

The Arbour of Amorous Devices, 1597

FROM *The Passionate Shepherd*

Who can live in heart so glad
As the merry country lad?
Who upon a fair green baulk
May at pleasure sit and walk;
And amidst the azure skies
See the morning sun arise,
While he hears in every spring
How the birds do chirp and sing;
Or, before the hounds in cry,
See the hare go stealing by;
Or along the shallow brook
Angling with a baited hook,
See the fishes leap and play
In a blessed sunny day;
Or to hear the partridge call
Till she have her covey all;
Or to see the subtle fox,
How the villain plays the box,
After feeding on his prey
How he closely sneaks away,
Through the hedge and down the furrow
Till he gets into his burrow;
Then the bee to gather honey,
And the little black-haired coney
On a bank for sunny place
With her fore-feet wash her face:
Are not these with thousands moe
Than the court of kings do know?

Phillida and Coridon

In the merry month of May,
In a morn by break of day,
Forth I walked by the wood side
Whenas May was in his pride.
There I spiéd all alone
Phillida and Coridon.
Much ado there was, Got wot,
He would love and she would not.
She said, never man was true;
He said, none was false to you.
He said, he had loved her long;
She said, Love should have no wrong.
Coridon would kiss her then.
She said, maids must kiss no men
Till they did for good and all.
Then she made the shepherd call
All the heavens to witness truth,
Never loved a truer youth.
Thus with many a pretty oath,
Yea and nay, and faith and troth,
Such as silly shepherds use
When they will not love abuse;
Love, which had been long deluded,
Was with kisses sweet concluded.
And Phillida, with garlands gay,
Was made the lady of the May.

England's Helicon, 1600

FROM An Invective against the Wicked of the World

Let but a fellow in a fox-furred gown,
A greasy night-cap and a drivelled beard,
Grow but a bailiff of a fisher-town,
And have a matter 'fore him to be heard,
Will not his frown make half a street afeared?
    Yea, and the greatest Codshead gape for fear
    He shall be swallowed by this ugly bear.

Look but on beggars going to the stocks,
How master constable can march before them,
And while the beadle maketh fast the locks,
How bravely he can knave them and be-whore them,
And not afford one word of pity for them,
　　When it may be poor honest silly people
　　Must make the church make curtsy to the steeple.

Note but the beadle of a beggars' Spittle,
How in his place he can himself advance,
And will not of his title lose a tittle,
If any matter come in variance,
To try the credit of his countenance;
　　For whatsoever the poor beggars say
　　His is the word must carry all away.

Find out a villain, born and bred a knave,
That never knew what honesty became,
A drunken rascal and a doggéd slave,
That all his wits to wickedness doth frame,
And only lives in infamy and shame;
　　Yet let him tink upon the golden pan,
　　His word may pass yet for an honest man.

Look on old Beatrice with her beetle brows,
Begot betwixt a tinker and his Tib,
And but of late a silly cobbler's spouse;
If she have played the thrifty prowling scrib
To purchase grass to grase the bullock's rib,
　　She shall be fed with fine and dainty fare,
　　And wooed and wedded ere she be aware.

But for a poor wench, be she ne'er so fair,
Gracious and virtuous, wise and nobly born,
And worthy well to sit in Honour's chair,
Yet, if her kirtle or her gown be torn,
All her good gifts shall but be held in scorn,
　　And she, poor soul, in sorrow and disgrace,
　　Be forced to give a filthy baggage place.

So that by all these consequents I see
It is the money makes or mars the man,
And yet where judges will indifferent be
The hobby-horse best fits Maid Marian,
While greedy dogs may lick the dripping pan;
  For though that money may do many things,
  Yet virtue makes the truest kings and queens.

THOMAS DELONEY

(1543?–1607?)

Song

The primrose in the green forest,
  The violets, they be gay;
The double daisies, and the rest
  That trimly decks the way,
Doth move the spirits with brave delights,
  Who Beauty's darlings be:
With hey tricksy, trim-go-tricksy,
  Under the greenwood tree.

FROM A Joyful New Ballad

O noble England,
  Fall down upon thy knee,
And praise thy God with thankful heart,
  Which still maintaineth thee.
The foreign forces
  That seek thy utter spoil,
Shall then through His especial grace
  Be brought to shameful foil,
With mighty power
  They come unto our coast;
To over-run our country quite,
  They make their brag and boast.
In strength of men
  They set their only stay;
But we upon the Lord our God
  Will put our trust alway.

Great is their number
  Of ships upon the sea,
And their provision wonderful;
  But, Lord, Thou art our stay.
Their armed soldiers
  Are many by account;
Their aiders eke in this attempt
  Do sundry ways surmount.
The Pope of Rome
  With many blessed grains,
To sanctify their bad pretence
  Bestowed both cost and pains.
But little land
  Is not dismayed at all;
The Lord, no doubt, is on our side,
  Which soon will work their fall.

Our pleasant country,
  So fruitful and so fair,
They do intend by deadly war
  To make both poor and bare.
Our towns and cities
  To rack and sack likewise,
To kill and murder man and wife,
  As malice doth arise.
And to deflower
  Our virgins in our sight,
And in the cradle cruelly
  The tender babe to smite.
God's holy truth
  They mean for to cast down,
And to deprive our noble Queen
  Both of her life and crown.

But God Almighty
  Be blessed evermore,
Who doth encourage Englishmen
  To beat them from the shore,
With roaring cannons,
  Their hasty steps to stay,
And with the force of thundering shot
  To make them fly away.

Who made account,
　Before this time or day,
Against the walls of fair London
　Their banners to display.
But their intent
　The Lord will bring to naught,
If faithfully we call and cry
　For succour as we ought.

And you, dear brethren,
　Which beareth arms this day,
For safeguard of your native soil,
　Mark well what I shall say.
Regard your duties,
　Think on your country's good,
And fear not in defence thereof
　To spend your dearest blood;
Desiring you,
　True English hearts to bear,
To God, to Her, and to the land
　Wherein you nursed were.

SIR EDWARD DYER

(1545?–1607)

My Mind to Me a Kingdom Is

My mind to me a kingdom is;
　Such present joys therein I find,
That it excels all other bliss
　That earth affords or grows by kind:
Though much I want which most would have
Yet still my mind forbids to crave.

No princely pomp, no wealthy store,
　No force to win the victory,
No wily wit to salve a sore,
　No shape to feed a loving eye;
To none of these I yield as thrall:
For why? My mind doth serve for all.

I see how plenty suffers oft,
   And hasty climbers down do fall;
I see that those which are aloft,
   Mishap doth threaten most of all;
They get with toil, they keep with fear:
Such cares my mind could never bear.

Content I live, this is my stay,
   I seek no more than may suffice;
I press to bear no haughty sway;
   Look what I lack my mind supplies:
Lo, thus I triumph like a king,
Content with that my mind doth bring.

Some have too much, yet still do crave;
   I little have, and seek no more.
They are but poor though much they have,
   And I am rich with little store;
They poor, I rich; they beg, I give;
They lack, I leave; they pine, I live.

I laugh not at another's loss,
   I grudge not at another's gain;
No worldly waves my mind can toss:
   My state at one doth still remain:
I fear no foe, I fawn no friend;
I loathe not life nor dread my end.

Some weigh their pleasure by their lust,
   Their wisdom by their rage of will;
Their treasure is their only trust,
   A cloakéd craft their store of skill.
But all the pleasure that I find
Is to maintain a quiet mind.

My wealth is health and perfect ease;
   My conscience clear my choice defence;
I neither seek by bribes to please
   Nor by deceit to breed offence;
Thus do I live, thus will I die;
Would all did so as well as I.

BARTHOLOMEW GRIFFIN
(15—?–1602)
"*Venus, with Young Adonis*..."

Venus, with young Adonis sitting by her
Under a myrtle shade, began to woo him:
She told the youngling how god Mars did try her,
And as he fell to her, so fell she to him.
"Even thus," quoth she, "the warlike god embraced me,"
And then she clipped Adonis in her arms;
"Even thus," quoth she, "the warlike god unlaced me,"
As if the boy should use like loving charms;
"Even thus," quoth she, "he seizéd on my lips,"
And with her lips on his did act the seizure:
And as she fetchéd breath, away he skips,
And would not take her meaning nor her pleasure.
Ah, that I had my lady at this bay,
To kiss and clip me till I run away!

The Passionate Pilgrim, 1599

FROM *Sonnets*

Fair is my love that feeds among the lilies,
The lilies growing in that pleasant garden,
Where Cupid's mount, that well-beloved hill is,
And where the little god himself is warden.

See where my love sits in the bed of spices,
Beset all round with camphor, myrrh and roses,
And interlaced with curious devices,
Which her from all the world apart incloses.

ANONYMOUS
(16TH CENTURY)
"*Crabbed Age and Youth*..."

Crabbed age and youth cannot live together:
Youth is full of pleasance, age is full of care;
Youth like summer morn, age like winter weather;

Youth like summer brave, age like winter bare.
Youth is full of sport, age's breath is short;
   Youth is nimble, age is lame;
Youth is hot and bold, age is weak and cold;
   Youth is wild, and age is tame.
Age, I do abhor thee; youth, I do adore thee;
   O, my love, my love is young!
Age, I do defy thee: O, sweet shepherd, hie thee,
   For methinks thou stay'st too long.

[Attributed to WILLIAM SHAKESPEARE]
The Passionate Pilgrim, 1599

SIR WALTER RALEIGH
[See also page 169]

(1552–1618)

The Shepherd's Description of Love

Meliboeus: Shepherd, what's love, I pray thee tell?

Faustus: It is that fountain and that well,
Where pleasure and repentance dwell;
It is perhaps that sauncing bell,
   That tolls all in to heaven or hell:
   And this is love as I heard tell.

Meliboeus: Yet what is love, I prithee say?

Faustus: It is a work on holiday,
It is December match'd with May,
When lusty bloods in fresh array
   Hear ten months after of the play:
   And this is love, as I hear say.

Meliboeus: Yet what is Love, good shepherd, sain?

Faustus: It is a sunshine mix'd with rain,
It is a tooth-ache, or like pain,
It is a game, where none doth gain;
   The lass saith no, and would full fain:
   And this is Love, as I hear sain.

Meliboeus: Yet, shepherd, what is Love, I pray?

Faustus: It is a yea, it is a nay,
        A pretty kind of sporting fray,
        It is a thing will soon away,
           Then, nymphs, take vantage while ye may:
           And this is Love, as I hear say.

Meliboeus: Yet what is love, good shepherd, show?

Faustus: A thing that creeps, it cannot go,
        A prize that passeth to and fro,
        A thing for one, a thing for moe,
           And he that proves shall find it so:
           And, shepherd, this is love, I trow.

                    [Authorship uncertain]

The Faery Queen

Methought I saw the grave where Laura lay,
  Within that temple where the vestal flame
Was wont to burn; and passing by that way,
  To see that buried dust of living fame,
Whose tomb fair Love and fairer Virtue kept,
  All suddenly I saw the Faery Queen,
At whose approach the soul of Petrarch wept;
  And from thenceforth those graces were not seen,
For they this queen attended; in whose stead
  Oblivion laid him down on Laura's hearse.
Hereat the hardest stones were seen to bleed,
  And groans of buried ghosts the heavens did pierce:
Where Homer's sprite did tremble all for grief,
And cursed th' access of that celestial thief.

The Silent Lover

Passions are likened best to floods and streams:
  The shallow murmur, but the deep are dumb;
So, when affections yield discourse, it seems
  The bottom is but shallow whence they come.
They that are rich in words, in words discover
That they are poor in that which makes a lover.

Wrong not, sweet empress of my heart,
   The merit of true passion,
With thinking that he feels no smart,
   That sues for no compassion;

Since, if my plaints serve not to approve
   The conquest of thy beauty,
It comes not from defect of love,
   But from excess of duty.

For, knowing that I sue to serve
   A saint of such perfection,
As all desire, but none deserve,
   A place in her affection,

I rather choose to want relief
   Than venture the revealing;
Where glory recommends the grief,
   Despair distrusts the healing.

Thus those desires that aim too high
   For any mortal lover,
When reason cannot make them die,
   Discretion doth them cover.

Yet, when discretion doth bereave
   The plaints that they should utter,
Then thy discretion may perceive
   That silence is a suitor.

Silence in love bewrays more woe
   Than words, though ne'er so witty:
A beggar that is dumb, you know,
   May challenge double pity.

Then wrong not, dearest to my heart,
   My true, though secret, passion:
He smarteth most that hides his smart,
   And sues for no compassion.

The Lie

Go, Soul, the body's guest,
  Upon a thankless arrant;
Fear not to touch the best;
  The truth shall be thy warrant:
Go, since I needs must die,
And give the world the lie.

Say to the Court, it glows
  And shines like rotten wood;
Say to the Church, it shows
  What's good, and doth no good:
If Church and Court reply,
Then give them both the lie.

Tell potentates, they live
  Acting by others' action;
Not loved unless they give,
  Not strong but by a faction:
If potentates reply,
Give potentates the lie.

Tell men of high condition
  That manage the Estate,
Their purpose is ambition,
  Their practice only hate:
And if they once reply,
Then give them all the lie.

Tell them that brave it most,
  They beg for more by spending,
Who, in their greatest cost,
  Seek nothing but commending:
And if they make reply,
Then give them all the lie.

Tell zeal it wants devotion;
  Tell love it is but lust;
Tell time it is but motion;

Tell flesh it is but dust:
And wish them not reply,
For thou must give the lie.

Tell age it daily wasteth;
　Tell honour how it alters;
Tell beauty how she blasteth;
　Tell favour how it falters:
And as they shall reply,
Give every one the lie.

Tell wit how much it wrangles
　In tickle points of niceness;
Tell wisdom she entangles
　Herself in over-wiseness:
And when they do reply,
Straight give them both the lie.

Tell physic of her boldness;
　Tell skill it is pretention;
Tell charity of coldness;
　Tell law it is contention:
And as they do reply,
So give them still the lie.

Tell Fortune of her blindness;
　Tell Nature of decay;
Tell friendship of unkindness;
　Tell justice of delay;
And if they will reply,
Then give them all the lie.

Tell arts they have no soundness,
　But vary by esteeming;
Tell schools they want profoundness,
　And stand too much on seeming:
If arts and schools reply,
Give arts and schools the lie.

Tell faith it's fled the city;
　Tell how the country erreth;
Tell manhood shakes off pity;

Tell virtue least preferreth:
And if they do reply,
Spare not to give the lie.

So when thou hast, as I
    Commanded thee, done blabbing—
Although to give the lie
    Deserves no less than stabbing—
Stab at thee he that will,
No stab the soul can kill.

FROM *The Pilgrimage*

Give me my scallop-shell of quiet,
    My staff of faith to walk upon,
My scrip of joy, immortal diet,
    My bottle of salvation,
My gown of glory, hope's true gage;
And thus I'll take my pilgrimage.

Blood must be my body's balmer;
    No other balm will there be given;
Whilst my soul, like quiet palmer,
    Travelleth towards the land of heaven;
Over the silver mountains,
Where spring the nectar fountains:
        There will I kiss
        The bowl of bliss;
And drink mine everlasting fill
Upon every milken hill.
My soul will be a-dry before;
But after, it will thirst no more.

Verses Written in His Bible

Even such is Time, that takes in trust
Our youth, our joys, our all we have,
And pays us but with earth and dust;
Who in the dark and silent grave

When we have wandered all our ways,
Shuts up the story of our days;
But from this earth, this grave, this dust,
My God shall raise me up, I trust.

EDMUND SPENSER

(1552–1599)

FROM *The Shepherd's Calender, April*

See where she sits upon the grassy green,
    (O seemly sight!)
Yclad in scarlet, like a maiden Queen,
    And ermines white:
Upon her head a crimson coronet
With damask roses and daffadillies set,
    Bay leaves between,
    And primroses green,
Embellish the sweet violet.

Bring hither the pink and purple columbine,
    With gillyflowers;
Bring coronations and sops-in-wine
    Worn of paramours;
Strew me the ground with daffadowdillies
And cowslips and kingcups and lovéd lilies;
    The pretty pawnce
    And the chevisaunce
Shall match with the fair flower de lys.

FROM *Sonnets*

LXX

Fresh spring, the herald of Love's mighty king,
In whose coat-armour richly are displayed
All sorts of flowers, the which on earth do spring,
In goodly colours gloriously arrayed;
Go to my love, where she is careless laid,
Yet in her winter's bower will not awake;

Tell her the joyous time will not be stayed
Unless she do him by the forelock take;
Bid her therefore herself soon ready make
To wait on Love among his lovely crew;
Where every one that misseth then her make
Shall be by him amerced with penance due.
Make haste, therefore, sweet love, whilst it is prime,
For none can call again the passéd time.

LXXV

One day I wrote her name upon the strand;
But came the waves and washéd it away;
Again I wrote it with a second hand;
But came the tide, and made my pains his prey.
"Vain man," said she, "that dost in vain essay
A mortal thing so to immortalise,
For I myself shall like to this decay,
And eke my name be wipéd out likewise."
"Not so," quoth I, "let baser things devise
To die in dust, but you shall live by fame;
My verse your virtues rare shall eternise,
And in the heavens write your glorious name.
Where, whenas death shall all the world subdue,
Our love shall live, and later life renew."

LXXVIII

Lacking my love, I go from place to place,
Like a young fawn, that late hath lost the hind,
And seek each where, where last I saw her face,
Whose image yet I carry fresh in mind.
I seek the fields with her late footing signed,
I seek her bower with her late presence decked;
Yet nor in field nor bower I her can find,
Yet field and bower are full of her aspect.
But when mine eyes I thereunto direct
They idly back return to me again;
And when I hope to see their true objéct
I find myself but fed with fancies vain.
Cease then, mine eyes, to seek herself to see
And let my thoughts behold herself in me.

Prothalamion

Calm was the day, and through the trembling air
Sweet-breathing Zephyrus did softly play
A gentle spirit, that lightly did delay
Hot Titan's beams, which then did glister fair;
When I, (whom sullen care,
Through discontent of my long fruitless stay
In Prince's Court, and expectation vain
Of idle hopes, which still do fly away,
Like empty shadows, did afflict my brain,)
Walked forth to ease my pain
Along the shore of silver streaming Thames;
Whose rutty bank, the which his river hems,
Was painted all with variable flowers,
And all the meads adorned with dainty gems
Fit to deck maidens' bowers,
And crown their paramours
Against the bridal day, which is not long:
   Sweet Thames! run softly, till I end my song.

There, in a meadow, by the river's side,
A flock of nymphs I chancéd to espy,
All lovely daughters of the flood thereby,
With goodly greenish locks, all loose untied,
As each had been a bride;
And each one had a little wicker basket,
Made of the twigs, entailéd curiously,
In which they gathered flowers to fill their flasket,
And with fine fingers cropt full feateously
The tender stalks on high.
Of every sort, which in that meadow grew,
They gathered some; the violet, pallid blue,
The little daisy, that at evening closes,
The virgin lily, and the primrose true,
With store of vermeil roses,
To deck their bridegrooms' posies
Against the bridal day, which was not long:
   Sweet Thames! run softly, till I end my song.

With that I saw two swans of goodly hue
Come softly swimming down along the lea;
Two fairer birds I yet did never see;
The snow, which doth the top of Pindus strew,
Did never whiter show;
Nor Jove himself, when he a swan would be
For love of Leda, whiter did appear;
Yet Leda was (they say) as white as he,
Yet not so white as these, nor nothing near;
So purely white they were,
That even the gentle stream, the which them bare,
Seemed foul to them, and bade his billows spare
To wet their silken feathers, lest they might
Soil their fair plumes with water not so fair,
And mar their beauties bright,
That shone as heaven's light,
Against their bridal day, which was not long:
    Sweet Thames! run softly, till I end my song.

Eftsoons the Nymphs, which now had flowers their fill,
Ran all in haste to see that silver brood,
As they came floating on the crystal flood;
Whom when they saw, they stood amazéd still,
Their wondering eyes to fill;
Them seemed they never saw a sight so fair,
Of fowls, so lovely, that they sure did deem
Them heavenly born, or to be that same pair
Which through the sky draw Venus' silver team;
For sure they did not seem
To be begot of any earthly seed,
But rather angels, or of angels' breed;
Yet were they bred of summer's heat, they say,
In sweetest season, when each flower and weed
The earth did fresh array;
So fresh they seemed as day,
Even as their bridal day, which was not long:
    Sweet Thames! run softly, till I end my song.

Then forth they all out of their baskets drew
Great store of flowers, the honour of the field,
That to the sense did fragrant odours yield,

All which upon those goodly birds they threw
And all the waves did strew,
That like old Peneus' waters they did seem,
When down along by pleasant Tempe's shore,
Scattered with flowers, through Thessaly they stream.
That they appear, through lilies' plenteous store,
Like a bride's chamber floor.
Two of those Nymphs, meanwhile, two garlands bound
Of freshest flowers which in that mead they found,
The which presenting all in trim array,
Their snowy foreheads therewithal they crowned,
Whilst one did sing this lay,
Prepared against that day,
Against their bridal day, which was not long:
   Sweet Thames! run softly, till I end my song.

"Ye gentle birds! the world's fair ornament,
And heaven's glory, whom this happy hour
Doth lead unto your lovers' blissful bower,
Joy may you have, and gentle heart's content
Of your love's couplement;
And let fair Venus, that is queen of love,
With her heart-quelling son upon you smile,
Whose smile, they say, hath virtue to remove
All Love's dislike, and friendship's faulty guile
For ever to assoil.
Let endless Peace your steadfast hearts accord,
And blessèd Plenty wait upon your board;
And let your bed with pleasures chaste abound,
That fruitful issue may to you afford,
Which may your foes confound,
And make your joys redound
Upon your bridal day, which is not long:
   Sweet Thames! run softly, till I end my song."

So ended she; and all the rest around
To her redoubled that her undersong,
Which said their bridal day should not be long:
And gentle Echo from the neighbour ground
Their accents did resound.
So forth those joyous birds did pass along,

Adown the lea, that to them murmured low,
As he would speak, but that he lacked a tongue,
Yet did by signs his glad affection show,
Making his stream run slow.
And all the fowl which in his flood did dwell
'Gan flock about these twain, that did excel
The rest, so far as Cynthia doth shend
The lesser stars. So they, enrangéd well,
Did on these two attend,
And their best service lend
Against their wedding day, which was not long:
   Sweet Thames! run softly, till I end my song.

At length they all to merry London came,
To merry London, my most kindly nurse,
That to me gave this life's first native source,
Though from another place I take my name,
A house of ancient fame:
There when they came, whereas those bricky towers
The which on Thames' broad agéd back do ride,
Where now the studious lawyers have their bowers,
There whilom wont the Templar knights to bide,
Till they decayed through pride:
Next whereunto there stands a stately place,
Where oft I gainéd gifts and goodly grace
Of that great Lord, which therein wont to dwell,
Whose want too well now feels my friendless case;
But ah! here fits not well
Old woes, but joys, to tell
Against the bridal day, which is not long:
   Sweet Thames! run softly, till I end my song.

Yet therein now doth lodge a noble peer,
Great England's glory, and the world's wide wonder,
Whose dreadful name late through all Spain did thunder,
And Hercules' two pillars standing near
Did make to quake and fear:
Fair branch of Honour, flower of Chivalry!
Thou fillest England with thy triumph's fame,
Joy have thou of thy noble victory,
And endless happiness of thine own name

That promiseth the same;
That through thy prowess, and victorious arms,
Thy country may be freed from foreign harms;
And great Eliza's glorious name may ring
Through all the world, filled with thy wide alarms,
Which some brave muse may sing
To ages following
Upon the bridal day, which is not long:
    Sweet Thames! run softly, till I end my song.

From those high towers this noble Lord issuing,
Like radiant Hesper, when his golden hair
In th' ocean billows he hath bathéd fair,
Descended to the river's open viewing,
With a great train ensuing.
Above the rest were goodly to be seen
Two gentle knights of lovely face and feature,
Beseeming well the bower of any queen,
With gifts of wit, and ornaments of nature,
Fit for so goodly stature,
That like the twins of Jove they seemed in sight,
Which deck the baldrick of the heavens bright;
They two, forth pacing to the river's side,
Received those two fair brides, their love's delight;
Which, at th' appointed tide,
Each one did make his bride
Against their bridal day, which is not long:
    Sweet Thames! run softly, till I end my song.

Epithalamion

Ye learned sisters, which have oftentimes
Been to me aiding others to adorn,
Whom ye thought worthy of your graceful rhymes
That even the greatest did not greatly scorn
To hear their names sung in your simple lays,
But joyéd in their praise;
And when ye list your own mishaps to mourn,
Which death or love or fortune's wreck did raise,
Your string could soon to sadder tenor turn

And teach the woods and waters to lament
Your doleful dreariment;
Now lay those sorrowful complaints aside
And, having all your heads with garlands crowned,
Help me my own love's praises to resound;
Nor let the same of any be envied;
So Orpheus did for his own bride,
So I unto myself alone will sing;
The woods shall to me answer, and my echo ring.

Early, before the world's light-giving lamp
His early beam upon the hills doth spread,
Having dispersed the night's uncheerful damp,
Do ye awake; and with fresh lustihead
Go to the bower of my beloved love,
My truest turtle dove.
Bid her awake, for Hymen is awake
And long since ready forth his masque to move,
With his bright tead that flames with many a flake,
And many a bachelor to wait on him
In their fresh garments trim.
Bid her awake therefore, and soon her dight,
For lo! the wishéd day is come at last
That shall, for all the pains and sorrows past,
Pay to her usury of long delight;
And, while she doth her dight,
Do ye to her of joy and solace sing
That all the woods may answer, and your echo ring.

Bring with you all the nymphs that you can hear
Both of the rivers and the forests green
And of the sea that neighbours to her near,
All with gay garlands goodly well beseen.
And let them also with them bring in hand
Another gay garland,
For my fair love, of lilies and of roses,
Bound true-love wise with a blue silk riband.
And let them make great store of bridal posies,
And let them eke bring store of other flowers

Tead, torch.

To deck the bridal bowers.
And let the ground whereas her foot shall tread,
For fear the stones her tender foot should wrong,
Be strewed with fragrant flowers all along
And diapered like the discoloured mead.
Which done, do at her chamber door await,
For she will waken straight;
The whiles do ye this song unto her sing,
The woods shall to you answer, and your echo ring.

Ye Nymphs of Mulla, which with careful heed
The silver scaly trouts do tend full well
And greedy pikes which use therein to feed;
(These trouts and pikes all others do excel;)
And ye likewise, which keep the rushy lake,
Where none do fishes take;
Bind up the locks the which hang scattered light,
And in the waters, which your mirror make,
Behold your faces as the crystal bright,
That when you come whereas my love doth lie,
No blemish she may spy.
And eke ye lightfoot maids, which keep the deer
That on the hoary mountain used to tower,
And the wild wolves which seek them to devour
With your steel darts do chase from coming near;
Be also present here
To help to deck her and to help to sing,
That all the woods may answer, and your echo ring.

Wake now, my love, awake! for it is time;
The rosy Morn long since left Tithon's bed,
All ready to her silver coach to climb;
And Phoebus 'gins to show his glorious head.
Hark! how the cheerful birds do chant their lays
And carol of Love's praise.
The merry lark her matins sings aloft,
The thrush replies, the mavis descant plays,
The ousel shrills, the ruddock warbles soft;
So goodly all agree, with sweet consent,
To this day's merriment.
Ah! my dear love, why do you sleep thus long

When meeter were that you should now awake,
T'await the coming of your joyous make
And hearken to the birds' love-learned song
The dewy leaves among!
Now they of joy and pleasance to you sing
That all the woods may answer, and their echo ring.

My love is now awake out of her dreams,
And her fair eyes, like stars that dimméd were
With darksome cloud, now show their goodly beams
More bright than Hesperus his head doth rear.
Come now, ye damsels, daughters of delight,
Help quickly her to dight.
But first come ye fair hours, which were begot
In Jove's sweet paradise of Day and Night,
Which do the seasons of the year allot,
And all that ever in this world is fair
Do make and still repair.
And ye three handmaids of the Cyprian Queen,
The which do still adorn her beauty's pride,
Help to adorn my beautifullest bride;
And, as ye her array, still throw between
Some graces to be seen;
And, as ye use to Venus, to her sing
The whiles the woods shall answer, and your echo ring.

Now is my love all ready forth to come.
Let all the virgins therefore well await;
And ye, fresh boys, that tend upon 'her groom,
Prepare yourselves; for he is coming straight.
Set all your things in seemly good array,
Fit for so joyful day,
The fairest day that ever sun did see.
Fair Sun! shew forth thy favourable ray,
And let thy lifefull heat not fervent be,
For fear of burning her sunshiny face,
Her beauty to disgrace.
O fairest Phoebus! father of the Muse!
If ever I did honour thee aright
Or sing the thing that mote thy mind delight,
Do not thy servant's simple boon refuse;

But let this day, let this one day be mine;
Let all the rest be thine.
Then I thy sovereign praises loud will sing
That all the woods shall answer, and their echo ring.

Hark how the minstrels 'gin to shrill aloud
Their merry music that resounds from far,
The pipe, the tabor, and the trembling croud,
That well agree withouten breach or jar.
But most of all the damsels do delight
When they their timbrels smite,
And thereunto do dance and carol sweet
That all the senses they do ravish quite;
The whiles the boys run up and down the street,
Crying aloud with strong confused noise,
As if it were one voice,
"Hymen, io Hymen, Hymen", they do shout;
That even to the heavens their shouting shrill
Doth reach, and all the firmament doth fill;
To which the people standing all about,
As in approvance, do thereto applaud,
And loud advance her laud;
And evermore they "Hymen, Hymen" sing
That all the woods them answer, and their echo ring.

Lo! where she comes along with portly pace,
Like Phoebe from her chamber of the East,
Arising forth to run her mighty race,
Clad all in white, that 'seems a virgin best.
So well it her beseems that ye would ween
Some angel she had been.
Her long loose yellow locks like golden wire,
Sprinkled with pearl and pearling flowers atween,
Do like a golden mantle her attire;
And, being crownéd with a garland green,
Seem like some maiden queen.
Her modest eyes, abashéd to behold
So many gazers as do at her stare,
Upon the lowly ground affixéd are;
Nor dare lift up her countenance too bold,
But blush to hear her praises sung so loud,

So far from being proud.
Nathless do ye still loud her praises sing
That all the woods may answer, and your echo ring.

Tell me, ye merchants' daughters, did ye see
So fair a creature in your town before,
So sweet, so lovely, and so mild as she,
Adorned with beauty's grace and virtue's store?
Her goodly eyes like sapphires shining bright,
Her forehead ivory white,
Her cheeks like apples which the sun hath rudded,
Her lips like cherries charming men to bite,
Her breast like to a bowl of cream uncrudded,
Her paps like lilies budded,
Her snowy neck like to a marble tower;
And all her body like a palace fair
Ascending up with many a stately stair
To honour's seat and chastity's sweet bower.
Why stand ye still, ye virgins, in amaze
Upon her so to gaze,
Whiles ye forget your former lay to sing,
To which the woods did answer, and your echo ring?

But if ye saw that which no eyes can see,
The inward beauty of her lively spright,
Garnished with heavenly gifts of high degree,
Much more then would ye wonder at that sight
And stand astonished like to those which read
Medusa's mazeful head.
There dwells sweet love and constant chastity,
Unspotted faith and comely womanhood,
Regard of honour and mild modesty.
There virtue reigns as queen in royal throne
And giveth laws alone,
The which the base affections do obey
And yield their services unto her will;
Nor thought of thing uncomely ever may
Thereto approach to tempt her mind to ill.
Had ye once seen these her celestial treasures
And unrevealéd pleasures,
Then would ye wonder and her praises sing
That all the woods should answer, and your echo ring.

Open the temple gates unto my love,
Open them wide that she may enter in,
And all the post adorn as doth behove,
And all the pillars deck with garlands trim,
For to receive this saint with honour due,
That cometh in to you.
With trembling steps and humble reverence
She cometh in before th'Almighty's view;
Of her, ye virgins, learn obedience,
When so ye come into those holy places,
To humble your proud faces.
Bring her up to th'high altar that she may
The sacred ceremonies there partake,
And let the roaring organs loudly play
The praises of the Lord in lively notes;
The whiles, with hollow throats,
The choristers the joyous anthem sing
That all the woods may answer, and their echo ring.

Behold, whiles she before the altar stands,
Hearing the holy priest that to her speaks,
And blesseth her with his two happy hands,
How the red roses flush up in her cheeks,
And the pure snow, with goodly vermeil stain
Like crimson dyed in grain;
That even th'angels, which continually
About the sacred altar do remain,
Forget their service and about her fly,
Oft peeping in her face, that seems more fair
The more they on it stare.
But her sad eyes, still fastened on the ground,
Are governéd with goodly modesty,
That suffers not one look to glance awry,
Which may let in a little thought unsound.
Why blush you, love, to give to me your hand,
The pledge of all our band!
Sing, ye sweet angels, alleluia sing,
That all the woods may answer, and your echo ring.

Now all is done. Bring home the bride again,
Bring home the triumph of our victory,

Bring home with you the glory of her gain,
With joyance bring her and with jollity.
Never had man more joyful day than this,
Whom heaven would heap with bliss,
Make feast therefore now all this live-long day;
This day for ever to me holy is.
Pour out the wine without restraint or stay,
Pour not by cups but by the bellyful,
Pour out to all that wull,
And sprinkle all the post and walls with wine
That they may sweat and drunken be withal.
Crown ye god Bacchus with a coronal,
And Hymen also crown with wreaths of vine;
And let the Graces dance unto the rest,
For they can do it best;
The whiles the maidens do their carol sing,
To which the woods shall answer, and their echo ring.

Ring ye the bells, ye young men of the town,
And leave your wonted labours for this day.
This day is holy; do ye write it down
That ye for ever it remember may.
This day the sun is in his chiefest height,
With Barnaby the bright,
From whence declining daily by degrees
He somewhat loseth of his heat and light,
When once the Crab behind his back he sees.
But for this time it ill ordainéd was
To choose the longest day in all the year
And shortest night, when longest fitter were;
Yet never day so long but late would pass.
Ring ye the bells to make it wear away
And bonfires make all day,
And dance about them and about them sing,
That all the woods may answer, and your echo ring.

Ah! when will this long weary day have end,
And lend me leave to come unto my love?
How slowly do the hours their numbers spend!
How slowly does sad Time his feathers move!
Haste thee, O fairest planet, to thy home

Within the western foam;
Thy tired steeds long since have need of rest.
Long though it be, at last I see it gloom
And the bright evening star with golden crest
Appear out of the East.
Fair child of beauty! glorious lamp of love!
That all the host of heaven in ranks dost lead
And guidest lovers through the night's sad dread,
How cheerfully thou lookest from above
And seem'st to laugh atween thy twinkling light,
As joining in the sight
Of these glad many, which for joy do sing
That all the woods them answer, and their echo ring!

Now cease, ye damsels, your delights fore-past,
Enough it is that all the day was yours;
Now day is done, and night is nighing fast,
Now bring the bride into the bridal bowers.
The night is come; now soon her disarray
And in her bed her lay;
Lay her in lilies and in violets,
And silken curtains over her display,
And odoured sheets and Arras coverlets.
Behold how goodly my fair love does lie
In proud humility!
Like unto Maia whenas Jove her took
In Tempe, lying on the flowery grass
'Twixt sleep and wake, after she weary was
With bathing in the Acidalian brook.
Now it is night, ye damsels may be gone
And leave my love alone,
And leave likewise your former lay to sing.
The woods no more shall answer, nor your echo ring.

Now welcome night! thou night so long expected,
That long days' labour dost at last defray,
And all my cares which cruel Love collected
Hast summed in one and cancelléd for aye.
Spread thy broad wing over my love and me
That no man may us see,
And in thy sable mantle us enwrap

From fear of peril and foul horror free.
Let no false treason seek us to entrap,
Nor any dread disquiet once annoy
The safety of our joy;
But let the night be calm and quietsome
Without tempestuous storms or sad affray;
Like as when Jove with fair Alcmena lay
When he begot the great Tirynthian groom;
Or like as when he with thyself did lie
And begot Majesty.
And let the maids and young men cease to sing;
Nor let the woods them answer, nor their echo ring.

Let no lamenting cries nor doleful tears
Be heard all night within, nor yet without;
Nor let false whispers breeding hidden fears
Break gentle sleep with misconceivéd doubt.
Let no deluding dreams nor dreadful sights
Make sudden sad affrights;
Nor let house fires nor lightnings' helpless harms,
Nor let the Puck nor other evil sprights,
Nor let mischievous witches with their charms,
Nor let hobgoblins, names whose sense we see not,
Fray us with things that be not;
Let not the screech owl nor the stork be heard,
Nor the night raven that still deadly yells,
Nor damnéd ghosts called up with mighty spells,
Nor grisly vultures, make us once afeared;
Nor let th'unpleasant choir of frogs still croaking
Make us to wish their choking.
Let none of these their dreary accents sing,
Nor let the woods them answer, nor their echo ring.

But let still Silence true night-watches keep
That sacred Peace may in assurance reign;
And timely Sleep, when it is time to sleep,
May pour his limbs forth on your pleasant plain;
The whiles an hundred little wingéd Loves,
Like divers-feathered doves,
Their pretty stealths shall work, and snares shall spread
To filch away sweet snatches of delight,

Concealed through covert night.
Ye sons of Venus, play your sports at will!
For greedy pleasure, careless of your toys,
Thinks more upon her paradise of joys
Than what ye do, albeit good or ill.
All night therefore attend your merry play,
For it will soon be day;
Now none doth hinder you that say or sing,
Nor will the woods now answer, nor their echo ring.

Who is the same which at my window peeps?
Or whose is that fair face that shines so bright?
Is it not Cynthia, she that never sleeps,
But walks about high heaven all the night?
O! fairest goddess, do thou not envy
My love with me to spy;
For thou likewise didst love, though now unthought,
And for a fleece of wool which privily
The Latmian shepherd once unto thee brought,
His pleasures with thee wrought.
Therefore to us be favourable now;
And sith of women's labours thou hast charge
And goodly generation dost enlarge,
Incline thy will t'effect our wishful vow,
And the chaste womb inform with timely seed
That may our comfort breed.
Till which we cease our hopeful hap to sing;
Nor let the woods us answer, nor our echo ring.

And thou, great Juno! which with awful might
The laws of wedlock still dost patronise,
And the religion of the faith first plight
With sacred rites hast taught to solemnise,
And eke for comfort often calléd art
Of women in their smart;
Eternally bind thou this lovely band,
And all thy blessings unto us impart.
And thou, glad Genius! in whose gentle hand
The bridal bower and genial bed remain
Without blemish or stain,
And the sweet pleasures of their love's delight

With secret aid dost succour and supply
Till they bring forth the fruitful progeny,
Send us the timely fruit of this same night.
And thou, fair Hebe! and thou, Hymen free!
Grant that it so may be.
Till which we cease your further praise to sing;
Nor any woods shall answer, nor your echo ring.

And ye high heavens, the temple of the gods,
In which a thousand torches flaming bright
Do burn, that to us wretched earthly clods
In dreadful darkness lend desired light;
And all ye powers that in the same remain,
More than we men can feign!
Pour out your blessing on us plenteously,
And happy influence upon us rain,
That we may raise a large posterity,
Which from the earth, which they may long possess
With lasting happiness,
Up to your haughty palaces may mount;
And for the guerdon of their glorious merit
May heavenly tabernacles there inherit,
Of blessed saints for to increase the count.
So let us rest, sweet love, in hope of this,
And cease till then our timely joys to sing;
     The woods no more us answer, nor our echo ring!

   Song! made in lieu of many ornaments,
   With which my love should duly have been decked,
   Which cutting off through hasty accidents,
   You would not stay your due time to expect,
   But promised both to recompense;
   Be unto her a goodly ornament,
   And for short time an endless monument.

FROM *The Faery Queen*

1.

The noble heart that harbours virtuous thought
And is with child of glorious great intent,
Can never rest until it forth have brought
Th'eternal brood of glory excellent;
Such restless passion did all night torment
The flaming courage of that Faery knight,
Devising how that doughty tournament
With greatest honour he achieven might:
Still did he wake, and still did watch for dawning light.

At last, the golden oriental gate
Of greatest heaven 'gan to open fair,
And Phoebus, fresh as bridegroom to his mate,
Came dancing forth shaking his dewy hair
And hurled his glistering beams through gloomy air.
Which when the wakeful Elf perceived, straightway
He started up, and did himself prepare
In sun-bright arms and battailous array;
For with that pagan proud he combat will that day.

And forth he comes into the common hall,
Where early waits him many a gazing eye,
To weet what end to stranger knight may fall.
There many minstrels maken melody
To drive away the dull melancholy,
And many bards that to the trembling cord
Can tune their timely voices cunningly,
And many chroniclers that can record
Old loves and wars for ladies done by many a lord.

Soon after comes the cruel Sarazin
In woven mail all arméd warily,
And sternly looks at him who not a pin
Does care for look of living creature's eye.
They bring them wines of Greece and Araby
And dainty spices fetched from furthest Ind
To kindle heat of courage privily;
And in the wine a solemn oath they bind
T'observe the sacred laws of arms that are assigned.

At last forth comes that far renownéd Queen.
With royal pomp and princely majesty
She is ybrought unto a paléd green,
And placéd under stately canopy,
The warlike feats of both those knights to see.
On th'other side in all men's open view
Duessa placéd is, and on a tree
Sansfoy his shield is hanged with bloody hue;
Both those the laurel garlands to the victor due.

A shrilling trumpet sounded from on high
And unto battle bade themselves address;
Their shining shields about their wrists they tie,
And burning blades about their heads do bless,
The instruments of wrath and heaviness,
With greedy force each other doth assail
And strike so fiercely that they do impress
Deep dinted furrows in the battered mail;
The iron walls to ward their blows are weak and frail.

The Sarazin was stout and wondrous strong,
And heapéd blows like iron hammers great,
For after blood and vengeance he did long;
The knight was fierce and full of youthful heat,
And doubled strokes like dreaded thunder's threat;
For all for praise and honour he did fight.
Both stricken strike, and beaten both do beat,
That from their shields forth flyeth fiery light,
And hewen helmets deep shew marks of either's might.

So th'one for wrong, the other strives for right,
And each to deadly shame would drive his foe;
The cruel steel so greedily doth bite
In tender flesh that streams of blood down flow,
With which the arms that erst so bright did show
Into a pure vermilion now are dyed.
Great ruth in all the gazers' hearts did grow,
Seeing the goréd wounds to gape so wide,
That victory they dare not wish to either side.

Book 1, Canto 5

2.

Mammon emovéd was with inward wrath;
Yet, forcing it to feign, him forth thence led
Through grisly shadows by a beaten path,
Into a garden goodly garnishéd
With herbs and fruits, whose kinds mote not be read;
Not such as earth out of her fruitful womb
Throws forth to men, sweet and well savouréd,
But direful deadly black both leaf and bloom,
Fit to adorn the dead and deck the dreary tomb.

There mournful cypress grew in greatest store,
And trees of bitter gall and ebon sad,
Dead sleeping poppy and black hellebore,
Cold coloquintida and tetra mad,
Mortal samnitis and cicuta bad,
With which th'unjust Athenians made to die
Wise Socrates, who therof quaffing glad,
Poured out his life and last philosophy
To the fair Critias, his dearest belamy!

The Garden of Proserpina this hight;
And in the midst thereof a silver seat,
With a thick arbour goodly over-dight,
In which she often used from open heat
Herself to shroud, and pleasures to entreat;
Next thereunto did grow a goodly tree,
With branches broad dispread and body great,
Clothéd with leaves, that none the wood might see,
And loaden all with fruit as thick as it might be.

Their fruit were golden apples glistering bright,
That goodly was their glory to behold;
On earth like never grew, nor living wight
Like ever saw, but they from hence were sold;
For those which Hercules with conquest bold
Got from great Atlas' daughters hence began,
And planted there did bring forth fruit of gold;
And those with which th'Euboean young man wan
Swift Atalanta, when through craft he her outran.

Here also sprung that goodly golden fruit
With which Acontius got his lover true,
Whom he had long time sought with fruitless suit;
Here eke that famous golden apple grew,
The which amongst the gods false Até threw,
For which th'Idaean ladies disagreed
Till partial Paris deemed it virtue's due,
And had of her fair Helen for his meed,
That many noble Greeks and Trojans made to bleed.

Book 2, Canto 7

3.

Eftsoons they heard a most melodious sound,
Of all that mote delight a dainty ear,
Such as at once might not on living ground,
Save in this paradise, be heard elsewhere;
Right hard it was for wight which did it hear
To read what manner music that mote be;
For all that pleasing is to living ear
Was there consorted in one harmony;
Birds, voices, instruments, winds, waters all agree.

The joyous birds shrouded in cheerful shade
Their notes unto the voice attempered sweet;
Th'angelical soft trembling voices made
To th'instruments divine respondence meet;
The silver sounding instruments did meet
With the bass murmur of the water's fall;
The water's fall with difference discreet
Now soft, now loud, unto the wind did call;
The gentle warbling wind low answeréd to all.

The whiles some one did chant this lovely lay:
Ah! see, whoso fair thing dost fain to see,
In springing flower the image of thy day.
Ah! see the virgin rose how sweetly she
Doth first peep forth with bashful modesty,
That fairer seems the less ye see her may.
Lo! see soon after how more bold and free
Her baréd bosom she doth broad display;
Lo! see soon after how she fades and falls away.

So passeth in the passing of a day
Of mortal life the leaf, the bud, the flower;
Nor more doth flourish after first decay
That erst was sought to deck both bed and bower
Of many a lady' and many a paramour.
Gather therefore the rose whilst yet is prime,
For soon comes age that will her pride deflower;
Gather the rose of love whilst yet is time,
Whilst loving thou mayst lovéd be with equal crime.

                                    Book 2, Canto 12

ANTHONY MUNDAY
                                    (1553–1633)
To Colin Clout

Beauty sat bathing by a spring,
    Where fairest shades did hide her,
The winds blew calm, the birds did sing,
    The cool streams ran beside her.
My wanton thoughts enticed mine eye
    To see what was forbidden,
But better memory said, fie,
    So vain desire was chidden.
            Hey nonny nonny O!
            Hey nonny nonny!

Into a slumber then I fell,
    When fond imagination
Seeméd to see, but could not tell
    Her feature or her fashion.
But even as babes in dreams do smile,
    And sometimes fall a-weeping,
So I awaked, as wise this while,
    As when I fell a-sleeping.

                                    England's Helicon, 1600

JOHN LYLY?

(1553–1606)

"What Bird So Sings…"

What bird so sings, yet does so wail?
O 'tis the ravished nightingale.
"Jug, jug, jug, jug, tereu," she cries,
And still her woes at midnight rise.
Brave prick-song! who is't now we hear?
None but the lark so shrill and clear;
Now at heaven's gates she claps her wings,
The morn not waking till she sings.
Hark, hark, with what a pretty throat,
Poor robin redbreast tunes his note;
Hark how the jolly cuckoos sing,
Cuckoo to welcome in the spring!
Cuckoo to welcome in the spring!

Alexander and Campaspe, 1584

"Cupid and My Campaspe Played"

Cupid and my Campaspe played
At cards for kisses—Cupid paid;
He stakes his quiver, bow and arrows,
His mother's doves, and team of sparrows;
Loses them too; then down he throws
The coral of his lip, the rose
Growing on's cheek (but none knows how);
With these, the crystal of his brow,
And then the dimple of his chin:
All these did my Campaspe win.
At last he set her both his eyes,
She won, and Cupid blind did rise.
O Love! has she done this to thee?
What shall, alas! become of me?

Alexander and Campaspe, 1584

"Pan's Syrinx Was a Girl..."

Pan's Syrinx was a girl indeed,
Though now she's turned into a reed;
From that dear reed Pan's pipe does come,
A pipe that strikes Apollo dumb;
Nor flute, nor lute, nor gittern can
So chant it as the pipe of Pan:
Cross-gartered swains and dairy girls,
With faces smug and round as pearls,
When Pan's shrill pipe begins to play,
With dancing wear out night and day;
The bagpipe's drone his hum lays by,
When Pan sounds up his minstrelsy;
His minstrelsy! O base! this quill,
Which at my mouth with wind I fill,
Puts me in mind, though her I miss,
That still my Syrinx' lips I kiss.

Midas, 1592

FULKE GREVILLE, LORD BROOKE
(1554–1628)

Song to His Cynthia

Away with these self-loving lads,
Whom Cupid's arrow never glads!
Away poor souls that sigh and weep
In love of them that lie and sleep!
  For Cupid is a meadow-god,
  And forceth none to kiss the rod.

God Cupid's shaft, like destiny,
Doth either good or ill decree;
Desert is borne out of his bow,
Reward upon his feet doth go.
  What fools are they that have not known
  That Love likes no laws but his own?

My songs they be of Cynthia's praise,
I wear her rings on holidays;
On every tree I write her name,
And every day I read the same.
    Where Honour Cupid's rival is,
    There miracles are seen of his.

If Cynthia crave her ring of me,
I blot her name out of the tree;
If doubt do darken things held dear,
Then welfare nothing once a year,
    For many run, but one must win;
    Fools only hedge the cuckoo in.

The worth that worthiness should move
Is love, which is the due of love;
And love as well the shepherd can
As can the mighty nobleman.
    Sweet nymph, 'tis true you worthy be,
    Yet without love naught worth to me.

To Myra

I, with whose colours Myra dressed her head,
I, that wear posies of her own hand-making,
I, that mine own name in the chimneys read
By Myra finely wrought ere I was waking;
    Must I look on, in hope time coming may
    With change bring back my turn again to play?

I, that on Sunday at the church-stile found
A garland sweet with true-love knots in flowers,
Which I to wear about mine arms was bound,
That each of us might know that all was ours;
    Must I now lead an idle life in wishes,
    And follow Cupid for his loaves and fishes?

I, that did wear the ring her mother left,
I, for whose love she gloried to be blamed,
I, with whose eyes her eyes committed theft,

I, who did make her blush when I was named;
 Must I lose ring, flowers, blush, theft, and go naked,
 Watching with sighs till dead love be awakéd?

I, that when drowsy Argus fell asleep,
Like jealousy o'erwatchéd with desire,
Was ever warnéd modesty to keep,
While her breath speaking kindled Nature's fire;
 Must I look on a-cold, while others warm them?
 Do Vulcan's brothers in such fine nets arm them?

Was it for this that I might Myra see
Washing the water with her beauties white?
Yet would she never write her love to me,
Thinks wit of change while thoughts are in delight?
 Mad girls must safely love, as they may leave;
 No man can print a kiss; lines may deceive.

Chorus

 O wearisome condition of humanity!
 Born under one law, to another bound;
 Vainly begot, and yet forbidden vanity,
 Created sick, commanded to be sound.
 What meaneth Nature by these diverse laws?
 Passion and reason self-division cause.
 Is it the mark or majesty of Power
 To make offences that it may forgive?
 Nature herself doth her own self deflower
 To hate those errors she herself doth give.
 For how should man think that he may not do
 If Nature did not fail and punish too?
 Tyrant to others, to herself unjust,
 Only commands things difficult and hard,
 Forbids us all things which it knows we lust,
 Makes easy pains, impossible reward.
 If Nature did not take delight in blood,
 She would have made more easy ways to good.
 We that are bound by vows and by promotion,
 With pomp of holy sacrifice and rites,

To preach belief in God and stir devotion,
To preach of Heaven's wonders and delights;
Yet when each of us in his own heart looks,
He finds the God there far unlike his books.

Mustapha, 1609

SIR PHILIP SIDNEY
(1554–1586)

"My True Love Hath My Heart..."

My true love hath my heart, and I have his,
By just exchange one for the other given.
I hold his dear, and mine he cannot miss;
There never was a better bargain driven.
His heart in me keeps me and him in one;
My heart in him his thoughts and senses guides;
He loves my heart, for once it was his own;
I cherish his, because in me it bides.
His heart his wound receivéd from my sight;
My heart was wounded with his wounded heart;
For as from me on him his hurt did light
So still methought in me his hurt did smart:
Both equal hurt, in this change sought our bliss;
My true love hath my heart, and I have his.

Arcadia

FROM *Astrophel and Stella*

1.   SONNET I

Loving in truth, and fain my love in verse to show,
That the dear she might take some pleasure of my pain:
Pleasure might cause her read, reading might make her know,
Knowledge might pity win, and pity grace obtain—
I sought fit words, to paint the blackest face of woe,
Studying inventions fine, her wits to entertain,
Oft turning others' leaves, to see if thence would flow
Some fresh and fruitful shower, upon my sun-burnt brain.
But words came halting out, wanting invention's stay,
Invention, nature's child, fled stepdame study's blows,

And others' feet still seemed but strangers in my way.
Thus great with child to speak, and helpless in my throes,
Biting my tongue and pen, beating myself for spite:
Fool! said my muse to me, look in thy heart and write.

2.   SONNET XXXI

With how sad steps, O moon, thou climb'st the skies!
How silently, and with how wan a face!
What! may it be that even in heavenly place
That busy archer his sharp arrows tries?
Sure, if that long-with-love-acquainted eyes
Can judge of love, thou feel'st a lover's case:
I read it in thy looks; thy languished grace
To me, that feel the like, thy state descries.
Then, even of fellowship, O Moon, tell me,
Is constant love deemed there but want of wit?
Are beauties there as proud as here they be?
Do they above love to be loved, and yet
Those lovers scorn whom that love doth possess?
Do they call virtue there ungratefulness?

3.   SONNET XXXIX

Come, Sleep; O Sleep! the certain knot of peace,
The baiting-place of wit, the balm of woe,
The poor man's wealth, the prisoner's release,
Th'indifferent judge between the high and low;
With shield of proof shield me from out the prease
Of those fierce darts Despair at me doth throw:
O make in me those civil wars to cease;
I will good tribute pay, if thou do so.
Take thou of me smooth pillows, sweetest bed,
A chamber deaf to noise and blind of light,
A rosy garland and a weary head;
And if these things, as being thine by right,
Move not thy heavy grace, thou shalt in me,
Livelier than elsewhere, Stella's image see.

4.

ELEVENTH SONG

"Who is it that, this dark night,
Underneath my window plaineth?"
"It is one, who from thy sight
Being, ah! exiled, disdaineth
Every other vulgar light."

"Why, alas! and are you he?
Be not yet those fancies changed?"
"Dear, when you find change in me,
Though from me you be estranged,
Let my change to ruin be."

"Well, in absence this will die;
Leave to see, and leave to wonder."
"Absence sure will help, if I
Can learn how myself to sunder
From what in my heart doth lie."

"But time will these thoughts remove;
Time doth work what no man knoweth."
"Time doth as the subject prove,
With time still the affection groweth
In the faithful turtle dove."

"What if you new beauties see?
Will they not stir new affections?"
"I will think they pictures be,
Image-like of saint's perfection,
Poorly counterfeiting thee."

"But your reason's purest light
Bids you leave such minds to nourish."
"Dear, do reason no such spite,
Never doth thy beauty flourish
More than in my reason's sight."

"But the wrongs love bears will make
Love at length leave undertaking."
"No, the more fools it do shake
In a ground of so firm making,
Deeper still they drive the stake."

"Peace, I think that some give ear;
Come no more lest I get anger."
"Bliss, I will my bliss forbear,
Fearing, sweet, you to endanger,
But my soul shall harbour there."

"Well, begone, begone I say,
Lest that Argus' eyes perceive you."
"O unjust Fortune's sway!
Which can make me thus to leave you
And from louts to run away!"

FROM *Certain Sonnets*

1.   "RING OUT YOUR BELLS! ..."

Ring out your bells! Let mourning shows be spread,
For Love is dead:
All love is dead, infected
With plague of deep disdain;
Worth as nought worth rejected,
And faith fair scorn doth gain.
    From so ungrateful fancy,
    From such a female frenzy,
    From them that use men thus,
    Good Lord deliver us.

Weep, neighbours, weep, do you not hear it said
That Love is dead?
His death-bed, peacock's folly;
His winding sheet is shame;
His will false-seeming holy;
His sole executor blame.

Let dirge be sung, and trentals rightly read,
For Love is dead.
Sir Wrong his tomb ordaineth;
My mistress Marble-heart,
Which epitaph containeth,
His eyes were once his dart.

Alas, I lie! Rage hath this error bred,
Love is not dead.
Love is not dead, but sleepeth
In her unmatchéd mind,
Where she his counsel keepeth
Till due desert she find.
   Therefore from so vile fancy,
   To call such wit a frenzy,
   Who love can temper thus,
   Good Lord, deliver us.

2.   "THOU BLIND MAN'S MARK..."

Thou blind man's mark, thou fool's self-chosen snare,
Fond Fancy's scum and dregs of scattered thought,
Band of all evils, cradle of causeless care,
Thou web of will whose end is never wrought;
Desire! desire, I have too dearly bought
With price of mangled mind thy worthless ware;
Too long, too long asleep thou hast me brought,
Who should my mind to higher things prepare.
But yet in vain thou hast my ruin sought,
In vain thou mad'st me to vain things aspire,
In vain thou kindlest all thy smoky fire.
For virtue hath this better lesson taught,
Within myself to seek my only hire,
Desiring nought but how to kill desire.

3.   "LEAVE ME, O LOVE..."

Leave me, O Love, which reachest but to dust;
And thou, my mind, aspire to higher things.
Grow rich in that which never taketh rust;
Whatever fades but fading pleasure brings.
Draw in thy beams, and humble all thy might,
To that sweet yoke where lasting freedom be,
Which breaks the clouds and opens forth the light,
That doth both shine and give us sight to see.
O take fast hold, let that light be thy guide
In this small course which birth draws out to death,
And think how evil becometh him to slide
Who seeketh heav'n, and comes of heav'nly breath.
Then, farewell world! thy uttermost I see;
Eternal Love, maintain thy life in me.

THOMAS LODGE

(1556?-1625)

Phoebe's Sonnet

"Down a down!"
    Thus Phyllis sung,
    By fancy once distress'd:
"Whoso by foolish Love are stung
    Are worthily oppress'd.
And so sing I, with a down a down."

"When Love was first begot,
And by the mother's will,
Did fall to human lot,
His solace to fulfil,
Devoid of all deceit,
A chaste and holy fire,
Did quicken men's conceit,
And women's breasts inspire.
The gods that saw the good,
That mortals did approve,

With kind and holy mood
Began to talk of Love.
   Down a down!"
     Thus Phyllis sung
     By fancy once distress'd.

"But during this accord,
A wonder strange to hear,
Whilst Love in deed and word,
Most faithful did appear,
False semblance came in place,
By jealousy attended,
And with a double face
Both love and fancy blended;
Which made the gods forsake,
And men from fancy fly,
And maidens scorn a make;
Forsooth, and so will I.
   Down a down!"
     Thus Phyllis sung,
     By fancy once distress'd:
     "Whoso by foolish Love are stung
     Are worthily oppress'd.
And so sing I, with a down a down."

Rosalind's Madrigal

Love in my bosom like a bee
   Doth suck his sweet;
Now with his wings he plays with me,
   Now with his feet.
Within mine eyes he makes his nest,
His bed amidst my tender breast;
My kisses are his daily feast,
And yet he robs me of my rest.
   Ah wanton, will ye?

And if I sleep, then percheth he,
   With pretty flight,
And makes his pillow of my knee
   The livelong night.

Strike I my lute, he tunes the string;
He music plays if so I sing;
He lends me every lovely thing;
Yet cruel he my heart doth sting.
   Whist, wanton, still ye!

Else I with roses every day
   Will whip you hence,
And bind you, when you long to play,
   For your offence.
I'll shut mine eyes to keep you in,
I'll make you fast it for your sin,
I'll count your power not worth a pin,
Alas, what hereby shall I win,
   If he gainsay me?

What if I beat the wanton boy
   With many a rod?
He will repay me with annoy,
   Because a god.
Then sit thou safely on my knee,
Then let thy bower my bosom be;
Lurk in mine eyes, I like of thee.
O Cupid, so thou pity me,
   Spare not, but play me.

"The Earth, Late Choked..."

The earth, late choked with showers,
   Is now arrayed in green,
Her bosom springs with flowers,
   The air dissolves her teen;
     The heavens laugh at her glory,
     Yet bide I sad and sorry.

The woods are decked with leaves,
   And trees are clothéd gay,
And Flora crowned with sheaves,
   With oaken boughs doth play;
     Where I am clad in black,
     The token of my wrack.

The birds upon the trees
  Do sing with pleasant voices,
And chant in their degrees
  Their loves and lucky choices;
    When I, whilst they are singing,
    With sighs mine arms am wringing.

The thrushes seek the shade,
  And I my fatal grave;
Their flight to heaven is made,
  My walk on earth I have;
    They free, I thrall; they jolly,
    I sad and pensive wholly.

Scilla's Metamorphosis, 1589

To Phyllis, the Fair Shepherdess

My Phyllis hath the morning sun,
  At first to look upon her;
And Phyllis hath morn-waking birds
  Her risings for to honour.

My Phyllis hath prime-feathered flowers
  That smile when she treads on them;
And Phyllis hath a gallant flock
  That leaps since she doth own them.

But Phyllis hath so hard a heart,
  Alas that she should have it,
As yields no mercy to desart,
  Nor grace to those that crave it.

Sweet sun, when thou look'st on,
Pray her regard my moan;
Sweet birds, when you sing to her,
To yield some pity, woo her;
Sweet flowers whenas she treads on,
Tell her, her beauty deads one,
And if in life her love she nill agree me,
Pray her before I die she will come see me.

To Phyllis

Love guards the roses of thy lips
   And flies about them like a bee;
If I approach he forward skips,
   And if I kiss he stingeth me.

Love in thine eyes doth build his bower,
   And sleeps within their pretty shine;
And if I look the boy will lower,
   And from their orbs shoot shafts divine.

Love works thy heart within his fire,
   And in my tears doth firm the same;
And if I tempt it will retire,
   And of my plaints doth make a game.

Love, let me cull her choicest flowers,
   And pity me, and calm her eye,
Make soft her heart, dissolve her lowers,
   Then will I praise thy deity.

But if thou do not, Love, I'll truly serve her
In spite of thee, and by firm faith deserve her.

GEORGE PEELE

(1558?–1597)

"Fair and Fair..."

Oenone: Fair and fair, and twice so fair,
            As fair as any may be;
            The fairest shepherd on our green,
            A love for any lady.

Paris: Fair and fair, and twice so fair,
            As fair as any may be;
            Thy love is fair for thee alone,
            And for no other lady.

Oenone: My love is fair, my love is gay,
  As fresh as bin the flowers in May,
And of my love my roundelay,
  My merry, merry, merry roundelay,
Concludes with Cupid's curse—
  They that do change old love for new,
Pray gods they change for worse!

Both: They that do change &c.

Oenone: Fair and fair &c.

Paris: Fair and fair &c.

Oenone: My love can pipe, my love can sing,
My love can many a pretty thing,
And of his lovely praises ring
My merry, merry roundelays,
  Amen to Cupid's curse,
  They that do change old love for new,
Pray gods they change for worse!

Both: Fair and fair, and twice so fair,
  As fair as any may be;
The fairest shepherd on our green,
  A love for any lady.

      The Arraignment of Paris, 1584

"His Golden Locks..."

His golden locks time hath to silver turned;
 O time too swift, O swiftness never ceasing!
His youth 'gainst time and age hath ever spurned,
 But spurned in vain; youth waneth by increasing:
Beauty, strength, youth, are flowers but fading seen;
Duty, faith, love, are roots, and ever green.

His helmet now shall make a hive for bees,
 And, lovers' sonnets turned to holy psalms,
A man-at-arms must now serve on his knees,

And feed on prayers, which are age his alms:
But though from court to cottage he depart,
His saint is sure of his unspotted heart.

And when he saddest sits in homely cell,
   He'll teach his swains this carol for a song—
"Blessed be the hearts that wish my sovereign well,
   Cursed be the souls that think her any wrong."
Goddess, allow this aged man his right,
To be your beadsman now that was your knight.

Polyhymnia, 1590

"Whenas the Rye..."

Whenas the rye reach to the chin,
And chopcherry, chopcherry ripe within,
Strawberries swimming in the cream,
And schoolboys playing in the stream;
Then, O then, O then, O, my true love said,
'Till that time come again
She could not live a maid.

The Old Wives' Tale, 1595

"Not Iris in Her Pride..."

Not Iris in her pride and bravery
Adorns her arch with such variety;
Nor doth the Milk-white Way in frosty night
Appear so fair and beautiful in sight,
As do these fields and groves and sweetest bowers
Bestrewed and decked with parti-coloured flowers.
Along the bubbling brooks and silver glide,
That at the bottom doth in silence slide,
The water-flowers and lilies on the banks
Like blazing comets burgeon all in ranks;
Under the hawthorn and the poplar tree,
Where sacred Phoebe may delight to be,
The primrose and the purple hyacinth,

The dainty violet and the wholesome minth,
The double daisy and the cowslip (Queen
Of summer flowers) do over-peer the green;
And round about the valley as ye pass,
Ye may not see, for peeping flowers, the grass.

The Arraignment of Paris, 1584

FROM *The Love of King David and Fair Bethsabe,* 1599

1.

Absalon: Now for the crown and throne of Israel,
To be confirmed with virtue of my sword,
And writ with David's blood upon the blade.
Now, Jove, let forth the golden firmament
And look on him with all thy fiery eyes,
Which thou hast made to give their glories light.
To show thou lovest the virtue of thy hand,
Let fall a wreath of stars upon my head,
Whose influence may govern Israel
With state exceeding all her other kings.
Fight, lords and captains, that your sovereign's face
May shine in honour brighter than the sun;
And with the virtue of my beauteous rays
Make this fair land as fruitful as the fields
That with sweet milk and honey overflowed.
God, in the whizzing of a pleasant wind,
Shall march upon the tops of mulberry-trees,
To cool all breasts that burn with any griefs;
As whilom he was good to Moses' men,
By day the Lord shall sit within a cloud,
To guide your footsteps to the fields of joy;
And in the night a pillar bright as fire
Shall go before you like a second sun,
Wherein the essence of his Godhead is;
That day and night you may be brought to peace,
And never swerve from that delightsome path
That leads your souls to perfect happiness.
This He shall do for joy when I am king.
Then fight, brave captains, that these joys may fly
Into your bosoms with sweet victory.

2.

Bethsabe: Come, gentle Zephyr, tricked with those perfumes
That erst in Eden sweetened Adam's love,
And stroke my bosom with thy silken fan.
This shade, sun-proof, is yet no proof for thee;
Thy body, smoother than this waveless spring,
And purer than the substance of the same,
Can creep through that his lances cannot pierce:
Thou and thy sister, soft and sacred Air,
Goddess of life and governess of health,
Keep every fountain fresh and arbour sweet;
No brazen gate her passage can repulse,
Nor bushy thicket bar thy subtle breath.
Then deck thee with thy loose delightsome robes,
And on thy wings bring delicate perfumes
To play the wanton with us through the leaves.

3.

David: Now comes my lover tripping like the roe,
And brings my longings tangled in her hair.
To joy her love I'll build a kingly bower,
Seated in hearing of a hundred streams,
That for their homage to her sovereign joys
Shall, as the serpents fold into their nests
In oblique turnings, wind their nimble waves
About the circles of her curious walks;
And with their murmur summon easeful sleep
To lay his golden sceptre on her brows.
Open the doors, and entertain my love;
Open, I say, and, as you open, sing:
Welcome fair Bethsabe, King David's darling.

CHIDIOCK TICHBOURNE
(1558?–1586)

Written the Night before His Execution

My prime of youth is but a frost of cares;
My feast of joy is but a dish of pain;
My crop of corn is but a field of tares;

And all my good is but vain hope of gain;
My life is fled, and yet I saw no sun;
And now I live, and now my life is done.

The spring is past, and yet it hath not sprung;
  The fruit is dead, and yet the leaves be green;
My youth is gone, and yet I am but young;
  I saw the world, and yet I was not seen;
My thread is cut, and yet it is not spun;
And now I live, and now my life is done.

I sought my death, and found it in my womb,
  I looked for life, and saw it was a shade,
I trod the earth and knew it was my tomb,
  And now I die, and now I am but made:
The glass is full, and now my glass is run,
And now I live, and now my life is done.

ROBERT GREENE

(1560?–1592)

The Shepherd's Wife's Song

Ah, what is love? It is a pretty thing,
As sweet unto a shepherd as a king;
    And sweeter too,
For kings have cares that wait upon a crown,
And cares can make the sweetest love to frown;
    Ah then, ah then,
If country loves such sweet desires do gain,
What lady would not love a shepherd swain?

His flocks are folded, he comes home at night,
As merry as a king in his delight;
    And merrier too,
For kings bethink them what the state require,
When shepherds careless carol by the fire:

Ah then, ah then,
If country loves such sweet desires do gain,
What lady would not love a shepherd swain?

He kisseth first, then sits as blithe to eat
His cream and curds as doth the king his meat;
    And blither too,
For kings have often fears when they do sup,
Where shepherds dread no poison in their cup:
    Ah then, ah then,
If country loves such sweet desires do gain,
What lady would not love a shepherd swain?

To bed he goes, as wanton then, I ween,
As is a king in dalliance with a queen;
    More wanton too,
For kings have many griefs affects to move,
Where shepherds have no greater grief than love:
    Ah then, ah then,
If country loves such sweet desires do gain,
What lady would not love a shepherd swain?

Upon his couch of straw he sleeps as sound,
As doth the king upon his bed of down;
    More sounder too,
For cares cause kings full oft their sleep to spill,
Where weary shepherds lie and snort their fill:
    Ah then, ah then,
If country loves such sweet desires do gain,
What lady would not love a shepherd swain?

Thus with his wife he spends the year, as blithe
As doth the king at every tide or sithe;
    And blither too,
For kings have wars and broils to take in hand,
Where shepherds laugh and love upon the land:
    Ah then, ah then,
If country loves such sweet desires do gain,
What lady would not love a shepherd swain?

Sithe, *time*.

Samela

Like to Diana in her summer-weed,
Girt with a crimson robe of brightest dye,
         Goes fair Samela;

Whiter than be the flocks that straggling feed,
When washed by Arethusa's Fount they lie,
         Is fair Samela;

As fair Aurora in her morning-grey,
Decked with the ruddy glister of her love,
         Is fair Samela;

Like lovely Thetis on a calméd day,
Whenas her brightness Neptune's fancy move,
         Shines fair Samela;

Her tresses gold, her eyes like glassy streams,
Her teeth are pearl, the breasts are ivory
         Of fair Samela;

Her cheeks like rose and lily, yield forth gleams,
Her brows bright arches framed of ebony:
         Thus fair Samela

Passeth fair Venus in her bravest hue,
And Juno in the show of majesty,
         For she's Samela;

Pallas in wit, all three, if you well view,
For beauty, wit and matchless dignity,
         Yield to Samela.

Weep Not, My Wanton

Weep not, my wanton, smile upon my knee;
When thou art old there's grief enough for thee.
  Mother's wag, pretty boy,
  Father's sorrow, father's joy;
  When thy father first did see

Such a boy by him and me,
He was glad, I was woe;
Fortune changéd made him so,
When he left his pretty boy,
Last his sorrow, first his joy.

Weep not, my wanton, smile upon my knee;
When thou art old there's grief enough for thee.
    Streaming tears that never stint,
    Like pearl-drops from a flint,
    Fell by course from his eyes,
    That one another's place supplies;
    Thus he grieved in every part,
    Tears of blood fell from his heart,
    When he left his pretty boy,
    Father's sorrow, father's joy.

Weep not, my wanton, smile upon my knee;
When thou art old there's grief enough for thee.
    The wanton smiled, father wept,
    Mother cried, baby lept;
    More he crowed, more we cried,
    Nature could not sorrow hide:
    He must go, he must kiss
    Child and mother, baby bliss,
    For he left his pretty boy,
    Father's sorrow, father's joy.
Weep not, my wanton, smile upon my knee;
When thou art old there's grief enough for thee.

A Mind Content

Sweet are the thoughts that savour of content;
    The quiet mind is richer than a crown;
Sweet are the nights in careless slumber spent;
    The poor estate scorns fortune's angry frown:
Such sweet content, such minds, such sleep, such bliss,
Beggars enjoy, when princes oft do miss.

The homely house that harbours quiet rest;
  The cottage that affords no pride nor care;
The mean that 'grees with country music best;
  The sweet consort of mirth and music's fare;
Obscuréd life sets down a type of bliss:
A mind content both crown and kingdom is.

"Ah, Were She Pitiful..."

Ah, were she pitiful as she is fair,
  Or but as mild as she is seeming so,
Then were my hopes greater than my despair,
  Then all the world were heaven, nothing woe.
Ah, were her heart relenting as her hand,
  That seems to melt even with the mildest touch,
Then knew I where to seat me in a land,
  Under wide heavens, but yet there is not such.
So as she shows, she seems the budding rose,
  Yet sweeter far than is an earthly flower,
Sovereign of beauty, like the spray she grows,
  Compassed she is with thorns and cankered bower,
Yet were she willing to be plucked and worn,
She would be gathered, though she grew on thorn.

Ah, when she sings, all music else be still,
  For none must be comparéd to her note;
Ne'er breathed such glee from Philomela's bill,
  Nor from the morning-singer's swelling throat.
Ah, when she riseth from her blissful bed,
  She comforts all the world, as doth the sun,
And at her sight the night's foul vapour's fled;
  When she is set, the gladsome day is done.
O glorious sun, imagine me the west,
Shine in my arms, and set thou on my breast!

Pandosto, the Triumph of Time, 1588?

FROM A *Madrigal*

The swans, whose pens as white as ivory,
Eclipsing fair Endymion's silver love,
Floating like snow down by the banks of Po,
Ne'er tuned their notes, like Leda once forlorn,
With more despairing sorts of madrigals,
Than I, when wanton Love hath with his gad
Pricked to the core of deep and restless thoughts.

"Sonnet"

Fair is my love, for April is her face,
   Her lovely breasts September claims his part,
And lordly July in her eyes takes place;
   But old December dwelleth in her heart.
Blest be the months that set my thoughts on fire,
Accursed that month that hind'reth my desire!

Like Phoebus' fire, so sparkle both her eyes;
   As air perfumed with amber is her breath;
Like swelling waves her lovely teats do rise;
   As earth her heart, cold, dateth me to death.
Ay me, poor man, that on the earth do live,
When unkind earth death and despair doth give!

In pomp sits Mercy seated in her face;
   Love 'twixt her breasts his trophies doth imprint;
Her eyes shine favour, courtesy and grace;
   But touch her heart, ah, that is framed of flint!
Therefore my harvest in the grass bears grain;
The rock will wear washed with a winter's rain.

GEORGE CHAPMAN
(1560–1634)

Song

O come, soft rest of cares! come, Night!
Come, naked Virtue's only tire,
The reapéd harvest of the light
Bound up in sheaves of sacred fire.
Love calls to war;
Sighs his alarms,
Lips his swords are,
The field his arms.

Come, Night, and lay thy velvet hand
On glorious Day's outfacing face;
And all thy crownéd flames command
For torches to our nuptial grace.
Love calls to war;
Sighs his alarms,
Lips his swords are,
The field his arms.

FROM *Bussy d'Ambois*, 1607

1.

Bussy   As cedars beaten with continual storms,
d'Ambois: So great men flourish; and do imitate
Unskilful statuaries, who suppose
In forming a Colossus, if they make him
Straddle enough, strut, and look big, and gape,
Their work is goodly: so men merely great
In their affected gravity of voice,
Sourness of countenance, manners' cruelty,
Authority, wealth, and all the spawn of fortune,
Think they bear all the kingdom's worth before
them;
Yet differ not from those colossic statues,
Which, with heroic forms without o'erspread,
Within are nought but mortar, flint and lead.

2.

Bussy   I long to know
d'Ambois: How my dear mistress fares, and be informed
          What hand she now doth hold on the troubled blood
          Of her incenséd lord. Methought the Spirit
          When he had uttered his perplexed presage,
          Threw his changed countenance headlong into clouds
          His forehead bent, as he would hide his face;
          He knocked his chin against his darkened breast,
          And struck a churlish silence through his powers.
          Terror of Darkness, O thou King of Flames,
          That with thy music-footed horse dost strike
          The clear light out of crystal, on dark earth;
          And hurl'st instructive fire about the world;
          Wake, wake the drowsy and enchanted night,
          That sleeps with dead eyes in this heavy riddle.
          Or thou, Great Prince of Shades, where never sun
          Sticks his far-darted beams; whose eyes are made
          To see in darkness and see ever best
          Where sense is blinded; open now the heart
          Of thy abashed oracle, that, for fear
          Of some ill it includes, would fain lie hid,
          And rise Thou with it in thy greater light.

FROM *Caesar and Pompey*, 1631

Cato: Poor slaves, how terrible this Death is to them!
         If men would sleep, they would be wroth with all
         That interrupt them; physic take, to take
         The golden rest it brings; both pay and pray
         For good and soundest naps; all friends consenting
         In those kind invocations; praying all
         "Good rest the Gods vouchsafe you." But when Death,
         Sleep's natural brother, comes, that's nothing worse
         But better (being more rich—and keeps the store—
         Sleep ever fickle, wayward still, and poor)
         O, how men grudge and shake and fear and fly
         His stern approaches! all their comforts, taken
         In faith and knowledge of the bliss and beauties

That watch their wakings in an endless life,
Drowned in the pains and horrors of their sense
Sustained but for an hour.

FROM *The Conspiracy of Charles,*
Duke of Byron, 1608

1.
Laffin: As when the moon hath comforted the night,
And set the world in silver of her light,
The planets, asterisms, and whole State of Heaven
In beams of gold descending; all the winds
Bound up in caves, charged not to drive abroad
Their cloudy heads; and universal peace
(Proclaimed in silence) of the quiet earth:
Soon as her hot and dry fumes are let loose,
Storms and clouds mixing suddenly put out
The eyes of all these glories; the creation
Turned into chaos; and we then desire
For all our joy of life the death of sleep.
So, when the glories of our lives (men's loves,
Clear consciences, our fames and loyalties)
That did us worthy comfort are eclipsed,
Grief and disgrace invade us; and for all
Our night of life besides, our misery craves
Dark earth would ope and hide us in our graves.

2.
Byron: Give me a spirit that on life's rough sea
Loves to have his sails filled with a lusty wind,
E'en till his sail-yards tremble, his masts crack,
And his rapt ship run on her side so low
That she drinks water and her keel ploughs air.
There is no danger to a man that knows
What life and death is; there's not any law
Exceeds his knowledge; neither is it lawful
That he should stoop to any other law.
He goes before them, and commands them all,
That to himself is a law rational.

FROM *The Sixth Book of Homer's Iliads*

She, with his sight made breathless haste to meet him; she,
    whose grace
Brought him withal so great a dower; she that of all the race
Of King Aetion only lived; Aetion whose house stood
Beneath the mountain Placius, environed with the wood
Of Theban Hypoplace, being court to the Cilician land.
She ran to Hector, and with her, tender of heart and hand
Her son, borne in his nurse's arms; when, like a heavenly sign
Compact of many golden stars, the princely child did shine,
Whom Hector called Scamandrius; but whom the town did
    name
Astyanax, because his sire did only prop the same.
Hector, though grief bereft his speech, yet smiled upon his joy.
Andromache cried out, mixed hands, and to the strength of
    Troy
Thus wept forth her affection: "O noblest in desire,
Thy mind, inflamed with others' good, will set thyself on fire;
Nor pitiest thou thy son, nor wife who must thy widow be,
If now thou issue; all the field will only run on thee.
Better my shoulders underwent the earth than thy decease;
For then would earth bear joys no more; then comes the black
    increase
Of griefs, like Greeks on Ilion. Alas, what one survives
To be my refuge? one black day bereft seven brothers' lives,
By stern Achilles; by his hand my father breathed his last,
His high-walled rich Cilician Thebes sacked by him and laid
    waste
The royal body yet he left unspoiled; religion charmed
That act of spoil; and all in fire he burned him complete
    armed;
Built over him a royal tomb; and to the monument
He left of him, th' Oreades (that are the high descent
Of aegis-bearing Jupiter) another of their own
Did add to it, and set it round with elms; by which is shown
In theirs the barrenness of death; yet might it serve beside
To shelter the sad monument from all the ruffinous pride
Of storms and tempests, used to hurt things of that noble kind.

The short life yet my mother lived he saved, and served his
    mind
With all the riches of the realm; which not enough esteemed
He kept her prisoner; whom small time but much more wealth
    redeemed;
And she in sylvan Hypoplace Cilicia ruled again,
But soon was overruled by death; Diana's chaste disdain
Gave her a lance, and took her life. Yet, all these gone from me
Thou amply render'st all; thy life makes still my father be,
My mother, brothers; and besides thou art my husband too,
Most loved, most worthy. Pity then, dear love, and do not go,
For, thou gone, all these go again; pity our common joy,
Lest, of a father's patronage, the bulwark of all Troy,
Thou leavest him a poor widow's charge; stay, stay then, in
    this tower,
And call up to the wild fig-tree all thy retired power;
For there the wall is easiest scaled, and fittest for surprise,
And there th' Ajaces, Idomen, th' Atrides, Diomed, thrice
Have both surveyed and made attempt; I know not if induced
By some wise augur, or the fact was naturally infused
Into their wits or courages." To this great Hector said:
"Be well assured, wife, all these things in my kind cares are
    weighed.
But what a shame and fear it is to think how Troy would
    scorn
(Both in her husbands and her wives, whom long-trained
    gowns adorn)
That I should cowardly fly off! The spirit I first did breathe
Did never teach me that; much less, since the contempt of
    death
Was settled in me, and my mind knew what a worthy was,
Whose office is to lead in fight, and give no danger pass
Without improvement. In this fire must Hector's trial shine;
Here must his country, father, friends, be in him made divine.
And such a stormy day shall come (in mind and soul I know)
When sacred Troy shall shed her towers, for tears of over-
    throw;
When Priam, all his birth and power, shall in those tears be
    drowned.
But neither Troy's posterity so much my soul doth wound,
Priam, nor Hecuba herself, nor all my brothers' woes

(Who though so many and so good must all be food for foes)
As thy sad state; when some rude Greek shall lead thee
    weeping hence,
These free days clouded, and a night of captive violence
Loading thy temples out of which thine eyes must never see,
But spin the Greek wives' webs of task, and their fetch-water
    be
To Argos, from Messeides, or clear Hyperia's spring;
Which howsoever thou abhorr'st, Fate's such a shrewish thing
She will be mistress; whose cursed hands, when they shall
    crush out cries
From thy oppressions (being beheld by other enemies)
Thus they will nourish thy extremes: 'This dame was Hector's
    wife,
A man that at the wars of Troy did breathe the worthiest life
Of all their army.' This again will rub thy fruitful wounds,
To miss the man that to thy bands could give such narrow
    bounds.
But that day shall not wound mine eyes; the solid heap of
    night
Shall interpose, and stop mine ears against thy plaints and
    plight."
This said, he reached to take his son; who, of his arms afraid,
And then the horse-hair plume, with which he so was overlaid,
Nodded so horribly, he clinged back to his nurse and cried.
Laughter affected his great sire, who doffed and laid aside
His fearful helm, that on the earth cast round about it light;
Then took and kissed his loving son, and, balancing his weight
In dancing him, these loving vows to living Jove he used. . . .

ROBERT SOUTHWELL

(1561?–1595)

The Burning Babe

    As I in hoary winter's night
      Stood shivering in the snow,
    Surprised I was with sudden heat
      Which made my heart to glow;
    And lifting up a fearful eye
      To view what fire was near,

A pretty babe all burning bright
  Did in the air appear;
Who, scorchéd with excessive heat,
  Such floods of tears did shed,
As though His floods should quench His flames,
  Which with His tears were fed.
"Alas!" quoth He, "but newly born
  In fiery heats I fry,
Yet none approach to warm their hearts
  Or feel my fire but I!
My faultless breast the furnace is,
  The fuel wounding thorns;
Love is the fire, and sighs the smoke,
  The ashes shame and scorns;
The fuel Justice layeth on,
  And Mercy blows the coals;
The metal in this furnace wrought
  Are men's defiléd souls.
For which, as now on fire I am,
  To work them to their good,
So will I melt into a bath
  To wash them in My blood."
With this He vanished out of sight,
  And swiftly shrunk away,
And straight I calléd unto mind
  That it was Christmas Day.

The Virgin Mary to Christ on the Cross

What mist hath dimmed that glorious face!
  What seas of grief my sun doth toss!
The golden rays of heavenly grace
  Lies now eclipséd on the cross.

Jesus! my Love, my Son, my God,
  Behold Thy mother washed in tears;
Thy bloody wounds be made a rod
  To chasten these my latter years.

You cruel Jews, come work your ire
　Upon this worthless flesh of mine;
And kindle not eternal fire
　By wounding Him which is divine.

Thou messenger that didst impart
　His first descent into my womb,
Come, help me now to cleave my heart,
　That there I may my Son entomb.

You angels all, that present were
　To show His birth with harmony,
Why are you not now ready here
　To make a mourning symphony?

The cause I know; you wail alone
　And shed your tears in secrecy,
Lest I should movéd be to moan
　By force of heavy company.

But wail, my soul, thy comfort dies;
　My woeful womb, lament thy fruit;
My heart, give tears unto my eyes,
　Let Sorrow string my heavy lute.

FROM *The Image of Death*

The gown which I do use to wear,
　The knife wherewith I cut my meat,
And eke that old and ancient chair
　Which is my only usual seat,
All these do tell me I must die,
And yet my life amend not I.

My ancestors are turned to clay,
　And many of my mates are gone;
My youngers daily drop away,
　And can I think to 'scape alone?
No, no, I know that I must die,
And yet my life amend not I.

Not Solomon, for all his wit,
  Nor Samson, though he were so strong,
No king nor person ever yet
  Could 'scape, but Death laid him along;
Wherefore I know that I must die,
And yet my life amend not I.

Though all the East did quake to hear
  Of Alexander's dreadful name,
And all the West did likewise fear
  To hear of Julius Caesar's fame,
Yet both by Death in dust now lie;
Who then can 'scape, but he must die?

If none can 'scape Death's dreadful dart,
  If rich and poor his beck obey;
If strong, if wise, if all do smart,
  Then I to 'scape shall have no way.
Oh! grant me grace, O God! that I
My life may mend, sith I must die.

HENRY CONSTABLE

(1562?–1613?)

Damelus' Song to His Diaphenia

Diaphenia, like the daffadowndilly,
White as the sun, fair as the lily,
  Heighho, how I do love thee!
I do love thee as my lambs
Are belovéd of their dams:
  How blest were I if thou wouldst prove me!

Diaphenia, like the spreading roses,
That in thy sweets all sweets encloses,
  Fair sweet, how I do love thee!
I do love thee as each flower
Loves the sun's life-giving power;
  For dead, thy breath to life might move me.

Diaphenia, like to all things blessèd,
When all thy praises are expressèd,
  Dear joy, how I do love thee!
As the birds do love the Spring,
Or the bees their careful king:
  Then in requite, sweet virgin, love me!

SAMUEL DANIEL

(1562–1619)

"Love Is a Sickness..."

Love is a sickness full of woes,
  All remedies refusing;
A plant that with most cutting grows,
  Most barren with best using.
                    Why so?
More we enjoy it, more it dies,
If not enjoyed, it sighing cries,
                    Heigh-ho!

Love is a torment of the mind,
  A tempest everlasting;
And Jove hath made it of a kind
  Not well, nor full nor fasting.
                    Why so?
More we enjoy it, more it dies,
If not enjoyed, it sighing cries,
                    Heigh-ho!

Ulysses and the Siren

Siren: Come, worthy Greek, Ulysses, come,
              Possess these shores with me;
            The winds and seas are troublesome,
              And here we may be free.
            Here may we sit and view their toil
              That travail in the deep,
            And joy the day in mirth the while,
              And spend the night in sleep.

Ulysses:　Fair nymph, if fame or honour were
　　　　　　　　To be attained with ease,
　　　　　　Then would I come and rest with thee,
　　　　　　　　And leave such toils as these.
　　　　　　But here it dwells, and here must I
　　　　　　　　With danger seek it forth,
　　　　　　To spend the time luxuriously
　　　　　　　　Becomes not men of worth.

Siren:　Ulysses, Oh be not deceived
　　　　　　　　With that unreal name;
　　　　　　This honour is a thing conceived,
　　　　　　　　And rests on others' fame;
　　　　　　Begotten only to molest
　　　　　　　　Our peace and to beguile,
　　　　　　The best thing of our life, our rest,
　　　　　　　　And give us up to toil.

Ulysses:　Delicious nymph, suppose there were
　　　　　　　　Nor honour, nor report,
　　　　　　Yet manliness would scorn to wear
　　　　　　　　The time in idle sport.
　　　　　　For toil doth give a better touch
　　　　　　　　To make us feel our joy;
　　　　　　And ease finds tediousness as much
　　　　　　　　As labour yields annoy.

Siren:　Then pleasure likewise seems the shore
　　　　　　　　Whereto tends all your toil,
　　　　　　Which you forgo to make it more,
　　　　　　　　And perish oft the while.
　　　　　　Who may disport them diversely
　　　　　　　　Find never tedious day,
　　　　　　And ease may have variety
　　　　　　　　As well as action may.

Ulysses:　But natures of the noblest frame
　　　　　　　　These toils and dangers please,
　　　　　　And they take comfort in the same
　　　　　　　　As much as you in ease.

And with the thought of actions past
    Are recreated still;
When pleasure leaves a touch at last
    To show that it was ill.

Siren: That doth opinion only cause,
    That's out of custom bred,
Which makes us many other laws
    Than ever Nature did.
No widows wail for our delights,
    Our sports are without blood,
The world we see by warlike wights
    Receives more ill than good.

Ulysses: But yet the state of things require
    These motions of unrest,
And these great Spirits of high desire
    Seem born to turn them best;
To purge the mischiefs that increase
    And all good order mar;
For oft we see a wicked peace
    To be well changed for war.

Siren: Well, well, Ulysses, then I see
    I shall not have thee here,
And therefore I will come to thee,
    And take my fortunes there.
I must be won that cannot win,
    Yet lost were I not won;
For beauty hath created been
    T' undo or be undone.

Sonnets

1.

Fair is my love and cruel as she's fair;
Her brow-shades frown, although her eyes are sunny.
Her smiles are lightning, though her pride despair,
And her disdains are gall, her favours honey;
A modest maid, decked with a blush of honour,
Whose feet do tread green paths of youth and love,

The wonder of all eyes that look upon her,
Sacred on earth, designed a saint above.
Chastity and beauty, which were deadly foes,
Live reconciléd friends within her brow;
And had she pity to conjoin with those,
Then who had heard the plaints I utter now?
For had she not been fair, and thus unkind,
My Muse had slept, and none had known my mind.

2.

Beauty, sweet love, is like the morning dew,
Whose short refresh upon the tender green
Cheers for a time, but till the sun doth show,
And straight 'tis gone as it had never been.
Soon doth it fade that makes the fairest flourish,
Short is the glory of the blushing rose;
The hue which thou so carefully dost nourish,
Yet which at length thou must be forced to lose.
When thou, surcharged with burthen of thy years,
Shall bend thy wrinkles homeward to the earth;
And that, in beauty's lease expired, appears
The date of age, the calends of our death—
But ah, no more!—this must not be foretold,
For women grieve to think they must be old.

3.

Let others sing of knights and paladins
In agéd accents and untimely words,
Paint shadows in imaginary lines,
Which well the reach of their high wit records;
But I must sing of thee, and those fair eyes
Authentic shall my verse in time to come;
When yet th'unborn shall say, Lo, where she lies!
Whose beauty made him speak that else was dumb!
These are the arcs, the trophies I erect,
That fortify thy name against old age;
And these thy sacred virtues must protect
Against the dark and time's consuming rage.
Though th'error of my youth in them appear,
Suffice they show I lived and loved thee dear.

4.

Care-charmer sleep, son of the sable night,
Brother to death, in silent darkness born,
Relieve my languish and restore the light,
With dark forgetting of my cares return.
And let the day be time enough to mourn
The shipwreck of my ill-adventured youth;
Let waking eyes suffice to wail their scorn,
Without the torment of the night's untruth.
Cease, dreams, the images of day desires,
To model forth the passions of the morrow;
Never let rising sun approve you liars,
To add more grief to aggravate my sorrow.
Still let me sleep, embracing clouds in vain,
And never wake to feel the day's disdain.

JOSHUA SYLVESTER

(1563–1618)

Sonnet

Were I as base as is the lowly plain
And you, my love, as high as heav'n above,
Yet should the thoughts of me your humble swain
Ascend to heav'n in honour of my love.
Were I as high as heav'n above the plain,
And you, my love, as humble and as low
As are the deepest bottoms of the main,
Wheresoe'er you were, with you my love should go.
Were you the earth, dear love, and I the skies,
My love should shine on you like to the sun,
And look upon you with ten thousand eyes,
Till heav'n waxed blind and till the world were dun.
Wheresoe'er I am, below or else above you,
Wheresoe'er you are, my heart shall truly love you.

MICHAEL DRAYTON

(1563–1631)

FROM *The Shepherd's Garland*

Batte: Gorbo, as thou cam'st this way
By yonder little hill,
Or as thou through the fields didst stray,
Saw'st thou my Daffodil?

She's in a frock of Lincoln green,
The colour maids delight,
And never hath her beauty seen
But through a veil of white;

Than roses richer to behold
That trim up lovers' bowers,
The pansy and the marigold
Though Phoebus' paramours.

Gorbo: Thou well describ'st the daffodil;
It is not full an hour
Since by the spring near yonder hill
I saw that lovely flower.

Batte: Yet my fair flower thou didst not meet,
Nor news of her didst bring,
And yet my Daffodil's more sweet
Than that by yonder spring.

Gorbo: I saw a shepherd that doth keep
In yonder field of lilies,
Was making, as he fed his sheep,
A wreath of daffodillies.

Batte: Yet, Gorbo, thou delud'st me still;
My flower thou didst not see;
For, know, my pretty Daffodil
Is worn of none but me.

To show itself but near her seat
No lily is so bold,
Except to shade her from the heat
Or keep her from the cold.

Gorbo: Through yonder vale as I did pass,
Descending from the hill,
I met a smirking bonny lass,
They call her Daffodil,

Whose presence as along she went
The pretty flowers did greet,
As though their heads they downward bent
With homage to her feet.

And all the shepherds that were nigh,
From top of every hill,
Unto the valleys low did cry:
"There goes sweet Daffodil!"

Batte: Ay, gentle shepherd, now with joy
Thou all my flocks dost fill,
That's she alone, kind shepherd's boy;
Let us to Daffodil.

To His Coy Love

I pray thee leave, love me no more,
    Call home the heart you gave me,
I but in vain that saint adore,
    That can, but will not save me.
These poor half kisses kill me quite;
    Was ever man thus served?
Amidst an ocean of delight
    For pleasure to be sterved.

Show me no more those snowy breasts
    With azure riverets branchéd,
Where, whilst mine eye with plenty feasts,
    Yet is my thirst not stanchéd.

O Tantalus, thy pains ne'er tell,
  By me thou art prevented,
'Tis nothing to be plagued in hell,
  But thus in heaven tormented.

Clip me no more in those dear arms,
  Nor thy life's comfort call me;
O, these are but too pow'rful charms,
  And do but more enthral me.
But see, how patient I am grown,
  In all this coil about thee;
Come, nice thing, let my heart alone,
  I cannot live without thee.

To the Virginian Voyage

You brave heroic minds,
Worthy your country's name,
  That honour still pursue;
  Go and subdue
Whilst loit'ring hinds
Lurk here at home with shame.

Britons, you stay too long;
Quickly abroad bestow you,
  And with a merry gale
  Swell your stretch'd sail,
With vows as strong
As the winds that blow you.

Your course securely steer,
West and by south forth keep;
  Rocks, lee-shores, nor shoals,
  When Eolus scowls,
You need not fear,
So absolute the deep

And, cheerfully at sea,
Success you still entice,
    To get the pearl and gold,
    And ours to hold,
VIRGINIA,
Earth's only paradise.

Where Nature hath in store
Fowl, venison and fish,
    And the fruitfull'st soil,
    Without your toil,
Three harvests more,
All greater than your wish.

And the ambitious vine
Crowns with his purple mass
    The cedar reaching high
    To kiss the sky,
The cypress, pine,
And useful sassafras.

To whom the golden age
Still Nature's laws doth give,
    No other cares that tend,
    But them to defend
From winter's rage,
That long there doth not live.

When as the luscious smell
Of that delicious land,
    Above the sea's that flows,
    The clear wind throws,
Your hearts to swell
Approaching the dear strand.

In kenning of the shore,
(Thanks to God first given)
    O you, the happiest men,
    Be frolic then,
Let cannons roar,
Frighting the wide heaven.

And as there plenty grows
Of laurel everywhere,
   Apollo's sacred tree,
   You may it see
A poet's brows
To crown, that may sing there.

Thy voyages attend
Industrious Hakluyt,
   Whose reading shall inflame
   Men to seek fame,
And much commend
To after-times thy wit.

FROM *Nimphidia, the Court of Fayrie*

Pigwiggen was this fairy knight,
One wondrous gracious in the sight
Of fair Queen Mab, which day and night
      He amorously observed;
Which made king Oberon suspect
His service took too good effect,
His sauciness and often checkt,
      And could have wished him starved.

Pigwiggen gladly would commend
Some token to queen Mab to send,
If sea or land him aught could lend
      Were worthy of her wearing;
At length this lover doth devise
A bracelet made of emmets' eyes,
A thing he thought that she would prize,
      No whit her state impairing.

And to the queen a letter writes,
Which he most curiously indites,
Conjuring her by all the rites
      Of love she would be pleased

To meet him, her true servant, where
They might without suspect or fear,
Themselves to one another clear,
      And have their poor hearts eased.

At midnight, the appointed hour,
And for the queen a fitting bower
(Quoth he) is that fair cowslip flower
      On Hipcut hill that groweth.
In all your train there's not a fay
That ever went to gather may
But she hath made it in her way,
      The tallest there that groweth.

When by Tom Thumb, a fairy page,
He sent it, and doth him engage
By promise of a mighty wage
      It secretly to carry;
Which done, the queen her maids doth call,
And bids them to be ready all,
She would go see her summer hall,
      She could no longer tarry.

Her chariot ready straight is made,
Each thing therein is fitting laid,
That she by nothing might be stayed,
      For naught must be her letting;
Four nimble gnats the horses were,
Their harnesses of gossamer,
Fly Cranion her charioteer,
      Upon the coach-box getting.

Her chariot of a snail's fine shell,
Which for the colours did excel,
The fair queen Mab becoming well,
      So lively was the limning;
The seat, the soft wool of the bee;
The cover, gallantly to see,
The wing of a pied butterfly,
      I trow 'twas simple trimming.

The wheels compos'd of crickets' bones,
And daintily made for the nones,
For fear of rattling on the stones,
　　With thistle-down they shod it;
For all her maidens much did fear,
If Oberon had chanced to hear
That Mab his queen should have been there,
　　He would not have abode it.

She mounts her chariot with a trice,
Nor would she stay for no advice,
Until her maids that were so nice,
　　To wait on her were fitted;
But run herself away alone,
Which, when they heard, there was not one
But hasted after to be gone,
　　As she had been diswitted.

Hop and Mop and Drop so clear,
Pip and Trip and Skip that were
To Mab their sovereign ever dear,
　　Her special maids of honour;
Fib and Tib and Pink and Pin,
Tick and Quick and Jill and Jin,
Tit and Nit and Wap and Win,
　　The train that wait upon her.

Upon a grasshopper they got,
And what with amble and with trot
For hedge nor ditch they sparéd not,
　　But after her they hie them.
A cobweb over them they throw
To shield the wind if it should blow,
Themselves they wisely could bestow,
　　Lest any should espy them.

Sonnets

1.

　　If chaste and pure devotion of my youth
Or glory of my April-springing years,
Unfeignéd love in naked simple truth,

A thousand vows, a thousand sighs and tears;
Or if a world of faithful service done,
Words, thoughts and deeds devoted to her honour,
Or eyes that have beheld her as their sun,
With admiration ever looking on her;
A life that never joyed but in her love,
A soul that ever hath adored her name,
A faith that time nor fortune could not move.
A Muse that unto heaven hath raised her fame:
Though these, nor these, deserve to be embraced,
Yet, fair unkind, too good to be disgraced.

2.

Sweet secrecy, what tongue can tell thy worth?
What mortal pen sufficiently can praise thee?
What curious pencil serves to limn thee forth?
What Muse hath power above thy height to raise thee?
Strong lock of kindness, closet of love's store,
Heart's mithridate, the soul's preservative,
O virtue! which all virtues do adore,
Chief good, from whom all good things we derive.
O rare effect! true bond of friendship's measure,
Conceit of angels, which all wisdom teachest,
O richest casket of all heavenly treasure,
In secret silence which such wonders preachest.
O purest mirror, wherein men may see
The lively image of divinity.

3.

Into these loves who but for passion looks,
At this first sight here let him lay them by,
And seek elsewhere in turning other books
Which better may his labour satisfy.
No far-fetched sigh shall ever wound my breast,
Love from mine eye a tear shall never wring,
Nor in Ah-mes! my whining sonnets drest,
A libertine fantastic'ly I sing;

My verse is the true image of my mind,
Ever in motion, still desiring change,
To choice of all variety inclined,
And in all humours sportively I range;
My active Muse is of the world's right strain,
That cannot long one fashion entertain.

4.

To nothing fitter can I thee compare
Than to the son of some rich pennyfather,
Who having now brought on his end with care
Leaves to his son all he had heaped together;
This new rich novice, lavish of his chest,
To one man gives, and on another spends,
Then here he riots, yet among the rest
Haps to lend some to one true honest friend.
Thy gifts thou in obscurity dost waste,
False friends thy kindness, born but to deceive thee,
Thy love, that is on the unworthy placed;
Time hath thy beauty which with age will leave thee:
Only that little which to me was lent
I give thee back, when all the rest is spent.

5.

Whilst thus my pen strives to eternise thee,
Age rules my lines with wrinkles in my face,
Where in the map of all my misery
Is modelled out the world of my disgrace;
Whilst in despite of tyrannising times,
Medea-like I make thee young again;
Proudly thou scorn'st my world-outwearing rhymes
And murder'st virtue with thy coy disdain.
And though in youth my youth untimely perish
To keep thee from oblivion and the grave,
Ensuing ages yet my rhymes shall cherish,
Where I entombed my better part shall save;
And though this earthly body fade and die,
My name shall mount upon eternity.

6.

Dear, why should you command me to my rest
When now the night doth summon all to sleep?
Methinks this time becometh lovers best,
Night was ordained together friends to keep.
How happy are all other living things,
Which though the day disjoin by several flight,
The quiet evening yet together brings
And each returns unto his love at night.
O thou that art so courteous unto all,
Why shouldst thou, Night, abuse me only thus,
That every creature to his kind dost call,
And yet 'tis thou dost only sever us?
Well could I wish it would be ever day,
If when night comes you bid me go away.

7.

Since there's no help, come, let us kiss and part.
Nay, I have done. You get no more of me.
And I am glad, yea, glad with all my heart,
That thus so cleanly I myself can free.
Shake hands for ever, cancel all our vows;
And when we meet at any time again,
Be it not seen in either of our brows
That we one jot of former love retain.
Now at the last gasp of Love's latest breath,
When, his pulse failing, Passion speechless lies,
When Faith is kneeling by his bed of death,
And Innocence is closing up his eyes,
Now, if thou would'st, when all have given him over,
From death to life thou might'st him yet recover.

CHRISTOPHER MARLOWE
(1564–1593)

The Passionate Shepherd to His Love

Come live with me, and be my love,
And we will all the pleasures prove
That hills and valleys, dales and fields,
And all the craggy mountains yields.

And we will sit upon the rocks,
Seeing the shepherds feed their flocks
By shallow rivers, to whose falls
Melodious birds sing madrigals.

And I will make thee beds of roses,
And a thousand fragrant posies,
A cap of flowers and a kirtle
Embroider'd all with leaves of myrtle.

A gown made of the finest wool
Which from our pretty lambs we pull,
Fair linéd slippers for the cold,
With buckles of the purest gold;

A belt of straw and ivy-buds,
With coral clasps and amber studs,
And if these pleasures may thee move,
Come live with me, and be my love.

Thy silver dishes for thy meat,
As precious as the gods do eat,
Shall on an ivory table be
Prepar'd each day for thee and me.

The shepherd swains shall dance and sing
For thy delight each May-morning;
If these delights thy mind may move,
Then live with me, and be my love.

Reply

By SIR WALTER RALEIGH

If all the world and love were young,
And truth in every shepherd's tongue,
These pretty pleasures might me move
To live with thee and be thy love.

But Time drives flocks from field to fold
When rivers rage and rocks grow cold,
And Philomel becometh dumb;
The rest complains of cares to come.

The flowers do fade, and wanton fields
To wayward winter reckoning yields;
A honey tongue, a heart of gall,
Is fancy's spring but sorrow's fall.

Thy gowns, thy shoes, the beds of roses,
Thy cap, thy kirtle, and thy posies,
Soon break, soon wither, soon forgotten
In folly ripe, in reason rotten.

Thy belt of straw and ivy-buds,
Thy coral clasps and amber studs,
All these in me no means can move
To come to thee and be thy love.

But could youth last and love still breed,
Had joy no date nor age no need,
Then these delights my mind might move
To live with thee and be thy love.

FROM *Hero and Leander*

On this feast day, O curséd day and hour,
Went Hero thorough Sestos, from her tower
To Venus' temple, where unhappily,
As after chanc'd, they did each other spy.
So fair a church as this, had Venus none:
The walls were of discoloured jasper stone,
Wherein was Proteus carvéd, and o'erhead
A lively vine of green sea-agate spread;
Where by one hand, light-headed Bacchus hung,
And with the other, wine from grapes outwrung.
Of crystal shining fair the pavement was;
The town of Sestos call'd it Venus' glass.
There might you see the gods in sundry shapes,

Committing heady riots, incest, rapes:
For know, that underneath this radiant floor
Was Danae's statue in a brazen tower,
Jove slily stealing from his sister's bed,
To dally with Idalian Ganymed;
And for his love, Europa, bellowing loud,
And tumbling with the Rainbow in a cloud:
Blood-quaffing Mars heaving the iron net
Which limping Vulcan and his Cyclops set:
Love kindling fire, to burn such towns as Troy,
Sylvanus weeping for the lovely boy
That now is turn'd into a cypress tree,
Under whose shade the wood-gods love to be.
And in the midst a silver altar stood;
There Hero sacrificing turtles' blood,
Vail'd to the ground, vailing her eyelids close,
And modestly they opened as she rose:
Thence flew Love's arrow with the golden head,
And thus Leander was enamouréd.
Stone still he stood, and evermore he gazed,
Till with the fire that from his count'nance blazed,
Relenting Hero's gentle heart was strook:
Such force and virtue hath an amorous look.

It lies not in our power to love, or hate,
For will in us is over-rul'd by fate.
When two are stript, long ere the course begin,
We wish that one should lose, the other win;
And one especially do we affect
Of two gold ingots, like in each respect.
The reason no man knows; let it suffice,
What we behold is censur'd by our eyes.
Where both deliberate, the love is slight;
Who ever lov'd, that lov'd not at first sight?

FROM *The First Part of Tamburlaine the Great*
1.

Tamburlaine: Disdains Zenocrate to live with me?
Or you, my lords, to be my followers?
Think you I weigh this treasure more than you?

Not all the wealth in India's wealthy arms
Shall buy the meanest soldier in my train.
Zenocrate, lovelier than the love of Jove,
Brighter than is the silver Rhodope,
Fairer than whitest snow on Scythian hills,
Thy person is more worth to Tamburlaine
Than the possession of the Persian crown,
Which gracious stars have promis'd at my birth.
A hundred Tartars shall attend on thee,
Mounted on steeds swifter than Pegasus.
Thy garments shall be made of Median silk,
Enchas'd with precious jewels of mine own,
More rich and valorous than Zenocrate's.
With milk-white harts upon an ivory sled
Thou shalt be drawn amidst the frozen pools,
And scale the icy mountains' lofty tops,
Which with thy beauty will be soon resolv'd.
My martial prizes, with five hundred men,
Won on the fifty-headed Volga's waves,
Shall we all offer to Zenocrate,
And then myself to fair Zenocrate.

2.

Tamburlaine: The thirst of reign and sweetness of a crown,
That caused the eldest son of heavenly Ops
To thrust his doting father from his chair
And place himself in the imperial heaven,
Mov'd me to manage arms against thy state,
What better precedent than mighty Jove?
Nature, that fram'd us of four elements
Warring within our breasts for regiment,
Doth teach us all to have aspiring minds:
Our souls, whose faculties can comprehend
The wondrous architecture of the world,
And measure every wandering planet's course,
Still climbing after knowledge infinite,
And always moving as the restless spheres,
Wills us to wear ourselves and never rest,
Until we reach the ripest fruit of all,
That perfect bliss and sole felicity,
The sweet fruition of an earthly crown.

3.

Tamburlaine: Those walléd garrisons will I subdue,
And write myself great lord of Africa.
So from the East unto the furthest West
Shall Tamburlaine extend his puissant arm.
The galleys and those pilling brigandines,
That yearly sail to the Venetian gulf,
And hover in the straits for Christians' wreck,
Shall lie at anchor in the Isle Asant,
Until the Persian fleet and men-of-war,
Sailing along the oriental sea,
Have fetched about the Indian continent,
Even from Persepolis to Mexico,
And thence unto the Straits of Jubalter,
Where they shall meet and join their force in
one
Keeping in awe the bay of Portingale,
And all the ocean by the British shore;
And by this means I'll win the world at last.

4.

Tamburlaine: Ah, fair Zenocrate, divine Zenocrate,
Fair is too foul an epithet for thee,
That in thy passion for thy country's love,
And fear to see thy kingly father's harm,
With hair dishevelled wip'st thy watery cheeks;
And like to Flora in her morning pride,
Shaking her silver tresses in the air,
Rain'st on the earth resolvéd pearl in showers,
And sprinklest sapphires on thy shining face,
Where Beauty, mother to the Muses, sits,
And comments volumes on her ivory pen,
Taking instructions from thy flowing eyes,
Eyes, when that Ebena steps to heaven,
In silence of thy solemn evening's walk,
Making the mantle of the richest night,
The moon, the planets, and the meteors, light.
There angels in their crystal armours fight
A doubtful battle with my tempted thoughts

For Egypt's freedom and the Soldan's life,
His life that so consumes Zenocrate;
Whose sorrows lay more siege unto my soul
Than all my army to Damascus' walls;
And neither Persia's sovereign nor the Turk
Troubled my senses with conceit of foil
So much by much as doth Zenocrate.
What is beauty, saith my sufferings, then?
If all the pens that ever poets held
Had fed the feeling of their masters' thoughts,
And every sweetness that inspir'd their hearts,
Their minds and muses on admiréd themes;
If all the heavenly quintessence they still
From the immortal flowers of poesy,
Wherein as in a mirror we perceive
The highest reaches of a human wit--
If these had made one poem's period,
And all combin'd in beauty's worthiness,
Yet should there hover in their restless heads
One thought, one grace, one wonder, at the
          least,
Which into words no virtue can digest.

FROM *The Second Part of Tamburlaine the Great*

1.

Tamburlaine: Black is the beauty of the brightest day;
The golden ball of heaven's eternal fire,
That danc'd with glory on the silver waves,
Now wants the fuel that inflamed his beams,
And all with faintness and for foul disgrace,
He binds his temples with a frowning cloud,
Ready to darken earth with endless night.
Zenocrate, that gave him light and life,
Whose eyes shot fire from their ivory bowers,
And tempered every soul with lively heat,
Now by the malice of the angry skies,
Whose jealousy admits no second mate,
Draws in the comfort of her latest breath,
All dazzled with the hellish mists of death.

Now walk the angels on the walls of heaven,
As sentinels to warn th'immortal souls
To entertain divine Zenocrate:
Apollo, Cynthia, and the ceaseless lamps
That gently look'd upon this loathsome earth,
Shine downwards now no more, but deck the
    heavens
To entertain divine Zenocrate:
The crystal springs, whose taste illuminates
Refinéd eyes with an eternal sight,
Like triéd silver run through Paradise
To entertain divine Zenocrate:
The cherubins and holy seraphins,
That sing and play before the King of Kings,
Use all their voices and their instruments
To entertain divine Zenocrate:
And in this sweet and curious harmony,
The god that tunes this music to our souls
Holds out his hand in highest majesty
To entertain divine Zenocrate.

2.

Tamburlaine: Forward, then, ye jades!
Now crouch, ye kings of greatest Asia,
And tremble when ye hear this scourge will
    come
That whips down cities and controlleth crowns,
Adding their wealth and treasure to my store.
The Euxine sea, north to Natolia;
The Terrene, west; the Caspian, north north-
    east;
And on the south, Sinus Arabicus;
Shall all be loaden with the martial spoils
We will convey with us to Persia.
Then shall my native city Samarcanda,
And crystal waves of fresh Jaertis' stream,
The pride and beauty of her princely seat,
Be famous through the furthest continents;
For there my palace royal shall be plac'd,
Whose shining turrets shall dismay the heavens,

And cast the fame of Ilion's tower to hell;
Thorough the streets, with troops of conquered
    kings,
I'll ride in golden armour like the sun;
And in my helm a triple plume shall spring,
Spangled with diamonds, dancing in the air,
To note me emperor of the three-fold world;
Like to an almond tree ymounted high
Upon the lofty and celestial mount
Of ever green Selinus, quaintly decked
With blooms more white than Herycina's
    brows,
Whose tender blossoms tremble every one
At every little breath that thorough heaven
    is blown.
Then in my coach, like Saturn's royal son
Mounted his shining chariot gilt with fire,
And drawn with princely eagles through the
    path
Pav'd with bright crystal and enchas'd with
    stars
Where all the gods stand gazing at his pomp,
So will I ride through Samarcanda streets,
Until my soul, dissevered from this flesh,
Shall mount the milk-white way, and meet him
    there.
To Babylon, my lords, to Babylon!

FROM *The Tragical History of Doctor Faustus*

1.

(*Enter Helen again, passing over the stage*)

Faustus: Was this the face that launch'd a thousand ships,
And burnt the topless towers of Ilium?—
Sweet Helen, make me immortal with a kiss.—
                      (*She kisses him*)
Her lips suck forth my soul: see where it flies!—
Come, Helen, come, give me my soul again.
Here will I dwell, for heaven is in those lips,
And all is dross that is not Helena.

I will be Paris, and for love of thee,
Instead of Troy, shall Wittenberg be sack'd;
And I will combat with meek Menelaus,
And wear thy colours on my pluméd crest:
Yea, I will wound Achilles in the heel,
And then return to Helen for a kiss.
O, thou art fairer than the evening air
Clad in the beauty of a thousand stars;
Brighter art thou than flaming Jupiter
When he appear'd to hapless Semele;
More lovely than the monarch of the sky
In wanton Arethusa's azured arms;
And none but thou shalt be my paramour!

2.

Faustus: Ah, Faustus,
Now hast thou but one bare hour to live,
And then thou must be damn'd perpetually!
Stand still, you ever-moving spheres of heaven,
That time may cease, and midnight never come;
Fair Nature's eye, rise, rise again, and make
Perpetual day; or let this hour be but
A year, a month, a week, a natural day,
That Faustus may repent and save his soul!
O lente, lente currite, noctis equi!
The stars move still, time runs, the clock will
strike,
The devil will come, and Faustus must be damn'd.
O, I'll leap up to my God!—Who pulls me down?—
See, see, where Christ's blood streams in the firma-
ment!
One drop would save my soul, half a drop: ah, my
Christ!—
Ah, rend not my heart for naming of my Christ!
Yet will I call on him: O, spare me, Lucifer!—
Where is it now! 'tis gone: and see, where God
Stretcheth out his arm, and bends his ireful brows!
Mountains and hills, come, come, and fall on me,
And hide me from the heavy wrath of God!

No, no!
Then will I headlong run into the earth:
Earth, gape! O, no, it will not harbour me!
You stars that reign'd at my nativity,
Whose influence hath allotted death and hell,
Now draw up Faustus, like a foggy mist,
Into the entrails of yon lab'ring cloud
That, when you vomit forth into the air,
My limbs may issue from your smoky mouths,
So that my soul may but ascend to heaven!
                              (*The watch strikes*)
Ah, half the hour is past! 'twill all be passed anon.
O God,
If thou wilt not have mercy on my soul,
Yet for Christ's sake, whose blood hath ransom'd me,
Impose some end to my incessant pain;
Let Faustus live in hell a thousand years,
A hundred thousand, and at last be sav'd!
O, no end is limited to damnéd souls!
Why wert thou not a creature wanting soul?
Or why is this immortal that thou hast?
Ah, Pythagoras' metempsychosis, were that true,
This soul should fly from me, and I be changed
Unto some brutish beast! all beasts are happy,
For, when they die,
Their souls are soon dissolved in elements;
But mine must live still to be plagu'd in hell.
Curs'd be the parents that engendered me!
No, Faustus, curse thyself, curse Lucifer
That hath depriv'd thee of the joys of heaven.
                              (*The clock striketh twelve*)
O, it strikes, it strikes! Now, body, turn to air,
Or Lucifer will bear thee quick to hell!
O soul, be changed into little water-drops,
And fall into the ocean, ne'er be found!
                              (*Thunder and enter the Devils*)
My God, my God, look not so fierce on me!
Adders and serpents, let me breathe a while!
Ugly hell, gape not! come not, Lucifer!
I'll burn my book!—Ah, Mephistophilis!
                              (*The Devils hale him off*)

3.

Chorus: Cut is the branch that might have grown full
    straight,
  And burnéd is Apollo's laurel-bough,
  That sometime grew within this learned man.
  Faustus is gone: regard his hellish fall,
  Whose fiendful fortune may exhort the wise,
  Only to wonder at unlawful things,
  Whose deepness doth entice such forward wits
  To practise more than heavenly power permits.

FROM *Edward the Second*

Gaveston: I must have wanton poets, pleasant wits,
  Musicians, that with touching of a string
  May draw the pliant king which way I please.
  Music and poetry are his delight;
  Therefore I'll have Italian masques by night,
  Sweet speeches, comedies, and pleasing shows;
  And in the day, when he shall walk abroad,
  Like sylvan nymphs my pages shall be clad;
  My men, like satyrs grazing on the lawns,
  Shall with their goat-feet dance the antic hay.
  Sometimes a lovely boy in Dian's shape,
  With hair that gilds the water as it glides,
  Crownets of pearl about his naked arms,
  And in his sportful hands an olive tree
  To hide those parts which men delight to see,
  Shall bathe him in a spring, and there hard by,
  One like Acteon, peeping through the grove,
  Shall by the angry goddess be transformed,
  And running in the likeness of a hart,
  By yelping hounds pulled down, shall seem to die;
  Such things as these best please his majesty.

WILLIAM SHAKESPEARE

(1564–1616)

Song

Who is Silvia? what is she,
    That all our swains commend her?
Holy, fair, and wise is she;
    The heaven such grace did lend her,
That she might admiréd be.

Is she kind as she is fair?
    For beauty lives with kindness.
Love doth to her eyes repair,
    To help him of his blindness,
And, being help'd, inhabits there.

Then to Silvia let us sing,
    That Silvia is excelling;
She excels each mortal thing
    Upon the dull earth dwelling:
To her let us garlands bring.

The Two Gentlemen of Verona

Sonnet

Did not the heavenly rhetoric of thine eye,
    'Gainst whom the world cannot hold argument,
Persuade my heart to this false perjury?
    Vows for thee broke deserve not punishment.
A woman I forswore; but I will prove,
    Thou being a goddess, I forswore not thee:
My vow was earthly, thou a heavenly love;
    Thy grace being gain'd cures all disgrace in me.
Vows are but breath, and breath a vapour is:
    Then thou, fair sun, which on my earth dost shine,
Exhalest this vapour-vow; in thee it is:
    If broken then, it is no fault of mine:
If by me broke, what fool is not so wise
To lose an oath to win a paradise?

Love's Labour's Lost

"On a Day—Alack the Day!"

On a day—alack the day!—
Love, whose month is ever May,
Spied a blossom passing fair
Playing in the wanton air:
Through the velvet leaves the wind,
All unseen, can passage find;
That the lover, sick to death,
Wish himself the heaven's breath.
Air, quoth he, thy cheeks may blow;
Air, would I might triumph so!

But, alack, my hand is sworn
Ne'er to pluck thee from thy thorn;
Vow, alack, for youth unmeet,
Youth so apt to pluck a sweet!
Do not call it sin in me,
That I am forsworn for thee;
Thou for whom e'en Jove would swear
Juno but an Ethiop were;
And deny himself for Jove,
Turning mortal for thy love.

Love's Labour's Lost

Spring

When daisies pied and violets blue
    And lady-smocks all silver-white
And cuckoo buds of yellow hue
    Do paint the meadows with delight,
The cuckoo then, on every tree,
Mocks married men; for thus sings he,
        Cuckoo;
Cuckoo, cuckoo: O word of fear,
Unpleasing to a married ear.

When shepherds pipe on oaten straws,
    And merry larks are ploughmen's clocks,
When turtles tread, and rooks, and daws,
    And maidens bleach their summer smocks,

The cuckoo then, on every tree,
Mocks married men; for thus sings he,
 Cuckoo;
Cuckoo, cuckoo; O word of fear,
Unpleasing to a married ear.

Love's Labour's Lost

Winter

When icicles hang by the wall,
 And Dick the shepherd blows his nail,
And Tom bears logs into the hall,
 And milk comes frozen home in pail,
When blood is nipp'd and ways be foul,
Then nightly sings the staring owl,
 Tu-whit;
Tu-who, a merry note,
While greasy Joan doth keel the pot.

When all aloud the wind doth blow,
 And coughing drowns the parson's saw,
And birds sit brooding in the snow,
 And Marion's nose looks red and raw,
When roasted crabs hiss in the bowl,
Then nightly sings the staring owl,
 Tu-whit;
Tu-who, a merry note,
While greasy Joan doth keel the pot.

Love's Labour's Lost

"Over Hill, over Dale"

Over hill, over dale,
 Thorough bush, thorough briar,
Over park, over pale,
 Thorough flood, thorough fire,
I do wander everywhere,
Swifter than the moonë's sphere;

And I serve the fairy queen,
To dew her orbs upon the green.
The cowslips tall her pensioners be:
In their gold coats spots you see;
Those be rubies, fairy favours,
In those freckles live their savours:
I must go seek some dewdrops here,
And hang a pearl in every cowslip's ear.
Farewell, thou lob of spirits; I'll be gone:
Our queen and all her elves come here anon.

A *Midsummer-Night's Dream*

"You Spotted Snakes..."

First Fairy: You spotted snakes with double tongue,
　　　　　Thorny hedgehogs, be not seen;
　　　　　Newts and blind-worms, do no wrong,
　　　　　Come not near our fairy queen.

Chorus:　　Philomel, with melody
　　　　　Sing in our sweet lullaby;
　　　Lulla, lulla, lullaby, lulla, lulla, lullaby:
　　　　　Never harm,
　　　　　　Nor spell, nor charm,
　　　　　Come our lovely lady nigh;
　　　　　So, good night, with lullaby.

First Fairy: Weaving spiders, come not here;
　　　　　Hence, you long-legg'd spinners, hence!
　　　　　Beetles black, approach not near;
　　　　　Worm nor snail, do no offence.

Chorus:　　Philomel, with melody
　　　　　Sing in our sweet lullaby.

A *Midsummer-Night's Dream*

"The Ousel Cock..."

The ousel cock so black of hue,
   With orange-tawny bill,
The throstle with his note so true,
   The wren with little quill;

The finch, the sparrow, and the lark,
   The plain-song cuckoo gray,
Whose note full many a man doth mark,
   And dares not answer nay.

A Midsummer-Night's Dream

"Now the Hungry Lion Roars"

Now the hungry lion roars,
   And the wolf behowls the moon;
Whilst the heavy ploughman snores,
   All with weary task foredone.
Now the wasted brands do glow,
   Whilst the screech-owl, screeching loud,
Puts the wretch that lies in woe
   In remembrance of a shroud.
Now it is the time of night,
   That the graves, all gaping wide,
Every one lets forth his sprite,
   In the church-way paths to glide:
And we fairies, that do run
   By the triple Hecate's team,
From the presence of the sun,
   Following darkness like a dream,
Now are frolic: not a mouse
Shall disturb this hallow'd house:
I am sent with broom before,
To sweep the dust behind the door.

A Midsummer-Night's Dream

"Tell Me Where Is Fancy Bred"

Tell me where is fancy bred,
Or in the heart or in the head?
How begot, how nourishéd?
      Reply, reply.
It is engender'd in the eyes,
With gazing fed; and fancy dies
In the cradle where it lies.
      Let us all ring fancy's knell;
      I'll begin it—Ding, dong, bell.

All: Ding, dong, bell.

                              The Merchant of Venice

"Sigh No More, Ladies..."

Sigh no more, ladies, sigh no more,
   Men were deceivers ever,
One foot in sea and one on shore,
   To one thing constant never:
Then sigh not so, but let them go,
   And be you blithe and bonny,
Converting all your sounds of woe
   Into Hey nonny, nonny.

Sing no more ditties, sing no moe,
   Of dumps so dull and heavy;
The fraud of men was ever so,
   Since summer first was leafy:
Then sigh not so, but let them go,
   And be you blithe and bonny,
Converting all your sounds of woe
   Into Hey nonny, nonny.

                              Much Ado about Nothing

"Pardon, Goddess of the Night"

Pardon, goddess of the night,
Those that slew thy virgin knight;
For the which, with songs of woe,
Round about her tomb they go.
　　Midnight, assist our moan;
　　Help us to sigh and groan,
　　　　Heavily, heavily:
　　Graves, yawn, and yield your dead,
　　Till death be utteréd,
　　　　Heavily, heavily.

Much Ado about Nothing

"Under the Greenwood Tree"

Under the greenwood tree
Who loves to lie with me,
And turn his merry note
Unto the sweet bird's throat,
Come hither, come hither, come hither:
Here shall he see
No enemy
But winter and rough weather.

Who doth ambition shun,
And loves to live i' the sun,
Seeking the food he eats,
And pleased with what he gets,
Come hither, come hither, come hither:
Here shall he see
No enemy
But winter and rough weather.

As You Like It

"If It Do Come to Pass"

If it do come to pass
That any man turn ass,
Leaving his wealth and ease
A stubborn will to please,
Ducdame, ducdame, ducdame:
Here shall he see
Gross fools as he,
And if he will come to me.

As You Like It

"Blow, Blow, Thou Winter Wind"

Blow, blow, thou winter wind,
Thou art not so unkind
   As man's ingratitude;
Thy tooth is not so keen,
Because thou art not seen,
   Although thy breath be rude.
Heigh-ho! sing, heigh-ho! unto the green holly:
Most friendship is feigning, most loving mere folly:
   Then, heigh-ho, the holly!
   This life is most jolly.

Freeze, freeze, thou bitter sky,
That dost not bite so nigh
   As benefits forgot:
Though thou the waters warp,
Thy sting is not so sharp
   As friends remember'd not.
Heigh-ho! sing, heigh-ho! unto the green holly:
Most friendship is feigning, most loving mere folly:
   Then, heigh-ho, the holly!
   This life is most jolly.

As You Like It

"What Shall He Have..."

What shall he have that kill'd the deer?
His leather skin and horns to wear.
  Then sing him home:
Take thou no scorn to wear the horn;
It was a crest ere thou wast born:
Thy father's father wore it,
And thy father bore it:
The horn, the horn, the lusty horn
Is not a thing to laugh to scorn.

As You Like It

"It Was a Lover and His Lass"

It was a lover and his lass,
  With a hey, and a ho, and hey nonino,
That o'er the green corn-field did pass
  In the spring time, the only pretty ring time,
When birds do sing, hey ding a ding, ding:
Sweet lovers love the spring.

Between the acres of the rye,
  With a hey, and a ho, and a hey nonino,
These pretty country folk would lie,
  In the spring time, the only pretty ring time,
When birds do sing, hey ding a ding, ding:
Sweet lovers love the spring.

This carol they began that hour,
  With a hey, and a ho, and a hey nonino,
How that a life was but a flower
  In the spring time, the only pretty ring time,
When birds do sing, hey ding a ding, ding,
Sweet lovers love the spring.

And therefore take the present time,
    With a hey, and a ho, and a hey nonino,
For love is crowned with the prime
    In the spring time, the only pretty ring time,
When birds do sing, hey ding a ding, ding,
Sweet lovers love the spring.

As You Like It

"Wedding Is Great Juno's Crown"

Wedding is great Juno's crown:
    O blessed bond of board and bed!
'Tis Hymen peoples every town:
    High wedlock then be honouréd:
Honour, high honour and renown,
To Hymen, god of every town!

As You Like It

"O Mistress Mine..."

O Mistress mine, where are you roaming?
O, stay and hear; your true love's coming,
    That can sing both high and low:
Trip no further, pretty sweeting;
Journeys end in lovers meeting,
    Every wise man's son doth know.

What is love? 'Tis not hereafter;
Present mirth hath present laughter;
    What's to come is still unsure:
In delay there lies no plenty;
Then, come kiss me, sweet and twenty,
    Youth's a stuff will not endure.

Twelfth Night

"Come Away, Come Away, Death"

Come away, come away, death,
  And in sad cypress let me be laid;
Fly away, fly away, breath;
  I am slain by a fair cruel maid.
My shroud of white, stuck all with yew,
      O, prepare it!
My part of death, no one so true
      Did share it.

Not a flower, not a flower sweet,
  On my black coffin let there be strown;
Not a friend, not a friend greet
  My poor corpse, where my bones shall be thrown:
A thousand thousand sighs to save,
      Lay me, O, where,
Sad true lover never find my grave,
      To weep there!

Twelfth Night

"When That I Was and a Little Tiny Boy"

When that I was and a little tiny boy,
  With hey, ho, the wind and the rain,
A foolish thing was but a toy,
  For the rain it raineth every day.

But when I came to man's estate,
  With hey, ho, the wind and the rain,
'Gainst knaves and thieves men shut the gate,
  For the rain it raineth every day.

But when I came, alas! to wive,
  With hey, ho, the wind and the rain,
By swaggering could I never thrive,
  For the rain it raineth every day.

But when I came unto my beds,
　　With hey, ho, the wind and the rain,
With toss-pots still had drunken heads,
　　For the rain it raineth every day.

A great while ago the world begun,
　　With hey, ho, the wind and the rain,
But that's all one, our play is done,
　　And we'll strive to please you every day.

Twelfth Night

"How Should I Your True Love Know"

How should I your true love know
　　From another one?
By his cockle hat and staff
　　And his sandal shoon.

He is dead and gone, lady,
　　He is dead and gone;
At his head a grass-green turf,
　　At his heels a stone.

White his shroud as the mountain snow,
　　Larded with sweet flowers;
Which bewept to the grave did go
　　With true-love showers.

Hamlet

"To-morrow Is Saint Valentine's Day"

To-morrow is Saint Valentine's day,
　　All in the morning betimes,
And I a maid at your window,
　　To be your Valentine.

Then up he rose, and donn'd his clothes,
　　And dupp'd the chamber-door;
Let in the maid, that out a maid
　　Never departed more.

Hamlet

"And Will A' Not Come Again?"

And will a' not come again?
And will a' not come again?
   No, no, he is dead,
   Go to thy death-bed,
He never will come again.

His beard was as white as snow,
All flaxen was his poll:
   He is gone, he is gone,
   And we cast away moan:
God ha' mercy on his soul!

Hamlet

"Fie on Sinful Fantasy!"

Fie on sinful fantasy!
Fie on lust and luxury!
Lust is but a bloody fire,
Kindled with unchaste desire,
Fed in heart, whose flames aspire,
As thoughts do blow them, higher and higher.
Pinch him, fairies, mutually;
Pinch him for his villany;
Pinch him, and burn him, and turn him about,
Till candles and starlight and moonshine be out.

The Merry Wives of Windsor

"For I the Ballad Will Repeat"

For I the ballad will repeat,
   Which men full true shall find;
Your marriage comes by destiny,
   Your cuckoo sings by kind.

All's Well That Ends Well

"Take, O Take Those Lips Away"

Take, O take those lips away,
  That so sweetly were forsworn;
And those eyes, the break of day,
  Lights that do mislead the morn:
But my kisses bring again, bring again;
Seals of love, but seal'd in vain, seal'd in vain.

Measure for Measure

"The Cod-Piece That Will House"

The cod-piece that will house
  Before the head has any,
The head and he shall louse;
  So beggars marry many.
The man that makes his toe
  What he his heart should make
Shall of a corn cry woe,
  And turn his sleep to wake.

King Lear

"He That Has and a Little Tiny Wit"

He that has and a little tiny wit,—
With hey, ho, the wind and the rain,—
Must make content with his fortune's fit,
For the rain it raineth every day.

King Lear

"When Priests Are More in Word..."

When priests are more in word than matter;
When brewers mar their malt with water;
When nobles are their tailors' tutors;
No heretics burn'd, but wenches' suitors;
When every case in law is right;

No squire in debt, nor no poor knight;
When slanders do not live in tongues,
Nor cutpurses come not to throngs;
When usurers tell their gold i' the field,
And bawds and whores do churches build;
Then shall the realm of Albion
Come to great confusion:
Then comes the time, who lives to see't,
That going shall be used with feet.

King Lear

"Come, Thou Monarch..."

Come, thou monarch of the vine,
Plumpy Bacchus with pink eyne!
In thy fats our cares be drown'd,
With thy grapes our hairs be crown'd:
Cup us, till the world go round,
Cup us, till the world go round!

Antony and Cleopatra

"Hark, Hark! the Lark..."

Hark, hark! the lark at heaven's gate sings,
  And Phoebus 'gins arise,
His steeds to water at those springs
  On chaliced flowers that lies;
And winking Mary-buds begin
  To ope their golden eyes;
With every thing that pretty is,
  My lady sweet, arise:
    Arise, arise!

Cymbeline

"Fear No More..."

Fear no more the heat o' the sun,
　Nor the furious winter's rages;
Thou thy worldly task hast done,
　Home art gone and ta'en thy wages:
Golden lads and girls all must,
As chimney-sweepers, come to dust.

Fear no more the frown o' the great;
　Thou art past the tyrant's stroke;
Care no more to clothe and eat;
　To thee the reed is as the oak:
The sceptre, learning, physic, must
All follow this and come to dust.

Fear no more the lightning-flash,
　Nor the all-dreaded thunder-stone;
Fear not slander, censure rash;
　Thou hast finish'd joy and moan:
All lovers young, all lovers must
Consign to thee and come to dust.

No exorciser harm thee!
Nor no witchcraft charm thee!
Ghost unlaid forbear thee!
Nothing ill come near thee!
Quiet consummation have;
And renownéd be thy grave!

Cymbeline

"When Daffodils Begin to Peer"

When daffodils begin to peer,
　With heigh! the doxy over the dale,
Why, then comes in the sweet o' the year;
　For the red blood reigns in the winter's pale.

The white sheet bleaching on the hedge,
    With heigh! the sweet birds, O, how they sing!
Doth set my pugging tooth on edge;
    For a quart of ale is a dish for a king.

The lark, that tirra-lyra chants,
    With heigh! with heigh! the thrush and the jay,
Are summer songs for me and my aunts,
    While we lie tumbling in the hay.

The Winter's Tale

"Jog On, Jog On..."

Jog on, jog on, the foot-path way,
    And merrily hent the stile-a:
A merry heart goes all the day,
    Your sad tires in a mile-a.

The Winter's Tale

"Lawn as White as Driven Snow"

Lawn as white as driven snow;
Cypress black as e'er was crow;
Gloves as sweet as damask roses;
Masks for faces and for noses;
Bugle bracelet, necklace amber,
Perfume for a lady's chamber;
Golden coifs and stomachers,
For my lads to give their dears;
Pins and poking-sticks of steel,
What maids lack from head to heel:
Come, buy of me, come; come buy, come buy;
Buy, lads, or else your lasses cry:
Come buy.

The Winter's Tale

"Will You Buy Any Tape"

Will you buy any tape,
  Or lace for your cape,
My dainty duck, my dear-a?
  Any silk, any thread,
  Any toys for your head,
Of the new'st, and finest, finest wear-a?
  Come to the pedlar;
  Money's a medlar,
That doth utter all men's ware-a.

The Winter's Tale

"Come unto These Yellow Sands"

Come unto these yellow sands,
  And then take hands:
Courtsied when you have and kiss'd
  The wild waves whist:
Foot it featly here and there;
And, sweet sprites, the burthen bear.
  Hark, hark!

Bow-wow.
The watch-dogs bark.
Bow-wow.
Hark, hark! I hear
The strain of strutting chanticleer
Cry, cock-a-diddle-dow.

The Tempest

"Full Fathom Five..."

Full fathom five thy father lies;
  Of his bones are coral made;
Those are pearls that were his eyes:
  Nothing of him that doth fade,
But doth suffer a sea-change

Into something rich and strange.
Sea-nymphs hourly ring his knell:
            Ding-dong.
Hark! now I hear them—Ding-dong, bell.

The Tempest

"No More Dams I'll Make..."

No more dams I'll make for fish;
    Nor fetch in firing
    At requiring;
Nor scrape trencher, nor wash dish:
    'Ban, 'Ban, Ca-Caliban
    Has a new master—get a new man.

The Tempest

"The Master, the Swabber..."

The master, the swabber, the boatswain, and I,
    The gunner, and his mate,
Loved Mall, Meg, and Marian, and Margery,
    But none of us cared for Kate;
    For she had a tongue with a tang,
    Would cry to a sailor, Go hang!
She loved not the savour of tar nor of pitch;
Yet a tailor might scratch her where'er she did itch.
    Then, to sea, boys, and let her go hang!

The Tempest

"You Nymphs, Call'd Naiads..."

You nymphs, call'd Naiads, of the windring brooks,
With your sedged crowns and ever-harmless looks,
Leave your crisp channels, and on this green land
Answer your summons; Juno does command:
Come, temperate nymphs, and help to celebrate
A contract of true love; be not too late.

You sunburn'd sicklemen, of August weary,
Come hither from the furrow, and be merry:
Make holiday; your rye-straw hats put on,
And these fresh nymphs encounter every one
In country footing.

The Tempest

"Where the Bee Sucks..."

Where the bee sucks, there suck I:
In a cowslip's bell I lie;
There I couch when owls do cry.
On the bat's back I do fly
After summer merrily.
Merrily, merrily shall I live now
Under the blossom that hangs on the bough.

The Tempest

Sonnets

VIII

Music to hear, why hear'st thou music sadly?
Sweets with sweets war not, joy delights in joy.
Why lovest thou that which thou receivest not gladly?
Or else receiv'st with pleasure thine annoy?
If the true concord of well tunéd sounds,
By unions married, do offend thine ear,
They do but sweetly chide thee, who confounds
In singleness the parts that thou shouldst bear.
Mark how one string, sweet husband to another,
Strikes each in each by mutual ordering;
Resembling sire and child and happy mother,
Who, all in one, one pleasing note do sing:
Whose speechless song, being many, seeming one,
Sings this to thee: "Thou single wilt prove none."

XII

When I do count the clock that tells the time,
And see the brave day sunk in hideous night;
When I behold the violet past prime,
And sable curls all silver'd o'er with white;
When lofty trees I see barren of leaves,
Which erst from heat did canopy the herd,
And summer's green all girded up in sheaves,
Borne on the bier with white and bristly beard,
Then of thy beauty do I question make,
That thou among the wastes of time must go,
Since sweets and beauties do themselves forsake
And die as fast as they see others grow;
And nothing 'gainst Time's scythe can make defence
Save breed, to brave him when he takes thee hence,

XVIII

Shall I compare thee to a summer's day?
Thou art more lovely and more temperate:
Rough winds do shake the darling buds of May,
And summer's lease hath all too short a date:
Sometimes too hot the eye of heaven shines,
And often is his gold complexion dimm'd;
And every fair from fair sometime declines,
By chance or nature's changing course untrimm'd;
But thy eternal summer shall not fade,
Nor lose possession of that fair thou owest;
Nor shall Death brag thou wander'st in his shade,
When in eternal lines to time thou growest:
So long as men can breathe, or eyes can see,
So long lives this, and this gives life to thee.

XXIX

When, in disgrace with fortune and men's eyes,
I all alone beweep my outcast state,
And trouble deaf heaven with my bootless cries,
And look upon myself, and curse my fate,
Wishing me like to one more rich in hope,
Featured like him, like him with friends possessed,
Desiring this man's art and that man's scope,

With what I most enjoy contented least;
Yet in these thoughts myself almost despising,
Haply I think on thee, and then my state,
Like to the lark at break of day arising
From sullen earth, sings hymns at heaven's gate;
For thy sweet love remembered such wealth brings
That then I scorn to change my state with kings.

XXX

When to the sessions of sweet silent thought
I summon up remembrance of things past,
I sigh the lack of many a thing I sought,
And with old woes new wail my dear time's waste:
Then can I drown an eye, unused to flow,
For precious friends hid in death's dateless night,
And weep afresh love's long since cancelled woe,
And moan the expense of many a vanished sight:
Then can I grieve at grievances foregone,
And heavily from woe to woe tell o'er
The sad account of fore-bemoaned moan,
Which I new pay as if not paid before.
But if the while I think on thee, dear friend,
All losses are restored and sorrows end.

XXXIII

Full many a glorious morning have I seen
Flatter the mountain-tops with sovereign eye,
Kissing with golden face the meadows green,
Gilding pale streams with heavenly alchemy;
Anon permit the basest clouds to ride
With ugly rack on his celestial face,
And from the forlorn world his visage hide,
Stealing unseen to west with this disgrace:
Even so my sun one early morn did shine
With all-triumphant splendour on my brow;
But, out, alack! he was but one hour mine,
The region cloud hath masked him from me now.
Yet him for this my love no whit disdaineth;
Suns of the world may stain when heaven's sun staineth.

LIII

What is your substance, whereof are you made,
That millions of fair shadows on you tend?
Since every one hath, every one, one shade,
And you, but one, can every shadow lend.
Describe Adonis, and the counterfeit
Is poorly imitated after you;
On Helen's cheek all art of beauty set,
And you in Grecian tires are painted new:
Speak of the spring and foison of the year,
The one doth shadow of your beauty show,
The other as your bounty doth appear;
And you in every blessed shape we know.
In all external grace you have some part,
But you like none, none you, for constant heart.

LIV

O, how much more doth beauty beauteous seem
By that sweet ornament which truth doth give!
The rose looks fair, but fairer we it deem
For that sweet odour which doth in it live.
The canker-blooms have full as deep a dye
As the perfuméd tincture of the roses,
Hang on such thorns, and play as wantonly
When summer's breath their maskéd buds discloses:
But, for their virtue only is their show,
They live unwoo'd and unrespected fade;
Die to themselves. Sweet roses do not so;
Of their sweet deaths are sweetest odours made:
And so of you, beauteous and lovely youth,
When that shall vade, my verse distils your truth.

LV

Not marble, nor the gilded monuments
Of princes, shall outlive this powerful rhyme;
But you shall shine more bright in these contents
Than unswept stone, besmeared with sluttish time.
When wasteful war shall statues overturn,
And broils root out the work of masonry,
Nor Mars his sword nor war's quick fire shall burn

The living record of your memory.
'Gainst death and all-oblivious enmity
Shall you pace forth; your praise shall still find room
Even in the eyes of all posterity
That wear this world out to the ending doom.
So, till the judgement that yourself arise,
You live in this, and dwell in lovers' eyes.

LVII

Being your slave, what should I do but tend
Upon the hours and times of your desire?
I have no precious time at all to spend,
Nor services to do, till you require.
Nor dare I chide the world-without-end hour
Whilst I, my sovereign, watch the clock for you.
Nor think the bitterness of absence sour
When you have bid your servant once adieu;
Nor dare I question with my jealous thought
Where you may be, or your affairs suppose,
But like a sad slave, stay and think of nought,
Save, where you are how happy you make those.
So true a fool is love that in your will,
Though you do anything, he thinks no ill.

LX

Like as the waves make toward the pebbled shore,
So do our minutes hasten to their end;
Each changing place with that which goes before,
In sequent toil all forwards do contend.
Nativity, once in the main of light,
Crawls to maturity, wherewith being crowned,
Crooked eclipses 'gainst his glory fight,
And Time that gave doth now his gift confound.
Time doth transfix the flourish set on youth
And delves the parallels in beauty's brow,
Feeds on the rarities of nature's truth,
And nothing stands but for his scythe to mow:
And yet to times in hope my verse shall stand,
Praising thy worth, despite his cruel hand.

LXIV

When I have seen by Time's fell hand defac'd
The rich-proud cost of outworn buried age;
When sometime lofty towers I see down-razed,
And brass eternal slave to mortal rage;
When I have seen the hungry ocean gain
Advantage on the kingdom of the shore,
And the firm soil win of the watery main,
Increasing store with loss, and loss with store;
When I have seen such interchange of state,
Or state itself confounded to decay;
Ruin hath taught me thus to ruminate—
That Time will come and take my love away.
This thought is as a death, which cannot choose
But weep to have that which it fears to lose.

LXVI

Tired with all these, for restful death I cry,
As, to behold desert a beggar born,
And needy nothing trimmed in jollity,
And purest faith unhappily forsworn,
And gilded honour shamefully misplaced,
And maiden virtue rudely strumpeted,
And right perfection wrongfully disgraced,
And strength by limping sway disabled,
And art made tongue-tied by authority,
And folly, doctor-like, controlling skill,
And simple truth miscalled simplicity,
And captive good attending captain ill:
Tired with all these, from these would I be gone,
Save that, to die, I leave my love alone.

LXXI

No longer mourn for me when I am dead
Than you shall hear the surly sullen bell
Give warning to the world that I am fled
From this vile world, with vilest worms to dwell:
Nay, if you read this line, remember not
The hand that writ it; for I love you so,
That I in your sweet thoughts would be forgot,

If thinking on me then should make you woe.
O, if, I say, you look upon this verse
When I perhaps compounded am with clay,
Do not so much as my poor name rehearse,
But let your love even with my life decay;
Lest the wise world should look into your moan
And mock you with me after I am gone.

LXXIII

That time of year thou mayst in me behold
When yellow leaves, or none, or few, do hang
Upon those boughs which shake against the cold,
Bare ruined choirs, where late the sweet birds sang.
In me thou see'st the twilight of such day
As after sunset fadeth in the west;
Which by and by black night doth take away,
Death's second self, that seals up all in rest.
In me thou see'st the glowing of such fire,
That on the ashes of his youth doth lie,
As the death-bed whereon it must expire,
Consumed with that which it was nourished by.
This thou perceivest, which makes thy love more strong,
To love that well which thou must leave ere long.

LXXXVII

Farewell! thou art too dear for my possessing,
And like enough thou know'st thy estimate:
The charter of thy worth gives thee releasing;
My bonds in thee are all determinate.
For how do I hold thee but by thy granting?
And for that riches where is my deserving?
The cause of this fair gift in me is wanting,
And so my patent back again is swerving.
Thyself thou gavest, thy own worth then not knowing,
Or me, to whom thou gavest it, else mistaking;
So thy great gift, upon misprision growing,
Comes home again, on better judgement making.
Thus have I had thee, as a dream doth flatter,
In sleep a king, but waking no such matter.

XCIV

They that have power to hurt and will do none,
That do not do the thing they most do show;
Who, moving others, are themselves as stone,
Unmovéd, cold and to temptation slow;
They rightly do inherit heaven's graces
And husband nature's riches from expense;
They are the lords and owners of their faces.
Others but stewards of their excellence.
The summer's flower is to the summer sweet,
Though to itself it only live and die,
But if that flower with base infection meet,
The basest weed outbraves his dignity:
For sweetest things turn sourest by their deeds;
Lilies that fester smell far worse than weeds.

XCVIII

From you have I been absent in the spring,
When proud-pied April, dressed in all his trim,
Hath put a spirit of youth in everything,
That heavy Saturn laughed and leaped with him.
Yet nor the lays of birds, nor the sweet smell
Of different flowers in odour and in hue,
Could make me any summer's story tell,
Or from their proud lap pluck them where they grew:
Nor did I wonder at the lily's white,
Nor praise the deep vermilion of the rose;
They were but sweet, but figures of delight,
Drawn after you, you pattern of all those.
Yet seemed it winter still, and, you away,
As with your shadow I with these did play.

CII

My love is strengthened, though more weak in seeming;
I love not less, though less the show appear:
That love is merchandized whose rich esteeming
The owner's tongue doth publish everywhere.
Our love was new, and then but in the spring,
When I was wont to greet it with my lays;
As Philomel in summer's front doth sing,

And stops her pipe in growth of riper days:
Not that the summer is less pleasant now
Than when her mournful hymns did hush the night,
But that wild music burthens every bough,
And sweets grown common lose their dear delight.
Therefore, like her, I sometime hold my tongue,
Because I would not dull you with my song.

CIV

To me, fair friend, you never can be old,
For as you were when first your eye I eyed,
Such seems your beauty still. Three winters cold
Have from the forests shook three summers' pride,
Three beauteous springs to yellow autumn turned
In process of the seasons have I seen,
Three April perfumes in three hot Junes burned,
Since first I saw you fresh, which yet are green.
Ah, yet doth beauty, like a dial-hand,
Steal from his figure, and no pace perceived;
So your sweet hue, which methinks still doth stand,
Hath motion, and mine eye may be deceived:
For fear of which, hear this, thou age unbred;
Ere you were born was beauty's summer dead.

CVI

When in the chronicle of wasted time
I see descriptions of the fairest wights,
And beauty making beautiful old rhyme
In praise of ladies dead and lovely knights,
Then, in the blazon of sweet beauty's best,
Of hand, of foot, of lip, of eye, of brow,
I see their antique pen would have expressed
Even such a beauty as you master now.
So all their praises are but prophecies
Of this our time, all you prefiguring;
And, for they looked but with divining eyes,
They had not skill enough your worth to sing:
For we, which now behold these present days,
Have eyes to wonder, but lack tongues to praise.

CX

Alas, 'tis true I have gone here and there,
And made myself a motley to the view,
Gored mine own thoughts, sold cheap what is most dear,
Made old offences of affections new;
Most true it is that I have looked on truth
Askance and strangely: but, by all above,
These blenches gave my heart another youth,
And worse essays proved thee my best of love.
Now all is done, have what shall have no end:
Mine appetite I never more will grind
On newer proof, to try an older friend,
A god in love, to whom I am confined.
Then give me welcome, next to my heaven the best,
Even to thy pure and most most loving breast.

CXVI

Let me not to the marriage of true minds
Admit impediments. Love is not love
Which alters when it alteration finds,
Or bends with the remover to remove:
O, no! it is an ever-fixéd mark,
That looks on tempests and is never shaken;
It is the star to every wandering bark,
Whose worth's unknown, although his height be taken.
Love's not Time's fool, though rosy lips and cheeks
Within his bending sickle's compass come;
Love alters not with his brief hours and weeks,
And bears it out even to the edge of doom.
If this be error and upon me proved,
I never writ, nor no man ever loved.

CXXIX

Th' expense of spirit in a waste of shame
Is lust in action; and till action, lust
Is perjured, murderous, bloody, full of blame,
Savage, extreme, rude, cruel, not to trust;
Enjoy'd no sooner but despiséd straight;
Past reason hunted; and, no sooner had,
Past reason hated, as a swallow'd bait

On purpose laid to make the taker mad:
Mad in pursuit, and in possession so;
Had, having, and in quest to have, extreme;
A bliss in proof, and proved, a very woe;
Before, a joy proposed; behind, a dream.
All this the world well knows; yet none knows well
To shun the heaven that leads men to this hell.

CXXXVIII

When my love swears that she is made of truth,
I do believe her, though I know she lies,
That she might think me some untutored youth,
Unlearnéd in the world's false subtleties.
Thus vainly thinking that she thinks me young,
Although she knows my days are past the best,
Simply I credit her false-speaking tongue:
On both sides thus is simple truth suppressed.
But wherefore says she not she is unjust?
And wherefore say not I that I am old?
O, love's best habit is in seeming trust,
And age in love loves not to have years told:
Therefore I lie with her and she with me,
And in our faults by lies we flattered be.

CXLVI

Poor soul, the centre of my sinful earth,
Pressed by these rebel powers that thee array,
Why dost thou pine within and suffer dearth,
Painting thy outward walls so costly gay?
Why so large cost, having so short a lease,
Dost thou upon thy fading mansion spend?
Shall worms, inheritors of this excess,
Eat up thy charge? Is this thy body's end?
Then, soul, live thou upon thy servant's loss,
And let that pine to aggravate thy store;
Buy terms divine in selling hours of dross;
Within be fed, without be rich no more:
So shalt thou feed on Death, that feeds on men;
And Death once dead, there's no more dying then.

RICHARD ROWLANDS, *alias* VERSTEGAN
(1565–1630)

"Upon My Lap My Sovereign Sits"

Upon my lap my sovereign sits
And sucks upon my breast;
Meantime his love maintains my life
And gives my sense her rest.
   Sing lullaby, my little boy,
   Sing lullaby, mine only joy!

When thou hast taken thy repast,
Repose, my babe, on me;
So may thy mother and thy nurse
Thy cradle also be.
   Sing lullaby, my little boy,
   Sing lullaby, mine only joy!

I grieve that duty doth not work
All that my wishing would,
Because I would not be to thee
But in the best I should.
   Sing lullaby, my little boy,
   Sing lullaby, mine only joy!

Yet as I am, and as I may,
I must and will be thine,
Though all too little for thyself
Vouchsafing to be mine.
   Sing lullaby, my little boy,
   Sing lullaby, mine only joy!

THOMAS NASHE
(1567–1601)

"Spring, the Sweet Spring..."

Spring, the sweet Spring, is the year's pleasant king;
Then blooms each thing, then maids dance in a ring,
Cold doth not sting, the pretty birds do sing,
Cuckoo, jug, jug, pu we, to witta woo.

The palm and may make country houses gay,
Lambs frisk and play, the shepherds pipe all day,
And we hear aye birds tune this merry lay,
Cuckoo, jug, jug, pu we, to witta woo.

The fields breathe sweet, the daisies kiss our feet,
Young lovers meet, old wives a-sunning sit,
In every street these tunes our ears do greet,
Cuckoo, jug, jug, pu we, to witta woo.
          Spring, the sweet spring!

Summer's Last Will and Testament, 1600

"Adieu; Farewell Earth's Bliss"

Adieu; farewell earth's bliss,
This world uncertain is:
Fond are life's lustful joys,
Death proves them all but toys.
None from his darts can fly:
I am sick, I must die.
     Lord have mercy on us!

Rich men, trust not in wealth,
Gold cannot buy you health;
Physic himself must fade;
All things to end are made;
The plague full swift goes by;
I am sick, I must die.
     Lord have mercy on us!

Beauty is but a flower,
Which wrinkles will devour:
Brightness falls from the air;
Queens have died young and fair;
Dust hath closed Helen's eye;
I am sick, I must die.
     Lord have mercy on us!

Strength stoops unto the grave:
Worms feed on Hector brave;
Swords may not fight with fate:
Earth still holds ope her gate.
Come, come, the bells do cry;
I am sick, I must die.
　　Lord have mercy on us!

Wit with his wantonness,
Tasteth death's bitterness.
Hell's executioner
Hath no ears for to hear
What vain art can reply;
I am sick, I must die.
　　Lord have mercy on us!

Haste therefore each degree
To welcome destiny:
Heaven is our heritage,
Earth but a player's stage.
Mount we unto the sky;
I am sick, I must die.
　　Lord have mercy on us!

Summer's Last Will and Testament, 1600

WILLIAM ALEXANDER, Earl of Stirling
(1567?–1640)
Sonnet

Then whilst that Latmos did contain her bliss
Chaste Phoebe left her church so much admired,
And when her brother from that bounds retired
Would of the sleepy shepherd steal a kiss;
But to no greater grace I crave to climb
Than of my goddess whiles whilst she reposes
That I might kiss the still-selfkissing roses,
And steal of her that which was stol'n of him:
And though I know that this would only prove
A maimed delight, whereof th'one half would want,

Yet whilst the light did Morpheus' power supplant;
If that my theft did her displeasure move,
I render would all that I robbed again
And for each kiss I take would give her twain.

THOMAS CAMPION
(1567–1619)
"Follow Your Saint..."

Follow your saint, follow with accents sweet!
Haste you, sad notes, fall at her flying feet!
There, wrapped in cloud of sorrow, pity move,
And tell the ravisher of my soul I perish for her love:
But, if she scorns my never-ceasing pain,
Then burst with sighing in her sight and ne'er return again.

All that I sang still to her praise did tend,
Still she was first, still she my songs did end;
Yet she my love and music both doth fly,
The music that her echo is and beauty's sympathy.
Then let my notes pursue her scornful flight!
It shall suffice that they were breathed and died for her
    delight.

"Follow Thy Fair Sun..."

Follow thy fair sun, unhappy shadow!
    Though thou be black as night,
    And she made all of light,
Yet follow thy fair sun, unhappy shadow!

Follow her, whose light thy light depriveth!
    Though here thou liv'st disgraced,
    And she in heaven is placed,
Yet follow her whose light the world reviveth!

Follow those pure beams, whose beauty burneth!
    That so have scorchéd thee
    As thou still black must be
Till her kind beams thy black to brightness turneth.

Follow her, while yet her glory shineth!
    There comes a luckless night
    That will dim all her light;
And this the black unhappy shade divineth.

Follow still, since so thy fates ordained!
    The sun must have his shade,
    Till both at once do fade,
The sun still proud, the shadow still disdained.

"Give Beauty All Her Right"

Give Beauty all her right,
    She's not to one form tied;
Each shape yields fair delight
    Where her perfections bide:
Helen, I grant might pleasing be,
And Ros'mund was as sweet as she.

Some the quick eye commends,
    Some swelling lips and red;
Pale looks have many friends,
    Through sacred sweetness bred:
Meadows have flowers that pleasures move,
Though roses are the flowers of love.

Free beauty is not bound
    To one unmovéd clime;
She visits every ground
    And favours every time.
Let the old loves with mine compare,
My sovereign is as sweet and fair.

"Thou Art Not Fair..."

Thou art not fair, for all thy red and white,
    For all those rosy ornaments in thee;
Thou art not sweet, tho' made of mere delight,
    Nor fair, nor sweet—unless thou pity me.
I will not soothe thy fancies, thou shalt prove
That beauty is no beauty without love.

Yet love not me, nor seek not to allure
  My thoughts with beauty were it more divine;
Thy smiles and kisses I cannot endure,
  I'll not be wrapped up in those arms of thine:
Now show it, if thou be a woman right,—
Embrace and kiss and love me in despite.

"Turn All Thy Thoughts..."

Turn all thy thoughts to eyes,
Turn all thy hairs to ears,
Change all thy friends to spies
And all thy joys to fears;
  True love will yet be free
  In spite of jealousy.

Turn darkness into day,
Conjectures into truth,
Believe what th' envious say,
Let age interpret youth:
  True love will yet be free
  In spite of jealousy.

Wrest every word and look,
Rack every hidden thought,
Or fish with golden hook;
True love cannot be caught:
  For that will still be free
  In spite of jealousy.

"Never Love..."

Never love unless you can
Bear with all the faults of man:
Men sometimes will jealous be
Though but little cause they see;
And hang the head as discontent,
And speak what straight they will repent.

Men that but one saint adore
Make a show of love to more;
Beauty must be scorned in none,
Though but truly served in one:
For what is courtship but disguise?
True hearts may have dissembling eyes.

Men, when their affairs require,
Must awhile themselves retire;
Sometimes hunt, and sometimes hawk,
And not ever sit and talk.
If these and such-like you can bear,
Then like, and love, and never fear!

"Thrice Toss These Oaken Ashes..."

Thrice toss these oaken ashes in the air,
Thrice sit thou mute in this enchanted chair,
Then thrice-three times tie up this true love's knot,
And murmur soft "She will or she will not."

Go, burn these poisonous weeds in yon blue fire,
These screech-owl's feathers and this prickling briar,
This cypress gathered at a dead man's grave,
That all my fears and cares an end may have.

Then come, you Fairies! dance with me a round!
Melt her hard heart with your melodious sound!
In vain are all the charms I can devise:
She hath an art to break them with her eyes.

"Love Me or Not..."

Love me or not, love her I must or die;
Leave me or not, follow her needs must I.
O that her grace would my wish'd comforts give!
How rich in her, how happy should I live!

All my desire, all my delight should be
Her to enjoy, her to unite to me;
Envy should cease, her would I love alone:
Who loves by looks is seldom true to one.

Could I enchant, and that it lawful were,
Her would I charm softly that none should hear;
But love enforced rarely yields firm content:
So would I love that neither should repent.

"Shall I Come, Sweet Love..."

Shall I come, sweet Love, to thee
    When the evening beams are set?
Shall I not excluded be,
    Will you find no feignéd let?
Let me not, for pity, more
Tell the long hours at your door.

Who can tell what thief or foe,
    In the covert of the night,
For his prey will work my woe,
    Or through wicked foul despite?
So may I die unredrest
Ere my long love be possest.

But to let such dangers pass,
    Which a lover's thoughts disdain,
'Tis enough in such a place
    To attend love's joys in vain:
Do not mock me in thy bed,
While these cold nights freeze me dead.

"There Is a Garden in Her Face"

There is a garden in her face
Where roses and white lilies grow;
A heavenly paradise is that place
Wherein all pleasant fruits do flow.
    There cherries grow which none may buy,
    Till "Cherry ripe" themselves do cry.

Those cherries fairly do enclose
Of orient pearl a double row,
Which when her lovely laughter shows,
They look like rose-buds filled with snow;
　　Yet them nor peer nor prince can buy,
　　Till "Cherry ripe" themselves do cry.

Her eyes like angels watch them still,
Her brows like bended bows do stand,
Threatening with piercing frowns to kill
All that attempt, with eye or hand,
　　Those sacred cherries to come nigh
　　Till "Cherry ripe" themselves do cry.

"When Thou Must Home..."

When thou must home to shades of underground,
And there arrived, a new admiréd guest,
The beauteous spirits do engirt thee round,
White Iope, blithe Helen and the rest,
To hear the stories of thy finished love
From that smooth tongue whose music hell can move;
Then wilt thou speak of banqueting delights,
Of masques and revels which sweet youth did make,
Of tourneys and great challenges of knights,
And all these triumphs for thy beauty's sake:
When thou hast told these honours done to thee,
Then tell, O tell, how thou didst murder me.

"Now Winter Nights..."

Now winter nights enlarge
The number of their hours,
And clouds their storms discharge
Upon the airy towers.
Let now the chimneys blaze,
And cups o'erflow with wine;

Let well-tuned words amaze
With harmony divine.
Now yellow waxen lights
Shall wait on honey love,
While youthful revels, masques and courtly sights
Sleep's leaden spells remove.

This time doth well dispense
With lovers' long discourse;
Much speech hath some defence,
Though beauty no remorse.
All do not all things well;
Some measures comely tread,
Some knotted riddles tell,
Some poems smoothly read.
The summer hath his joys
And winter his delights;
Though love and all his pleasures are but toys,
They shorten tedious nights.

"The Man of Life Upright"

The man of life upright,
  Whose guiltless heart is free
From all dishonest deeds,
  Or thought of vanity;

The man whose silent days
  In harmless joys are spent,
Whom hopes cannot delude
  Nor sorrow discontent:

That man needs neither towers
  Nor armour for defence,
Nor secret vaults to fly
  From thunder's violence.

He only can behold
  With unaffrighted eyes
The horrors of the deep
  And terrors of the skies.

Thus scorning all the cares
  That fate or fortune brings,
He makes the heaven his book,
  His wisdom heavenly things;

Good thoughts his only friends,
  His wealth a well-spent age,
The earth his sober inn
  And quiet pilgrimage.

"I Care Not for These Ladies"

I care not for these ladies
That must be wooed and prayed:
Give me kind Amarillis,
The wanton country maid!
Nature, art disdaineth,
Her beauty is her own,
    Her, when we court and kiss,
    She cries, "Forsooth, let go!"
    But when we come where comfort is,
    She never will say, "No!"

If I love Amarillis,
She gives me fruit and flowers:
But if we love these ladies,
We must give golden showers.
Give them gold, they sell love!
Give me the nut-brown lass!
    Who, when we court and kiss,
    She cries, "Forsooth, let go!"
    But when we come where comfort is,
    She never will say, "No!"

These ladies must have pillows
And beds, by strangers wrought;
Give me a bower of willows,
Of moss and leaves unbought!
And fresh Amarillis,

With milk and honey fed!
  Who, when we court and kiss,
  She cries, "Forsooth, let go!"
  But when we come where comfort is,
  She never will say, "No!"

"Rose-Cheek'd Laura, Come"

  Rose-cheek'd Laura, come;
  Sing thou smoothly with thy beauty's
  Silent music, either other
    Sweetly gracing.

  Lovely forms do flow
  From concent divinely framéd:
  Heaven is music, and thy beauty's
    Birth is heavenly.

  These dull notes we sing
  Discords need for helps to grace them;
  Only beauty purely loving
    Knows no discord;

  But still moves delight,
  Like clear springs renew'd by flowing,
  Ever perfect, ever in them-
    selves eternal.

SIR HENRY WOOTTON

(1568–1639)

The Character of a Happy Life

How happy is he born and taught
  That serveth not another's will;
Whose armour is his honest thought,
  And simple truth his utmost skill;

Whose passions not his masters are;
  Whose soul is still prepared for death,
Untied unto the world by care
  Of public fame or private breath;

Who envies none that chance doth raise,
  Nor vice; who never understood
How deepest wounds are given by praise;
  Nor rules of state, but rules of good;

Who hath his life from rumours freed;
  Whose conscience is his strong retreat;
Whose state can neither flatterers feed,
  Nor ruin make oppressors great;

Who God doth late and early pray
  More of his grace than gifts to lend;
And entertains the harmless day
  With a religious book or friend.

This man is free from servile bands
  Of hope to rise or fear to fall:
Lord of himself, though not of lands,
  And, having nothing, yet hath all.

On His Mistress, the Queen of Bohemia

You meaner beauties of the night,
  That poorly satisfy our eyes
More by your number than your light,
  You common people of the skies;
  What are you when the moon shall rise?

You curious chanters of the wood,
  That warble forth Dame Nature's lays,
Thinking your passions understood
  By your weak accents; what's your praise,
When Philomel her voice shall raise?

You violets that first appear,
    By your pure purple mantles known
Like the proud virgins of the year,
    As if the spring were all your own;
    What are you when the rose is blown?

So, when my mistress shall be seen
    In form and beauty of her mind,
By virtue first, then choice, a Queen,
    Tell me if she were not designed
    The eclipse and glory of her kind?

Upon the Death of Sir Albert Morton's Wife

He first deceased; she for a little tried
To live without him, liked it not, and died.

SIR JOHN DAVIES

(1569–1626)

FROM *The Immortality of the Soul*

For why should we the busy soul believe
    When boldly she concludes of that and this,
When of herself she can no judgment give,
    Nor how, nor whence, nor where, nor what she is?

All things without which round about we see,
    We seek to know, and how therewith to do;
But that whereby we reason, live and be
    Within ourselves, we strangers are thereto.

We seek to know the moving of each sphere
    And the strange cause of th'ebbs and floods of Nile
But of that clock within our breasts we bear
    The subtle motions we forget the while.

We that acquaint ourselves with every zone
    And pass both tropics and behold each pole,
When we come home are to ourselves unknown
    And unacquainted still with our own soul.

We study speech, but others we persuade;
   We leech-craft learn, but others cure with it;
We interpret laws which other men have made,
   But read not those which in our hearts are writ.

I know my body's of so frail a kind
   As force without, fevers within can kill;
I know the heavenly nature of my mind,
   But 'tis corrupted both in wit and will.

I know my soul hath power to know all things,
   Yet is she blind and ignorant in all;
I know I'm one of Nature's little kings,
   Yet to the least and vilest things am thrall.

I know my life's a pain and but a span;
   I know my sense is mocked in everything;
And, to conclude, I know myself a man,
   Which is a proud and yet a wretched thing.

SIR ROBERT AYTOUN

(1570–1638)

"I Loved Thee Once..."

I loved thee once; I'll love no more.
   Thine be the grief, as is the blame;
Thou art not what thou wast before,
   What reason I should be the same?
     He that can love unloved again,
     Hath better store of love than brain;
   God send me love my debts to pay
   While unthrifts fool their love away!

Nothing could have my love o'erthrown
   If thou hadst still continued mine;
Yea, if thou hadst remained thy own,
   I might perchance have yet been thine.
     But thou thy freedom did recall
     That it thou might elsewhere enthral;
   And then how could I but disdain
   A captive's captive to remain?

When new desires had conquered thee
  And changed the object of thy will,
It had been lethargy in me,
  Not constancy, to love thee still.
        Yea, it had been a sin to go
        And prostitute affection so;
    Since we are taught no prayers to say
    To such as must to others pray.

Yet do thou glory in thy choice,
  Thy choice of his good fortune boast;
I'll neither grieve nor yet rejoice
  To see him gain what I have lost;
        The height of my disdain shall be
        To laugh at him, to blush for thee;
    To love thee still, but go no more
    A-begging at a beggar's door.

THOMAS DEKKER

(1570?–1641?)

"O, the Month of May..."

O, the month of May, the merry month of May,
So frolic, so gay, and so green, so green, so green!
O, and then did I unto my true love say,
Sweet Peg, thou shalt be my Summer's Queen.

Now the nightingale, the pretty nightingale,
The sweetest singer in all the forest quire,
Entreats thee, sweet Peggy, to hear thy true love's tale:
Lo, yonder she sitteth, her breast against a brier.

But O, I spy the cuckoo, the cuckoo, the cuckoo;
See where she sitteth; come away, my joy:
Come away, I prithee, I do not like the cuckoo
Should sing where my Peggy and I kiss and toy.

O, the month of May, the merry month of May,
So frolic, so gay, and so green, so green, so green;
And then did I unto my true love say,
Sweet Peg, thou shalt be my Summer's Queen.

The Shoemaker's Holiday, 1600

"Cold's the Wind..."

Cold's the wind, and wet's the rain,
   Saint Hugh be our good speed!
Ill is the weather that bringeth no gain,
   Nor helps good hearts in need.

Troll the bowl, the jolly nut-brown bowl,
   And here, kind mate, to thee!
Let's sing a dirge for Saint Hugh's soul,
   And down it merrily.

Down-a-down, hey, down-a-down,
   Hey derry derry down-a-down!
Ho! well done, to me let come,
   Ring compass, gentle joy!

Cold's the wind, and wet's the rain,
   Saint Hugh be our good speed!
Ill is the weather that bringeth no gain,
   Nor helps good hearts in need.

The Shoemaker's Holiday, 1600

"Art Thou Poor..."

Art thou poor, yet hast thou golden slumbers?
   O, sweet content!
Art thou rich, yet is thy mind perplexed?
   O, punishment!
 Dost thou laugh to see how fools are vexed
To add to golden numbers golden numbers?
   O, sweet content!

Work apace, apace, apace, apace;
Honest labour bears a lovely face;
Then hey noney, noney, hey noney, noney!

Canst drink the waters of the crispéd spring?
        O, sweet content!
Swim'st thou in wealth, yet sink'st in thine own tears?
        O, punishment!
    Then he that patiently want's burden bears,
No burden bears, but is a king, a king!
        O, sweet content!

The Pleasant Comedy of Patient Grissill, 1603

"Golden Slumbers..."

Golden slumbers kiss your eyes,
Smiles awake you when you rise.
Sleep, pretty wantons, do not cry,
And I will sing a lullaby:
Rock them, rock them, lullaby.

Care is heavy, therefore sleep you;
You are care, and care must keep you.
Sleep, pretty wantons, do not cry,
And I will sing a lullaby:
Rock them, rock them, lullaby.

The Pleasant Comedy of Patient Grissill, 1603

"Haymakers, Rakers..."

Haymakers, rakers, reapers, and mowers,
    Wait on your summer queen.
Dress up with musk-rose her eglantine bowers,
    Daffodils strew the green.
        Sing, dance, and play,
        'Tis holiday.
    The sun does bravely shine
On our ears of corn.
        Rich as a pearl,
        Comes every girl,
    This is mine, this is mine, this is mine;
Let us die, ere away they be borne.

Bow to the sun, to our queen, and that fair one,
　　Come to behold our sports.
Each bonny lass here is counted a rare one,
　　As those in princes' courts.
　　　　These and we
　　　　With country glee,
　　Will teach the woods to resound
　　And the hills with echoes hollow;
　　　　Skipping lambs
　　　　Their bleating dams
　　'Mongst kids shall trip it round;
For joy thus our wenches we follow.

Wind, jolly huntsman, your neat bugles shrilly,
　　Hounds make a lusty cry;
Spring up, you falconers, the partridges freely,
　　Then let your brave hawks fly.
　　　　Horses amain
　　　　Over ridge, over plain,
　　The dogs have the stag in chase;
　　'Tis a sport to content a king:
　　　　So, ho! ho! through the skies
　　　　How the proud bird flies,
　　And sousing, kills with a grace.
Now the deer falls; hark! how they ring.

The Sun's Darling, 1632–4

FROM *Old Fortunatus,* 1600

1.

Fortune:　Behold you not this globe, this golden bowl,
　　This toy called world, at our imperial feet?
　　This world is Fortune's ball, wherewith she
　　　　sports.
　　Sometimes I strike it up into the air,
　　And then create I emperors and kings:
　　Sometimes I spurn it, at which spurn crawls
　　　　out
　　That wild beast Multitude. Curse on, you fools,—
　　'Tis I that tumble princes from their thrones,

And gild false brows with glittering diadems.
'Tis I that tread on necks of conquerors,
And when, like demi-gods, they have been drawn
In ivory chariots to the capitol,
Circled about with wonder of all eyes,
The shouts of every tongue, love of all hearts,
Being swoll'n with their own greatness, I have
    pricked
The bladder of their pride, and made them die,
As water-bubbles, without memory.
I thrust base cowards into Honour's chair,
While the true-spirited soldier stands by
Bare-headed, and all bare, whilst at his scars
They scoff, that ne'er durst view the face of
    wars.
I set an idiot's cap on Virtue's head,
Turn Learning out of doors, clothe Wit in rags,
And paint ten thousand images of loam
In gaudy silken colours. On the backs
Of mules and asses I make asses ride,
Only for sport, to see the apish world
Worship such beasts with sound idolatry.
This Fortune does, and when this is done,
She sits and smiles to hear some curse her name,
And some with adoration crown her fame.

2.

Fortune: Stay, Fortunatus, once more hear me speak;
If thou kiss Wisdom's cheek and make her thine,
She'll breathe into thy lips divinity,
And thou like Phoebus shalt speak oracle,
Thy Heaven-inspiréd soul, on Wisdom's wings,
Shall fly up to the Parliament of Jove,
And read the statutes of eternity,
And see what's past and learn what is to come.
If thou lay claim to strength, armies shall quake
To see thee frown: as kings at mine do lie,
So shall thy feet trample on empery.
Make health thine object, thou shalt be strong
    proof

'Gainst the deep searching darts of surfeiting,
Be ever merry, ever revelling.
Wish but for beauty, and within thine eyes
Two naked Cupids amorously shall swim,
And on thy cheeks I'll mix such white and red,
That Jove shall turn away young Ganymede,
And with immortal arms shall circle thee.
Are thy desires long life?—thy vital thread
Shall be stretched out, thou shalt behold the
          change
Of monarchies and see those children die,
Whose great great grandsires now in cradles
          lie.
If through gold's sacred hunger thou dost pine,
Those gilded wantons which in swarms do run,
To warm their tender bodies in the sun,
Shall stand for number of those golden piles,
Which in rich pride shall swell before thy
          feet;
As those are, so shall these be infinite.
Awaken then thy soul's best faculties,
And gladly kiss this bounteous hand of Fate,
Which strives to bless thy name of Fortunate.

3.

Fortunatus: Oh, whither am I rapt beyond myself?
More violent conflict fights in every thought,
Than his whose fatal choice Troy's downfall
          wrought.
Shall I contract myself to wisdom's love?
Then I lose riches: and a wise man poor,
Is like a sacred book that's never read,—
To himself he lives, and to all else seems dead.
This age thinks better of a gilded fool,
Than of a threadbare saint in wisdom's school.
I will be strong: then I refuse long life,
And though mine arm should conquer twenty
          worlds,
There's a lean fellow beats all conquerors:

The greatest strength expires with loss of
    breath;
The mightiest in one minute stoop to death.
Then take long life, or health: should I do so
I might grow ugly, and that tedious scroll
Of months and years, much misery may enroll.
Therefore I'll beg for beauty; yet I will not,
That fairest cheek hath oftentimes a soul
Leprous as sin itself; than hell more foul.
The wisdom of this world is idiotism,
Strength a weak reed: health sickness' enemy,
And it at length will have the victory.
Beauty is but a painting, and long life
Is a long journey in December gone,
Tedious and full of tribulation
Therefore, dread sacred Empress, make me rich,
My choice is store of gold; the rich are wise.
He that upon his back rich garments wears,
Is wise, though on his head grow Midas' ears.
Gold is the strength, the sinews of the world,
The health, the soul, the beauty most divine,
A mask of gold hides all deformities;
Gold is Heaven's physic, life's restorative,
Oh therefore make me rich: not as the wretch,
That only serves lean banquets to his eye,
Has gold, yet starves: is famished in his store:
No, let me ever spend, be never poor.

FROM *The Honest Whore, Part I*, 1604

Candido: Patience, my lord! why, 'tis the soul of peace;
    Of all the virtues, 'tis nearest kin to Heaven.
    It makes men look like gods. The best of men
    That e'er wore earth about him, was a sufferer,
    A soft, meek, patient, humble, tranquil spirit,
    The first true gentleman that ever breathed.
    The stock of patience then cannot be poor;
    All it desires, it has; what monarch more?
    It is the greatest enemy to law
    That can be: for it doth embrace all wrongs,

And so chains up lawyers' and women's tongues.
'Tis the perpetual prisoner's liberty,
His walks and orchards: 'tis the bond slave's freedom,
And makes him seem proud of each iron chain,
As though he wore it more for state than pain:
It is the beggars' music, and thus sings,
Although their bodies beg, their souls are kings.
O my dread liege! It is the sap of bliss
Rears us aloft, makes men and angels kiss.
And last of all, to end a household strife,
It is the honey 'gainst a waspish wife.

THOMAS MIDDLETON

(1570?–1627)

"Love for Such a Cherry Lip"

Love for such a cherry lip
　Would be glad to pawn his arrows;
Venus here to take a sip
　Would sell her doves and teams of sparrows.
　　But they shall not so;
　　　Hey nonny, nonny no!
　　None but I this lip must owe,
　　　Hey nonny, nonny no!

Did Jove see this wanton eye,
　Ganymede must wait no longer;
Phoebe here one night did lie,
　Would change her face and look much younger.
　　But they shall not so;
　　　Hey nonny, nonny no!
　　None but I this lip must owe;
　　　Hey nonny, nonny no!

Blurt, Master Constable, 1602

"O for a Bowl of Fat Canary"

O for a bowl of fat canary,
Rich Aristippus, sparkling sherry!
Some nectar else from Juno's dairy;
O these draughts would make us merry!

O for a wench! I deal in faces,
And in other daintier things;
Tickled am I with her embraces;
Fine dancing in such fairy rings!

O for a plump, fat leg of mutton,
Veal, lamb, capon, pig, and coney!
None is happy but a glutton,
None an ass, but who wants money.

Wines indeed, and girls are good;
But brave victuals feast the blood;
For wenches, wine and lusty cheer,
Jove would come down to surfeit here.

A Mad World, My Masters, 1608

BEN JONSON

(1573–1637)

An Epitaph on Salathiel Pavey,
a Child of Queen Elizabeth's Chapel

Weep with me all you that read
This little story;
And know, for whom a tear you shed,
Death's self is sorry.
'Twas a child, that so did thrive
In grace and feature,
As Heaven and Nature seemed to strive
Which owned the creature.
Years he numbered scarce thirteen
When Fates turned cruel,
Yet three filled zodiacs had he been
The stage's jewel;
And did act (what now we moan)
Old men so duly
As, sooth, the Parcae thought him one,
He played so truly.
So by error to his fate
They all consented;

But viewing him since (alas, too late)
  They have repented.
And have sought (to give new birth)
  In baths to steep him;
But, being so much too good for earth,
  Heaven vows to keep him.

Epitaph on Elizabeth, L.H.

Would'st thou hear what man can say
  In a little? Reader, stay.
Underneath this stone doth lie
  As much beauty as could die;
Which in life did harbour give
  To more virtue than doth live.
If at all she had a fault,
  Leave it buried in this vault.
One name was Elizabeth,
  Th' other let it sleep with death;
Fitter, where it died, to tell,
  Than that it lived at all. Farewell.

That Women Are but Men's Shadows

Follow a shadow, it still flies you;
  Seem to fly, it will pursue;
So court a mistress, she denies you;
  Let her alone, she will court you.
Say, are not women truly then
  Styled but the shadows of us men?
At morn and even shades are longest;
  At noon they are or short or none;
So men at weakest, they are strongest,
  But grant us perfect, they're not known.
Say, are not women truly then
  Styled but the shadows of us men?

To Celia

Drink to me only with thine eyes,
 And I will pledge with mine;
And leave a kiss but in the cup,
 And I'll not look for wine.

The thirst that from the soul doth rise
 Doth ask a drink divine,
But might I of Jove's nectar sup
 I would not change for thine.

I sent thee late a rosy wreath,
 Not so much honouring thee,
As giving it a hope that there
 It could not withered be.

But thou thereon did'st only breathe
 And sent'st it back to me,
Since when it breathes and smells, I swear,
 Not of itself but thee.

From the Greek of PHILOSTRATUS

Her Triumph

See the chariot at hand here of Love
 Wherein my lady rideth!
Each that draws is a swan or a dove,
 And well the car Love guideth;
As she goes all hearts do duty
 Unto her beauty;
And enamoured do wish, so they might
 But enjoy such a sight,
That they still were to run by her side
Through swords, through seas, whither she would ride.

Do but look on her eyes, they do light
    All that Love's world compriseth!
Do but look on her hair, it is bright
    As Love's star when it riseth!
Do but mark, her forehead's smoother
    Than words that soothe her!
And from her arched brows such a grace
    Sheds itself through her face,
As alone there triumphs to the life
All the gain, all the good, of the elements' strife.

Have you seen but a bright lily grow
    Before rude hands have touched it?
Ha' you marked but the fall o' the snow
    Before the soil hath smutched it?
Ha' you felt the wool of beaver
    Or swan's down ever?
Or have smelt o' the bud o' the briar?
    Or the nard in the fire?
Or have tasted the bag of the bee?
O so white! O so soft! O so sweet is she!

To the Memory of My Beloved, the Author, Mr. William Shakespeare

To draw no envy, Shakespeare, on thy name,
    Am I thus ample to thy book and fame;
While I confess thy writings to be such
    As neither man nor Muse can praise too much.
'Tis true, and all men's suffrage. But these ways
    Were not the paths I meant unto thy praise;
For silliest ignorance on these may light,
    Which, when it sounds at best, but echoes right;
Or blind affection, which doth ne'er advance
    The truth, but gropes and urgeth all by chance;
Or crafty malice might pretend this praise
    And think to ruin where it seemed to praise.
These are as some infamous bawd or whore
    Should praise a matron. What could hurt her more?

But thou art proof against them, and indeed
   Above th' ill fortune of them or the need.
I, therefore, will begin. Soul of the Age!
   The applause, delight, the wonder of our stage!
My Shakespeare, rise. I will not lodge thee by
   Chaucer or Spenser, or bid Beaumont lie
A little further to make thee a room;
   Thou art a monument without a tomb,
And art alive still while thy book doth live,
   And we have wits to read and praise to give.
That I not mix thee so, my brain excuses;
   I mean with great but disproportioned Muses;
For, if I thought my judgment were of years,
   I should commit thee surely with thy peers,
And tell how far thou didst our Lyly outshine,
   Or sporting Kyd or Marlowe's mighty line.
And though thou hadst small Latin and less Greek,
   From thence to honour thee I would not seek
For names, but call forth thundering Aeschylus,
   Euripides and Sophocles to us,
Paccuvius, Accius, him of Cordoba dead,
   To life again, to hear thy buskin tread
And shake a stage; or, when thy socks were on,
   Leave thee alone for the comparison
Of all that insolent Greece or haughty Rome
   Sent forth, or since did from their ashes come.
Triumph, my Britain, thou hast one to show
   To whom all scenes of Europe homage owe.
He was not of an age, but for all time!
   And all the Muses still were in their prime
When like Apollo forth he came to warm
   Our ears, or like a Mercury to charm.
Nature herself was proud of his designs,
   And joyed to wear the dressing of his lines;
Which were so richly spun and woven so fit
   As since she will vouchsafe no other wit.
The merry Greek, tart Aristophanes,
   Neat Terence, witty Plautus, now not please;
But antiquated and deserted lie,
   As they were not of Nature's family.

Yet must I not give Nature all; thy Art,
  My gentle Shakespeare, must enjoy a part.
For though the poet's matter Nature be,
  His art doth give the fashion. And that he
Who casts to write a living line must sweat,
  (Such as thine are) and strike the second heat
Upon the Muses' anvil; turn the same
  (And himself with it) that he thinks to frame;
Or for the laurel he may gain a scorn,
  For a good poet's made as well as born.
And such wert thou. Look, how the father's face
  Lives in his issue, even so the race
Of Shakespeare's mind and manners brightly shines
  In his well-turnéd and true-filéd lines;
In each of which he seems to shake a lance
  As brandished at the eyes of ignorance.
Sweet Swan of Avon! what a sight it were
  To see thee in our waters yet appear,
And make those flights upon the banks of Thames
  That did so take Eliza and our James!
But stay, I see thee in the hemisphere
  Advanced, and make a constellation there.
Shine forth, thou Star of Poets, and with rage
  Or influence chide or cheer the drooping stage,
Which since thy flight from hence hath mourned like night,
  And despairs day but for thy volume's light.

Song

Slow, slow, fresh fount, keep time with my salt tears;
  Yet slower, yet, O faintly gentle springs;
  List to the heavy part the music bears:
    Woe weeps out her division when she sings.
      Droop herbs and flowers,
      Fall grief in showers,
      Our beauties are not ours;
        O, I could still
  (Like melting snow upon some craggy hill)
      Drop, drop, drop, drop,
Since Nature's pride is now a withered daffodil.

Cynthia's Revels, 1616

Song

O, that joy so soon should waste!
  Or so sweet a bliss
      As a kiss
Might not for ever last!
So sugared, so melting, so soft, so delicious,
  The dew that lies on roses,
  When the Morn herself discloses,
      Is not so precious.
O, rather than I would it smother,
Were I to taste such another,
  It should be my wishing
  That I might die kissing.

Cynthia's Revels, 1616

Hymn

Queen and huntress, chaste and fair,
Now the sun is laid to sleep,
Seated in thy silver chair
State in wonted manner keep;
  Hesperus entreats thy light,
  Goddess excellently bright.

Earth, let not thy envious shade
Dare itself to interpose;
Cynthia's shining orb was made
Heaven to clear, when day did close;
  Bless us then with wishéd sight,
  Goddess excellently bright.

Lay thy bow of pearl apart
And thy crystal-shining quiver,
Give unto the flying hart
Space to breathe, how short soever;
  Thou that mak'st a day of night,
  Goddess excellently bright.

Cynthia's Revels, 1616

Song

Still to be neat, still to be dressed,
As you were going to a feast,
Still to be powdered, still perfumed,
Lady, it is to be presumed,
Though art's hid causes are not found,
All is not sweet, all is not sound.

Give me a look, give me a face,
That makes simplicity a grace,
Robes loosely flowing, hair as free;
Such sweet neglect more taketh me
Than all the adulteries of art.
They strike mine eye, but not my heart.

The Silent Woman, 1616

FROM *Volpone or The Fox,* 1605

Volpone:　If thou hast wisdom, hear me, Celia.
　　　　Thy baths shall be the juice of July-flowers,
　　　　Spirit of roses, and of violets,
　　　　The milk of unicorns, and panthers' breath
　　　　Gathered in bags, and mixt with Cretan wines.
　　　　Our drink shall be preparéd gold and amber;
　　　　Which we will take, until my roof whirl round
　　　　With the vertigo: and my dwarf shall dance,
　　　　My eunuch sing, my fool make up the antic,
　　　　Whilst we, in changéd shapes, act Ovid's tales,
　　　　Thou, like Europa now, and I like Jove,
　　　　Then I like Mars, and thou like Erycine:
　　　　So, of the rest, till we have quite run through,
　　　　And wearied all the fables of the gods.
　　　　Then will I have thee in more modern forms,
　　　　Attiréd like some sprightly dame of France,
　　　　Brave Tuscan lady, or proud Spanish beauty;
　　　　Sometimes, unto the Persian sophy's wife;
　　　　Or the grand signior's mistress; and, for change,
　　　　To one of our most artful courtezans,

Or some quick Negro, or cold Russian;
And I will meet thee in as many shapes:
Where we may so transfuse our wandering souls
Out at our lips, and score up sums of pleasure.

FROM *The Alchemist*, 1610

Sir Epicure   No. I'll have no bawds,
Mammon: But fathers and mothers: they will do it best,
Best of all others. And my flatterers
Shall be the pure and gravest of divines,
That I can get for money. My mere fools,
Eloquent burgesses, and then my poets
The same that writ so subtly of the fart,
Whom I will entertain still for that subject.
The few that would give out themselves to be
Court and town-stallions, and, each-where, belie
Ladies who are known most innocent for them;
Those will I beg, to make me eunuchs of:
And they shall fan me with ten estrich tails
A-piece, made in a plume to gather wind.
We will be brave, Puffe, now we have the
        med'cine.
My meat shall all come in, in Indian shells,
Dishes of agate set in gold, and studded
With emeralds, sapphires, hyacinths and rubies.
The tongues of carps, dormice, and camels' heels,
Boiled in the spirit of sol, and dissolved pearl,
Apicius' diet, 'gainst the epilepsy:
And I will eat these broths with spoons of amber,
Headed with diamond and carbuncle.
My foot-boy shall eat pheasants, calver'd
        salmons,
Knots, godwits, lampreys: I myself will have
The beards of barbels served, instead of salads;
Oil'd mushrooms; and the swelling unctuous
        paps
Of a fat pregnant sow, newly cut off,
Dressed with an exquisite and poignant sauce;

For which I'll say unto my cook, *There's gold,
Go forth, and be a knight.*

            . . . My shirts
I'll have of taffeta-sarsnet, soft and light
As cobwebs; and for all my other raiment,
It shall be such as might provoke the Persian,
Were he to teach the world riot anew.
My gloves of fishes' and birds' skins, perfumed
With gums of paradise and eastern air.

JOHN DAY

(15—?–1640?)

FROM *The Parliament of Bees,* 1607?

1.
Polypragmus: I will have one built
       Like Pompey's theatre; the ceiling gilt
       And interseamed with pearl, to make it shine
       Like high Jove's palace: my descent's divine.
       My great hall I'll have paved with clouds; which
            done
       By wondrous skill, an artificial sun
       Shall roll about, reflecting golden beams,
       Like Phoebus dancing on the wanton streams.
       And when 'tis night, just as that sun goes down,
       I'll have the stars draw up a silver moon
       In her full height of glory. Overhead
       A roof of woods and forests I'll have spread,
       Trees growing downwards, full of fallow-deer;
       When of the sudden, listening, you shall hear
       A noise of horns and hunting, which shall bring
       Actaeon to Diana in the spring,
       Where all shall see her naked skin; and there
       Actaeon's hounds shall their own master tear,
       As emblem of his folly that will keep
       Hounds to devour and eat him up asleep.
       All this I'll do that men with praise may crown
       My fame for turning the world upside-down.

2.

Iltriste: This baseness follows your profession:
    You are like common beadles, easily won
    To whip poor bees to death, scarce worth the striking,
    But fawn with slavish flattery and throw liking
    On great drones' vices; you clap hands at those,
    Which proves your vices friends and virtues foes;
    Where the true poet indeed doth scorn to gild
    A coward's tomb with glories, or to build
    A sumptuous pyramid of golden verse
    Over the ruins of an ignoble hearse.
    His lines like his invention are born free,
    And both live blameless to eternity:
    He holds his reputation so dear
    As neither flattering hope nor servile fear
    Can bribe his pen to temporize with kings;
    The blacker are their crimes, he louder sings.

3.

  Vintager: High steward of thy vines,
      Taster both of grapes and wines,
      In these ripe clusters that present
      Full bounty, on his knees low bent,
      Pays Oberon homage; and in this bowl
      Brimmed with grape blood, tender toll
      Of all thy vintage.

  Oberon: May thy grapes thrive
      In autumn, and the roots survive
      In churlish winter; may thy fence
      Be proof 'gainst wild boars' violence;
      As thou in service true shalt be
      To us and our high royalty.
      —A female bee: thy character?

  Flora: Flora, Oberon's gardener,
      (Housewife both of herbs and flowers,
      To strew thy shrine and trim thy bowers
      With violets, roses, eglantine,

Daffodil and blue columbine)
Hath forth the bosom of the spring
Plucked this nosegay, which I bring
From Eleusis, mine own shrine,
To thee a monarch all divine;
And, as true impost of my grove,
Present it to great Oberon's love.

Oberon: Honey-dew refresh thy meads,
Cowslips spring with golden heads;
July-flowers and carnations wear
Leaves double streaked with maiden-hair;
May thy lilies taller grow,
Thy violets fuller sweetness owe;
And, last of all, may Phoebus love
To kiss thee and frequent thy grove,
As thou in service true shalt be
Unto our crown and royalty.

JOHN DONNE

(1573–1631)

The Good-Morrow

I wonder by my troth what thou and I
Did till we loved? were we not weaned till then?
But sucked on country pleasures childishly?
Or snorted we in the seven sleepers' den?
'Twas so; but this, all pleasures fancies be.
If ever any beauty I did see,
Which I desired and got, 'twas but a dream of thee.

And now good morrow to our waking souls,
Which watch not one another out of fear;
For love all love of other sights controls,
And makes one little room an everywhere.
Let sea-discoverers to new worlds have gone,
Let maps to other worlds on worlds have shown,
Let us possess one world, each hath one, and is one.

My face in thine eye, thine in mine appears,
And true plain hearts do in the faces rest;
Where can we find two better hemispheres
Without sharp North, without declining West?
Whatever dies was not mixt equally;
If our two loves be one, or thou and I
Love so alike that none do slacken, none can die.

Song

Go and catch a falling star,
   Get with child a mandrake root,
Tell me, where all past years are,
   Or who cleft the Devil's foot,
Teach me to hear Mermaids singing,
   Or to keep off envy's stinging,
       And find
       What wind
Serves to advance an honest mind.

If thou be'st born to strange sights,
   Things invisible to see,
Ride ten thousand days and nights,
   Till age snow white hairs on thee;
Thou, when thou return'st, will tell me
All strange wonders that befell thee,
       And swear
       No where
Lives a woman true and fair.

If thou find'st one, let me know,
   Such a Pilgrimage were sweet;
Yet do not, I would not go,
   Though at next door we might meet;
Though she were true when you met her,
And last till you write your letter,
       Yet she
       Will be
False ere I come to two or three.

The Canonization

For God's sake hold your tongue, and let me love;
  Or chide my palsy, or my gout,
My five grey hairs, or ruined fortune flout;
    With wealth your state, your mind with arts improve,
      Take you a course, get you a place,
      Observe his Honour, or his Grace,
Or the King's real, or his stamped face
  Contemplate; what you will, approve,
  So you will let me love.

Alas, alas, who's injured by my love?
  What merchant's ships have my sighs drowned?
Who says my tears have overflowed his ground?
    When did my colds a forward spring remove?
      When did the heats which my veins fill
      Add one more to the plaguy bill?
Soldiers find wars, and lawyers find out still
  Litigious men, which quarrels move,
  Though she and I do love.

Call us what you will, we are made such by love;
  Call her one, me another fly,
We're tapers too, and at our own cost die,
    And we in us find the Eagle and the Dove.
      The Phoenix riddle hath more wit
      By us; we two being one, are it.
So to one neutral thing both sexes fit,
  We die and rise the same, and prove
  Mysterious by this love.

We can die by it, if not live by love,
  And if unfit for tombs and hearse
Our legend be, it will be fit for verse;
    And if no piece of Chronicle we prove,
      We'll build in sonnets pretty rooms;
      As well a well-wrought urn becomes
The greatest ashes, as half-acre tombs,
  And by these hymns all shall approve
  Us canonized for Love:

And thus invoke us: You whom reverend love
   Made one another's hermitage;
You, to whom love was peace, that now is rage;
   Who did the whole world's soul contract, and drove
     Into the glasses of your eyes
     (So made such mirrors, and such spies,
That they did all to you epitomise,)
   Countries, Towns, Courts: beg from above
   A pattern of your love!

Song

Sweetest love, I do not go,
   For weariness of thee,
Nor in hope the world can show
   A fitter love for me;
     But since that I
Must die at last, 'tis best
To use myself in jest
     Thus by feigned deaths to die.

Yesternight the sun went hence,
   And yet is here to-day;
He hath no desire nor sense,
   Nor half so short a way;
     Then fear not me,
But believe that I shall make
Speedier journeys, since I take
     More wings and spurs than he.

O how feeble is man's power,
   That if good fortune fall,
Cannot add another hour
   Nor a lost hour recall!
     But come bad chance,
And we join to it our strength,
And we teach it art and length,
     Itself o'er us to advance.

When thou sigh'st, thou sigh'st not wind,
　But sigh'st my soul away;
When thou weep'st, unkindly kind,
　My life's blood doth decay.
　　It cannot be
That thou lov'st me, as thou say'st,
If in thine my life thou waste,
　That art the best of me.

Let not thy divining heart
　Forethink me any ill,
Destiny may take thy part,
　And may thy fears fulfil;
　　But think that we
Are but turned aside to sleep;
They who one another keep
　Alive, ne'er parted be.

Love's Alchemy

Some that have deeper digged love's mine than I,
Say where his centric happiness doth lie.
　I have loved and got and told,
But should I love, get, tell, till I were old,
I should not find that hidden mystery;
　Oh, 'tis imposture all:
And as no chemic yet the Elixir got,
　But glorifies his pregnant pot,
　If by the way to him befall
Some odoriferous thing, or medicinal,
　So lovers dream a rich and long delight,
　But get a winter-seeming summer's night.

Our ease, our thrift, our honour, and our day,
Shall we, for this vain bubble's shadow pay?
　Ends love in this, that my man
Can be as happy as I can; if he can
Endure the short scorn of a bridegroom's play?
　The loving wretch that swears

'Tis not the bodies marry, but the minds,
   Which he in her angelic finds,
   Would swear as justly that he hears
In that day's rude hoarse minstrelsy, the spheres.
Hope not for mind in women; at their best
   Sweetness and wit they are but mummy possessed.

The Message

Send home my long strayed eyes to me,
Which O! too long have dwelt on thee;
Yet since there they have learned such ill,
    Such forced fashions,
    And false passions,
      That they be
      Made by thee
Fit for no good sight, keep them still.

Send home my harmless heart again,
Which no unworthy thought could stain;
But if it be taught by thine
    To make jestings
    Of protestings,
      And cross both
      Word and oath,
Keep it, for then 'tis none of mine.

Yet send me back my heart and eyes,
That I may know, and see thy lies,
And may laugh and joy, when thou
    Art in anguish
    And dost languish
      For some one
      That will none,
Or prove as false as thou art now.

The Apparition

When by thy scorn, O murd'ress, I am dead,
And that thou think'st thee free
From all solicitations from me,
Then shall my ghost come to thy bed,
And thee, feigned vestal, in worse arms shall see;
Then thy sick taper will begin to wink,
And he, whose thou art then, being tired before,
Will, if thou stir, or pinch to wake him, think
    Thou call'st for more,
And in false sleep will from thee shrink,
And then poor aspen wretch, neglected thou
Bathed in a cold quicksilver sweat wilt lie
    A verier ghost than I;
What I will say, I will not tell thee now,
Lest that preserve thee; and since my love is spent,
I'd rather thou should'st painfully repent,
Than by my threat'nings rest still innocent.

The Ecstasy

Where, like a pillow on a bed,
    A pregnant bank swelled up, to rest
The violet's reclining head,
    Sat we two, one another's best.
Our hands were firmly cemented
    With a fast balm, which thence did spring,
Our eye-beams twisted, and did thread
    Our eyes upon one double string;
So t'intergraft our hands, as yet
    Was all the means to make us one,
And pictures in our eyes to get
    Was all our propagation.
As 'twixt two equal armies, Fate
    Suspends uncertain victory,
Our souls (which to advance their state
    Were gone out,) hung 'twixt her and me.

And whilst our souls negotiate there,
    We like sepulchral statues lay;
All day, the same our postures were,
    And we said nothing all the day.
If any so by love refined
    That he soul's language understood,
And by good love were grown all mind,
    Within convenient distance stood,
He (though he knew not which soul spake,
    Because both meant, not spake the same)
Might thence a new concoction take,
    And part far purer than he came.
This Ecstasy doth unperplex
    (We said) and tell us what we love,
We see by this, it was not sex,
    We see, we saw not what did move:
But as all several souls contain
    Mixture of things, they knew not what,
Love these mixed souls doth mix again,
    And makes both one each this and that.
A single violet transplant,
    The strength, the colour, and the size,
(All which before was poor and scant)
    Redoubles still, and multiplies.
When love, with one another so
    Interinanimates two souls,
That abler soul, which thence doth flow,
    Defects of loneliness controls.
We then, who are this new soul, know
    Of what we are composed and made,
For th'atomies of which we grow
    Are souls, whom no change can invade.
But O alas, so long, so far
    Our bodies why do we forbear?
They are ours, though they are not we. We are
    The intelligences, they the spheres.
We owe them thanks, because they thus
    Did us to us at first convey,
Yielded their forces, sense, to us,
    Nor are dross to us, but allay.

On man heaven's influence works not so,
    But that it first imprints the air,
So soul into the soul may flow,
    Though it to body first repair.
As our blood labours to beget
    Spirits as like souls as it can,
Because such fingers need to knit
    That subtle knot which makes us man:
So must pure lovers' souls descend
    T' affections and to faculties,
Which sense may reach and apprehend,
    Else a great Prince in prison lies.
To our bodies turn we then, that so
    Weak men on love revealed may look;
Love's mysteries in souls do grow,
    But yet the body is his book,
And if some lover such as we
    Have heard this dialogue of one,
Let him still mark us, he shall see
    Small change when we're to bodies gone.

The Relique

When my grave is broke up again
Some second guest to entertain,
    (For graves have learned that woman-head
    To be to more than one a bed)
    And he that digs it spies
A bracelet of bright hair about the bone,
    Will he not let us alone,
And think that there a loving couple lies,
Who thought that this device might be some way
To make their souls, at the last busy day,
Meet at this grave and make a little stay?

If this fall in a time or land
Where mis-devotion doth command,
Then he that digs us up will bring
Us to the Bishop and the King
    To make us Reliques; then

Thou shalt be Mary Magdalen, and I
　　　A something else thereby;
All women shall adore us and some men;
And since at such time miracles are sought,
I would have that age by this paper taught
What miracles we harmless lovers wrought.

　　First, we loved well and faithfully,
　　Yet knew not what we loved nor why,
　　Difference of sex no more we knew
　　Than our Guardian Angels do;
　　　Coming and going, we
Perchance might kiss, but not between those meals;
　　Our hands ne'er touched the seals
Which nature, injured by late law, sets free:
These miracles we did; but now, alas,
All measure and all language I should pass,
Should I tell what a miracle she was.

Change

Although thy hand and faith and good works too,
Have sealed thy love which nothing should undo,
Yea, though thou fall back, that apostasy
Confirm thy love; yet much, much I fear thee.
Women are like the Arts, forced unto none,
Open to all searchers, unprized if unknown.
If I have caught a bird and let him fly,
Another fowler using these means, as I,
May catch the same bird; and, as these things be,
Women are made for men, not him, nor me.
Foxes and goats, all beasts change when they please;
Shall women, more hot, wily, wild than these,
Be bound to one man, and did Nature then
Idly make them apter to endure than men?
They're our clogs, not their own; if a man be
Chained to a galley, yet the galley's free;
Who hath a plough-land casts all his seed corn there,
And yet allows his ground more corn should bear;
Though Danube into the sea must flow,

The sea receives the Rhine, Volga, and Po.
By nature, which gave it, this liberty
Thou lov'st, but Oh! canst thou love it and me?
Likeness glues love: and if that thou so do,
To make us like and love, must I change too?
More than thy hate, I hate it, rather let me
Allow her change, than change as oft as she,
And so not teach, but force my opinion
To love not any one, nor every one.
To live in one land is captivity,
To run all countries a wild roguery;
Waters stink soon if in one place they bide,
And in the vast sea are more putrefied:
But when they kiss one bank and, leaving this,
Never look back but the next bank do kiss,
Then are they purest; Change is the nursery
Of music, joy, life and eternity.

The Autumnal

No Spring, nor Summer Beauty hath such grace
    As I have seen in one Autumnal face.
Young Beauties force our love, and that's a rape,
    This doth but counsel, yet you cannot 'scape.
If 'twere a shame to love, here 'twere no shame,
    Affection here takes Reverence's name.
Were her first years the Golden Age; that's true,
    But now she's gold oft-tried and ever new.
That was her torrid and inflaming time,
    This is her tolerable tropic clime.
Fair eyes, who asks more heat than come from hence,
    He in a fever wishes pestilence.
Call not these wrinkles, graves; if graves they were,
    They were Love's graves, for else he is no where.
Yet lies not Love dead here, but here doth sit
    Vowed to this trench like an anachorite.
And here, till hers, which must be his death, come,
    He doth not dig a grave, but build a tomb.
Here dwells he, though he sojourn everywhere
    In Progress, yet his standing house is here.

Here where still evening is, not noon nor night;
  Where no voluptuousness, yet all delight.
In all her words, unto all hearers fit,
  You may at Revels, you at Council, sit.
This is love's timber, youth his underwood;
  There he as wine in June enrages blood,
Which then comes seasonabliest, when our taste
  And appetite to other things is past.
Xerxes' strange Lydian love, the Platane tree,
  Was loved for age, none being so large as she,
Or else because, being young, nature did bless
  Her youth with age's glory, barrenness.
If we love things long sought, Age is a thing
  Which we are fifty years in compassing;
If transitory things which soon decay,
  Age must be loveliest at the latest day.
But name not Winter-faces, whose skin's slack,
  Lank as an unthrift's purse, but a soul's sack;
Whose eyes seek light within, for all here's shade;
  Whose mouths are holes rather worn out than made;
Whose every truth to a several place is gone
  To vex their souls at Resurrection;
Name not these living Death's-heads unto me,
  For these not ancient but antique be.
I hate extremes, yet I had rather stay
  With tombs than cradles to wear out a day.
Since such love's natural lation is, may still
  My love descend, and journey down the hill,
Not panting after growing beauties, so
  I shall ebb out with them who homeward go.

On His Mistress

    By our first strange and fatal interview,
    By all desires which thereof did ensue,
    By our long starving hopes, by that remorse
    Which my words' masculine persuasive force
    Begot in thee, and by the memory
    Of hurts, which spies and rivals threatened me,

Lation, *astronomical motion.*

I calmly beg; but by thy father's wrath,
By all pains, which want and divorcement hath,
I conjure thee, and all the oaths which I
And thou have sworn to seal joint constancy,
Here I unswear, and overswear them thus,
Thou shalt not love by ways so dangerous.
Temper, O fair Love, love's impetuous rage,
Be my true mistress still, not my feigned page;
I'll go, and by thy kind leave, leave behind
Thee, only worthy to nurse in my mind
Thirst to come back; O if thou die before,
My soul from other lands to thee shall soar.
Thy (else Almighty) beauty cannot move
Rage from the seas, nor thy love teach them love,
Nor tame wild Boreas' harshness; thou hast read
How roughly he in pieces shiveréd
Fair Orithea, whom he swore he loved.
Fall ill or good, 'tis madness to have proved
Dangers unurged; feed on this flattery,
That absent lovers one in th'other be.
Dissemble nothing, not a boy, nor change
Thy body's habit, nor mind's; be not strange
To thyself only; all will spy in thy face
A blushing womanly discovering grace;
Richly clothed apes are called apes, and as soon
Eclipsed as bright we call the moon the moon.
Men of France, changeable chameleons,
Spitals of diseases, shops of fashions,
Love's fuellers, and the rightest company
Of players, which upon the world's stage be,
Will quickly know thee, and no less, alas!
Th'indifferent Italian, as we pass
His warm land, well content to think thee page,
Will hunt thee with such lust and hideous rage
As Lot's fair guests were vexed. But none of these
Nor spongy hydroptic Dutch shall thee displease,
If thou stay here. O stay here, for to thee
England is only a worthy gallery,
To walk in expectation, till from thence
Our greatest King call thee to his presence.
When I am gone, dream me some happiness,

Nor let thy looks our long-hid love confess,
Nor praise, nor dispraise me, nor bless nor curse
Openly love's force, nor in bed fright thy nurse
With midnight startings, crying out: Oh, oh,
Nurse, O my love is slain, I saw him go
O'er the white Alps alone; I saw him, I,
Assailed, fight, taken, stabbed, bleed, fall, and die.
Augur me better chance, except great Jove
Think it enough for me to have had thy love.

Love's Progress

Whoever loves, if he do not propose
The right true end of love, he's one that goes
To sea for nothing but to make him sick.
Love is a bear-whelp born, if we o'er-lick
Our love, and force it new strange shapes to take,
We err, and of a lump a monster make.
Were not a calf a monster that were grown
Faced like a man, though better than his own?
Perfection is in unity; prefer
One woman first, and then one thing in her.
I, when I value gold, may think upon
The ductileness, the application,
The wholesomeness, the ingenuity,
From rust, from soil, from fire ever free:
But if I love it, 'tis because 'tis made
By our new nature (Use) the soul of trade.

All these in women we might think upon
(If women had them) and yet love but one.
Can men more injure women than to say
They love for that, by which they're not they?
Makes virtue women? Must I cool my blood
Till I both be, and find one, wise and good?
May barren angels love so. But if we
Make love to woman, virtue is not she,
As beauty's not, nor wealth; he that strays thus
From her to hers is more adulterous
Than if he took the maid. Search every sphere

And firmament, our Cupid is not there;
He's an infernal god, and underground
With Pluto dwells, where gold and fire abound;
Men to such gods their sacrificing coals
Did not in altars lay, but pits and holes.
Although we see the celestial bodies move
Above the earth, the earth we till and love;
So we her airs contemplate, words and heart,
And virtues, but we love the centric part.

Nor is the soul more worthy, or more fit
For love than this, as infinite it is.
But in attaining this desiréd place
How much they err that set out at the face.
The hair a forest is of ambushes,
Of springs, snares, fetters and manacles;
The brow becalms us when 'tis smooth and plain,
And when 'tis wrinkled shipwrecks us again.
Smooth, 'tis a paradise where we would have
Immortal stay, and wrinkled 'tis our grave.
The nose (like to the first meridian) runs
Not 'twixt an East and West, but 'twixt two suns;
It leaves a cheek, a rosy hemisphere
On either side, and then directs us where
Upon the Islands Fortunate we fall,
(Not faint Canaries, but ambrosial)
Her swelling lips; to which when we are come,
We anchor there and think ourselves at home,
For they seem all; there sirens' songs and there
Wise Delphic oracles to fill the ear,
There in a creek where chosen pearls do swell,
The remora, her cleaving tongue, doth dwell.
These and the glorious promontory, her chin,
O'erpast, and the strait Hellespont between
The Sestos and Abydos of her breasts,
(Not of two lovers, but two loves the nests)
Succeeds a boundless sea, but yet thine eye
Some island moles may scattered there descry,
And sailing toward her India in that way
Shall at her fair Atlantic navel stay;
Though thence the current be thy pilot made,

Yet ere thou be where thou wouldst be embayed
Thou shalt upon another forest set,
Where many shipwreck and no further get.
When thou art there, consider what this chase
Misspent by thy beginning at the face.

Rather set out below; practise my art,
Some symmetry the foot hath with that part
Which thou dost seek, and is thy map for that
Lovely enough to stoop, but not stay at;
Least subject to disguise and change it is;
Men say the Devil never can change his.
It is the emblem that hath figuréd
Firmness; 'tis the first part that comes to bed.
Civility we see refined; the kiss
Which at the face began, transplanted is,
Since to the hand, since to the Imperial knee,
Now at the Papal foot delights to be.
If kings think that the nearer way, and do
Rise from the foot, lovers may do so too;
For as free spheres move faster far than can
Birds, whom the air resists, so may that man
Which goes this empty and aethereal way,
Than if at beauty's elements he stay.
Rich Nature hath in woman wisely made
Two purses, and their mouths aversely laid;
They then which to the lower tribute owe,
That way which that Exchequer looks must go.
He that doth not, his error is as great
As who by clyster gave the stomach meat.

Satire II

Sir: though (I thank God for it) I do hate
Perfectly all this town, yet there's one state
In all ill things so excellently best
That hate toward them breeds pity toward the rest.
Though poetry indeed be such a sin
As I think that brings dearth and Spaniards in,
Though like the pestilence and old-fashioned love
Riddlingly it catch men, and doth remove

Never till it be starved out, yet their state
Is poor, disarmed, like papists, not worth hate.
One (like a wretch which at Bar judged as dead,
Yet prompts him which stands next, and cannot read,
And saves his life) gives idiot actors means
(Starving himself) to live by his laboured scenes;
As in some organ puppets dance above
And bellows pant below, which them do move.
One would move Love by rhythms; but witchcraft's charms
Bring not now their old fears nor their old harms;
Rams and slings now are silly battery,
Pistolets are the best artillery.
And they who write to Lords, rewards to get,
Are they not like singers at doors for meat?
And they who write, because all write, have still
That excuse for writing and for writing ill;
But he is worst who beggarly doth chaw
Others' wits' fruits, and in his ravenous maw
Rankly digested doth those things out spew
As his own things; and they are his own, 'tis true,
For if one eat my meat, though it be known
The meat was mine, th'excrement is his own.
But these do me no harm, nor they which use
To out-do dildos and out-usure Jews,
To out-drink the sea, to out-swear the litany;
Who with sins all kinds as familiar be
As confessors, and for whose sinful sake
Schoolmen new tenements in hell must make,
Whose strange sins Canonists could hardly tell
In which Commandment's large receipt they dwell.
But these punish themselves. The insolence
Of Coscus only breeds my just offence,
Whom time (which rots all, and makes botches pox,
And, plodding on, must make a calf an ox)
Hath made a Lawyer, which was, alas, of late
But a scarce poet; jollier of this state
Than are now beneficed ministers, he throws
Like nets or lime-twigs wheresoever he goes
His title of Barrister on every wench,
And woos in language of the Pleas and Bench.
A motion, Lady. Speak, Coscus. I have been

In love ever since tricesimo of the Queen,
Continual claims I have made, injunctions got
To stay my rival's suit that he should not
Proceed. Spare me. In Hilary term I went;
You said, if I returned next 'size in Lent
I should be in remitter of your grace;
In th'interim my letters should take place
Of affidavits; words, words, which would tear
The tender labyrinth of a soft maid's ear
More, more than ten Sclavonians scolding, more
Than when winds in our ruined abbeys roar.
When sick with poetry and possessed with Muse
Thou wast and mad, I hoped; but men which choose
Law-practice for mere gain, bold soul, repute
Worse than embrothelled strumpets prostitute.
Now like an owl-like watchman, he must walk
His hand still at a bill, now he must talk
Idly like prisoners, which whole months will swear
That only suretyship hath brought them there,
And to every suitor lie in everything
Like a King's favourite, yea, like a King;
Like a wedge in a block, wring to the bar,
Bearing like asses; and more shameless far
Than carted whores, lie to the grave Judge; for
Bastardy abounds not in King's titles nor
Simony and Sodomy in churchmen's lives,
As these things do in him; by these he thrives.
Shortly (as the sea) he will compass all our land,
From Scots to Wight, from Mount to Dover strand.
And spying heirs melting with luxury,
Satan will not joy at their sins, as he.
For as a thrifty wench scrapes kitchen stuff,
And barrelling the droppings and the snuff
Of wasting candles, which in thirty years
(Relique-like kept) perchance buys wedding gear;
Piecemeal he gets lands, and spends as much time
Wringing each acre as men pulling prime.
In parchments then, large as his fields, he draws
Assurances big as glossed civil laws,
So huge that men (in our time's forwardness)
Are Fathers of the Church for writing less.

These he writes not, nor for those written pays,
Therefore spares no length; as in those first days
When Luther was professed he did desire
Short Pater nosters, saying as a friar
Each day his beads; but having left those laws
Adds to Christ's prayer the Power and glory clause.
And when he sells or changes land he impairs
His writings, and unwatched leaves out "ses heires,"
As slily as any commentator goes by
Hard words or sense; or in divinity
As controverters in vouched texts leave out
Shrewd words, which might against them clear the doubt.
Where are those spread woods which clothed heretofore
Those bought lands? Not built, nor burnt within door.
Where's th'old landlord's troops and alms? In great halls
Carthusian fasts and fulsome bacchanals
Equally I hate; means bless; in rich men's homes
I bid kill some beasts but no hecatombs;
None starve, none surfeit so; but Oh, we allow
Good works as good, but out of fashion now,
Like old rich wardrobes; but my words none draws
Within the vast reach of the huge statute laws.

Holy Sonnets

VII

At the round earth's imagined corners, blow
Your trumpets, Angels, and arise, arise
From death, you numberless infinities
Of souls, and to your scattered bodies go,
All whom the flood did, and fire shall o'erthrow,
All whom war, dearth, age, agues, tyrannies,
Despair, law, chance, hath slain, and you whose eyes
Shall behold God and never taste death's woe.
But let them sleep, Lord, and me mourn a space,
For if above all these my sins abound,
'Tis late to ask abundance of Thy grace,
When we are there; here on this lowly ground,
Teach me how to repent; for that's as good
As if Thou hadst seal'd my pardon with Thy blood.

X

Death, be not proud though some have called thee
Mighty and dreadful, for thou art not so,
For those, whom thou think'st thou dost overthrow,
Die not, poor Death, nor yet canst thou kill me.
From rest and sleep, which but thy pictures be,
Much pleasure, then from thee much more must flow,
And soonest our best men with thee do go,
Rest of their bones and soul's delivery.
Thou art slave to Fate, Chance, kings and desperate men,
And dost with poison, war, and sickness dwell,
And poppy or charms can make us sleep as well,
And better than thy stroke; why swell'st thou then?
One short sleep past, we wake eternally,
And death shall be no more; Death, thou shalt die.

A Hymn to Christ at the Author's Last Going into Germany

In what torn ship soever I embark,
That ship shall be my emblem of Thy Ark;
What sea soever swallow me, that flood
Shall be to me an emblem of Thy blood;
Though Thou with clouds of anger do disguise
Thy face, yet through that mask I know those eyes,
    Which, though they turn away sometimes,
        They never will despise.

I sacrifice this Island unto Thee,
And all whom I loved there and who loved me;
When I have put our seas 'twixt them and me,
Put Thou Thy sea betwixt my sins and Thee.
As the tree's sap doth seek the root below
In winter, in my winter now I go,
    Where none but Thee, th'Eternal root
        Of true Love, I may know.

Nor Thou nor Thy religion dost control
The amorousness of an harmonious soul,
But Thou would'st have that love Thyself; as Thou
Art jealous, Lord, so I am jealous now,

Thou lov'st not till from loving more Thou free
My soul; who ever gives, takes liberty.
  O, if Thou car'st not whom I love,
    Alas, Thou lov'st not me.

Seal then this bill of my Divorce to All,
On whom those fainter beams of love did fall;
Marry those loves, which in youth scattered be
On Fame, Wit, Hopes (false mistresses) to Thee.
Churches are best for prayer that have least light;
To see God only I go out of sight.
  And to 'scape stormy days, I choose
    An everlasting night.

A Hymn to God the Father

Wilt Thou forgive that sin where I begun,
  Which is my sin though it were done before?
Wilt Thou forgive that sin through which I run
  And do run still, though still I do deplore?
    When Thou hast done, Thou hast not done,
      For I have more.

Wilt Thou forgive that sin by which I have won
  Others to sin? and made my sin their door?
Wilt Thou forgive that sin which I did shun
  A year or two, but wallowed in a score?
    When Thou hast done, Thou hast not done,
      For I have more.

I have a sin of fear, that when I have spun
  My last thread I shall perish on the shore;
Swear by Thyself that at my death Thy son
  Shall shine as He shines now and heretofore;
    And having done that Thou hast done,
      I fear no more.

RICHARD BARNEFIELD

(1574–1627)

"As It Fell upon a Day"

As it fell upon a day
In the merry month of May,
Sitting in a pleasant shade
Which a grove of myrtles made,
Beasts did leap and birds did sing,
Trees did grow and plants did spring;
Every thing did banish moan,
Save the nightingale alone:
She, poor bird, as all forlorn,
Lean'd her breast up-till a thorn,
And there sung the dolefull'st ditty,
That to hear it was great pity:
"Fie, fie, fie," now would she cry;
"Tereu, Tereu!" by and by;
That to hear her so complain,
Scarce I could from tears refrain;
For her griefs so lively shown
Made me think upon mine own.
Ah, thought I, thou mourn'st in vain!
None takes pity on thy pain:
Senseless trees they cannot hear thee;
Ruthless beasts they will not cheer thee:
King Pandion he is dead;
All thy friends are lapped in lead;
All thy fellow birds do sing,
Careless of thy sorrowing.
Even so, poor bird, like thee,
None alive will pity me.
Whilst as fickle Fortune smiled,
Thou and I were both beguiled.

Every one that flatters thee
Is no friend to misery.
Words are easy, like the wind;
Faithful friends are hard to find:
Every man will be thy friend

Whilst thou hast wherewith to spend;
But if store of crowns be scant,
No man will supply thy want.
If that one be prodigal,
Bountiful they will him call,
And with such-like flattering,
"Pity but he were a king;"
If he be addict to vice,
Quickly him they will entice;
If to women he be bent,
They have at commandment:
But if Fortune once do frown,
Then farewell his great renown;
They that fawn'd on him before
Use his company no more.
He that is thy friend indeed,
He will help thee in thy need:
If thou sorrow, he will weep;
If thou wake, he cannot sleep;
Thus of every grief in heart
He with thee doth bear a part.
These are certain signs to know
Faithful friend from flattering foe.

The Passionate Pilgrim, 1599

"If Music and Sweet Poetry..."

If music and sweet poetry agree,
As they needs must, the sister and the brother,
Then must the love be great 'twixt thee and me,
Because thou lovest the one and I the other.
Dowland to thee is dear, whose heavenly touch
Upon the lute doth ravish human sense;
Spenser to me, whose deep conceit is such
As passing all conceit needs no defence.
Thou lovest to hear the sweet melodious sound
That Phoebus' lute, the queen of music, makes;
And I in deep delight am chiefly drown'd

Whenas himself to singing he betakes.
One god is god of both, as poets feign;
One knight loves both, and both in thee remain.

The Passionate Pilgrim, 1599

JOSEPH HALL

(1574–1656)

FROM *Vergidemiarum*

1.

PROLOGUE

I first adventure, with foolhardy might,
To tread the steps of perilous despite:
I first adventure; follow me who list,
And be the second English satirist.
Envy waits at my back, Truth on my side;
Envy will be my page, and Truth my guide.
Envy the margent holds, and Truth the line;
Truth doth approve, but Envy doth repine.
For in this smoothing age who durst indite,
Hath made his pen an hired parasite,
To claw the back of him that beastly lives,
And prank base men in proud superlatives.
Whence damnéd vice is shrouded quite from shame
And crowned with Virtue's meed, immortal name;
Infamy dispossest of native due
Ordained of old on looser life to sue:
The world's eye blearéd with those shameless lies,
Masked in the shew of meal-mouthed poesies.
Go, daring Muse, on with thy thankless task,
And do the ugly face of vice unmask;
And if thou canst not thine high flight remit,
So as it may a lowly satire fit,
Let lowly satires rise aloft to thee:
Truth be thy speed, and Truth thy patron be.

2.

A Gentle Squire would gladly entertain
Into his house some trencher-chaplain,
Some willing man that might instruct his sons,
And that would stand to good conditions:

First, that he lie upon the truckle-bed,
While his young master lieth o'er his head;
Secondly, that he do, on no default,
Ever presume to sit above the salt;
Third, that he never charge his trencher twice;
Fourth, that he use all comely courtesies,
Sit bare at meals, and one half rise and wait;
Last, that he never his young master beat,
But he must ask his mother to define
How many yerks she would his breech should line.
All these observed, he would contented be
To give five marks and winter livery.

Book 2, Satire 6

JOHN MARSTON
(1575?–1634)

FROM *Antonio and Mellida*, 1602

Andrugio: My thoughts are fixed in contemplation
    Why this huge earth, this monstrous animal
    That eats her children, should not have eyes and
        ears.
    Philosophy maintains that Nature's wise
    And forms no useless nor unperfect thing.
    Did Nature make the earth, or the earth Nature?
    For earthly dirt makes all things, makes the man,
    Moulds me up honour, and, like a cunning Dutch-
        man
    Paints me a puppet e'en with seeming breath,
    And gives a sot appearance of a soul.
    Go to, go to; thou liest, Philosophy.
    Nature forms things unperfect, useless, vain.
    Why made she not the earth with eyes and ears
    That she might see desert and hear men's plaints
    That when a soul is splitted, sunk with grief,
    He might fall thus upon the breast of earth
    And in her ear halloo his misery,
    Exclaiming thus: O thou all-bearing Earth,
    Which men do gape for till thou cramm'st their
        mouths

And chok'st their throats with dust, open thy breast,
And let me sink into thee; look who knocks;
Andrugio calls. But O, she's deaf and blind.
A wretch but lean relief on earth can find.

FROM *Antonio's Revenge*, 1602

PROLOGUE

The rawish dank of clumsy winter ramps
The fluent summer's vein; and drizzling sleet
Chilleth the wan bleak cheek of the numbed earth,
While snarling gusts nibble the juiceless leaves
From the nak'd shuddering branch, and pills the skin
From off the soft and delicate aspects.
O now methinks a sullen tragic scene
Would suit the time with pleasing congruence.
May we be happy in our weak devoir,
And all part pleased in most wished content.
But sweat of Hercules can ne'er beget
So blest an issue. Therefore we proclaim,
If any spirit breathes within this round
Uncapable of weighty passion,
(As from his birth being hugged in the arms
And nuzzled 'twixt the breasts of Happiness)
Who winks and shuts his apprehension up
Of common sense of what men were, and are;
Who would not know what men must be; let such
Hurry amain from our black-visaged shows,
We shall affright their eyes. But if a breast
Nailed to the earth with grief, if any heart
Pierced through with anguish pant within this ring,
If there be any blood whose heat is choked
And stifled with true sense of misery;
If aught of these strains fill his consort up,
They arrive most welcome. O that our power
Could lackey or keep wing with our desires,
That with unused poise of style and sense
We might weigh massy in judicious scale!
Yet here's the prop that doth support our hopes;
When our scenes falter or invention halts,
Your favour will give crutches to our faults.

FROM *Satire V*

Ambitious Gorgons, wide-mouthed Lamians,
Shape-changing Proteans, damned Briarians,
Is Minos dead, is Rhadamanth asleep?
That ye thus dare unto Jove's palace creep?
What, hath Rhamnusia spent her knotted whip,
That ye dare strive on Hebe's cup to sip?
Yet know, Apollo's quiver is not spent,
But can abate your daring hardiment.
Python is slain, yet his accursèd race
Dare look divine Astraea in the face;
Chaos returns, and with confusion;
Involves the world with strange disunion;
For Pluto sits in that adorèd chair
Which doth belong unto Minerva's heir.
O hecatombe! O catastrophe!
From Midas' pomp to Irus' beggary!
Prometheus, who celestial fire
Did steal from heaven, therewith to inspire
Our earthly bodies with a senseful mind,
Whereby we might the depth of nature find,
Is dinged to hell, and vulture eats his heart,
Which did such deep philosophy impart
To mortal men; when thieving Mercury,
That even in his new-born infancy
Stole fair Apollo's quiver and Jove's mace,
And would have filched the lightning from his place,
But that he feared he should have burned his wing
And singed his downy feathers' new-come spring;
He that in ghastly shade of night doth lead
Our souls unto the empire of the dead;
When he that better doth deserve a rope
Is a fair planet in our horoscope,
And now hath caduceus in his hand,
Of life and death that hath the sole command.
Thus petty thefts are paid and soundly whipped.
But greater crimes are slightly overslipped;
Nay, he's a god that can do villainy
With a good grace and glib facility.

THOMAS HEYWOOD

(1575?–1650?)

"Pack, Clouds, Away..."

Pack, clouds, away, and welcome, day!
With night we banish sorrow.
Sweet air, blow soft; mount, lark, aloft
To give my love good morrow.
Wings from the wind to please her mind,
Notes from the lark I'll borrow:
Bird, prune thy wing, nightingale, sing,
To give my love good morrow.
To give my love good morrow,
Notes from them all I'll borrow.

Wake from thy nest, robin redbreast!
Sing, birds, in every furrow,
And from each bill let music shrill
Give my fair love good morrow.
Black-bird and thrush in every bush,
Stare, linnet, and cock-sparrow,
You pretty elves, among yourselves
Sing my fair love good morrow.
To give my love good morrow
Sing, birds, in every furrow.

The Rape of Lucrece, 1608

JOHN CHALKHILL

(15—?–16—?)

Coridon's Song

Oh, the sweet contentment
The countryman doth find.
    High trolollie lolly loe,
    High trolollie lee,
That quiet contemplation
Possesseth all my mind:
    Then care away,
    And wend along with me.

For courts are full of flattery,
As hath too oft been tried;
   High trolollie lollie loe,
   High trolollie lee,
The city full of wantonness,
And both are full of pride.
   Then care away,
   And wend along with me.

But oh, the honest countryman
Speaks truly from his heart,
   High trolollie lollie loe,
   High trolollie lee,
His pride is in his tillage,
His horses and his cart:
   Then care away,
   And wend along with me.

Our clothing is good sheepskins,
Grey russet for our wives,
   High trolollie lollie loe,
   High trolollie lee.
'Tis warmth and not gay clothing
That doth prolong our lives;
   Then care away,
   And wend along with me.

The ploughman though he labour hard,
Yet on the holy-day,
   High trolollie lollie loe,
   High trolollie lee,
No emperor so merrily
Does pass his time away;
   Then care away,
   And wend along with me.

To recompense our tillage
The heavens afford us showers;
   High trolollie lollie loe,
   High trolollie lee.

And for our sweet refreshments
The earth affords us bowers:
   Then care away,
   And wend along with me.

The cuckoo and the nightingale
Full merrily do sing,
   High trolollie lollie loe,
   High trolollie lee.
And with their pleasant roundelays
Bid welcome in the spring:
   Then care away,
   And wend along with me.

This is not half the happiness
The countryman enjoys;
   High trolollie lollie loe,
   High trolollie lee.
Though others think they have as much
Yet he that says so lies:
   Then come away, turn
   Countryman with me.

CYRIL TOURNEUR
(1575?–1626)
FROM *The Atheist's Tragedy*, 1611

Borachio: Walking next day upon the fatal shore,
Among the slaughtered bodies of their men
Which the full-stomached sea had cast upon
The sands, it was my unhappy chance to light
Upon a face, whose favour when it lived,
My astonished mind informed me I 'had seen.
He lay in's armour, as if that had been
His coffin; and the weeping sea, like one
Whose milder temper doth lament the death
Of him whom in his rage he slew, runs up
The shore, embraces him, kisses his cheek,
Goes back again, and forces up the sands
To bury him, and every time it parts

Sheds tears upon him, till at last (as if
It could no longer endure to see the man
Whom it had slain, yet loath to leave him) with
A kind of unresolved unwilling pace,
Winding her waves one in another, like
A man that folds his arms or wrings his hands
For grief, ebbed from the body, and descends
As if it would sink down into the earth,
And hide itself for shame of such a deed.

FROM *The Revenger's Tragedy*, 1607
1.

Vendice (addressing his mistress' skull):

My study's ornament, thou shell of death,
Once the bright face of my betrothéd lady,
When life and beauty naturally filled out
These ragged imperfections;
When two heaven-pointed diamonds were set
In those unsightly rings—then 'twas a face
So far beyond the artificial shine
Of any woman's bought complexion,
That the uprightest man (if such there be,
That sin but seven times a day) broke custom,
And made up eight with looking after her.
O, she was able to ha' made a usurer's son
Melt all his patrimony in a kiss;
And what his father fifty yearës told,
To have consumed, and yet his suit been cold.
But, O accurséd palace!
Thee, when thou wert apparelled in the flesh,
The old duke poisoned,
Because thy purer part would not consent
Unto his palsied lust; for old men lustful
Do show like young men angry, eager, violent,
Outbidden like their limited performances.
O, 'ware an old man hot and vicious!
"Age, as in gold, in lust is covetous."
Vengeance, thou murder's quit-rent, and whereby
Thou show'st thyself tenant to tragedy,

O keep thy day, hour, minute, I beseech,
For those thou hast determined. Hum! who e'er
    knew
Murder unpaid? faith, give revenge her due,
She has kept touch hitherto; be merry, merry,
Advance thee, O thou terror to fat folks,
To have their costly three-piled flesh worn off
As bare as this; for banquets, ease and laughter
Can make great men, as greatness goes by clay;
But wise men little are more great than they.

2.

Vendice: And now methinks I could e'en chide myself
For doating on her beauty, though her death
Shall be revenged after no common action.
Does the silkworm expend her yellow labours
For thee? For thee does she undo herself?
Are lordships sold to maintain ladyships,
For the poor benefit of a bewildering minute?
Why does yon fellow falsify highways,
And put his life between the judge's lips,
To refine such a thing—keeps horse and men
To beat their valours for her?
Surely we are all mad people, and they
Whom we think are, are not; we mistake those;
'Tis we are mad in sense, they but in clothes.

Does every proud and self-affecting dame
Camphire her face for this, and grieve her Maker
In sinful baths of milk, when many an infant starves
For her superfluous outside—all for this?
Who now bids twenty pounds a night? prepares
Music, perfumes, and sweetmeats? All are hushed.
Thou may'st lie chaste now! it were fine, methinks,
To have thee seen at revels, forgetful feasts,
And unclean brothels! sure, 'twould fright the sin-
    ner,
And make him a good coward; put a reveller
Out of his antic amble,
And cloy an epicure with empty dishes.

Here might a scornful and ambitious woman
Look through and through herself. See, ladies, with
    false forms
You deceive men, but cannot deceive worms.

HENRY FARLEY

(15—?–16—?)

"To See a Quaint Outlandish Fowl"

To see a quaint outlandish fowl,
A quaint baboon, an ape, an owl,
A dancing bear, a giant's bone,
A foolish engine move alone,
A morris dance, a puppet-play,
Mad Tom to sing a roundelay,
A woman dancing on a rope,
Bull-baiting also at the *Hope,*
A rimer's jests, a juggler's cheats,
A tumbler showing cunning feats,
Or players acting on the stage—
There goes the bounty of our age:
    But unto any pious motion
    There's little coin and less devotion.

    St. Paul's Church, Her Bill for the Parliament, 1621

JOHN FLETCHER

(1579–1625)

"Hold Back Thy Hours..."

Hold back thy hours, dark Night, till we have done;
    The Day will come too soon;
Young maids will curse thee, if thou steal'st away
And leav'st their losses open to the day:
    Stay, stay, and hide
    The blushes of the bride.

Stay, gentle Night, and with thy darkness cover
    The kisses of her lover;
Stay, and confound her tears and her shrill cryings,
Her weak denials, vows, and often-dyings;
    Stay, and hide all:
    But help not, though she call.

The Maid's Tragedy, 1619

"Lay a Garland on My Hearse"

    Lay a garland on my hearse
        Of the dismal yew;
    Maidens, willow branches bear;
        Say, I died true.

    My love was false, but I was firm
        From my hour of birth.
    Upon my buried body lie
        Lightly, gentle earth!

The Maid's Tragedy, 1619

"Sing His Praises..."

    Sing his praises that doth keep
        Our flocks from harm,
    Pan, the father of our sheep;
        And arm in arm
    Tread we softly in a round,
    Whilst the hollow murmuring ground
    Fills the music with her sound.

    Pan, oh, great god Pan, to thee
        Thus do we sing!
    Thou that keep'st us chaste and free
        As the young spring;
    Ever be thy honour spoke,
    From that place the morn is broke,
    To that place day doth unyoke!

The Faithful Shepherdess, 1609–10

"Now the Lusty Spring..."

Now the lusty spring is seen;
  Golden yellow, gaudy blue,
  Daintily invite the view.
Everywhere on every green,
Roses blushing as they blow,
  And enticing men to pull,
Lilies whiter than the snow,
  Woodbines of sweet honey full:
    All love's emblems, and all cry,
    "Ladies, if not plucked, we die."

Yet the lusty spring hath stayed;
  Blushing red and purest white
  Daintily to love invite
Every woman, every maid.
Cherries kissing as they grow,
  And inviting men to taste,
Apples even ripe below,
  Winding gently to the waist:
    All love's emblems, and all cry,
    "Ladies, if not plucked, we die."

The Tragedy of Valentinian, 1619?

"Hear, Ye Ladies..."

Hear, ye ladies that despise,
  What the mighty Love has done;
Fear examples, and be wise:
  Fair Callisto was a nun;
Leda, sailing on the stream
  To deceive the hopes of man,
Love accounting but a dream,
  Doted on a silver swan;
    Danaë, in a brazen tower,
    Where no love was, loved a shower.

Hear, ye ladies that are coy,
    What the mighty Love can do;
Fear the fierceness of the boy:
    The chaste moon he makes to woo;
Vesta, kindling holy fires,
    Circled round about with spies,
Never dreaming loose desires,
    Doting at the altar dies;
        Ilion, in a short hour, higher
        He can build, and once more fire.

The Tragedy of Valentinian, 1619?

"Care-Charming Sleep..."

Care-charming Sleep, thou easer of all woes,
Brother to Death, sweetly thyself dispose
On this afflicted prince; fall like a cloud,
In gentle showers; give nothing that is loud,
Or painful to his slumbers; easy, light,
And as a purling stream, thou son of Night,
Pass by his troubled senses; sing his pain,
Like hollow murmuring wind or silver rain;
Into this prince gently, oh, gently slide,
And kiss him into slumbers like a bride.

The Tragedy of Valentinian, 1619?

"God Lyaeus, Ever Young"

God Lyaeus, ever young,
Ever honoured, ever sung,
Stained with blood of lusty grapes,
In a thousand lusty shapes,
Dance upon the mazer's brim,
In the crimson liquor swim;
From thy plenteous hand divine,
Let a river run with wine:
    God of youth, let this day here
    Enter neither care nor fear.

The Tragedy of Valentinian, 1619?

"Cast Our Caps and Cares Away"

Cast our caps and cares away:
This is beggars' holiday!
At the crowning of our king,
Thus we ever dance and sing.
In the world look out and see,
Where so happy a prince as he?
Where the nation lives so free,
And so merry as do we?
Here at liberty we are,
And enjoy our ease and rest:
To the field we are not pressed;
Nor are called into the town,
To be troubled with the gown.
Hang all offices, we cry,
And the magistrate too, by!
When the subsidy's increased,
We are not a penny sessed;
Nor will any go to law
With the beggar for a straw.
All which happiness, he brags,
He doth owe unto his rags.

Beggars' Bush, 1622

"Dearest, Do Not You Delay Me"

Dearest, do not you delay me,
  Since, thou knowest, I must be gone;
Wind and tide, 'tis thought, doth stay me,
  But 'tis wind that must be blown
    From that breath, whose native smell
    Indian odours far excel.

Oh, then speak, thou fairest fair!
  Kill not him that vows to serve thee;
But perfume this neighbouring air,
  Else dull silence, sure, will sterve me:
    'Tis a word that's quickly spoken,
    Which being restrained, a heart is broken.

The Spanish Curate, 1622

"'*Tis Late and Cold...*"

'Tis late and cold; stir up the fire;
Sit close, and draw the table nigher;
Be merry, and drink wine that's old,
A hearty medicine 'gainst a cold:
Your beds of wanton down the best,
Where you shall tumble to your rest;
I could wish you wenches too,
But I am dead, and cannot do.
Call for the best the house may ring,
Sack, white, and claret, let them bring,
And drink apace, while breath you have;
You'll find but cold drink in the grave:
Plover, partridge, for your dinner,
And a capon for the sinner,
You shall find ready when you're up,
And your horse shall have his sup:
Welcome, welcome, shall fly round,
And I shall smile, though under ground.

The Lovers' Progress, 1623?

"*Hence, All You Vain Delights*"

Hence, all you vain delights,
As short as are the nights
Wherein you spend your folly!
There's nought in this life sweet,
If man were wise to see't,
 But only melancholy,
  Oh, sweetest melancholy!
Welcome, folded arms, and fixéd eyes,
A sight that piercing mortifies,
A look that's fastened to the ground,
A tongue chained up without a sound!

Fountain-heads, and pathless groves,
Places which pale passion loves!
Moonlight walks, when all the fowls

Are warmly housed, save bats and owls!
A midnight bell, a parting groan!
These are the sounds we feed upon;
Then stretch our bones in a still gloomy valley,
Nothing's so dainty sweet as lovely melancholy.

The Nice Valour, 16—?

"Beauty Clear and Fair"

Beauty clear and fair,
    Where the air
Rather like a perfume dwells;
    Where the violet and rose
    Their blue veins and blush disclose,
And come to honour nothing else.

Where to live near,
    And planted there,
Is to live, and still live new;
    Where to gain a favour is
    More than light, perpetual bliss—
Make me live by serving you.

Dear, again back recall
    To this light,
A stranger to himself and all;
    Both the wonder and the story
    Shall be yours, and eke the glory:
I am your servant, and your thrall.

The Elder Brother, 1637

"Drink To-day..."

Drink to-day, and drown all sorrow,
You shall perhaps not do't to-morrow.
Best while you have it use your breath;
There is no drinking after death.

Wine works the heart up, wakes the wit,
There is no cure 'gainst age but it.
It helps the head-ache, cough and phthisic,
And is for all diseases physic.

Then let us swill, boys, for our health;
Who drinks well, loves the commonwealth.
And he that will to bed go sober,
Falls with the leaf, still in October.

The Bloody Brother, 1639

"Hide, Oh, Hide Those Hills..."

Hide, oh, hide those hills of snow,
    Which thy frozen bosom bears,
On whose tops the pinks that grow
    Are of those that April wears;
But first set my poor heart free,
Bound in those icy chains by thee.

The Bloody Brother, 1639

"Tell Me, Dearest..."

Tell me, dearest, what is love?
'Tis a lightning from above;
    'Tis an arrow, 'tis a fire,
    'Tis a boy they call Desire.
        'Tis a grave
        Gapes to have
Those poor fools that long to prove.

Tell me more, are women true?
Yes, some are, and some as you.
    Some are willing, some are strange,
    Since you men first taught to change.
        And till troth
        Be in both,
All shall love, to love anew.

Tell me more yet, can they grieve?
Yes, and sicken sore, but live:
And be wise, and delay,
When you men are as wise as they.
Then I see,
Faith will be,
Never till they both believe.

The Captain, 1613?

"Away, Delights..."

Away, delights; go seek some other dwelling,
For I must die:
Farewell, false love; thy tongue is ever telling
Lie after lie.
For ever let me rest now from thy smarts;
Alas, for pity go,
And fire their hearts
That have been hard to thee; mine was not so.

Never again deluding Love shall know me,
For I will die;
And all those griefs that think to overgrow me,
Shall be as I:
For ever will I sleep, while poor maids cry,
"Alas, for pity stay,
And let us die
With thee; men cannot mock us in the clay."

The Captain, 1613?

"Weep No More..."

Weep no more, nor sigh nor groan,
Sorrow calls no time that's gone;
Violets plucked, the sweetest rain
Makes not fresh nor grow again;
Trim thy locks, look cheerfully,

Fate's hidden ends eyes cannot see.
Joys as wingéd dreams fly fast,
Why should sadness longer last?
Grief is but a wound to woe;
Gentlest fair, mourn, mourn no moe.

The Queen of Corinth, 1617?

"Roses Their Sharp Spines..."

Roses their sharp spines being gone,
Not royal in their smells alone,
    But in their hue;
Maiden pinks of odour faint,
Daisies smell-less, yet most quaint,
    And sweet thyme true;

Primrose, first-born child of Ver,
Merry spring-time's harbinger,
    With her bells dim;
Oxlips in their cradles growing,
Marigolds on death-beds blowing,
    Lark-heels trim;

All, dear Nature's children sweet,
Lie 'fore bride and bridegroom's feet,
    Blessing their sense!
Not an angel of the air,
Bird melodious or bird fair,
    Be absent hence!

The crow, the slanderous cuckoo, nor
The boding raven, nor chough hoar,
    Nor chattering pie,
May on our bridehouse perch or sing,
Or with them any discord bring,
    But from it fly.

[*Also attributed to* WILLIAM SHAKESPEARE]
The Two Noble Kinsmen, 1634

"Orpheus with His Lute..."

Orpheus with his lute made trees,
And the mountain tops that freeze,
    Bow themselves when he did sing:
To his music plants and flowers
Ever sprung, as sun and showers,
    There had made a lasting spring.

Every thing that heard him play,
Even the billows of the sea,
    Hung their heads, and then lay by.
In sweet music is such art,
Killing care and grief of heart
    Fall asleep, or hearing die.

[Also attributed to WILLIAM SHAKESPEARE]
King Henry VIII, 1613

FROM *The Faithful Shepherdess*

1.

Here be grapes, whose lusty blood
Is the learned poets' good,
Sweeter yet did never crown
The head of Bacchus; nuts more brown
Than the squirrel's teeth that crack them;
Deign, oh, fairest fair, to take them.
For these black-eyed Dryope
Hath often times commanded me
With my claspéd knee to climb:
See how well the lusty time
Hath decked their rising cheeks in red,
Such as on your lips is spread.
Here be berries for a queen,
Some be red, some be green;
These are of that luscious meat,
The great god Pan himself doth eat:
All these, and what the woods can yield,
The hanging mountain or the field,
I freely offer, and ere long
Will bring you more, more sweet and strong.

2.

> Here be woods as green
> As any, air likewise as fresh and sweet
> As where smooth Zephyrus plays on the fleet
> Face of the curléd streams, with flowers as many
> As the young spring gives, and as choice as any;
> Here be all new delights, cool streams and wells,
> Arbours o'ergrown with woodbines; caves, and dells;
> Choose where thou wilt, whilst I sit by and sing,
> Or gather rushes, to make thee a ring
> For thy pale fingers; tell thee tales of love,
> How the pale Phoebe, hunting in a grove,
> First saw the boy Endymion, from whose eyes
> She took eternal fire that never dies;
> How she convey'd him softly in a sleep,
> His temples bound with poppy, to the steep
> Head of old Latmus, where she stoops each night,
> Gilding the mountain with her brother's light,
> To kiss her sweetest.

3.

> Shall I stray
> In the middle air, and stay
> The sailing rack, or nimbly take
> Hold by the moon, and gently make
> Suit to the pale queen of night
> For a beam to give thee light?
> Shall I dive into the sea,
> And bring thee coral, making way
> Through the rising waves that fall
> In snowy fleeces? Dearest, shall
> I catch thee wanton fawns, or flies
> Whose woven wings the summer dyes
> Of many colours? get thee fruit,
> Or steal from Heaven old Orpheus' lute?
> All these I'll venture for, and more,
> To do her service all these woods adore.

Holy virgin, I will dance
Round about these woods as quick
As the breaking light, and prick
Down the lawns, and down the vales
Faster than the windmill-sails.
So I take my leave, and pray
All the comforts of the day,
Such as Phoebus' heat doth send
On the earth, may still befriend
Thee and this arbour!

JOHN WEBSTER

(1580–1630?)

"Call for the Robin..."

Call for the robin redbreast and the wren,
Since o'er shady groves they hover,
And with leaves and flowers do cover
The friendless bodies of unburied men.
Call unto his funeral dole
The ant, the field-mouse and the mole,
To rear him hillocks that shall keep him warm,
And (when gay tombs are robbed) sustain no harm;
But keep the wolf far thence, that's foe to men,
For with his nails he'll dig them up again.

The White Devil, 1612

"Hark, Now Everything Is Still"

Hark, now everything is still,
The screech-owl and the whistler shrill,
Call upon our dame aloud,
And bid her quickly don her shroud!
Much you had of land and rent;
Your length in clay's now competent:
A long war disturbed your mind;
Here your perfect peace is signed.
Of what is't fools make such vain keeping?

Sin their conception, their birth weeping,
Their life a general mist of error,
Their death a hideous storm of terror.
Strew your hair with powders sweet,
Don clean linen, bathe your feet,
And (the foul fiend more to check)
A crucifix let bless your neck:
'Tis now full tide 'tween night and day;
End your groan, and come away.

The Duchess of Malfi, 1623

"All the Flowers of the Spring"

All the flowers of the spring
Meet to perfume our burying;
These have but their growing prime,
And man does flourish but his time:
Survey our progress from our birth;
We are set, we grow, we turn to earth.
Courts adieu, and all delights,
All bewitching appetites!
Sweetest breath and clearest eye,
Like perfumes, go out and die;
And consequently this is done
As shadows wait upon the sun.
Vain the ambition of kings
Who seek by trophies and dead things
To leave a living name behind,
And weave but nets to catch the wind.

The Devil's Law Case, 1623

RICHARD CORBET
(1582–1635)

FROM *The Fairies' Farewell*

Farewell, rewards and fairies,
    Good housewives now may say,
For now foul sluts in dairies
    Do fare as well as they.

And though they sweep their hearths no less
    Than maids were wont to do,
Yet who of late for cleanliness
    Finds sixpence in her shoe?

Lament, lament, old abbeys,
    The fairies' lost command;
They did but change priests' babies,
    But some have changed your land;
And all your children sprung from thence
    Are now grown puritans,
Who live as changelings ever since
    For love of your demesnes.

At morning and at evening both
    You merry were and glad,
So little care of sleep or sloth
    These pretty ladies had;
When Tom came home from labour
    Or Ciss to milking rose,
Then merrily went their tabor
    And nimbly went their toes.

Witness those rings and roundelays
    Of theirs, which yet remain,
Were footed in queen Mary's days
    On many a grassy plain;
But since of late Elizabeth
    And later James came in,
They never danced on any heath
    As when the time hath bin.

PHINEAS FLETCHER

(1582–1650)

FROM *The Purple Island*

But ah! let me under some Kentish hill
Near rolling Medway 'mong my shepherd peers,
With fearless merry-make and piping still,

Securely pass my few and slow-paced years:
  While yet the great Augustus of our nation
  Shuts up old Janus in this long cessation,
Strengthening our pleasing ease, and gives us sure vacation.

There may I, master of a little flock,
Feed my poor lambs, and often change their fare:
My lovely mate shall tend my sparing stock,
And nurse my little ones with pleasing care;
  Whose love and look shall speak their father plain.
  Health be my feast, Heaven hope, content my gain:
So in my little house my lesser heart shall reign.

The beech shall yield a cool safe canopy,
While down I sit, and chant to th'echoing wood:
Ah, singing might I live and singing die!
So by fair Thames or silver Medway's flood,
  The dying swan, when years her temples pierce,
  In music-strains breathes out her life and verse;
And chanting her own dirge rides on her wat'ry hearse.

What shall I then need seek a patron out,
Or beg a favour from a mistress' eyes,
To fence my song against the vulgar rout,
Or shine upon me with her Geminis?
  What care I, if they praise my slender song?
  Or reck I, if they do me right or wrong?
A shepherd's bliss nor stands nor falls to ev'ry tongue.

FROM *Elisa, or an Elegy upon the Unripe Decease*
of Sir Antony Irby

My dearest Betty, my more lovéd heart,
I leave thee now; with thee all earthly joying:
Heaven knows, with thee alone I sadly part:
All other earthly sweets have had their cloying;
  Yet never full of thy sweet love's enjoying,
  Thy constant loves, next Heaven I did refer them:
Had not much grace prevailed 'fore Heaven I should prefer
  them.

I leave them now the trumpet calls away;
In vain thine eyes beg for some time's reprieving;
Yet in my children here immortal stay:
In one I die, in many ones am living:
   In them and for them stay thy too much grieving:
   Look but on them, in them thou still wilt see
Married with thee again thy twice-two Antony.

And when with little hands they stroke thy face,
As in thy lap they sit (ah careless) playing,
And stammering ask a kiss, give them a brace;
The last from me: and then a little staying
   And in their face some part of me surveying,
   In them give me a third, and with a tear
Show thy dear love to him who loved thee ever dear.

And now our falling house leans all on thee;
This little nation to thy care commend them:
In thee it lies that hence they want not me;
Themselves yet cannot, thou the more, defend them;
   And when green age permits to goodness bend them:
   A mother were you once, now both you are:
Then with this double style double your love and care.

Turn their unwary steps into the way:
What first the vessel drinks, it long retaineth;
No bars will hold when they have used to stray:
And when for me one asks and weeping plaineth,
   Point thou to Heaven, and say, he there remaineth:
   And if they live in grace, grow and persever,
There shall they live with me: else shall they see me never.

My God, oh, in Thy fear here let them live;
Thy wards are they, take them to Thy protection:
Thou gav'st them first, now back to Thee I give;
Direct then Thou, and help her weak direction;
   That reunited by Thy strong election,
   Thou now in them, they then may live in Thee;
And seeing here Thy will, may there Thy glory see.

Betty, let these last words long with thee dwell:
If yet a second hymen do expect thee,
Though well he love thee, once I loved as well:
Yet if his presence make thee less respect me,
   Ah, do not in my children's good neglect me:
   Let me this faithful hope departing have;
More easy shall I die, and sleep in careless grave.

Farewell, farewell; I feel my long long rest,
And iron sleep my leaden heart oppressing:
Night after day, sleep after labour's best;
Port after storms, joy after long distressing:
   So weep thy loss, as knowing 'tis my blessing:
   Both as a widow and a Christian grieve:
Still live I in thy thoughts, but as in Heaven I live.

SIR JOHN BEAUMONT

(1583–1627)

FROM *Of My Dear Son, Gervase Beaumont*

Can I, who have for others oft compiled
The songs of Death, forget my sweetest child,
Which like a flower crushed, with a blast is dead,
And ere full time hangs down his smiling head,
Expecting with clear hope to live anew,
Among the angels fed with heavenly dew?

Dear Lord, receive my son, whose winning love
To me was like a friendship, far above
The course of nature or his tender age,
Whose looks could all my bitter griefs assuage;
Let his pure soul ordained sev'n years to be
In that frail body, which was part of me,
Remain my pledge in Heav'n, as sent to show
How to this port at ev'ry step I go.

LORD HERBERT OF CHERBURY
(1583–1648)

Sonnet

Thus ends my love, but this doth grieve me most
    That so it ends; but that ends too; this yet
Besides the wishes, hopes and time I lost
    Troubles my mind awhile, that I am set
Free, worse than denied. I can neither boast
    Choice nor success, as my case is, nor get
Pardon from myself that I loved not
    A better mistress, or her worse. This debt
Only's her due still, that she be forgot
    Ere changed lest I love none; this done, the taint
    Of foul inconstancy is cleared at least
In me. There only rests but to unpaint
    Her form in my mind, that so dispossest
It be a temple, but without a saint.

Madrigal

    How should I love my best?
What though my love unto that height be grown
    That taking joy in you alone
    I utterly this world detest;
Should I not love it as the only place
    Where beauty hath his perfect grace
    And is possest?

    But I beauties despise;
You universal beauty seem to me,
    Giving and showing form and degree
    To all the rest in your fair eyes;
Yet should I not love them as parts whereon
    Your beauty, their perfection
    And top, doth rise?

But even myself I hate;
So far my love is from the least delight
  That at my very self I spite,
    Senseless of any happy state;
Yet may I not with justest reason fear
  How hating her I truly her
    Can celebrate?

  Thus unresolvéd still
Although world, life, nay what is fair beside
  I cannot for your sake abide,
    Methinks I love not to my fill;
Yet if a greater love you can devise
  In love you some other wise,
    Believe't, I will.

Kissing

Come hither Womankind and all their worth,
Give me thy kisses as I call them forth.
Give me the billing-kiss, that of the dove,
    A kiss of love;
The melting-kiss, a kiss that doth consume
    To a perfume;
The extract-kiss, of every sweet a part,
    A kiss of art;
The kiss which ever stirs some new delight,
    A kiss of might;
The twaching smacking kiss, and when you cease
    A kiss of peace;
The music-kiss, crotchet and quaver time,
    The kiss of rhyme;
The kiss of eloquence, which doth belong
    Unto the tongue;
The kiss of all the sciences in one,
    The Kiss alone.
So 'tis enough.

Elegy over a Tomb

Must I then see, alas! eternal night
  Sitting upon those fairest eyes,
And closing all those beams, which once did rise
  So radiant and bright,
That light and heat in them to us did prove
  Knowledge and Love?

Oh, if you did delight no more to stay
  Upon this low and earthly stage,
But rather chose an endless heritage,
  Tell us at least, we pray,
Where all the beauties that those ashes owed
  Are now bestowed?

Doth the Sun now his light with yours renew?
  Have Waves the curling of your hair?
Did you restore unto the Sky and Air,
  The red and white and blue?
Have you vouchsafed to flowers since your death
  That sweetest breath?

Had not Heaven's Lights else in their houses slept,
  Or to some private life retired?
Must not the Sky and Air have else conspired,
  And in their Regions wept?
Must not each flower else the earth could breed
  Have been a weed?

But thus enriched, may we not yield some cause
  Why they themselves lament no more?
That must have changed the course they held before,
  And broke their proper laws,
Had not your beauties given this second birth
  To Heaven and Earth?

Tell us, for Oracles must still ascend,
  For those that crave them at your tomb;
Tell us, where are those beauties now become,
  And what they now intend;
Tell us, alas, that cannot tell our grief,
  Or hope relief.

FROM *An Ode upon a Question Moved,* *Whether Love Should Continue for Ever?*

> O no, beloved, I am most sure
>   Those virtuous habits we acquire,
>   As being with the Soul entire,
> Must with it evermore endure.
>
> For if where sins and vice reside
>   We find so foul a guilt remain,
>   As never dying in his stain
> Still punished in the Soul doth bide;
>
> Much more that true and real joy
>   Which in a virtuous love is found
>   Must be more solid in its ground
> Than Fate or Death can e'er destroy.
>
> Else should our Souls in vain elect,
>   And vainer yet were Heaven's laws,
>   When to an everlasting Cause
> They gave a perishing Effect.
>
> Nor here on earth, then, nor above,
>   Our good affection can impair;
>   For where God doth admit the fair,
> Think you that he excludeth Love?

WILLIAM BASSE

(1583?–1653?)

On Mr. Wm. Shakespeare

Renowned Spenser lie a thought more nigh
To learned Chaucer, and rare Beaumont lie
A little nearer Spenser, to make room
For Shakespeare in your threefold, fourfold tomb.
To lodge all four in one bed make a shift
Until doomsday, for hardly will a fift
Betwixt this day and that by Fate be slain,
For whom your curtains may be drawn again.

If your precedency in death doth bar
A fourth place in your sacred sepulchre,
Under this carvéd marble of thine own,
Sleep, rare tragedian, Shakespeare, sleep alone;
Thy unmolested peace, unsharéd cave,
Possess as Lord, not tenant, of thy grave,
That unto us and others it may be
Honour hereafter to be laid by thee.

PHILIP MASSINGER

(1583–1640)

Song

The blushing rose and purple flower,
  Let grow too long, are soonest blasted;
Dainty fruit, though sweet, will sour,
  And rot in ripeness, left untasted.
Yet here is one more sweet than these;
The more you taste, the more she'll please.

Beauty that's enclosed with ice,
  Is a shadow chaste as rare;
Then how much those sweets entice,
  That have issue full as fair!
Earth cannot yield from all her powers
One equal for dame Venus' bowers.

The Picture, 1629

Song

Why art thou slow, thou rest of trouble, Death,
  To stop a wretch's breath,
That calls on thee, and offers her sad heart
  A prey unto thy dart?
I am nor young nor fair; be, therefore, bold;
  Sorrow hath made me old,
Deformed and wrinkled; all that I can crave
  Is, quiet in my grave.

Such as live happy hold long life a jewel;
    But to me thou art cruel,
If thou end not my tedious misery;
    And I soon cease to be.
Strike, and strike home, then; pity unto me
    In one short hour's delay, is tyranny.

The Emperor of the East, 1631

FRANCIS BEAUMONT

(1584–1616)

"Shake Off Your Heavy Trance!"

Shake off your heavy trance!
    And leap into a dance
Such as no mortals use to tread:
    Fit only for Apollo
To play to, for the moon to lead,
    And all the stars to follow!

The Masque of the Inner Temple, 1612–3

"Ye Should Stay Longer..."

Ye should stay longer if we durst:
    Away! Alas that he that first
Gave Time wild wings to fly away—
Hath now no power to make him stay!
And though these games must needs be played,
I would this pair, when they are laid,
    And not a creature nigh 'em,
Could catch his scythe, as he doth pass,
And clip his wings, and break his glass,
    And keep him ever by 'em.

The Masque of the Inner Temple, 1612–3

On the Marriage of a Beauteous Young Gentlewoman with an Ancient Man

Fondly, too curious Nature, to adorn
Aurora with the blushes of the morn:
Why do her rosy lips breathe gums and spice
Unto the East, and sweet to Paradise?
Why do her eyes open the day? her hand
And voice entrance the panther, and command
Incenséd winds; her breasts, the tents of love,
Smooth as the godded swan or Venus' dove,
Soft as the balmy dew whose every touch
Is pregnant—but why those rich spoils, when such
Wonder and perfection must be led
A bridal captive unto Tithon's bed?
Aged and deforméd Tithon! Must thy twine
Circle and blast at once what care and time
Had made for wonder? Must pure beauty have
No other foil but ruin and a grave?
So have I seen the pride of Nature's store,
The orient pearl, chained to the sooty Moor;
So hath the diamond's bright ray been set
In night and wedded to the negro jet.
See, see, how thick those showers of pearl do fall
To weep her ransom or her funeral;
Whose every treasured drop congealed might bring
Freedom and ransom to a fettered king;
While tyrant Wealth stands by, and laughs to see
How he can wed love and antipathy.
Hymen, thy pine burns with adulterate fire.
Thou and thy quivered boy did once conspire
To mingle equal flames, and then no shine
Of gold, but beauty dressed the Paphian shrine.
Roses and lilies kissed; the amorous vine
Did with the fair and straight-limbed elm entwine.

On the Tombs in Westminster Abbey

Mortality, behold and fear,
What a change of flesh is here!
Think how many royal bones
Sleep within this heap of stones;
Here they lie had realms and lands,
Who now want strength to stir their hands;
Where, from their pulpits sealed with dust,
They preach: "In greatness is no trust."
Here's an acre sown indeed
With the richest royalest seed
That the earth did e'er suck in
Since the first man died for sin.
Here the bones of birth have cried:
"Though gods they were, as men they died."
Here are sands, ignoble things,
Dropt from the ruined sides of kings.
Here's a world of pomp and state
Buried in dust, once dead by fate.

FROM Mr. Francis Beaumont's Letter to Ben Jonson

The sun, which doth the greatest comfort bring
To absent friends, because the self-same thing
They know they see, however absent, is
Here our best hay-maker—forgive me this!
It is our country style. In this warm shine
I lie and dream of your full Mermaid wine.

Methinks the little wit I had is lost
Since I saw you; for wit is like a rest
Held up at tennis, which men do the best
With the best gamesters. What things have we seen
Done at the Mermaid! Heard words that have been
So nimble and so full of subtle flame
As if that every one from whence they came
Had meant to put his whole wit in a jest,
And had resolved to live a fool the rest

Of his dull life. Then when there hath been thrown
Wit able enough to justify the town
For three days past, wit that might warrant be
For the whole city to talk foolishly
Till that were cancelled, and when that was gone
We left an air behind us which alone
Was able to make the two next companies
Right witty, though but downright fools mere wise.

WILLIAM DRUMMOND OF HAWTHORNDEN

(1585-1649)

Madrigal

Like the Idalian Queen,
Her hair about her eyne,
With neck and breasts' ripe apples to be seen,
At first glance of the Morn
In Cyprus' gardens gathering those fair flowers
Which of her blood were born,
I saw, but fainting saw, my paramours.
The Graces naked danced about the place,
The winds and trees amazed
With silence on her gazed,
The flowers did smile, like those upon her face,
And as their aspen stalks those fingers band,
That she might read my case,
A hyacinth I wished me in her hand.

Sonnet

Dear quirister, who from those shadows sends,
Ere that the blushing dawn dare show her light,
Such sad lamenting strains that night attends
Become all ear, stars stay to hear thy plight;
If one whose grief even reach of thought transcends,
Who ne'er, not in a dream, did taste delight,
May thee importune who like case pretends
And seems to joy in woe, in woe's despite;

Tell me, so may thou Fortune milder try
And long, long sing, for what thou thus complains?
Sith, winter gone, the sun in dappled sky
Now smiles on meadows, mountains, woods and plains?
The bird, as if my questions did her move,
With trembling wings sobbed forth, *I love, I love.*

Song

Phoebus, arise,
And paint the sable skies
With azure, white and red:
Rouse Memnon's mother from her Tithon's bed
That she thy cariere may with roses spread,
The nightingales thy coming each where sing,
Make an eternal spring,
Give life to this dark world which lieth dead.
Spread forth thy golden hair
In larger locks than thou wast wont before,
And emperor-like decore
With diadem of pearl thy temples fair;
Chase hence the ugly night
Which serves but to make dear thy glorious light.
This is that happy morn,
That day, long-wished day,
Of all my life so dark,
(If cruel stars have not my ruin sworn,
And fates not hope betray)
Which, only white, deserves
A diamond for ever should it mark:
This is the morn should bring into this grove
My love to hear and recompense my love.
Fair king, who all preserves,
But show thy blushing beams,
And thou two sweeter eyes
Shalt see than those which by Peneus' streams
Did once thy heart surprise,
Nay, suns which shine as clear
As thou when two thou did to Rome appear.
Now, Flora, deck thyself in fairest guise;

If that ye, winds, would hear
A voice surpassing far Amphion's lyre,
Your stormy chiding stay,
Let zephyr only breathe
And with her tresses play,
Kissing sometimes those purple ports of death.
The winds all silent are,
And Phoebus in his chair,
Ensaffroning sea and air,
Makes vanish every star:
Night like a drunkard reels
Beyond the hills to shun his flaming wheels.
The fields with flowers are decked in every hue,
The clouds bespangle with bright gold their blue:
Here is the pleasant place
And everything save Her who all should grace.

Sonnet

My lute, be as thou wast when thou didst grow
With thy green mother in some shady grove,
When immelodious winds but made thee move,
And birds on thee their ramage did bestow.
Sith that dear voice which did thy sounds approve,
Which used in such harmonious strains to flow,
Is reft from earth to tune those spheres above,
What art thou but a harbinger of woe?
Thy pleasing notes, be pleasing notes no more,
But orphan wailings to the fainting ear,
Each stop a sigh, each sound draws forth a tear,
Be therefore silent as in woods before;
Or if that any hand to touch thee deign,
Like widowed turtle still her loss complain.

Sonnet

A passing glance, a lightning long the skies
That ush'ring thunder dies straight to our sight,
A spark, of contraries which doth arise,

Then drowns in the huge depths of day and night,
Is this small Small called life, held in such price
Of blinded wights who nothing judge aright:
Of Parthian shaft so swift is not the flight
As life, that wastes itself and living dies.
Oh, what is human greatness, valour, wit?
What fading beauty, riches, honour, praise?
To what doth serve in golden thrones to sit,
Thrall earth's vast round, triumphal arches raise?
All is a dream, learn in this prince's fall,
In whom, save death, naught mortal was at all.

GILES EARLE

(15—?-16—?)

Tom o' Bedlam's Song

From the hag and hungry goblin
That into rags would rend ye,
    And the spirit that stands
    By the naked man
In the book of moons defend ye,
That of your five sound senses
You never be forsaken,
    Nor wander from
    Yourselves with Tom
Abroad to beg your bacon.

While I do sing, "Any food, any feeding,
*   Feeding, drink or clothing?*
*   Come, dame or maid,*
*   Be not afraid,*
*   Poor Tom will injure nothing."*

Of thirty bare years have I
Twice twenty been enragéd,
    And of forty been
    Three times fifteen
In durance sadly cagéd

On the lordly lofts of Bedlam
With stubble soft and dainty,
 Brave bracelets strong,
 Sweet whips, ding-dong,
With wholesome hunger plenty.

And now I do sing, &c.

With a thought I took for Maudlin,
And a cruse of cockle pottage,
 With a thing thus tall,
 Sky bless you all!
I befell into this dotage.
I slept not since the conquest,
Till then I never wakéd,
 Till the roguish boy
 Of love where I lay
Me found and stript me naked.

And now I do sing, &c.

When I short have shorn my sow's face
And swigged my horny barrel
 In an oaken inn
 I pound my skin
As a suit of gilt apparel.
The moon's my constant mistress
And the lowly owl my morrow;
 The flaming drake
 And the night-crow make
Me music to my sorrow.

While I do sing, &c.

The palsy plagues my pulses
When I prig your pigs or pullen,
 Your culvers take,
 Or matchless make
Your chanticleer or sullen—

When I want provant with Humphrey
I sup, and when benighted,
    I repose in Paul's
    With waking souls
Yet never am affrighted.

But I do sing, &c.

I know more than Apollo,
For oft, when he lies sleeping,
    I see the stars
    At bloody wars
In the wounded welkin weeping,
The moon embrace her shepherd
And the queen of love her warrior,
    While the first doth horn
    The star of the morn
And the next the heavenly farrier.

While I do sing, &c.

The gipsy Snap, and Pedro,
Are none of Tom's comradoes;
    The punk I scorn
    And the cutpurse sworn
And the roaring-boys' bravadoes;
The meek, the white, the gentle,
Me handle, touch, and spare not,
    But those that cross
    Tom Rhinoceros
Do what the panther dare not.

Although I do sing, &c.

With a heart of furious fancies
Whereof I am commander,
    With a burning spear
    And a horse of air
To the wilderness I wander;

By a knight of ghosts and shadows
I summoned am to tourney
   Ten leagues beyond
   The wide world's end
—Methinks it is no journey.

Yet will I sing, "Any food, any feeding,
   Feeding, drink or clothing?
    Come, dame or maid,
     Be not afraid,
   Poor Tom will injure nothing."

JOHN FORD

(1586–1639)

"Fly Hence, Shadows ..."

Fly hence, shadows, that do keep
Watchful sorrows, charmed in sleep!
Though the eyes be overtaken,
Yet the heart doth ever waken
Thoughts, chained up in busy snares
Of continual woes and cares;
Love and griefs are so expressed,
As they rather sigh than rest.
Fly hence, shadows, that do keep
Watchful sorrows, charmed in sleep.

The Lover's Melancholy, 1628

"Can You Paint a Thought? ..."

Can you paint a thought? or number
Every fancy in a slumber?
Can you count soft minutes roving
From a dial's point by moving?
Can you grasp a sigh? or, lastly,
Rob a virgin's honour chastely?
No, oh no! yet you may
   Sooner do both that and this,
   This and that, and never miss,

Than by any praise display
  Beauty's beauty; such a glory
  As beyond all fate, all story,
    All arms, all arts,
    All loves, all hearts,
Greater than those or they,
Do, shall, and must obey.

The Broken Heart, 1639

"Oh, No More, No More..."

Oh, no more, no more, too late
  Sighs are spent; the burning tapers
Of a life as chaste as fate,
  Pure as are unwritten papers,
Are burned out; no heat, no light
Now remains; 'tis ever night.

Love is dead; let lovers' eyes,
  Locked in endless dreams,
  Th' extremes of all extremes,
Ope no more, for now Love dies.
Now Love dies—implying
Love's martyrs must be ever, ever dying.

The Broken Heart, 1639

"Glories, Pleasures..."

Glories, pleasures, pomps, delights and ease
    Can but please
The outward senses, when the mind
Is or untroubled or by peace refined.

Crowns may flourish and decay,
Beauties shine, but fade away.

Youth may revel, but it must
Lie down in a bed of dust.

Earthly honours flow and waste,
Time alone doth change and last.

Sorrows mingled with contents, prepare
    Rest for care;
Love only reigns in death; though art
Can find no comfort for a broken heart.

The Broken Heart, 1639

"*Pleasures, Beauty...*"

Pleasures, beauty, youth attend ye,
    Whilst the Spring of nature lasteth;
Love and melting thoughts befriend ye,
    Use the time ere Winter hasteth.
        Active blood and free delight
        Place and privacy invite.
Do, do! be kind as fair,
Lose not opportunity for air.

She is cruel that denies it,
    Bounty best appears in granting,
Stealth of sport as soon supplies it,
    Whilst the dues of love are wanting.
        Here's the sweet exchange of bliss
        When each whisper proves a kiss.
In the game are felt no pains,
For in all the loser gains.

The Lady's Trial, 1638

SIR FRANCIS KYNASTON

(1587–1642)

To Cynthia
(ON CONCEALMENT OF HER BEAUTY)

Do not conceal thy radiant eyes,
The star-light of serenest skies,
Lest wanting of their heavenly light,
They turn to Chaos' endless night.

Do not conceal those tresses fair,
The silken snares of thy curled hair,
Lest finding neither gold nor ore
The curious silkworm work no more.

Do not conceal those breasts of thine,
More snow-white than the Apennine,
Lest if there be like cold or frost
The lily be for ever lost.

Do not conceal that fragrant scent,
Thy breath, which to all flowers hath lent
Perfumes, lest it being supprest
No spices grow in all the East.

Do not conceal thy heavenly voice,
Which makes the hearts of gods rejoice,
Lest Music hearing no such thing
The nightingale forget to sing.

Do not conceal nor yet eclipse
Thy pearly teeth with coral lips,
Lest that the seas cease to bring forth
Gems which from thee have all their worth.

Do not conceal no beauty-grace,
That's either in thy mind or face,
Lest virtue overcome by vice
Make men believe no Paradise.

GEORGE WITHER

(1588–1667)

The Author's Resolution

Shall I wasting in despair
Die because a woman's fair?
Or make pale my cheeks with care
'Cause another's rosy are?
Be she fairer than the day,
Or the flowery meads in May,
    If she think not well of me
    What care I how fair she be?

Shall my silly heart be pined
'Cause I see a woman kind?
Or a well-disposéd nature
Joinéd with a lovely feature?
Be she meeker, kinder than
Turtle-dove or pelican,
    If she be not so to me
    What care I how kind she be?

Shall a woman's virtues move
Me to perish for her love?
Or her well-deservings known
Make me quite forget mine own?
Be she with that goodness blessed
Which may merit name of best,
    If she be not such to me
    What care I how good she be?

'Cause her fortune seems too high,
Shall I play the fool and die?
She that bears a noble mind,
If not outward helps she find,
Thinks what with them he would do
That without them dares her woo;
    And unless that mind I see
    What care I how great she be?

Great, or good, or kind, or fair,
I will ne'er the more despair;
If she loves me, this believe,
I will die, ere she shall grieve;
If she slight me when I woo
I can scorn and let her go,
    For if she be not for me
    What care I for whom she be?

A Love Sonnet

I loved a lass, a fair one,
    As fair as e'er was seen;
She was indeed a rare one,
    Another Sheba queen.

But fool as then I was,
   I thought she loved me too;
But now, alas! sh' 'as left me,
   Falero, lero, loo.

Her hair like gold did glister,
   Each eye was like a star;
She did surpass her sister,
   Which passed all others far.
She would me honey call;
   She'd, O she'd kiss me too;
But now, alas! sh' 'as left me,
   Falero, lero, loo.

In summer time to Medley,
   My love and I would go;
The boatmen there stood ready,
   My love and I to row.
For cream there would we call,
   For cakes, and for prunes too;
But now, alas! sh' 'as left me,
   Falero, lero, loo.

Many a merry meeting
   My love and I have had;
She was my only sweeting,
   She made my heart full glad.
The tears stood in her eyes,
   Like to the morning dew;
But now, alas! sh' 'as left me,
   Falero, lero, loo.

And as abroad we walked,
   As lovers' fashion is,
Oft as we sweetly talked
   The sun should steal a kiss.
The wind upon her lips
   Likewise most sweetly blew;
But now, alas! sh' 'as left me,
   Falero, lero, loo.

Her cheeks were like the cherry,
   Her skin as white as snow;
When she was blithe and merry,
   She angel-like did show.
Her waist exceeding small,
   The fives did fit her shoe;
But now, alas! sh' 'as left me,
   Falero, lero, loo.

In summer time or winter
   She had her heart's desire;
I still did scorn to stint her
   From sugar, sack, or fire.
The world went round about,
   No cares we ever knew;
But now, alas! sh' 'as left me,
   Falero, lero, loo.

As we walked home together
   At midnight through the town,
To keep away the weather
   O'er her I'd cast my gown.
No cold my love should feel,
   Whate'er the heavens could do;
But now, alas! sh' 'as left me,
   Falero, lero, loo.

Like doves we would be billing,
   And clip and kiss so fast;
Yet she would be unwilling
   That I should kiss the last.
They're Judas-kisses now,
   Since that they proved untrue;
For now, alas! sh' 'as left me,
   Falero, lero, loo.

To maidens' vows and swearing
   Henceforth no credit give;
You may give them the hearing,
   But never them believe.

They are as false as fair,
　Unconstant, frail, untrue;
For mine, alas! has left me,
　Falero, lero, loo.

'Twas I that paid for all things,
　'Twas others drank the wine;
I cannot now recall things,
　Live but a fool to pine.
'Twas I that beat the bush,
　The bird to others flew;
For she, alas! hath left me,
　Falero, lero, loo.

If ever that dame Nature,
　For this false lover's sake,
Another pleasing creature
　Like unto her would make,
Let her remember this,
　To make the other true;
For this, alas! hath left me,
　Falero, lero, loo.

No riches now can raise me,
　No want make me despair;
No misery amaze me,
　Not yet for want I care.
I have lost a world itself.
　My earthly heaven, adieu,
Since she, alas! hath left me,
　Falero, lero, loo.

A Christmas Carol

So now is come our joyful'st feast;
Let every man be jolly.
Each room with ivy-leaves is dressed,
And every post with holly.
　Though some churls at our mirth repine
　Round your foreheads garlands twine,
　Drown sorrow in a cup of wine,
And let us all be merry.

Now all our neighbours' chimneys smoke,
And Christmas blocks are burning;
The ovens they with baked meats choke,
And all their spits are turning.
   Without the door let sorrow lie,
   And if for cold it hap to die,
   We'll bury 't in a Christmas pie,
And evermore be merry.

Now every lad is wondrous trim,
And no man minds his labour;
Our lasses have provided them
A bag-pipe and a tabor.
   Young men, and maids, and girls and boys,
   Give life to one another's joys,
   And you anon shall by their noise
Perceive that they are merry.

Rank misers now do sparing shun,
Their hall of music soundeth,
And dogs thence with whole shoulders run,
So all things there aboundeth.
   The country-folk themselves advance,
   For crowdy-mutton's come out of France;
   And Jack shall pipe, and Jill shall dance,
And all the town be merry.

Ned Swash hath fetched his bands from pawn,
And all his best apparel;
Brisk Nell hath bought a ruff of lawn
With droppings of the barrel;
   And those that hardly all the year
   Had bread to eat or rags to wear,
   Will have both clothes and dainty fare,
And all the day be merry.

Now poor men to the justices
With capons make their arrants,
And if they hap to fail of these
They plague them with their warrants.

But now they feed them with good cheer,
And what they want they take in beer,
For Christmas comes but once a year,
And then they shall be merry.

Good farmers in the country nurse
The poor, that else were undone.
Some landlords spend their money worse,
On lust and pride in London.
    There the roysters they do play,
    Drab and dice their land away,
    Which may be ours another day;
And therefore let's be merry.

The client now his suit forbears,
The prisoner's heart is eased,
The debtor drinks away his cares,
And for the time is pleased.
    Though others' purses be more fat,
    Why should we pine or grieve at that?
    Hang sorrow, care will kill a cat,
And therefore let's be merry.

Hark how the wags abroad do call
Each other forth to rambling;
Anon you'll see them in the hall
For nuts and apples scrambling.
    Hark how the roofs with laughters sound!
    Anon they'll think the house goes round,
    For they the cellar's depths have found,
And there they will be merry.

The wenches with their wassail bowls
About the streets are singing,
The boys are come to catch the owls,
The wild mare in is bringing.
    Our kitchen-boy hath broke his box,
    And to the dealing of the ox
    Our honest neighbours come by flocks,
And here they will be merry.

Now kings and queens poor sheepcotes have,
And mate with everybody;
The honest now may play the knave,
And wise men play at noddy.
    Some youths will now a-mumming go,
    Some others play at rowland-hoe,
    And twenty other gameboys moe,
Because they will be merry.

Then wherefore in these merry days
Should we, I pray, be duller?
No; let us sing our roundelays
To make our mirth the fuller.
    And, whilst thus inspired we sing,
    Let all the streets with echoes ring;
    Woods, and hills, and everything,
Bear witness we are merry.

GILES FLETCHER THE YOUNGER
(1588?–1623)
FROM *Christ's Victory in Heaven*
(JUSTICE)

She was a Virgin of austere regard,
Not as the world esteems her, deaf and blind,
But as the eagle, that hath oft compared
Her eye with Heav'n's, so, and more brightly shined
Her lamping sight: for she the same could wind
    Into the solid heart, and with her ears
    The silence of the thought loud speaking hears,
And in one hand a pair of even scales she wears.

The wingéd Lightning is her Mercury,
And round about her mighty thunders sound:
Impatient of himself lies pining by
Pale Sickness, with his kerchered head upwound,
And thousand noisome plagues attend her round,
    But if her cloudy brow but once grow foul,
    The flints do melt and rocks to water roll,
And aery mountains shake and frighted shadows howl.

Upon two stony tables spread before her
She leaned her bosom, more than stony hard,
There slept th' impartial judge and strict restorer
Of wrong or right, with pain or with reward,
There hung the score of all our debts, the card
   Where good and bad, and life and death were painted:
   Was never heart of mortal so untainted,
But when that scroll was read with thousand terrors fainted.

Witness the thunder that Mount Sinai heard,
When all the hill with fiery clouds did flame,
And wandering Israel, with the sight afeared,
Blinded with seeing, durst not touch the same,
But like a wood of shaking leaves became.
   On this dead Justice, she, the living law,
   Bowing herself with a majestic awe,
All Heaven, to hear her speech, did into silence draw.

FROM *Christ's Victory on Earth*

Love is the blossom where there blows
Everything that lives or grows,
Love doth make the heavens to move,
And the Sun doth burn in love;
Love the strong and weak doth yoke,
And makes the ivy climb the oak,
Under whose shadows lions wild,
Softened by love, grow tame and mild;
Love no medicine can appease,
He burns the fishes in the seas,
Not all the skill his wounds can stanch,
Not all the sea his fire can quench;
Love did make the bloody spear
Once a leafy coat to wear,
While in his leaves there shrouded lay
Sweet birds, for love that sing and play;
And of all Love's joyful flame
I the bud and blossom am.
   Only bend thy knee to me,
   Thy wooing shall thy winning be.

See, see the flowers that below
Now as fresh as morning blow,
And of all the virgin rose,
That as bright Aurora shows,
How they all unleavéd die,
Losing their virginity:
Like unto a summer shade,
But now born, and now they fade.
Everything doth pass away,
There is danger in delay,
Come, come gather then the rose,
Gather it, or it you lose.
All the sand of Tagus' shore
Into my bosom casts his ore;
All the valley's swimming corn
To my house is yearly borne;
Every grape of every vine
Is gladly bruised to make me wine.
While ten thousand kings, as proud
To carry up my train have bowed,
And a world of ladies send me
In my chambers to attend me:
All the stars in heaven that shine
And ten thousand more are mine:
    Only bend thy knee to me,
    Thy wooing shall thy winning be.

WILLIAM BROWNE OF TAVISTOCK
(1591–1643?)

FROM *Britannia's Pastorals*

1.

Gentle nymphs, be not refusing,
Love's neglect is time's abusing,
    They and beauty are but lent you,
Take the one and keep the other;
Love keeps fresh what age doth smother;
    Beauty gone, you will repent you.

'Twill be said when ye have proved,
Never swains more truly loved;
    Oh then, fly all nice behaviour.
Pity fain would, as her duty,
Be attending still on beauty,
    Let her not be out of favour.

2.

So shuts the marigold her leaves
    At the departure of the sun;
So from the honeysuckle sheaves
    The bee goes when the day is done;
So sits the turtle when she is but one,
And so all woe, as I, since she is gone.

To some few birds kind Nature hath
    Made all the summer as one day;
Which once enjoyed, cold winter's wrath
    As night they sleeping pass away.
Those happy creatures are that know not yet
The pain to be deprived or to forget.

I oft have heard men say there be
    Some that with confidence profess
The helpful Art of Memory;
    But could they teach forgetfulness
I'd learn, and try what further art could do
To make me love her and forget her too.

FROM *The Inner Temple Masque*

1.

Steer hither, steer your wingéd pines,
    All beaten mariners,
Here lie Love's undiscovered mines,
    A prey to passengers;
Perfumes far sweeter than the best
Which make the Phoenix' urn and nest.
        Fear not your ships,
Nor any to oppose you save our lips,
        But come on shore,
Where no joy dies till love hath gotten more.

2.

> Son of Erebus and Night,
> Hie away; and aim thy flight
> Where consort none other fowl
> Than the bat and sullen owl;
> Where upon thy limber grass
> Poppy and mandragoras,
> With like simples not a few,
> Hang for ever drops of dew.
> Where flows Lethe without coil
> Softly like a stream of oil,
> Hie thee thither, gentle Sleep;
> With this Greek no longer keep.
> Thrice I charge thee by my wand,
> Thrice with moly from my hand
> Do I touch Ulysses' eyes,
> And with the jaspis. Then arise,
> Sagest Greek . . .

"Shall I Love Again..."

Shall I love again, and try
   If I still must love to lose,
And make weak mortality
   Give new birth unto my woes?
No, let me ever live from Love's enclosing,
Rather than love to live in fear of losing.

One whom hasty Nature gives
   To the world without his sight,
Not so discontented lives,
   As a man deprived of light;
'Tis knowledge that gives vigour to our woe,
And not the want but loss that pains us so.

With the Arabian bird then be
   Both the lover and beloved;
Be thy lines thy progeny
   By some gracious fair approved;
So may'st thou live, and be beloved of many,
Without the fear of loss or want of any.

"Welcome, Welcome, Do I Sing"

Welcome, welcome, do I sing,
　　Far more welcome than the spring;
He that parteth from you never
　　Shall enjoy a spring for ever.

Love, that to the voice is near,
　　Breaking from your iv'ry pale,
Need not walk abroad to hear
　　The delightful nightingale.
　　　　　　Welcome, welcome, then I sing, &c.

Love, that looks still on your eyes
　　Though the winter have begun
To benumb our arteries,
　　Shall not want the summer's sun.
　　　　　　Welcome, welcome, then I sing, &c.

Love, that still may see your cheeks
　　Where all rareness still reposes,
Is a fool if e'er he seeks
　　Other lilies, other roses.
　　　　　　Welcome, welcome, then I sing, &c.

Love, to whom your soft lips yields,
　　And perceives your breath in kissing,
All the odours of the fields
　　Never, never shall be missing.
　　　　　　Welcome, welcome, then I sing, &c.

Love, that question would anew
　　What fair Eden was of old,
Let him rightly study you
　　And a brief of that behold.
　　　　　　Welcome, welcome, then I sing, &c.

A Round

Now that the Spring hath filled our veins
　　With kind and active fire,
And made green liveries for the plains,
　　And every grove a choir;

Sing we a song of merry glee,
    And Bacchus fill the bowl.
Then here's to thee! And thou to me
    And every thirsty soul.

Nor care nor sorrow e'er paid debt,
    Nor never shall do mine;
I have no cradle going yet,
    Not I, by this good wine.

No wife at home to send for me,
    No hogs are in my ground,
No suit at law to pay a fee;
    Then round, old jockey, round!

Shear sheep that have them, cry we still,
    But see that no man 'scape
        To drink of the sherry
        That makes us so merry,
    And plump as the lusty grape.

FROM Visions

A rose, as fair as ever saw the north,
Grew in a little garden all alone;
A sweeter flower did Nature ne'er put forth,
Nor fairer garden yet was never known.
The maidens danced about it more and more,
And learned bards of it their ditties made;
The nimble fairies by the pale-faced moon
Watered the root and kissed her pretty shade.
But well-a-day, the gardener careless grew,
The maids and fairies both were kept away,
And in a drought the caterpillars threw
Themselves upon the bud and every spray.
God shield the stock! if Heaven send no supplies,
The fairest blossom of the garden dies.

On the Dowager Countess of Pembroke

Underneath this sable hearse
Lies the subject of all verse,
Sidney's sister, Pembroke's mother;
Death, ere thou hast slain another
Fair and learn'd and good as she,
Time shall throw a dart at thee.

ROBERT HERRICK

(1591–1674)

The Argument of His Book

I sing of Brooks, of Blossoms, Birds and Bowers:
Of April, May, of June, and July-Flowers.
I sing of May-poles, Hock-carts, Wassails, Wakes,
Of Bride-grooms, Brides, and of their Bridal-cakes.
I write of Youth, of Love, and have access
By these, to sing of cleanly-Wantonness.
I sing of Dews, of Rains, and piece by piece
Of Balm, of Oil, of Spice and Ambergris.
I sing of Times trans-shifting; and I write
How Roses first came red, and Lilies white.
I write of Groves, of Twilights, and I sing
The Court of Mab, and of the Fairy-King.
I write of Hell; I sing (and ever shall)
Of Heaven, and hope to have it after all.

Delight in Disorder

A sweet disorder in the dress
Kindles in clothes a wantonness:
A Lawn about the shoulders thrown
Into a fine distraction:
An erring lace, which here and there
Enthralls the crimson stomacher:
A cuff neglectful, and thereby
Ribbons to flow confusedly:

A winning wave (deserving note)
In the tempestuous petticoat:
A careless shoe-string, in whose tie
I see a wild civility:
Do more bewitch me, than when art
Is too precise in every part.

To His Mistress

Choose me your Valentine;
　　Next, let us marry:
Love to the death will pine,
　　If we long tarry.

Promise, and keep your vows,
　　Or vow ye never:
Love's doctrine disallows
　　Troth-breakers ever.

You have broke promise twice
　　(Dear) to undo me;
If you prove faithless thrice,
　　None then will woo ye.

To Dianeme

Sweet, be not proud of those two eyes,
Which star-like sparkle in their skies:
Nor be you proud, that you can see
All hearts your captives; yours, yet free:
Be you not proud of that rich hair,
Which wantons with the love-sick air:
When as that ruby, which you wear,
Sunk from the tip of your soft ear,
Will last to be a precious stone,
When all your world of beauty's gone.

To Violets

Welcome Maids of Honour,
　　You do bring
　　In the Spring;
And wait upon her.

She has virgins many,
　　Fresh and fair;
　　Yet you are
More sweet than any.

Y'are the maiden posies,
　　And so grac'd,
　　To be plac'd,
'Fore damask roses.

Yet though thus respected,
　　By and by
　　Ye do lie
Poor girls, neglected.

The Primrose

Ask me why I send you here
This sweet Infanta of the year?
Ask me why I send to you
This Primrose, thus bepearl'd with dew?
I will whisper in your ears,
The sweets of love are mixed with tears.

Ask me why this flower does show
So yellow-green, and sickly too?
Ask me why the stalk is weak,
And bending, (yet it doth not break?)
I will answer, These discover
What fainting hopes are in a lover.

Upon Julia's Clothes

Whenas in silks my Julia goes,
Then, then, methinks, how sweetly flows
The liquefaction of her clothes!

Next, when I cast mine eyes and see
That brave vibration each way free,
—O how that glittering taketh me!

To the Virgins, to Make Much of Time

Gather ye rose-buds while ye may,
    Old Time is still a-flying:
And this same flower that smiles to-day,
    To-morrow will be dying.

The glorious lamp of Heaven, the sun,
    The higher he's a-getting;
The sooner will his race be run,
    And nearer he's to setting.

That age is best, which is the first,
    When youth and blood are warmer;
But being spent, the worse, and worst
    Times, still succeed the former.

Then be not coy, but use your time;
    And while ye may, go marry:
For having lost but once your prime,
    You may for ever tarry.

FROM The Hock-Cart or Harvest Home

Come sons of Summer, by whose toil,
We are the lords of wine and oil:
By whose tough labours, and rough hands,
We rip up first, then reap our lands.

Crown'd with the ears of corn, now come,
And, to the pipe, sing harvest home.
Come forth, my lord, and see the cart
Dressed up with all the country art.
See, here a maukin, there a sheet,
As spotless pure, as it is sweet:
The horses, mares, and frisking fillies,
Clad, all, in linen, white as Lilies.
The harvest swains, and wenches bound
For joy, to see the Hock-cart crowned.
About the cart, hear, how the rout
Of rural younglings raise the shout;
Pressing before, some coming after,
Those with a shout, and these with laughter.
Some bless the cart; some kiss the sheaves;
Some prank them up with oaken leaves:
Some cross the fill-horse; some with great
Devotion, stroke the home-borne wheat:
While other rustics, less attent
To prayers, than to merriment,
Run after with their breeches rent.
Well, on, brave boys, to your lord's hearth,
Glitt'ring with fire; where for your mirth,
Ye shall see first the large and chief
Foundation of your feast, fat beef:
With upper stories, mutton, veal
And bacon, (which makes full the meal)
With sev'ral dishes standing by,
As here a custard, there a pie,
And here all-tempting frumenty.
And for to make the merry cheer,
If smirking wine be wanting here,
There's that, which drowns all care, stout beer.

To Primroses Fill'd with Morning-Dew

Why do ye weep, sweet babes? Can tears
        Speak grief in you,
        Who were but born
    Just as the modest Morn
    Teem'd her refreshing dew?

Alas, you have not known that shower,
          That mars a flower;
          Nor felt th'unkind
Breath of a blasting wind;
Nor are ye worn with years;
          Or warped, as we,
          Who think it strange to see,
Such pretty flowers, (like to orphans young)
To speak by tears, before ye have a tongue.

Speak, whimp'ring younglings, and make known
          The reason, why
          Ye droop, and weep;
Is it for want of sleep?
Or childish lullaby?
Or that ye have not seen as yet
          The violet?
          Or brought a kiss
From that sweetheart, to this?
No, no, this sorrow shown
          By your tears shed,
          Would have this lecture read,
The things of greatest, so of meanest worth,
Conceiv'd with grief are, and with tears brought forth.

FROM *Oberon's Feast*

A little mushroom table spread,
After short prayers, they set on bread;
A moon-parch'd grain of purest wheat,
With some small glitt'ring grit, to eat
His choice bits with; then in a trice
They make a feast less great than nice.
But all this while his eye is serv'd,
We must not think his ear was starv'd:
But that there was in place to stir
His spleen, the chirring grasshopper;
The merry cricket, puling fly,
The piping gnat for minstrelsy.

And now, we must imagine first,
The elves present to quench his thirst
A pure seed-pearl of infant dew,
Brought and besweetened in a blue
And pregnant violet; which done,
His kitling eyes begin to run
Quite through the table, where he spys
The horns of papery butterflies,
Of which he eats, and tastes a little
Of that we call the cuckoo's spittle.
A little fuzz-ball pudding stands
By, yet not blessed by his hands,
That was too coarse; but then forthwith
He ventures boldly on the pith
Of sugared rush, and eats the sag
And well bestrutted bee's sweet bag:
Gladding his palate with some store
Of emmit's eggs; what would he more?

To Virgins

Hear ye virgins, and I'll teach,
What the times of old did preach.
Rosamund was in a bower
Kept, as Danaë in a tower:
But yet Love (who subtle is)
Crept to that, and came to this.

Be ye locked up like to these,
Or the rich Hesperides;
Or those babies in your eyes,
In their crystal nunneries;
Notwithstanding Love will win,
Or else force a passage in:
And as coy be, as you can,
Gifts will get ye, or the man.

To Daffodils

Fair daffodils, we weep to see
    You haste away so soon:
As yet the early-rising sun
    Has not attain'd his noon.
        Stay, stay,
    Until the hasting day
        Has run
    But to the even-song;
And, having pray'd together, we
    Will go with you along.

We have short time to stay, as you.
    We have as short a Spring;
As quick a growth to meet decay,
    As you, or any thing.
        We die,
    As your hours do, and dry
        Away,
    Like to the Summer's rain;
Or as the pearls of morning's dew
    Ne'er to be found again.

To the Most Fair and Lovely Mistress, Anne Soame,
Now Lady Abdie

So smell those odours that do rise
From out the wealthy spiceries:
So smells the flower of blooming clove;
Or roses smother'd in the stove:
So smells the air of spicéd wine;
Or essences of jessamine:
So smells the breath about the hives,
When all the work of honey thrives;
And all the basic factors come
Laden with wax and honey home:
So smell those neat and woven bowers,
All over-arched with orange flowers;

And almond blossoms, that do mix
To make rich these aromatics:
So smell those bracelets, and those bands
Of amber chaf'd between the hands,
When thus enkindled they transpire
A noble perfume from the fire.
The wine of cherries, and to these
The cooling breath of respasses;
The smell of morning's milk, and cream;
Butter of cowslips mixed with them;
Of roasted warden, or bak'd pear,
These are not to be reckon'd here;
When as the meanest part of her,
Smells like the maiden-pomander.
Thus sweet she smells, or what can be
More lik'd by her, or lov'd by me.

The Mad Maid's Song

Good morrow to the day so fair;
   Good morrow Sir to you:
Good morrow to mine own torn hair
   Bedabbled with the dew.

Good morrow to this primrose too;
   Good morrow to each maid;
That will with flowers the tomb bestrew,
   Wherein my love is laid.

Ah woe is me, woe, woe is me,
   Alack and well-a-day!
For pity, Sir, find out that bee,
   Which bore my love away.

I'll seek him in your bonnet brave;
   I'll seek him in your eyes;
Nay, now I think they've made his grave
   I' th' bed of strawberries.

I'll seek him there; I know, ere this,
　　The cold, cold earth doth shake him;
But I will go, or send a kiss
　　By you, Sir, to awake him.

Pray hurt him not; though he be dead,
　　He knows well who do love him,
And who with green turfs rear his head,
　　And who do rudely move him.

He's soft and tender (pray take heed)
　　With bands of cowslips bind him;
And bring him home, but 'tis decreed,
　　That I shall never find him.

Upon the Nipples of Julia's Breast

Have ye beheld (with much delight)
A red rose peeping through a white?
Or else a cherry (double grac'd)
Within a lily? Centre plac'd?
Or ever mark'd the pretty beam,
A strawberry shows half drown'd in cream?
Or seen rich rubies blushing through
A pure smooth pearl, and orient too?
So like to this, nay all the rest,
Is each neat niplet of her breast.

To the Water Nymphs, Drinking at the Fountain

Reach, with your whiter hands, to me,
　　Some crystal of the spring;
And I, about the cup shall see
　　Fresh lilies flourishing.

Or else sweet nymphs do you but this;
　　To th' glass your lips incline;
And I shall see by that one kiss,
　　The water turn'd to wine.

Upon Her Feet

Her pretty feet
Like snails did creep
A little out, and then,
As if they started at bo-peep,
Did soon draw in again.

To Anthea, Who May Command Him
in Anything

Bid me to live, and I will live
  Thy Protestant to be:
Or bid me love, and I will give
  A loving heart to thee.

A heart as soft, a heart as kind,
  A heart as sound and free,
As in the whole world thou canst find,
  That heart I'll give to thee.

Bid that heart stay, and it will stay,
  To honour thy decree:
Or bid it languish quite away,
  And 't shall do so for thee.

Bid me to weep, and I will weep,
  While I have eyes to see:
And having none, yet I will keep
  A heart to weep for thee.

Bid me despair, and I'll despair
  Under that cypress tree:
Or bid me die, and I will dare
  E'en death to die for thee.

Thou art my life, my love, my heart,
  The very eyes of me:
And hast command of every part,
  To live and die for thee.

To Meadows

Ye have been fresh and green,
  Ye have been fill'd with flowers:
And ye the walks have been
  Where maids have spent their hours.

You have beheld, how they
  With wicker arks did come
To kiss, and bear away
  The richer cowslips home.

Y'ave heard them sweetly sing,
  And seen them in a round:
Each virgin, like a Spring,
  With honeysuckles crown'd.

But now, we see, none here,
  Whose silv'ry feet did tread,
And with dishevell'd hair,
  Adorn'd this smoother mead.

Like unthrifts, having spent
  Your stock, and needy grown,
Y'are left here to lament
  Your poor estate, alone.

Grace for a Child

Here a little child I stand,
Heaving up my either hand;
Cold as paddocks though they be,
Here I lift them up to Thee,
For a benison to fall
On our meat, and on us all. *Amen.*

A Thanksgiving to God, for His House

Lord, Thou hast given me a cell
    Wherein to dwell,
A little house, whose humble roof
    Is weather-proof;
Under the spars of which I lie
    Both soft, and dry;
Where Thou my chamber for to ward
    Hast set a guard
Of harmless thoughts, to watch and keep
    Me, while I sleep.
Low is my porch, as is my fate,
    Both void of state;
And yet the threshold of my door
    Is worn by th' poor,
Who thither come, and freely get
    Good words, or meat:
Like as my parlour, so my hall
    And kitchen's small:
A little buttery, and therein
    A little bin,
Which keeps my little loaf of bread
    Unchipp'd, unflead:
Some brittle sticks of thorn or briar
    Make me a fire,
Close by whose living coal I sit,
    And glow like it.
Lord, I confess too, when I dine,
    The pulse is thine,
And all those other bits, that be
    There plac'd by thee;
The worts, the purslain, and the mess
    Of water-cress,
Which of Thy kindness Thou has sent;
    And my content
Makes those, and my beloved beet,
    To be more sweet.
'Tis Thou that crown'st my glittering hearth
    With guiltless mirth;

And giv'st me wassail bowls to drink,
      Spic'd to the brink.
Lord, 'tis Thy plenty-dropping hand,
      That soils my land;
And giv'st me, for my bushel sown,
      Twice ten for one:
Thou mak'st my teeming hen to lay
      Her egg each day:
Besides my healthful ewes to bear
      Me twins each year:
The while the conduits of my kine
      Run cream, (for wine.)
All these, and better Thou dost send
      Me, to this end,
That I should render, for my part,
      A thankful heart;
Which, fir'd with incense, I resign,
      As wholly Thine;
But the acceptance, that must be,
      My Christ, by Thee.

HENRY KING

(1592–1669)

"Sonnet"

Tell me no more how fair she is,
      I have no mind to hear
The story of that distant bliss
      I never shall come near:
By sad experience I have found
That her perfection is my wound.

And tell me not how fond I am
      To tempt a daring fate,
From whence no triumph ever came,
      But to repent too late:
There is some hope ere long I may
In silence dote myself away.

I ask no pity, Love, from thee,
  Nor will thy justice blame,
So that thou wilt not envy me
  The glory of my flame:
Which crowns my heart whene'er it dies,
In that it falls her sacrifice.

FROM *The Exequy*
(ON HIS WIFE'S DEATH)

Accept, thou shrine of my dead saint,
Instead of dirges this complaint;
And for sweet flowers to crown thy hearse,
Receive a strew of weeping verse
From thy grieved friend, whom thou might'st see
Quite melted into tears for thee.

Sleep on, my Love, in thy cold bed,
Never to be disquieted!
My last good night! Thou wilt not wake
Till I thy fate shall overtake:
Till age or grief or sickness must
Marry my body to that dust
It so much loves; and fill the room
My heart keeps empty in thy tomb.
Stay for me there; I will not fail
To meet thee in that hollow vale;
And think not much of my delay;
I am already on the way,
And follow thee with all the speed
Desire can make or sorrows breed.
Each minute is a short degree,
And ev'ry hour a step towards thee.
At night, when I betake to rest,
Next morn I rise nearer my West
Of Life, almost by eight hours' sail
Than when sleep breathed his drowsy gale.

The thought of this bids me go on,
And wait my dissolution
With hope and comfort. Dear (forgive
The crime) I am content to live
Divided, with but half a heart,
Till we shall meet and never part.

GEORGE HERBERT

(1593-1633)

Man's Medley

Hark, how the birds do sing,
    And woods do ring!
All creatures have their joy, and man hath his.
    Yet if we rightly measure,
    Man's joy and pleasure
Rather hereafter than in present is.

To this life things of sense
    Make their pretence;
In th' other angels have a right by birth.
    Man ties them both alone,
    And makes them one,
With th' one hand touching Heav'n, with th' other earth.

In soul he mounts and flies,
    In flesh he dies.
He wears a stuff whose thread is coarse and round,
    But trimmed with curious lace,
    And should take place
After the trimming, not the stuff and ground.

Not that he may not here
    Taste of the cheer;
But as birds drink and straight lift up their head,
    So must he sip and think
    Of better drink
He may attain to after he is dead.

But as his joys are double,
  So is his trouble.
He hath two winters, other things but one.
  Both frosts and thoughts do nip
  And bite his lip,
And he of all things fears two deaths alone.

  Yet ev'n the greatest griefs
    May be reliefs,
Could he but take them right and in their ways.
  Happy is he whose heart
  Hath found the art
To turn his double pains to double praise.

The Collar

  I struck the board, and cried, No more!
    I will abroad.
What? Shall I ever sigh and pine?
My lines and life are free, free as the road,
  Loose as the wind, as large as store.
    Shall I be still in suit?
Have I no harvest but a thorn
To let me blood, and not restore
What I have lost with cordial fruit?
      Sure there was wine
  Before my sighs did dry it. There was corn
  Before my tears did drown it.
Is the year only lost to me?
    Have I no bays to crown it?
No flowers, no garlands gay? All blasted?
      All wasted?
  Not so, my heart! But there is fruit,
    And thou hast hands.
    Recover all thy sigh-blown age
On double pleasures. Leave thy cold dispute
Of what is fit and not. Forsake thy cage,
    Thy rope of sands,

Which petty thoughts have made, and made to thee
      Good cable, to enforce and draw,
            And be thy law,
      While thou didst wink and wouldst not see.
            Away! Take heed!
            I will abroad.
Call in thy death's head there. Tie up thy fears.
            He that forbears
            To suit and serve his need
            Deserves his load.
But as I raved and grew more fierce and wild
            At every word,
      Methought I heard one calling, *Child!*
      And I replied, *My Lord.*

Discipline

Throw away Thy rod,
Throw away Thy wrath.
      O my God,
Take the gentle path.

For my heart's desire
Unto Thine is bent.
      I aspire
To a full consent.

Not a word or look
I affect to own,
      But by book,
And Thy book alone.

Though I fail, I weep.
Though I halt in pace,
      Yet I creep
To the throne of grace.

Then let wrath remove.
Love will do the deed:
      For with love
Stony hearts will bleed.

Love is swift of foot.
Love's a man of war,
            And can shoot,
And can hit from far.

Who can 'scape his bow?
That which wrought on Thee,
            Brought Thee low,
Needs must work on me.

Throw away Thy rod,
Though man frailties hath,
            Thou art God.
Throw away Thy wrath.

Virtue

Sweet day, so cool, so calm, so bright,
    The bridal of the earth and sky;
The dew shall weep thy fall to night,
            For thou must die.

Sweet rose, whose hue angry and brave
    Bids the rash gazer wipe his eye;
Thy root is ever in its grave,
            And thou must die.

Sweet spring, full of sweet days and roses,
    A box where sweets compacted lie;
My music shows ye have your closes,
            And all must die.

Only a sweet and virtuous soul,
    Like seasoned timber, never gives;
But though the whole world turn to coal,
            Then chiefly lives.

Sin

Lord, with what care hast Thou begirt us round!
  Parents first season us; then schoolmasters
Deliver us to laws; they send us bound
  To rules of reason, holy messengers,
Pulpits and Sundays, sorrow dogging sin,
  Afflictions sorted, anguish of all sizes,
Fine nets and stratagems to catch us in.
  Bibles laid open, millions of surprises,
Blessings beforehand, ties of gratefulness,
  The sound of glory ringing in our ears;
Without, our shame; within, our consciences;
  Angels and grace, eternal hopes and fears.
Yet all these fences and their whole array
One cunning bosom-sin blows quite away.

Love

Love bade me welcome; yet my soul drew back,
        Guilty of dust and sin.
But quick-eyed Love, observing me grow slack
        From my first entrance in,
Drew nearer to me, sweetly questioning
        If I lacked any thing.

A guest, I answered, worthy to be here.
        Love said, You shall be he.
I, the unkind, ungrateful? Ah, my dear,
        I cannot look on thee.
Love took my hand and smiling did reply,
        Who made the eyes but I?

Truth, Lord, but I have marred them; let my shame
        Go where it doth deserve.
And know you not, says Love, who bore the blame?
        My dear, then I will serve.
You must sit down, says Love, and taste my meat.
        So I did sit and eat.

Mortification

How soon doth man decay!
When clothes are taken from a chest of sweets
  To swaddle infants, whose young breath
    Scarce knows the way,
  Those clouts are little winding sheets,
Which do consign and send them unto death.

When boys go first to bed,
They step into their voluntary graves;
  Sleep binds them fast; only their breath
    Makes them not dead.
  Successive nights, like rolling waves,
Convey them quickly who are bound for death.

When youth is frank and free,
And calls for music, while his veins do swell,
  All day exchanging mirth and breath
    In company,
  That music summons to the knell
Which shall befriend him at the house of death.

When man grows staid and wise,
Getting a house and home, where he may move
  Within the circle of his breath,
    Schooling his eyes,
  That dumb inclosure maketh love
Unto the coffin that attends his death.

When age grows low and weak,
Marking his grave, and thawing ev'ry year,
  Till all do melt and drown his breath
    When he would speak,
  A chair or litter shows the bier
Which shall convey him to the house of death.

Man, ere he is aware,
Hath put together a solemnity,
  And drest his hearse, while he has breath
    As yet to spare;
  Yet, Lord, instruct us so to die,
That all these dyings may be life in death.

The Pulley

When God at first made man,
Having a glass of blessings standing by,
"Let us," said he, "pour on him all we can;
Let the world's riches, which dispersèd lie,
   Contract into a span."

So strength first made a way,
Then beauty flowed, then wisdom, honour, pleasure;
When almost all was out, God made a stay,
Perceiving that, alone of all his treasure,
   Rest in the bottom lay.

"For if I should," said he,
"Bestow this jewel also on my creature,
He would adore my gifts instead of me,
And rest in Nature, not the God of Nature;
   So both should losers be.

Yet let him keep the rest,
But keep them with repining, restlessness;
Let him be rich and weary, that at least,
If goodness lead him not, yet weariness
   May toss him to my breast."

THOMAS MAY?

(1595–1650)

"Dear, Do Not Your Fair Beauty Wrong"

Dear, do not your fair beauty wrong
In thinking still you are too young;
The rose and lily in your cheek
Flourish, and no more ripening seek;
Inflaming beams shot from your eye
Do show Love's midsummer is nigh;
Your cherry lip, red, soft and sweet,
Proclaims such fruit for taste is meet;
Love is still young, a buxom boy,
And younglings are allowed to toy:
Then lose no time, for love hath wings,
   And flies away from aged things.

JAMES SHIRLEY

(1596–1666)

"You Virgins..."

You virgins, that did late despair
　To keep your wealth from cruel men,
Tie up in silk your careless hair:
　Soft peace is come again.

Now lovers' eyes may gently shoot
　A flame that will not kill;
The drum was angry, but the lute
　Shall whisper what you will.

Sing Io, Io! for his sake
　That hath restored your drooping heads;
With choice of sweetest flowers make
　A garden where he treads;

Whilst we whole groves of laurel bring,
　A petty triumph for his brow,
Who is the master of our spring
　And all the bloom we owe.

The Imposture, 1640?

"The Glories of Our Blood..."

The glories of our blood and state
　Are shadows, not substantial things;
There is no armour against Fate;
　Death lays his icy hand on kings:
　　　Sceptre and crown
　　　Must tumble down,
And in the dust be equal made
With the poor crooked scythe and spade.

Some men with swords may reap the field,
　And plant fresh laurels where they kill;
But their strong nerves at last must yield;
　They tame but one another still:

Early or late,
They stoop to fate,
And must give up their murmuring breath,
When they, pale captives, creep to death.

The garlands wither on your brow,
   Then boast no more your mighty deeds;
Upon Death's purple altar now
   See where the victor-victim bleeds:
         Your heads must come
         To the cold tomb;
Only the actions of the just
Smell sweet and blossom in the dust.

The Contention of Ajax and Ulysses, 1659

THOMAS CAREW

(1598?–1639?)

FROM *Persuasions to Love*

For that lovely face will fail,
Beauty's sweet, but beauty's frail;
'Tis sooner past, 'tis sooner done
Than summer's rain or winter's sun,
Most fleeting when it is most dear;
'Tis gone, while we but say 'tis here.
These curious locks so aptly twined,
Whose every hair a soul doth bind,
Will change their auburn hue and grow
White and cold as winter's snow.
That eye which now is Cupid's nest
Will prove his grave, and all the rest
Will follow; in the cheek, chin, nose,
Nor lily shall be found nor rose;
And what will then become of all
Those whom now you servants call?
Like swallows, when your summer's done
They'll fly and seek some warmer sun.

For when the storms of time have moved
Waves on that cheek that was beloved,
When a fair lady's face is pined

And yellow spread where red once shined,
When beauty, youth and all sweets leave her,
Love may return, but lovers never.

Oh, love me then, and now begin it,
Let us not lose this present minute.

Song

Give me more love or more disdain,
   The torrid or the frozen zone
Bring equal ease unto my pain,
   The temperate affords me none;
Either extreme of love or hate
Is sweeter than a calm estate.

Give me a storm; if it be love,
   Like Danaë in that golden shower
I swim in pleasure; if it prove
   Disdain, that torrent will devour
My vulture hopes; and he's possessed
Of heaven that's but from hell released.

Then crown my joys or cure my pain,
Give me more love or more disdain.

FROM *Disdain Returned*

He that loves a rosy cheek
   Or a coral lip admires,
Or from star-like eyes doth seek
   Fuel to maintain his fires;
As old Time makes these decay,
So his flames must waste away.

But a smooth and stedfast mind,
   Gentle thoughts and calm desires,
Hearts with equal love combined,
   Kindle never-dying fires.
Where these are not, I despise
Lovely cheeks or lips or eyes.

Song

Ask me no more where Jove bestows
When June is past, the fading rose;
For in your beauties' orient deep
These flowers as in their causes sleep.

Ask me no more whither do stray
The golden atoms of the day;
For in pure love Heaven did prepare
These powders to enrich your hair.

Ask me no more whither doth haste
The nightingale when May is past;
For in your sweet dividing throat
She winters and keeps warm her note.

Ask me no more where those stars light
That downwards fall in dead of night;
For in your eyes they sit and there
Fixéd become, as in their sphere.

Ask me no more if east or west
The phoenix builds her spicy nest;
For unto you at last she flies
And in your fragrant bosom dies.

Epitaph on the Lady Mary Villiers

The Lady Mary Villiers lies
Under this stone; with weeping eyes
The parents that first gave her breath,
And their sad friends, laid her in earth.
If any of them, reader, were
Known unto thee, shed a tear.
Or if thyself possess a gem
As dear to thee as this to them,
Though a stranger to this place
Bewail in theirs thine own hard case,
For thou perhaps at thy return
May'st find thy darling in an urn.

FROM A Rapture

I will enjoy thee now, my Celia, come,
And fly with me to Love's Elysium.
The giant, Honour, that keeps cowards out
Is but a masquer, and the servile rout
Of baser subjects only bend in vain
To the vast idol; whilst the nobler train
Of valiant lovers daily sail between
The huge Colossus' legs, and pass unseen
Unto the blissful shore. Be bold and wise,
And we shall enter; the grim Swiss denies
Only to tame fools a passage, that not know
He is but form and only frights in show
The duller eyes that look from far; draw near
And thou shalt scorn what we were wont to fear.
We shall see how the stalking pageant goes
With borrow'd legs, a heavy load to those
That made and bear him; not, as we once thought,
The seed of gods, but a weak model wrought
By greedy men, that seek to enclose the common,
And within private arms empale free woman.

Come, then, and mounted on the wings of Love
We'll cut the flitting air and soar above
The monster's head, and in the noblest seats
Of those blest shades quench and renew our heats.
There shall the queens of love and innocence,
Beauty and Nature, banish all offence
From our close ivy-twines; there I'll behold
Thy baréd snow and thy unbraided gold;
There my enfranchised hand on every side
Shall o'er thy naked polish'd ivory slide.
No curtain there, though of transparent lawn,
Shall be before thy virgin-treasure drawn;
But the rich mine, to the enquiring eye
Exposed, shall ready still for mintage lie,
And we will coin young Cupids. There a bed
Of roses and fresh myrtles shall be spread,
Under the cooler shades of cypress groves;
Our pillows of the down of Venus' doves,

Whereon our panting limbs we'll gently lay,
In the faint respites of our active play;
That so our slumbers may in dreams have leisure
To tell the nimble fancy our past pleasure,
And so our souls, that cannot be embraced,
Shall the embraces of our bodies taste.
Meanwhile the bubbling stream shall court the shore,
Th' enamour'd chirping wood-choir shall adore
In varied tunes the deity of love;
The gentle blasts of western winds shall move
The trembling leaves, and through their close boughs breathe
Still music, whilst we rest ourselves beneath
Their dancing shade; till a soft murmur, sent
From souls entranced in amorous languishment,
Rouse us, and shoot into our veins fresh fire,
Till we in their sweet ecstasy expire.

Then, as the empty bee that lately bore
Into the common treasure all her store,
Flies 'bout the painted field with nimble wing,
Deflow'ring the fresh virgins of the spring,
So will I rifle all the sweets that dwell
In my delicious paradise, and swell
My bag with honey, drawn forth by the power
Of fervent kisses from each spicy flower.
I'll seize the rose-buds in their perfumed bed,
The violet knots, like curious mazes spread
O'er all the garden, taste the ripen'd cherry,
The warm firm apple, tipp'd with coral berry;
Then will I visit with a wand'ring kiss
The vales of lilies and the bower of bliss;
And where the beauteous region doth divide
Into two milky ways, my lips shall slide
Down those smooth alleys, wearing as they go
A track for lovers on the printed snow;
Thence climbing o'er the swelling Apennine,
Retire into thy grove of eglantine,
Where I will all those ravish'd sweets distill
Through Love's alembic, and with chemic skill
From the mix'd mass one sovereign balm derive,
Then bring that great elixir to thy hive.

ANONYMOUS
(17TH CENTURY)

"Art Thou That She..."

"Art thou that she than whom no fairer is,
Art thou that she desire so strives to kiss?"
    "Say I am: how then?
    Maids may not kiss
    Such wanton-humour'd men."

"Art thou that she the world commends for wit?
Art thou so wise and makest no use of it?"
    "Say I am: how then?
    My wit doth teach me shun
    Such foolish foolish men."

ANONYMOUS
(17TH CENTURY)

"Hey Nonny No!"

Hey nonny no!
Men are fools that wish to die!
Is't not fine to dance and sing
When the bells of death do ring?
Is't not fine to swim in wine,
And turn upon the toe
And sing hey nonny no,
When the winds blow and the seas flow?
Hey nonny no!

ANONYMOUS
(17TH CENTURY)

"Yet If His Majesty..."

Yet if his majesty our sovereign lord
Should of his own accord
Friendly himself invite,
And say "I'll be your guest to morrow night",

How should we stir ourselves, call and command
All hands to work! "Let no man idle stand.
Set me fine Spanish tables in the hall,
See they be fitted all;
Let there be room to eat,
And order taken that there want no meat.
See every sconce and candlestick made bright,
That without tapers they may give a light.
Look to the presence: are the carpets spread,
The dais o'er the head,
The cushions in the chairs,
And all the candles lighted on the stairs?
Perfume the chambers, and in any case
Let each man give attendance in his place."
Thus if the king were coming would we do,
And 'twere good reason too;
For 'tis a duteous thing
To show all honour to an earthly king,
And after all our travail and our cost,
So he be pleased, to think no labour lost.
But at the coming of the King of Heaven
All's set at six and seven:
We wallow in our sin,
Christ cannot find a chamber in the inn.
We entertain Him always like a stranger,
And as at first still lodge Him in the manger.

ANONYMOUS

(17TH CENTURY)

"Daphnis Came on a Summer's Day"

Daphnis came on a summer's day
   Where fair Phyllis sleeping lay,
   With breast half naked bare:
He ran and gathered stores of lilies,
Wherewith he covered his fair Phyllis,
   She being nought aware.
   Fond youth, why dost thou mar
Those lily bowers and lose the pain!
   Her lily breast doth stain
All flowers and lilies far.

ANONYMOUS

(17TH CENTURY)

"On a Fair Morning..."

On a fair morning, as I came by the way,
Met I with a merry maid in the merry month of May,
When a sweet love song sings his lovely lay
And every bird upon the bush bechirps it up so gay,
With a heave and ho! with a heave and ho!
Thy wife shall be thy master, I trow.
Sing, care away, care away, let the world go!
Hey, lustily all in a row, all in a row,
Sing, care away, care away, let the world go!

Thomas Morley's Madrigals to Four Voices, 1600

ANONYMOUS

(17TH CENTURY)

"I Saw My Lady Weep"

I saw my lady weep,
And Sorrow proud to be advancéd so
In those fair eyes where all perfections keep.
Her face was full of woe,
But such a woe (believe me) as wins more hearts
Than Mirth can do with her enticing parts.

Sorrow was there made fair,
And Passion wise; Tears a delightful thing;
Silence beyond all speech, a wisdom rare;
She made her sighs to sing,
And all things with so sweet a sadness move
As made my heart at once both grieve and love.

O fairer than aught else
The world can show, leave off in time to grieve.
Enough, enough; your joyful look excels:
Tears kill the heart, believe.
O strive not to be excellent in woe,
Which only breeds your beauty's overthrow.

John Dowland's Second Book of Songs or Airs, 1600

ANONYMOUS

(17TH CENTURY)

"Fine Knacks for Ladies..."

Fine knacks for ladies, cheap choice, brave and new,
Good pennyworths—but money cannot move:
I keep a fair but for the Fair to view,—
    A beggar may be liberal of love.
Though all my wares be trash, the heart is true,
                The heart is true.

Great gifts are guiles and look for gifts again,
    My trifles come as treasures from my mind;
It is a precious jewel to be plain;
    Sometimes in shell the orient'st pearls we find:
Of others take a sheaf, of me a grain!
                Of me a grain.

Within this pack pins, points, laces, and gloves,
    And divers toys fitting a country fair,
But my heart, wherein duty serves and loves,
    Turtles and twins, court's brood, a heavenly pair—
Happy the heart that thinks of no removes!
              Of no removes!

John Dowland's Second Book of Songs or Airs, 1600

ANONYMOUS

(17TH CENTURY)

"My Love in Her Attire..."

My love in her attire doth show her wit,
    It doth so well become her:
For every season she hath dressings fit,
    For winter, spring, and summer.
    No beauty she doth miss,
    When all her robes are on:
    But Beauty's self she is,
    When all her robes are gone.

Davison's Poetical Rhapsody, 1602

ANONYMOUS
(17TH CENTURY)

"Flow Not so Fast..."

Flow not so fast, ye fountains,
What needeth all this haste?
Swell not above your mountains,
Nor spend your time in waste!
  Gentle springs! freshly your salt tears
  Must still fall, dropping from their spheres.

Weep not apace, whom Reason
Or lingering Time can ease;
My sorrow can no season,
Nor ought beside appease.
  Gentle springs! freshly your salt tears
  Must still fall, dropping from their spheres.

Time can abate the terror
Of every common pain:
But common grief is error,
True grief will still remain.
  Gentle springs! freshly your salt tears
  Must still fall, dropping from their spheres.

John Dowland's Third and Last Book of Songs or Airs, 1603

ANONYMOUS
(17TH CENTURY)

"Weep You No More..."

Weep you no more, sad fountains;
  What need you flow so fast?
Look how the snowy mountains
  Heaven's sun doth gently waste!
But my sun's heavenly eyes,
  View not your weeping,
  That now lies sleeping
Softly, now softly lies
      Sleeping.

Sleep is a reconciling,
    A rest that peace begets;
Doth not the sun rise smiling
    When fair at ev'n he sets?
Rest you then, rest, sad eyes!
    Melt not in weeping,
    While she lies sleeping
Softly, now softly lies
                Sleeping.

John Dowland's *Third and Last Book of Songs or Airs*, 1603

ANONYMOUS

(17TH CENTURY)

"Fain Would I Change..."

Fain would I change that note
To which fond love hath charm'd me
Long long to sing by rote,
Fancying that that harm'd me:
Yet when this thought doth come,
"Love is the perfect sum
Of all delight,"
I have no other choice
Either for pen or voice
To sing or write.

O Love, they wrong thee much
That say thy sweet is bitter,
When thy rich fruit is such
As nothing can be sweeter.
Fair house of joy and bliss,
Where truest pleasure is,
I do adore thee;
I know thee what thou art,
I serve thee with my heart,
And fall before thee.

Captain Tobias Hume's *The First Part of Airs*, 1605

ANONYMOUS

(17TH CENTURY)

"Ye Little Birds..."

Ye little birds that sit and sing
  Amidst the shady valleys,
And see how Phyllis sweetly walks
  Within her garden-alleys;
Go, pretty birds, about her bower;
Sing, pretty birds, she may not lower;
Ah me! methinks I see her frown!
  Ye pretty wantons, warble.

Go, tell her through your chirping bills,
  As you by me are bidden,
To her is only known my love,
  Which from the world is hidden.
Go, pretty birds, and tell her so;
See that your notes strain not too low,
For still, methinks, I see her frown;
  Ye pretty wantons, warble.

Go, tune your voices' harmony,
  And sing, I am her lover;
Strain loud and sweet, that every note
  With sweet content may move her:
And she that hath the sweetest voice,
Tell her I will not change my choice;
Yet still, methinks, I see her frown!
  Ye pretty wantons, warble.

Oh, fly! make haste! see, see, she falls
  Into a pretty slumber.
Sing round about her rosy bed,
  That waking, she may wonder.
So to her, 'tis her lover true
That sendeth love to you, to you;
And when you hear her kind reply,
  Return with pleasant warblings.

Fair Maid of the Exchange, 1607 [THOMAS HEYWOOD?]

ANONYMOUS

(17TH CENTURY)

"Ha Ha! Ha Ha! This World..."

Ha ha! ha ha! this world doth pass
　　Most merrily, I'll be sworn;
For many an honest Indian ass
　　Goes for an Unicorn.
　　　　　　　Fara diddle dino;
　　　　　　　This is idle fino.

Ty hye! ty hye! O sweet delight!
　　He tickles this age that can
Call Tullia's ape a marmosyte
　　And Leda's goose a swan.
　　　　　　　Fara diddle dino;
　　　　　　　This is idle fino.

So so! so so! fine English days!
　　When false play's no reproach;
For he that doth the coachman praise,
　　May safely use the coach.
　　　　　　　Fara diddle dino;
　　　　　　　This is idle fino.

　　　　　Thomas Weelkes's *Airs or Fantastic Spirits*, 1608

ANONYMOUS

(17TH CENTURY)

"Love Not Me..."

Love not me for comely grace,
For my pleasing eye or face,
Nor for any outward part:
No, nor for a constant heart!
For these may fail or turn to ill:
　　So thou and I shall sever.
Keep therefore a true woman's eye,
And love me still, but know not why!
So hast thou the same reason still
　　To doat upon me ever.

　　　　　John Wilbye's *Second Set of Madrigals*, 1609

ANONYMOUS

(17TH CENTURY)

"The Sea Hath Many Thousand Sands"

The sea hath many thousand sands,
The sky hath motes as many;
The sky is full of stars, and love
As full of woes as any:
Believe me, that do know the elf,
And make no trial by thyself.

It is in truth a pretty toy
For babes to play withal;
But O the honies of our youth
Are oft our age's gall!
Self-proof in time will make thee know
He was a prophet told thee so:

A prophet that, Cassandra-like,
Tells truth without belief;
For headstrong youth will run his race,
Although his goal be grief:
Love's martyr, when his heat is past,
Proves Care's confessor at the last.

Robert Jones's *The Muses' Garden of Delights*, 1610

ANONYMOUS

(17TH CENTURY)

"Sweet, Let Me Go!"

Sweet, let me go! sweet, let me go!
What do you mean to vex me so?
Cease your pleading force!
Do you think thus to extort remorse?
Now, now! no more! alas, you overbear me,
And I would cry—but some would hear, I fear me.

William Corkine's *Airs*, 1610

ANONYMOUS

(17TH CENTURY)

"Sweet Cupid, Ripen Her Desire"

Sweet Cupid, ripen her desire,
Thy joyful harvest may begin;
If age approach a little nigher,
'Twill be too late to get it in.

Cold winter storms lay standing corn,
Which once too ripe will never rise,
And lovers wish themselves unborn,
When all their joys lie in their eyes.

Then, sweet, let us embrace and kiss:
Shall beauty shale upon the ground?
If age bereave us of this bliss,
Then will no more such sport be found.

William Corkine's Airs, 1610

ANONYMOUS

(17TH CENTURY)

"On a Time the Amorous Silvy"

On a time the amorous Silvy
Said to her shepherd, "Sweet, how do you?
Kiss me this once and then God be wi' you,
           My sweetest dear!
Kiss me this once and then God be wi' you,
For now the morning draweth near."

With that her fairest bosom showing,
Opening her lips, rich perfumes blowing,
She said, "Now kiss me and be going,
           My sweetest dear!
Kiss me this once and then be going,
For now the morning draweth near."

With that the shepherd waked from sleeping,
And, spying where the day was peeping,
He said, "Now take my soul in keeping,
                    My sweetest dear!
Kiss me, and take my soul in keeping,
Since I must go, now day is near."

John Attye's *First Book of Airs*, 1622

ANONYMOUS

(17TH CENTURY)

"Love in Thy Youth..."

Love in thy youth, fair maid; be wise,
    Old Time will make thee colder,
And though each morning new arise
    Yet we each day grow older.

Thou as heaven art fair and young,
    Thine eyes like twin stars shining:
But ere another day be sprung,
    All these will be declining.

Then winter comes with all his fears
    And all thy sweets shall borrow;
Too late then wilt thou shower thy tears,
    And I too late shall sorrow.

Walter Porter's *Madrigals and Airs*, 1632

ANONYMOUS

(17TH CENTURY)

Phillada Flouts Me

O! what a plague is love!
    How shall I bear it?
She will inconstant prove,
    I greatly fear it.
She so torments my mind,
    That my strength faileth,

And wavers with the wind,
    As a ship saileth.
Please her the best I may,
She loves still to gainsay:
Alack and well a day!
        Phillada flouts me.

At the fair yesterday,
    She did pass by me;
She looked another way,
    And would not spy me.
I wooed her for to dine,
    But could not get her.
Will had her to the wine—
    He might intreat her.
With Daniel she did dance,
On me she looked askance.
O thrice unhappy chance!
        Phillada flouts me.

Fair maid, be not so coy,
    Do not disdain me:
I am my mother's joy,
    Sweet, entertain me.
She'll give me when she dies
    All that is fitting,
Her poultry and her bees
    And her geese sitting.
A pair of mattress beds,
And a bag full of shreds.
And yet for all this guedes,
        Phillada flouts me.

She hath a clout of mine
    Wrought with blue Coventry,
Which she keeps for a sign
    Of my fidelity.
But i' faith, if she flinch,
    She shall not wear it;

Guedes, goods.

To Tibb, my t'other wench,
  I mean to bear it.
And yet it grieves my heart,
So soon from her to part.
Death strikes me with his dart!
    Phillada flouts me.

Thou shalt eat curds and cream,
  All the year lasting:
And drink the crystal stream,
  Pleasant in tasting;
Whig and whey whilst thou lust
  And bramble-berries;
Pie-lid and pasty-crust,
  Pears, plums and cherries.
Thy raiment shall be thin,
Made of a weaver's skin:
Yet all's not worth a pin,
    Phillada flouts me.

In the last month of May
  I made her posies;
I heard her often say
  That she loved roses.
Cowslips and gillyflowers
  And the white lily
I brought to deck the bowers
  For my sweet Philly.
But she did all disdain,
And threw them back again;
Therefore 'tis flat and plain
    Phillada flouts me.

Fair maiden, have a care,
  And in time take me;
I can have those as fair
  If you forsake me.
For Doll the dairy-maid
  Laughed on me lately,

And wanton Winifred
  Favours me greatly.
One throws milk on my clothes,
  T'other plays with my nose;
What wanton signs are those?
    Phillada flouts me.

I cannot work nor sleep
  At all in season;
Love wounds my heart so deep
  Without all reason.
I gin to pine away,
  In my love's shadow,
Like as a fat beast may,
  Penned in a meadow.
I shall be dead, I fear,
  Within this thousand year:
And all for that my dear
    Phillada flouts me.

      Wit Restored, 1658, but written much earlier

ANONYMOUS
             (17TH CENTURY)

FROM *The New Jerusalem*

Hierusalem, my happy home,
  When shall I come to thee?
When shall my sorrows have an end?
  Thy joys when shall I see?

O happy harbour of the saints,
  O sweet and pleasant soil,
In thee no sorrow may be found,
  No grief, no care, no toil.

In thee no sickness may be seen,
  No hurt, no ache, no sore,
There is no death nor ugly devil,
  There is life for evermore.

No dampish mist is seen in thee,
   No cold nor darksome night,
There every soul shines as the sun,
   There God Himself gives light.

There lust and lucre cannot dwell,
   There envy bears no sway,
There is no hunger, heat nor cold,
   But pleasure every way.

Hierusalem, Hierusalem,
   God grant I once may see
Thy endless joys and of the same
   Partaker aye to be.

Thy walls are made of precious stones,
   Thy bulwarks diamonds square,
Thy gates are of right orient pearl
   Exceeding rich and rare.

Thy turrets and thy pinnacles
   With carbuncles do shine,
Thy very streets are paved with gold
   Surpassing clear and fine.

Thy houses are of ivory,
   Thy windows crystal clear,
Thy tiles are made of beaten gold—
   O God, that I were there!

Ah! my sweet home, Hierusalem,
   Would God I were in thee,
Would God my woes were at an end,
   Thy joys that I might see.

Thy saints are crowned with glory great,
   They see God face to face,
They triumph still, they still rejoice,
   Most happy is their case.

Thy vineyards and thy orchards are
   Most beautiful and fair,
Full furnishéd with trees and fruits
   Most wonderful and rare.

Thy gardens and thy gallant walks
   Continually are green,
There grows such sweet and pleasant flowers
   As nowhere else are seen.

There is nectar and ambrosia made,
   There is musk and civet sweet,
There many a fair and dainty drug
   Are trodden under feet.

There cinnamon, there sugar grows,
   There nard and balm abound;
What tongue can tell or heart conceive
   The joys that there are found.

Quiet through the streets with silver sound
   The flood of life does flow,
Upon whose bank at every side
   The wood of life doth grow.

There trees for evermore bear fruit
   And evermore do spring,
There evermore the angels sit
   And evermore do sing.

Hierusalem, my happy home,
   Would God I were in thee,
Would God my woes were at an end
   Thy joys that I might see.

ANONYMOUS
(17TH CENTURY)
The Old and Young Courtier

An old song made by an agéd old pate,
Of an old worshipful gentleman, who had a great estate,
That kept a brave old house at a bountiful rate,
And an old porter to relieve the poor at his gate;
  Like an old courtier of the Queen's,
  And the Queen's old courtier.

With an old lady, whose anger one word assuages;
They every quarter paid their old servants their wages,
And never knew what belonged to coachman, footmen, nor
  pages,
But kept twenty old fellows with blue coats and badges;
  Like an old courtier &c.

With an old study filled full of learnéd old books,
With an old reverend chaplain, you might know him by his
  looks.
With an old buttery hatch quite worn off the hooks,
And an old kitchen, that maintained half a dozen old cooks:
  Like an old courtier &c.

With an old hall hung about with pikes, guns and bows,
With old swords, and bucklers, that had borne many shrewd
  blows,
And an old frieze coat to cover his worship's trunk hose,
And a cup of old sherry, to comfort his copper nose:
  Like an old courtier &c.

With a good old fashion, when Christmas was come,
To call in all his neighbours with bagpipe and drum,
With good cheer enough to furnish every old room,
And old liquor able to make a cat speak, and man dumb,
  Like an old courtier &c.

With an old falconer, huntsman, and a kennel of hounds,
That never hawked, nor hunted, but in his own grounds,
Who, like a wise man, kept himself within his own bounds,
And when he died gave every child a thousand good pounds:
  Like an old courtier &c.

But to his eldest son his house and lands he assigned,
Charging him in his will to keep the old bountiful mind,
To be good to his old tenants, and to his neighbours be kind:
But in the ensuing ditty you shall hear how he was inclined;
   Like a young courtier of the King's,
   And the King's young courtier.

Like a flourishing young gallant, newly come to his land,
Who keeps a brace of painted madams at his command,
And takes up a thousand pound upon his father's land,
And gets drunk in a tavern, till he can neither go nor stand;
   Like a young courtier &c.

With a new-fangled lady, that is dainty, nice, and spare,
Who never knew what belonged to good housekeeping, or
  care,
Who buys gaudy-coloured fans to play with wanton air,
And seven or eight different dressings of other women's hair;
   Like a young courtier &c.

With a new-fashioned hall, built where the old one stood,
Hung round with new pictures, that do the poor no good,
With a fine marble chimney, wherein burns neither coal nor
  wood,
And a new smooth shovelboard, whereon no victuals ne'er
  stood;
   Like a young courtier &c.

With a new study, stuffed full of pamphlets, and plays,
And a new chaplain, that swears faster than he prays,
With a new buttery hatch, that opens once in four or five days,
And a new French cook, to devise fine kickshaws, and toys;
   Like a young courtier &c.

With a new fashion, when Christmas is drawing on,
On a new journey to London straight we all must begone,
And leave none to keep house, but our new porter John,
Who relieves the poor with a thump on the back with a stone;
   Like a young courtier &c.

With a new gentleman-usher, whose carriage is complete,
With a new coachman, footmen, and pages to carry up the
    meat,
With a waiting-gentlewoman, whose dressing is very neat,
Who when her lady has dined, lets the servants not eat;
        Like a young courtier &c.

With new titles of honour bought with his father's old gold,
For which sundry of his ancestors' old manors are sold;
And this is the course most of our new gallants hold,
Which makes that good house-keeping is now grown so cold,
        Among the young courtiers of the King,
        Or the King's young courtiers.

ANONYMOUS
(17TH CENTURY?)

Robin Goodfellow

From Oberon, in fairy land,
    The king of ghosts and shadows there,
Mad Robin I, at his command,
    Am sent to view the night-sports here.
        What revel rout
        Is kept about,
    In every corner where I go,
        I will o'ersee,
        And merry be,
    And make good sport, with ho, ho, ho!

More swift than lightning can I fly
    About this airy welkin soon,
And, in a minute's space, descry
    Each thing that's done beneath the moon.
        There's not a hag
        Or ghost shall wag,
    Or cry, 'ware goblins! where I go;
        But Robin I
        Their feats will spy,
    And send them home with ho, ho, ho!

Whene'er such wanderers I meet,
  As from their night-sports they trudge home,
With counterfeiting voice I greet,
  And call them on with me to roam:
      Through woods, through lakes,
      Through bogs, through brakes;
  Or else, unseen, with them I go,
      All in the nick,
      To play some trick,
  And frolic it, with ho, ho, ho!

Sometimes I meet them like a man,
  Sometimes an ox, sometimes a hound;
And to a horse I turn me can,
  To trip and trot about them round.
      But if to ride
      My back they stride,
More swift than wind away I go:
      O'er hedge and lands,
      Through pools and ponds
I hurry laughing, ho, ho, ho!

When lads and lasses merry be,
  With possets and with junkets fine;
Unseen of all the company,
  I eat their cakes and sip their wine!
      And, to make sport,
      I puff and snort:
And out the candles I do blow:
      The maids I kiss,
      They shriek—Who's this?
I answer nought but ho, ho, ho!

Yet now and then, the maids to please,
  At midnight I card up their wool;
And, while they sleep and take their ease,
  With wheel to threads their flax I pull.
      I grind at mill
      Their malt up still;

I dress their hemp; I spin their tow;
   If any wake,
   And would me take,
I wend me laughing, ho, ho, ho!

When any need to borrow aught,
  We lend them what they do require:
And for the use demand we nought;
  Our own is all we do desire.
   If to repay
   They do delay,
Abroad amongst them then I go,
   And night by night
   I them affright
With pinchings, dreams, and ho, ho, ho!

When lazy queans have nought to do,
  But study how to cheat and lie:
To make debate and mischief too,
  'Twixt one another secretly:
   I mark their gloze,
   And it disclose
To them whom they have wrongéd so:
   When I have done,
   I get me gone,
And leave them scolding, ho, ho, ho!

When men do traps and engines set
  In loop-holes, where the vermin creep,
Who from their folds and houses get
  Their ducks and geese, and lambs and sheep;
   I spy the gin,
   And enter in,
And seem a vermin taken so;
   But when they there
   Approach me near,
I leap out laughing, ho, ho, ho!

By wells and rills, in meadows green,
  We nightly dance our heyday guise;
And to our fairy king and queen

We chant our moonlight minstrelsies.
    When larks 'gin sing,
    Away we fling;
And babes newborn steal as we go;
    And elf in bed
    We leave instead,
And wend us laughing, ho, ho, ho!

From hag-bred Merlin's time, have I
  Thus nightly revelled to and fro;
And for my pranks men call me by
  The name of Robin Goodfellow.
    Fiends, ghosts, and sprites,
    Who haunt the nights,
The hags and goblins do me know;
    And beldames old
    My feats have told,
So vale, vale; ho, ho, ho!

ANONYMOUS

(17TH CENTURY)

The Queen of Fairies

    Come follow, follow me,
    You, fairy elves that be,
    Which circle on the green;
    Come follow me, your queen.
Hand in hand, let's dance a round,
For this place is fairy ground.

    When mortals are at rest,
    And snoring in their nest;
    Unheard and unespied,
    Through key-holes we do glide;
Over tables, stools, and shelves,
We trip it with our fairy elves.

    And, if the house be foul,
    Or platter, dish, or bowl,
    Up stairs we nimbly creep,

And find the sluts asleep:
There we pinch their arms and thighs—
None escapes; nor none espies.

But if the house be swept,
And from uncleanness kept,
We praise the household maid,
And surely she is paid:
For we do use before we go,
To drop a tester in her shoe.

Upon a mushroom's head,
Our table we do spread;
A grain of rye, or wheat,
Is manchet, which we eat;
Pearly drops of dew we drink
In acorn cups filled to the brink.

The brains of nightingales,
With unctuous dew of snails,
Between two nutshells stewed,
Is meat that's easily chewed;
And the beards of little mice
Do make a feast of wondrous price.

On tops of dewy grass,
So nimbly do we pass,
The young and tender stalk
Ne'er bends where we do walk;
Yet in the morning may be seen
Where we, the night before, have been.

The grasshopper, gnat and fly,
Serve for our minstrelsy;
Grace said, we dance a while,
And so the time beguile:
And when the moon doth hide her head,
The glow-worm lights us home to bed.

ANONYMOUS

(17TH CENTURY)

In Praise of Ale

When the chill Charoko blows,
  And Winter tells a heavy tale,
And pyes and daws and rooks and crows
Do sit and curse the frosts and snows;
      Then give me ale.

Ale in a Saxon rumkin then,
  Such as will make grim Malkin prate;
Bids valour burgeon in tall men,
Quickens the poet's wits and pen,
      Despises fate.

Ale, that the absent battle fights,
  And forms the march of Swedish drum,
Disputes the princes' laws, and rights,
What's past and done tells mortal wights,
      And what's to come.

Ale, that the plowman's heart up-keeps,
  And equals it to tyrant's thrones,
That wipes the eye that ever weeps,
And lulls in sweet and dainty sleeps
      Their very bones.

Grandchild of Ceres, Bacchus' daughter,
  Wine's emulous neighbour, though but stale,
Ennobling all the nymphs of water,
And filling each man's heart with laughter—
      Ha! Ha! give me ale!

ANONYMOUS

(17TH CENTURY)

The Farewell

It was a' for our rightfu' King
  We left fair Scotland's strand;
It was a' for our rightfu' King
  We e'er saw Irish land,
        My dear—
  We e'er saw Irish land.

Now a' is done that men can do,
  And a' is done in vain;
My love and native land, farewell!
  For I maun cross the main,
        My dear—
  For I maun cross the main.

He turned him right and round about
  Upon the Irish shore;
And gave his bridle-reins a shake,
  With Adieu for evermore,
        My dear—
  With Adieu for evermore!

The sodger frae the wars returns,
  The sailor frae the main;
But I hae parted frae my love,
  Never to meet again,
        My dear—
  Never to meet again.

When day is gane, and night is come,
  And a' folk bound to sleep,
I think on him that's far awa',
  The lee-lang night, and weep,
        My dear—
  The lee-lang night, and weep.

                    [Also attributed to ROBERT BURNS]

WILLIAM HABINGTON

(1605–1654)

To Roses in the Bosom of Castara

Ye blushing virgins happy are
In the chaste nunnery of her breasts,
For he'd profane so chaste a fair
Who e'er should call them Cupid's nests.

Transplanted thus, how bright ye grow,
How rich a perfume do ye yield!
In some close garden cowslips so
Are sweeter than i' th' open field.

In these white cloisters live secure
From the rude blasts of wanton breath,
Each hour more innocent and pure,
Till you shall wither into death.

Then that which living gave you room,
Your glorious sepulchre shall be;
There wants no marble for a tomb,
Whose breast hath marble been to me.

THOMAS RANDOLPH

(1605–1635)

An Ode to Mr. Anthony Stafford
to Hasten Him into the Country

Come, spur away,
I have no patience for a longer stay;
       But must go down
And leave the chargeable noise of this great town.
       I will the country see,
       Where old simplicity,
           Though hid in grey,
           Doth look more gay
Than foppery in plush and scarlet clad.
    Farewell, you City wits, that are
       Almost at civil war;
'Tis time that I grow wise, when all the world grows mad.

More of my days
I will not spend to gain an idiot's praise;
    Or to make sport
For some slight puisne of the Inns of Court.
    Then worthy Stafford, say
    How shall we spend the day,
        With what delights
        Shorten the nights?
When from the tumult we are got secure;
    Where mirth with all her freedom goes,
        Yet shall no finger lose;
Where every word is thought, and every thought is pure.

    There from the tree
We'll cherries pluck, and pick the strawberry.
    And every day
Go see the wholesome country girls make hay;
    Whose brown hath lovelier grace
    Than any painted face
        That I do know
        Hyde Park can show.
Where I had rather gain a kiss than meet
    (Though some of them in greater state
        Might court my love with plate)
The beauties of the Cheap and wives of Lombard Street.

    But think upon
Some other pleasures, these to me are none.
    Why do I prate
Of women, that are things against my fate?
    I never mean to wed
    That torture to my bed.
        My Muse is she
        My love shall be.
Let clowns get wealth and heirs; when I am gone,
    And the great bugbear, grisly death,
        Shall take this idle breath,
If I a poem leave, that poem is my son.

Of this, no more;
We'll rather taste the bright Pomona's store.
No fruit shall 'scape
Our palates, from the damson to the grape.
Then full we'll seek a shade
And hear what music's made;
How Philomel
Her tale doth tell;
And how the other birds do fill the choir;
The thrush and blackbird lend their notes,
Warbling melodious notes;
We will all sports enjoy which others but desire.

Ours is the sky,
Where at what fowl we please our hawk shall fly;
Nor will we spare
To hunt the crafty fox or timorous hare;
But let our hounds run loose
In any ground they choose,
The buck shall fall,
The stag and all.
Our pleasures must from our own warrants be,
For to my Muse, if not to me,
I'm sure all game is free;
Heaven, earth are all but parts of her great royalty.

And when we mean
To taste of Bacchus' blessings now and then,
And drink by stealth
A cup or two to noble Berkeley's health.
I'll take my pipe and try
The Phrygian melody,
Which he that hears
Lets through his ears
A madness to distemper all the brain.
Then I another pipe will take
And Doric music make
To civilize with graver notes our wits again.

To One Admiring Herself in a Looking Glass

Fair lady, when you see the grace
Of beauty in your looking glass:
A stately forehead smooth and high
And full of princely majesty;
A sparkling eye, no gem so fair,
Whose lustre dims the Cyprian star;
A glorious cheek divinely sweet
Wherein both roses kindly meet;
A cherry lip that would entice
Even gods to kiss at any price;
You think no beauty is so rare
That with your shadow might compare,
That your reflection is alone
The thing that men most dote upon.
Madam, alas, your glass doth lie,
And you are much deceived; for I
A beauty know of richer grace.
Sweet, be not angry—'tis your face.
Hence then, oh learn more mild to be,
And leave to lay your blame on me;
If me your real substance move
When you so much your shadow love.
Wise nature would not let your eye
Look on her own bright majesty,
Which had you once but gazed upon,
You could except yourself love none.
What then you cannot love, let me,
That face I can, you cannot see.
Now you have what to love, you'll say,
What then is left for me, I pray?
My face, sweetheart, if it please thee;
That which you can, I cannot see.
So either love shall gain his due;
Yours, sweet, in me, and mine in you.

FROM A *Pastoral Courtship*

Being set, let's sport a while, my fair;
I will tie love-knots in thy hair.
See, Zephyr through the leaves doth stray
And has free liberty to play,
And braids thy locks; and shall I find
Less favour than a saucy wind?
Now let me sit and fix my eyes
On thee that art my paradise.
Thou art my all. The Spring remains
In the fair violets of thy veins;
And that it is a Summer's day,
Ripe cherries in thy lips display;
And when for Autumn I would seek,
'Tis in the apples of thy cheek;
But that which only moves my smart,
Is to see Winter in thy heart.
Strange, when at once in one appear
All the four seasons of the year!
I'll clasp that neck, where should be set
A rich and orient carcanet;
But swains are poor; admit of, then,
More natural chains, the arms of men.
Come, let me touch those breasts that swell
Like two fair mountains, and may well
Be styled the Alps, but that I fear
The snow has less of whiteness there.
But stay, my love; a fault I spy.
Why are these two fair fountains dry?
Which, if they run, no Muse would please
To taste of any spring but these.
And Ganymede employed should be
To fetch his Jove nectar from thee.
Thou shalt be nurse, fair Venus swears,
To the next Cupid that she bears.
Were it not then discreetly done
To ope one spring to let two run?
Fie, fie, this belly, beauty's mint,
Blushes to see no coin stamped in't.

Employ it then, for though it be
Our wealth, it is your royalty;
And beauty will have current grace
That bears the image of your face.
How to the touch the ivory thighs
Vail gently, and again do rise,
As pliable to impression
As virgin wax or Parian stone
Dissolved to softness, plump and full,
More white and soft than Cotswold wool,
Or cotton from the Indian tree,
Or pretty silkworm's housewifery.
These on two marble pillars raised,
Make me in doubt which should be praised,
They or their columns, most; but when
I view those feet which I have seen
So nimbly trip it o'er the lawns
That all the satyrs and the fawns
Have stood amazed when they would pass
Over the leas, and not a grass
Would feel the weight, nor rush nor bent,
Drooping betray which way you went;
Oh then I felt my hot desires
Burn more and flame with double fires.

Now let us kiss. Would you be gone?
Manners at least allows me one.
Blush you at this, pretty one? Stay,
And I will take that kiss away
Thus, with a second, and that too
A third wipes off; so will we go
To numbers that the stars outrun
And all the atoms in the sun.
For though we kiss till Phoebus' ray
Sink in the seas, and kissing stay
Till his bright beams return again,
There can of all but one remain;
And if for one good manners call.
In one good manners grant me all.

SIR WILLIAM DAVENANT

(1606–1668)

"The Lark Now Leaves..."

The lark now leaves his watery nest,
  And climbing shakes his dewy wings;
He takes this window for the East,
  And to implore your light he sings—
Awake, awake, the morn will never rise
Till she can dress her beauty at your eyes.

The merchant bows unto the seaman's star,
  The ploughman from the sun his season takes;
But still the lover wonders what they are
  Who look for day before his mistress wakes.
Awake, awake! break through your veils of lawn!
Then draw your curtains, and begin the dawn!

FROM *Song*

Roses and pinks will be strewn where you go;
Whilst I walk in shades of willow, willow.
  When I am dead let him that did slay me
  Be but so good as kindly to lay me
  There where neglected lovers mourn,
  Where lamps and hallowed tapers burn,
  Where clerks in choirs sad dirges sing,
  Where sweetly bells at burials ring.

  My rose of youth is gone,
  Withered as soon as blown.
  Lovers, go ring my knell.
  Beauty and love, farewell.
  And lest virgins forsaken
  Should perhaps be mistaken
In seeking my grave, alas! let them know
I lie near a shade of willow, willow.

The Unfortunate Lovers, 1638

EDMUND WALLER

(1606–1687)

To a Very Young Lady

Why came I so untimely forth
Into a world which, wanting thee,
Could entertain us with no worth
Or shadow of felicity,
That time should me so far remove
From that which I was born to love?

Yet, fairest blossom! do not slight
That age which you may know so soon;
The rosy morn resigns her light,
And milder glory, to the noon;
And then what wonders shall you do,
Whose dawning beauty warms us so?

Hope waits upon the flowery prime;
And summer, though it be less gay,
Yet is not looked on as a time
Of declination or decay;
For with a full hand that doth bring
All that was promised by the spring.

On a Girdle

That which her slender waist confined,
Shall now my joyful temples bind;
No monarch but would give his crown,
His arms might do what this has done.

It was my heaven's extremest sphere,
The pale which held that lovely deer.
My joy, my grief, my hope, my love,
Did all within this circle move!

A narrow compass! and yet there
Dwelt all that's good and all that's fair;
Give me but what this ribband bound,
Take all the rest the sun goes round.

Go, Lovely Rose!

Go, lovely Rose!
Tell her that wastes her time and me
That now she knows,
When I resemble her to thee,
How sweet and fair she seems to be.

Tell her that's young,
And shuns to have her graces spied,
That hadst thou sprung
In deserts, where no men abide,
Thou must have uncommended died.

Small is the worth
Of beauty from the light retired;
Bid her come forth,
Suffer herself to be desired,
And not blush so to be admired.

Then die! that she
The common fate of all things rare
May read in thee;
How small a part of time they share
That are so wondrous sweet and fair!

Of the Last Verses in the Book

When we for age could neither read nor write,
The subject made us able to indite;
The soul, with nobler resolutions decked,
The body stooping, does herself erect.
No mortal parts are requisite to raise
Her that, unbodied, can her Maker praise.

The seas are quiet when the winds give o'er;
So, calm are we when passions are no more!
For then we know how vain it was to boast
Of fleeting things, so certain to be lost.
Clouds of affection from our younger eyes
Conceal that emptiness which age descries.

The soul's dark cottage, battered and decayed,
Lets in new light through chinks that time has made;
Stronger by weakness, wiser men become,
As they draw near to their eternal home.
Leaving the old, both worlds at once they view,
That stand upon the threshold of the new.

JOHN MILTON

(1608–1674)

Sonnet

O Nightingale, that on yon bloomy spray
Warbl'st at eve, when all the woods are still,
Thou with fresh hope the lover's heart dost fill,
While the jolly hours lead on propitious May,
Thy liquid notes that close the eye of Day,
First heard before the shallow cuckoo's bill
Portend success in love: O if Jove's will
Have linked that amorous power to thy soft lay,
Now timely sing, ere the rude bird of hate
Foretell my hopeless doom in some grove nigh:
As thou from year to year hast sung too late
For my relief; yet hadst no reason why,
Whether the Muse, or Love call thee his mate,
Both them I serve, and of their train am I.

An Epitaph on the Admirable Dramatic Poet William Shakespeare

What needs my Shakespeare for his honoured bones
The labour of an age in piléd stones,
Or that his hallowed relics should be hid
Under a star-ypointing pyramid?
Dear son of memory, great heir of fame,
What need'st thou such weak witness of thy name?
Thou in our wonder and astonishment
Hast built thyself a live-long monument.
For whilst to th' shame of slow-endeavouring art,

Thy easy numbers flow, and that each heart
Hath from the leaves of thy unvalued book
Those Delphic lines with deep impression took,
Then thou our fancy of itself bereaving,
Dost make us marble with too much conceiving:
And so sepulchred in such pomp dost lie,
That kings for such a tomb would wish to die.

Sonnet

How soon hath Time the subtle thief of youth,
Stol'n on his wing my three and twentieth year!
My hasting days fly on with full career,
But my late spring no bud or blossom shew'th.
Perhaps my semblance might deceive the truth,
That I to manhood am arriv'd so near,
And inward ripeness doth much less appear,
That some more timely-happy spirits endu'th.
Yet be it less or more, or soon or slow,
It shall be still in strictest measure ev'n,
To that same lot, however mean, or high,
Toward which Time leads me, and the will of Heav'n;
All is, if I have grace to use it so,
As ever in my great Task-Master's eye.

FROM Arcades

SECOND SONG

O'er the smooth enamelled green
Where no print of step hath been,
Follow me as I sing,
And touch the warbled string.
Under the shady roof
Of branching elm star-proof,
Follow me;
I will bring you where she sits
Clad in splendour as befits
Her deity.
Such a rural queen
All Arcadia hath not seen.

THIRD SONG

Nymphs and shepherds dance no more
 By sandy Ladon's lilied banks.
On old Lycaeus or Cyllene hoar
 Trip no more in twilight ranks.
Though Erymanth your loss deplore
 A better soil shall give ye thanks.
From the stony Maenalus
Bring your flocks, and live with us,
Here ye shall have greater grace,
To serve the Lady of this place.
Though Syrinx your Pan's mistress were,
Yet Syrinx well might wait on her.
  Such a rural queen
All Arcadia hath not seen.

L'Allegro

Hence loathéd Melancholy
 Of Cerberus and blackest midnight born,
In Stygian cave forlorn
 'Mongst horrid shapes, and shrieks, and sights unholy,
Find out some uncouth cell,
 Where brooding darkness spreads his jealous wings,
And the night-raven sings;
 There under ebon shades, and low-browed rocks,
As ragged as thy locks,
 In dark Cimmerian desert ever dwell.
But come thou goddess fair and free,
In Heaven yclept Euphrosyne,
And by men, heart-easing Mirth,
Whom lovely Venus at a birth
With two sister Graces more
To ivy-crownéd Bacchus bore;
Or whether (as some sager sing)
The frolic wind that breathes the spring,
Zephyr with Aurora playing,
As he met her once a-maying,
There on beds of violets blue,

And fresh-blown roses washed in dew,
Filled her with thee a daughter fair,
So buxom, blithe, and debonair.
Haste thee nymph and bring with thee
Jest and youthful jollity,
Quips and cranks, and wanton wiles,
Nods, and becks, and wreathéd smiles,
Such as hang on Hebe's cheek,
And love to live in dimple sleek;
Sport that wrinkled care derides,
And laughter holding both his sides.
Come, and trip it as ye go
On the light fantastic toe,
And in thy right hand lead with thee,
The mountain nymph, sweet Liberty;
And if I give thee honour due,
Mirth, admit me of thy crew
To live with her, and live with thee,
In unreprovéd pleasures free;
To hear the lark begin his flight,
And singing startle the dull night,
From his watch-tower in the skies,
Till the dappled dawn doth rise;
Then to come in spite of sorrow,
And at my window bid good morrow,
Through the sweet-briar, or the vine,
Or the twisted eglantine;
While the cock with lively din,
Scatters the rear of darkness thin,
And to the stack, or the barn door,
Stoutly struts his dames before;
Oft listening how the hounds and horn
Cheerly rouse the slumbering morn,
From the side of some hoar hill,
Through the high wood echoing shrill.
Some time walking not unseen
By hedge-row elms, on hillocks green,
Right against the eastern gate,
Where the great sun begins his state,
Robed in flames, and amber light,
The clouds in thousand liveries dight.

While the ploughman near at hand,
Whistles o'er the furrowed land,
And the milkmaid singeth blithe,
And the mower whets his scythe,
And every shepherd tells his tale
Under the hawthorn in the dale.

Straight mine eye hath caught new pleasures
While the landskip round it measures,
Russet lawns, and fallows gray,
Where the nibbling flocks do stray;
Mountains on whose barren breast
The labouring clouds do often rest;
Meadows trim with daisies pied,
Shallow brooks, and rivers wide.
Towers, and battlements it sees
Bosomed high in tufted trees,
Where perhaps some beauty lies,
The cynosure of neighbouring eyes.
Hard by, a cottage chimney smokes,
From betwixt two aged oaks,
Where Corydon and Thyrsis met,
Are at their savoury dinner set
Of herbs, and other country messes,
Which the neat-handed Phyllis dresses;
And then in haste her bower she leaves,
With Thestylis to bind the sheaves;
Or if the earlier season lead
To the tanned haycock in the mead.

Sometimes with secure delight
The upland hamlets will invite,
When the merry bells ring round,
And the jocund rebecks sound
To many a youth, and many a maid
Dancing in the chequered shade;
And young and old come forth to play
On a sunshine holiday,
Till the live-long daylight fail;
Then to the spicy nut-brown ale,
With stories told of many a feat,

How Faery Mab the junkets eat;
She was pinched, and pulled she said,
And he by friar's lanthorn led;
Tells how the drudging goblin sweat,
To earn his cream-bowl duly set,
When in one night, ere glimpse of morn,
His shadowy flail hath threshed the corn
That ten day-labourers could not end;
Then lies him down the lubber fiend,
And stretched out all the chimney's length,
Basks at the fire his hairy strength;
And crop-full out of doors he flings,
Ere the first cock his matin rings.
Thus done the tales, to bed they creep,
By whispering winds soon lulled asleep.

Towered cities please us then,
And the busy hum of men,
Where throngs of knights and barons bold,
In weeds of peace high triumphs hold,
With store of ladies, whose bright eyes
Rain influence, and judge the prize
Of wit, or arms, while both contend
To win her grace, whom all commend.
There let Hymen oft appear
In saffron robe, with taper clear,
And pomp, and feast, and revelry,
With mask, and antique pageantry,
Such sights as youthful poets dream
On summer eves by haunted stream.
Then to the well-trod stage anon,
If Jonson's learned sock be on,
Or sweetest Shakespeare, fancy's child,
Warble his native wood-notes wild.
And ever against eating cares,
Lap me in soft Lydian airs,
Married to immortal verse,
Such as the meeting soul may pierce
In notes, with many a winding bout
Of linkéd sweetness long drawn out,
With wanton heed, and giddy cunning,

The melting voice through mazes running;
Untwisting all the chains that tie
The hidden soul of harmony:
That Orpheus' self may heave his head
From golden slumber on a bed
Of heaped Elysian flowers, and hear
Such strains as would have won the ear
Of Pluto, to have quite set free
His half-regained Eurydice.
These delights if thou canst give,
Mirth, with thee I mean to live.

Il Penseroso

Hence, vain deluding joys,
    The brood of folly without father bred,
How little you bested,
    Or fill the fixéd mind with all your toys;
Dwell in some idle brain,
    And fancies fond with gaudy shapes possess,
As thick and numberless
    As the gay motes that people the sun-beams,
Or likest hovering dreams
    The fickle pensioners of Morpheus' train.
But hail thou goddess, sage and holy,
Hail divinest Melancholy,
Whose saintly visage is too bright
To hit the sense of human sight;
And therefore to our weaker view,
O'er-laid with black, staid wisdom's hue:
Black, but such as in esteem
Prince Memnon's sister might beseem,
Or that starred Ethiop queen that strove
To set her beauty's praise above
The sea nymphs, and their power offended.
Yet thou art higher far descended,
Thee bright-haired Vesta long of yore,
To solitary Saturn bore;
His sister she (in Saturn's reign,
Such mixture was not held a stain).

Oft in glimmering bowers and glades
He met her, and in secret shades
Of woody Ida's inmost grove,
While yet there was no fear of Jove.
Come pensive nun, devout and pure,
Sober, stedfast, and demure,
All in a robe of darkest grain,
Flowing with majestic train,
And sable stole of cypress lawn,
Over thy decent shoulders drawn.
Come, but keep thy wonted state,
With even step and musing gait,
And looks commercing with the skies,
Thy rapt soul sitting in thine eyes:
There held in holy passion still,
Forget thyself to marble, till
With a sad leaden downward cast,
Thou fix them on the earth as fast.
And join with thee calm peace, and quiet,
Spare fast, that oft with gods doth diet,
And hears the Muses in a ring,
Aye round about Jove's altar sing.
And add to these retiréd leisure,
That in trim gardens takes his pleasure;
But first, and chiefest, with thee bring
Him that yon soars on golden wing,
Guiding the fiery-wheeléd throne,
The cherub, contemplation;
And the mute silence hist along,
'Less Philomel will deign a song,
In her sweetest, saddest plight,
Smoothing the rugged brow of night,
While Cynthia checks her dragon yoke,
Gently o'er th' accustomed oak;
Sweet bird that shunn'st the noise of folly,
Most musical, most melancholy!
Thee chauntress oft the woods among,
I woo to hear thy even-song;
And missing thee, I walk unseen
On the dry smooth-shaven green,
To behold the wandering moon,

Riding near her highest noon,
Like one that hath been led astray
Through the heav'ns wide pathless way;
And oft, as if her head she bowed,
Stooping through a fleecy cloud.
Oft on a plat of rising ground,
I hear the far-off curfew sound,
Over some wide-watered shore,
Swinging slow with sullen roar;
Or if the air will not permit,
Some still removéd place will fit,
Where glowing embers through the room
Teach light to counterfeit a gloom,
Far from all resort of mirth,
Save the cricket on the hearth,
Or the bellman's drowsy charm,
To bless the doors from nightly harm:
Or let my lamp at midnight hour
Be seen in some high lonely tower,
Where I may oft out-watch the Bear,
With thrice-great Hermes, or unsphere
The spirit of Plato to unfold
What worlds, or what vast regions hold
The immortal mind that hath forsook
Her mansion in this fleshly nook:
And of those daemons that are found
In fire, air, flood, or under ground,
Whose power hath a true consent
With planet or with element.
Sometimes let gorgeous tragedy
In sceptered pall come sweeping by,
Presenting Thebes', or Pelops' line,
Or the tale of Troy divine,
Or what (though rare) of later age,
Ennobled hath the buskined stage.

But, O sad virgin, that thy power
Might raise Musaeus from his bower,
Or bid the soul of Orpheus sing
Such notes as warbled to the string
Drew iron tears down Pluto's cheek,

And made hell grant what love did seek.
Or call up him that left half told
The story of Cambuscan bold,
Of Camball, and of Algarsife,
And who had Canace to wife,
That owned the virtuous ring and glass,
And of the wond'rous horse of brass,
On which the Tartar king did ride;
And if aught else, great bards beside,
In sage and solemn tunes have sung,
Of tourneys and of trophies hung;
Of forests, and enchantments drear,
Where more is meant than meets the ear.
Thus night oft see me in thy pale career,
Till civil-suited morn appear,
Not tricked and frounced as she was wont,
With the Attic boy to hunt,
But kerchiefed in a comely cloud,
While rocking winds are piping loud,
Or ushered with a shower still,
When the gust hath blown his fill,
Ending on the rustling leaves,
With minute drops from off the eaves.
And when the sun begins to fling
His flaring beams, me goddess bring
To archéd walks of twilight groves,
And shadows brown that Sylvan loves
Of pine, or monumental oak,
Where the rude axe with heavéd stroke,
Was never heard the nymphs to daunt,
Or fright them from their hallowed haunt.
There in close covert by some brook,
Where no profaner eye may look,
Hide me from day's garish eye,
While the bee with honied thigh,
That at her flower work doth sing,
And the waters murmuring
With such consort as they keep,
Entice the dewy-feathered sleep;
And let some strange mysterious dream,
Wave at his wings in airy stream,

Of lively portraiture displayed,
Softly on my eye-lids laid.
And as I wake, sweet music breathe
Above, about, or underneath,
Sent by some spirit to mortals good,
Or th' unseen genius of the wood.

But let my due feet never fail
To walk the studious cloisters pale,
And love the high embowéd roof,
With antic pillars massy proof,
And storied windows richly dight,
Casting a dim religious light.
There let the pealing organ blow,
To the full-voiced choir below,
In service high, and anthems clear,
As may with sweetness, through mine ear,
Dissolve me into ecstasies,
And bring all heav'n before mine eyes.
And may at last my weary age
Find out the peaceful hermitage,
The hairy gown and mossy cell,
Where I may sit and rightly spell
Of every star that heav'n doth show,
And every herb that sips the dew;
Till old experience do attain
To something like prophetic strain.
These pleasures, Melancholy, give,
And I with thee will choose to live.

FROM A Mask Presented at Ludlow Castle
(Comus)

1.

Comus: The star that bids the shepherd fold,
Now the top of heav'n doth hold,
And the gilded car of day
His glowing axle doth allay
In the steep Atlantic stream,
And the slope sun his upward beam

Shoots against the dusky pole,
Pacing toward the other goal
Of his chamber in the east.
Meanwhile, welcome joy, and feast,
Midnight shout, and revelry,
Tipsy dance, and jollity.
Braid your locks with rosy twine
Dropping odours, dropping wine.
Rigour now is gone to bed,
And advice with scrupulous head,
Strict age, and sour severity,
With their grave saws in slumber lie.
We that are of purer fire
Imitate the starry choir,
Who in their nightly watchful spheres
Lead in swift round the months and years.
The sounds and seas with all their finny drove
Now to the moon in wavering morris move,
And on the tawny sands and shelves
Trip the pert fairies and the dapper elves;
By dimpled brook and fountain brim
The wood nymphs decked with daisies trim
Their merry wakes and pastimes keep:
What hath night to do with sleep?
Night hath better sweets to prove,
Venus now wakes, and wakens Love.
Come, let us our rites begin,
'Tis only daylight that makes sin
Which these dun shades will ne'er report.
Hail goddess of nocturnal sport,
Dark-veiled Cotytto, t' whom the secret flame
Of midnight torches burns; mysterious dame
That ne'er art called but when the dragon womb
Of Stygian darkness spits her thickest gloom,
And makes one blot of all the air,
Stay thy cloudy ebon chair,
Wherein thou rid'st with Hecat', and befriend
Us thy vowed priests, till utmost end
Of all thy dues be done, and none left out,
Ere the blabbing eastern scout,
The nice morn on the Indian steep

From her cabined loop-hole peep,
And to the tell-tale sun descry
Our concealed solemnity.
Come, knit hands, and beat the ground,
In a light fantastic round.

2.   SONG
   Sweet Echo, sweetest nymph that liv'st unseen
                Within thy airy shell
             By slow Meander's margent green,
      And in the violet-embroidered vale
             Where the love-lorn nightingale
   Nightly to thee her sad song mourneth well,
   Canst thou not tell me of a gentle pair
             That likest thy Narcissus are?
                O if thou have
             Hid them in some flowery cave,
                Tell me but where,
   Sweet queen of parley, daughter of the sphere,
   So mayst thou be transplanted to the skies,
   And give resounding grace to all Heav'n's harmonies.

3.

Comus: O foolishness of men! that lend their ears
             To those budge doctors of the Stoic fur,
             And fetch their precepts from the Cynic tub,
             Praising the lean and sallow abstinence.
             Wherefore did Nature pour her bounties forth,
             With such a full and unwithdrawing hand,
             Covering the earth with odours, fruits and flocks,
             Thronging the seas with spawn innumerable,
             But all to please and sate the curious taste?
             And set to work millions of spinning worms,
             That in their green shops weave the smooth-haired
                silk
             To deck her sons, and that no corner might
             Be vacant of her plenty, in her own loins
             She hutched th'all-worshipped ore, and precious gems

To store her children with; if all the world
Should in a pet of temperance feed on pulse,
Drink the clear stream, and nothing wear but frieze,
Th'all-giver would be unthanked, would be un-
          praised,
Not half his riches known, and yet despised,
And we should serve him as a grudging master,
As a penurious niggard of his wealth,
And live like Nature's bastards, not her sons,
Who would be quite surcharged with her own
          weight,
And strangled with her waste fertility;
Th'earth cumbered, and the winged air darked with
          plumes,
The herds would over-multitude their lords,
The sea o'erfraught would swell, and th'unsought
          diamonds
Would so emblaze the forehead of the deep,
And so bestud with stars, that they below
Would grow inured to light, and come at last
To gaze upon the sun with shameless brows.

4.   SONG
Sabrina fair
    Listen where thou art sitting
Under the glassy, cool, translucent wave,
    In twisted braids of lilies knitting
The loose train of thy amber-dropping hair;
    Listen for dear honour's sake,
    Goddess of the silver lake,
                         Listen and save.

Listen and appear to us
In name of great Oceanus,
By the earth-shaking Neptune's mace,
And Tethys' grave majestic pace,
By hoary Nereus' wrinkled look,
And the Carpathian wizard's hook,
By scaly Triton's winding shell,
And old sooth-saying Glaucus' spell,

By Leucothea's lovely hands,
And her son that rules the strands,
By Thetis' tinsel-slippered feet,
And the song of sirens sweet,
By dead Parthenope's dear tomb,
And fair Ligea's golden comb,
Wherewith she sits on diamond rocks
Sleeking her soft alluring locks,
By all the nymphs that nightly dance
Upon thy streams with wily glance,
Rise, rise, and heave thy rosy head
From thy coral-paven bed,
And bridle in thy headlong wave,
Till thou our summons answered have.
                              Listen and save.

5.   "TO THE OCEAN NOW I FLY"

Spirit: To the ocean now I fly,
And those happy climes that lie
Where day never shuts his eye,
Up in the broad fields of the sky:
There I suck the liquid air
All amidst the gardens fair
Of Hesperus, and his daughters three
That sing about the golden tree:
Along the crispéd shades and bowers
Revels the spruce and jocund Spring,
The Graces, and the rosy-bosomed Hours,
Thither all their bounties bring.
There eternal Summer dwells,
And west winds, with musky wing
About the cedarn alleys fling
Nard, and cassia's balmy smells.
Iris there with humid bow
Waters the odorous banks that blow
Flowers of more mingled hue
Than her purfled scarf can show,
And drenches with Elysian dew
(List mortals, if your ears be true)

Beds of hyacinth and roses
Where young Adonis oft reposes,
Waxing well of his deep wound
In slumber soft, and on the ground
Sadly sits th' Assyrian queen;
But far above in spangled sheen
Celestial Cupid, her famed son advanced,
Holds his dead Psyche sweet entranced
After her wandering labours long,
Till free consent the gods among
Make her his eternal bride,
And from her fair unspotted side
Two blissful twins are to be born,
Youth and Joy; so Jove has sworn.

But now my task is smoothly done,
I can fly, or I can run
Quickly to the green earth's end,
Where the bowed welkin slow doth bend,
And from thence can soar as soon
To the corners of the moon.

Mortals that would follow me,
Love virtue, she alone is free,
She can teach ye how to climb
Higher than the sphery chime;
Or if Virtue feeble were,
Heaven itself would stoop to her.

Lycidas

Yet once more, O ye laurels, and once more
Ye myrtles brown, with ivy never sere,
I come to pluck your berries harsh and crude,
And with forced fingers rude,
Shatter your leaves before the mellowing year.
Bitter constraint, and sad occasion dear,
Compels me to disturb your season due:
For Lycidas is dead, dead ere his prime
Young Lycidas, and hath not left his peer:

Who would not sing for Lycidas? he knew
Himself to sing, and build the lofty rhyme.
He must not float upon his watery bier
Unwept, and welter to the parching wind,
Without the meed of some melodious tear.
Begin then, Sisters of the sacred well,
That from beneath the seat of Jove doth spring,
Begin, and somewhat loudly sweep the string.
Hence with denial vain, and coy excuse,
So may some gentle Muse
With lucky words favour my destined urn,
And as he passes turn,
And bid fair peace be to my sable shroud.
For we were nursed upon the self-same hill,
Fed the same flock, by fountain, shade, and rill.
　　Together both, ere the high lawns appeared
Under the opening eye-lids of the morn,
We drove afield, and both together heard
What time the gray-fly winds her sultry horn,
Battening our flocks with the fresh dews of night,
Oft till the star that rose at evening, bright
Toward heaven's descent had sloped his westering wheel.
Meanwhile the rural ditties were not mute,
Tempered to th' oaten flute,
Rough satyrs danced, and fauns with cloven heel,
From the glad sound would not be absent long,
And old Damaetas loved to hear our song.
　　But O the heavy change, now thou art gone,
Now thou art gone, and never must return!
Thee shepherd, thee the woods and desert caves,
With wild thyme and the gadding vine o'ergrown,
And all their echoes mourn.
The willows, and the hazel copses green,
Shall now no more be seen,
Fanning their joyous leaves to thy soft lays.
As killing as the canker to the rose,
Or taint-worm to the weanling herds that graze,
Or frost to flowers, that their gay wardrobe wear,
When first the white thorn blows;
Such, Lycidas, thy loss to shepherd's ear.
　　Where were ye, nymphs, when the remorseless deep

Closed o'er the head of your loved Lycidas?
For neither were ye playing on the steep,
Where your old bards, the famous Druids lie,
Nor on the shaggy top of Mona high,
Nor yet where Deva spreads her wizard stream:
Ay me, I fondly dream!
Had ye been there—for what could that have done?
What could the Muse herself that Orpheus bore,
The Muse herself, for her enchanting son
Whom universal Nature did lament,
When by the rout that made the hideous roar,
His gory visage down the stream was sent,
Down the swift Hebrus to the Lesbian shore?

   Alas! What boots it with incessant care
To tend the homely slighted shepherd's trade,
And strictly meditate the thankless Muse?
Were it not better done as others use,
To sport with Amaryllis in the shade,
Or with the tangles of Neaera's hair?
Fame is the spur that the clear spirit doth raise
(That last infirmity of noble mind)
To scorn delights, and live laborious days;
But the fair guerdon when we hope to find,
And think to burst out into sudden blaze,
Comes the blind Fury with th' abhorréd shears,
And slits the thin spun life. But not the praise,
Phoebus replied, and touched my trembling ears;
Fame is no plant that grows on mortal soil,
Nor in the glistering foil
Set off to th' world, nor in broad rumour lies,
But lives and spreads aloft by those pure eyes,
And perfect witness of all judging Jove;
As He pronounces lastly on each deed,
Of so much fame in Heav'n expect thy meed.

   O fountain Arethuse, and thou honoured flood,
Smooth-sliding Mincius, crowned with vocal reeds,
That strain I heard was of a higher mood:
But now my oat proceeds,
And listens to the herald of the sea,
That came in Neptune's plea.
He asked the waves, and asked the felon winds,

What hard mishap hath doomed this gentle swain?
And questioned every gust of rugged wings
That blows from off each beakéd promontory,
They knew not of his story,
And sage Hippotades their answer brings,
That not a blast was from his dungeon strayed,
The air was calm, and on the level brine
Sleek Panope with all her sisters played.
It was that fatal and perfidious bark
Built in th' eclipse, and rigged with curses dark,
That sunk so low that sacred head of thine.

   Next Camus, reverend sire, went footing slow,
His mantle hairy, and his bonnet sedge,
Inwrought with figures dim, and on the edge
Like to that sanguine flower inscribed with woe.
Ah! Who hath reft (quoth he) my dearest pledge?
Last came, and last did go,
The pilot of the Galilean lake,
Two massy keys he bore of metals twain,
(The golden opes, the iron shuts amain)
He shook his mitred locks, and stern bespake:
How well could I have spared for thee, young swain,
Enow of such as for their belly's sake
Creep and intrude, and climb into the fold?
Of other care they little reckoning make,
Than how to scramble at the shearers' feast,
And shove away the worthy bidden guest.
Blind mouths! that scarce themselves know how to hold
A sheep-hook, or have learned aught else the least
That to the faithful herdman's art belongs!
What recks it them? What need they? They are sped;
And when they list, their lean and flashy songs
Grate on their scrannel pipes of wretched straw.
The hungry sheep look up, and are not fed,
But swoll'n with wind, and the rank mist they draw,
Rot inwardly, and foul contagion spread:
Beside what the grim wolf with privy paw
Daily devours apace, and nothing said,
But that two-handed engine at the door,
Stands ready to smite once, and smite no more.
   Return, Alpheus, the dread voice is past,

That shrunk thy streams; return, Sicilian Muse,
And call the vales, and bid them hither cast
Their bells and flow'rets of a thousand hues.
Ye valleys low, where the mild whispers use
Of shades and wanton winds and gushing brooks,
On whose fresh lap the swart star sparely looks,
Throw hither all your quaint enameled eyes,
That on the green turf suck the honied showers,
And purple all the ground with vernal showers.
Bring the rathe primrose that forsaken dies,
The tufted crow-toe, and pale jessamine,
The white pink, and the pansy freaked with jet,
The glowing violet,
The musk-rose, and the well-attired woodbine,
The cowslips wan that hang the pensive head,
And every flower that sad embroidery wears:
Bid Amaranthus all his beauty shed,
And daffadillies fill their cups with tears,
To strew the laureate hearse where Lycid lies.
For so to interpose a little ease,
Let our frail thoughts dally with false surmise.
Ay me! Whilst thee the shores and sounding seas
Wash far away, where'er thy bones are hurled,
Whether beyond the stormy Hebrides,
Where thou perhaps under the whelming tide
Visit'st the bottom of the monstrous world;
Or whether thou to our moist vows denied,
Sleep'st by the fable of Bellerus old,
Where the great vision of the guarded mount
Looks toward Namancos and Bayona's hold;
Look homeward Angel now, and melt with ruth,
And, O ye dolphins, waft the hapless youth.
    Weep no more, woeful shepherds, weep no more,
For Lycidas your sorrow is not dead,
Sunk though he be beneath the watery floor,
So sinks the day-star in the ocean bed,
And yet anon repairs his drooping head,
And tricks his beams, and with new spangled ore
Flames in the forehead of the morning sky:
So Lycidas sunk low, but mounted high,
Through the dear might of him that walked the waves,

Where other groves, and other streams along,
With nectar pure his oozy locks he laves,
And hears the unexpressive nuptial song,
In the blest kingdoms meek of joy and love.
There entertain him all the saints above,
In solemn troops, and sweet societies
That sing, and singing in their glory move,
And wipe the tears for ever from his eyes.
Now Lycidas the shepherds weep no more;
Henceforth thou art the genius of the shore,
In thy large recompense, and shalt be good
To all that wander in that perilous flood.

   Thus sang the uncouth swain to th' oaks and rills,
While the still morn went out with sandals gray,
He touched the tender stops of various quills,
With eager thought warbling his Doric lay:
And now the sun had stretched out all the hills,
And now was dropped into the western bay;
At last he rose, and twitched his mantle blue:
To morrow to fresh woods, and pastures new.

To the Lord General Cromwell

Cromwell, our chief of men, who through a cloud
Not of war only, but detractions rude,
Guided by faith and matchless fortitude,
To peace and truth thy glorious way hast plough'd,
And on the neck of crownéd Fortune proud
Hast rear'd God's trophies, and His work pursu'd,
While Darwen stream with blood of Scots imbru'd,
And Dunbar field resounds thy praises loud,
And Worcester's laureate wreath; yet much remains
To conquer still; peace hath her victories
No less renown'd than war, new foes arise
Threat'ning to bind our souls with secular chains:
Help us to save free Conscience from the paw
Of hireling wolves whose Gospel is their maw.

On the Late Massacre in Piedmont

Avenge O Lord Thy slaughtered saints, whose bones
Lie scattered on the Alpine mountains cold,
Ev'n them that kept Thy truth so pure of old
When all our fathers worshipped stocks and stones,
Forget not: in Thy book record their groans
Who were Thy sheep and in their ancient fold
Slain by the bloody Piedmontese that rolled
Mother with infant down the rocks. Their moans
The vales redoubled to the hills, and they
To Heav'n. Their martyred blood and ashes sow
O'er all th' Italian fields where still doth sway
The triple tyrant; that from these may grow
A hundred-fold, who having learnt Thy way
Early may fly the Babylonian woe.

"When I Consider..."

When I consider how my light is spent,
Ere half my days, in this dark world and wide,
And that one talent which is death to hide,
Lodged with me useless, though my soul more bent
To serve therewith my Maker, and present
My true account, lest He returning chide:
Doth God exact day-labour, light denied,
I fondly ask; but patience to prevent
That murmur, soon replies, God doth not need
Either man's works or His own gifts; who best
Bear His mild yoke, they serve Him best; His state
Is kingly; thousands at His bidding speed
And post o'er land and ocean without rest:
They also serve who only stand and wait.

FROM *Paradise Lost*

1.

Hail holy light, offspring of Heav'n's first-born,
Or of th' Eternal co-eternal beam,
May I express thee unblamed? since God is light,

And never but in unapproachéd light
Dwelt from Eternity, dwelt then in thee,
Bright effluence of bright essence increate.
Or hear'st thou rather pure ethereal stream,
Whose fountain who shall tell? before the sun,
Before the heavens thou wert, and at the voice
Of God, as with a mantle didst invest
The rising world of waters dark and deep,
Won from the void and formless infinite.
Thee I revisit now with bolder wing,
Escaped the Stygian pool, though long detained
In that obscure sojourn, while in my flight
Through utter and through middle darkness borne,
With other notes than to th' Orphean lyre
I sung of Chaos and Eternal Night,
Taught by the heavenly Muse to venture down
The dark descent, and up to reascend,
Though hard and rare; thee I revisit safe,
And feel thy sovereign vital lamp; but thou
Revisit'st not these eyes, that roll in vain
To find thy piercing ray, and find no dawn;
So thick a drop serene hath quenched their orbs,
Or dim suffusion veiled. Yet not the more
Cease I to wander where the Muses haunt
Clear spring, or shady grove, or sunny hill,
Smit with the love of sacred song; but chief
Thee, Sion, and the flowery brooks beneath
That wash thy hallowed feet, and warbling flow,
Nightly I visit: nor sometimes forget
Those other two equalled with me in fate,
So were I equalled with them in renown,
Blind Thamyris and blind Maeonides,
And Tiresias and Phineus prophets old:
Then feed on thoughts, that voluntary move
Harmonious numbers; as the wakeful bird
Sings darkling, and in shadiest covert hid
Tunes her nocturnal note. Thus with the year
Seasons return, but not to me returns
Day, or the sweet approach of ev'n or morn,
Or sight of vernal bloom, or summer's rose,
Or flocks, or herds, or human face divine;

But cloud instead, and ever-during dark
Surrounds me, from the cheerful ways of men
Cut off, and from the book of knowledge fair
Presented with a universal blank
Of Nature's works to me expunged and razed,
And wisdom at one entrance quite shut out.
So much the rather thou celestial light
Shine inward, and the mind through all her powers
Irradiate, there plant eyes, all mist from thence
Purge and disperse, that I may see and tell
Of things invisible to mortal sight.

2.

Southward through Eden went a river large,
Nor changed his course, but through the shaggy hill
Passed underneath engulfed, for God had thrown
That mountain as His garden mould high raised
Upon the rapid current, which through veins
Or porous earth with kindly thirst updrawn,
Rose a fresh fountain, and with many a rill
Watered the garden; thence united fell
Down the steep glade, and met the nether flood,
Which from his darksome passage now appears,
And now divided into four main streams,
Runs diverse, wand'ring many a famous realm
And country whereof here needs no account,
But rather to tell how, if art could tell,
How from that sapphire fount the crispéd brooks,
Rolling on orient pearl and sands of gold,
With mazy error under pendant shades
Ran nectar, visiting each plant, and fed
Flowers worthy of Paradise which not nice art
In beds and curious knots, but Nature boon
Poured forth profuse on hill and dale and plain,
Both where the morning sun first warmly smote
The open field, and where the unpierced shade
Embrowned the noontide bow'rs: Thus was this place
A happy rural seat of various view:
Groves whose rich trees wept odorous gums and balm,
Others whose fruit burnished with golden rind

Hung amiable, Hesperian fables true,
If true, here only, and of delicious taste:
Betwixt them lawns, or level downs, and flocks
Grazing the tender herb, were interposed,
Or palmy hillock, or the flowery lap
Of some irriguous valley spread her store,
Flowers of all hue, and without thorn the rose:
Another side, umbrageous grots and caves
Of cool recess, o'er which the mantling vine
Lays forth her purple grape, and gently creeps
Luxuriant; meanwhile murmuring waters fall
Down the slope hills, dispersed, or in a lake,
That to the fringéd bank with myrtle crowned,
Her crystal mirror holds, unite their streams.
The birds their choir apply; airs, vernal airs,
Breathing the smell of field and grove, attune
The trembling leaves, while universal Pan
Knit with the Graces and the Hours in dance
Led on th' eternal spring. Not that fair field
Of Enna, where Proserpin gathering flowers
Herself a fairer flower by gloomy Dis
Was gathered, which cost Ceres all that pain
To seek her through the world; nor that sweet grove
Of Daphne by Orontes, and th' inspired
Castalian spring might with this Paradise
Of Eden strive; nor that Nyseian isle
Girt with the river Triton, where old Cham,
Whom gentiles Ammon call and Lybian Jove,
Hid Amalthea and her florid son
Young Bacchus from his stepdame Rhea's eye;
Nor where Abassin kings their issue guard,
Mount Amara, though this by some supposed
True Paradise under the Ethiop line
By Nilus' head, enclosed with shining rock,
A whole day's journey high, but wide remote
From this Assyrian garden, where the fiend
Saw undelighted all delight, all kind
Of living creatures new to sight and strange:
Two of far nobler shape erect and tall,
Godlike erect, with native honour clad
In naked majesty seemed lords of all,

And worthy seemed, for in their looks divine
The image of their glorious Maker shone,
Truth, wisdom, sanctitude severe and pure,
Severe, but in true filial freedom placed;
Whence true authority in men; though both
Not equal, as their sex not equal seemed;
For contemplation he and valour formed,
For softness she and sweet attractive grace,
He for God only, she for God in him:
His fair large front and eye sublime declared
Absolute rule; and hyacinthine locks
Round from his parted forelock manly hung
Clust'ring, but not beneath his shoulders broad:
She as a veil down to the slender waist
Her unadornéd golden tresses wore
Dishevelled, but in wanton ringlets waved
As the vine curls her tendrils, which implied
Subjection, but required with gentle sway,
And by her yielded, by him best received,
Yielded with coy submission, modest pride,
And sweet reluctant amorous delay.

FROM *Paradise Regained*

Look once more ere we leave this specular Mount
Westward, much nearer by southwest, behold
Where on the Aegean shore a city stands
Built nobly, pure the air, and light the soil,
Athens the eye of Greece, mother of arts
And eloquence, native to famous wits
Or hospitable, in her sweet recess,
City or suburban, studious walks and shades;
See there the olive grove of Academe,
Plato's retirement, where the Attic bird
Trills her thick-warbled notes the summer long;
There flowery hill Hymettus with the sound
Of bees' industrious murmur, oft invites
To studious musing; there Ilissus rolls
His whispering stream; within the walls then view
The schools of ancient sages; his who bred

Great Alexander to subdue the world,
Lyceum there, and painted Stoa next;
There shalt thou hear and learn the secret power
Of harmony in tones and numbers hit
By voice or hand, and various-measured verse,
Aeolian charms and Dorian lyric odes,
And his who gave them breath, but higher sung,
Blind Melesigenes thence Homer called,
Whose poem Phoebus challenged for his own.
Thence what the lofty grave tragedians taught
In chorus or iambic, teachers best
Of moral prudence, with delight received
In brief sententious precepts, while they treat
Of fate, and chance, and change in human life;
High actions, and high passions best describing:
Thence to the famous orators repair,
Those ancient, whose resistless eloquence
Wielded at will that fierce democracy,
Shook the Arsenal and fulmined over Greece,
To Macedon, and Artaxerxes' throne;
To sage philosophy next lend thine ear,
From Heaven descended to the low-roofed house
Of Socrates, see there his tenement,
Whom well inspired the oracle pronounced
Wisest of men; from whose mouth issued forth
Mellifluous streams that watered all the schools
Of Academics old and new, with those
Surnamed Peripatetics, and the sect
Epicurean, and the Stoic severe;
These here revolve, or, as thou lik'st, at home,
Till time mature thee to a kingdom's weight;
These rules will render thee a king complete
Within thyself, much more with empire joined.

FROM *Samson Agonistes*

Samson: A little onward lend thy guiding hand
           To these dark steps, a little further on;
           For yonder bank hath choice of sun or shade,
           There I am wont to sit, when any chance

Relieves me from my task of servile toil,
Daily in the common prison else enjoined me,
Where I a prisoner chained, scarce freely draw
The air imprisoned also, close and damp,
Unwholesome draught: but here I feel amends
The breath of heaven fresh-blowing, pure and
  sweet,
With day-spring born; here leave me to respire.
This day a solemn feast the people hold
To Dagon their sea-idol, and forbid
Laborious works, unwillingly this rest
Their superstition yields me; hence with leave
Retiring from the popular noise, I seek
This unfrequented place to find some ease,
Ease to the body some, none to the mind
From restless thoughts, that like a deadly swarm
Of hornets armed, no sooner found alone,
But rush upon me thronging, and present
Times past, what once I was, and what am now.
O wherefore was my birth from Heaven foretold
Twice by an angel, who at last in sight
Of both my parents all in flames ascended
From off the altar, where an offering burned,
As in a fiery column charioting
His Godlike presence, and from some great act
Or benefit revealed to Abraham's race?
Why was my breeding ordered and prescribed
As of a person separate to God,
Designed for great exploits; if I must die
Betrayed, captive, and both my eyes put out,
Made of my enemies the scorn and gaze;
To grind in brazen fetters under task
With this heaven-gifted strength? O glorious
  strength
Put to the labour of a beast, debased
Lower than bondslave! Promise was that I
Should Israel from Philistian yoke deliver;
Ask for this great deliverer now, and find him
Eyeless in Gaza at the mill with slaves,
Himself in bonds under Philistian yoke;
Yet stay, let me not rashly call in doubt

Divine prediction; what if all foretold
Had been fulfilled but through mine own default,
Whom have I to complain of but myself?
Who this high gift of strength committed to me,
In what part lodged, how easily bereft me,
Under the seal of silence could not keep,
But weakly to a woman must reveal it
O'ercome with importunity and tears.
O impotence of mind, in body strong!
But what is strength without a double share
Of wisdom? vast, unwieldy, burdensome,
Proudly secure, yet liable to fall
By weakest subtleties, not made to rule,
But to subserve where wisdom bears command.
God, when He gave me strength, to show withal
How slight the gift was, hung it in my hair.
But peace, I must not quarrel with the will
Of highest dispensation, which herein
Haply had ends above my reach to know:
Suffices that to me strength is my bane,
And proves the source of all my miseries;
So many, and so huge, that each apart
Would ask a life to wail, but chief of all,
O loss of sight, of thee I most complain!
Blind among enemies, O worse than chains,
Dungeon, or beggary, or decrepit age!
Light the prime work of God to me is extinct,
And all her various objects of delight
Annulled, which might in part my grief have eased,
Inferior to the vilest now become
Of man or worm; the vilest here excel me,
They creep, yet see, I dark in light exposed
To daily fraud, contempt, abuse and wrong,
Within doors, or without, still as a fool,
In power of others, never in my own;
Scarce half I seem to live, dead more than half.
O dark, dark, dark, amid the blaze of noon,
Irrecoverably dark, total eclipse
Without all hope of day!
O first created beam, and thou great Word,
Let there be light, and light was over all;

Why am I thus bereaved thy prime decree?
The sun to me is dark
And silent as the moon,
When she deserts the night
Hid in her vacant interlunar cave.
Since light so necessary is to life,
And almost life itself, if it be true
That light is in the soul,
She all in every part; why was the sight
To such a tender ball as th' eye confined?
So obvious and so easy to be quenched,
And not as feeling through all parts diffused,
That she might look at will through every pore?
Then had I not been thus exiled from light;
As in the land of darkness yet in light,
To live a life half dead, a living death,
And buried; but O yet more miserable!
Myself my sepulchre, a moving grave,
Buried, yet not exempt
By privilege of death and burial
From worst of other evils, pains and wrongs,
But made hereby obnoxious more
To all the miseries of life,
Life in captivity
Among inhuman foes.

SIR JOHN SUCKLING

(1609–1642)

The Siege

'Tis now, since I sat down before
    That foolish fort, a heart,—
Time strangely spent—a year or more,
    And still I did my part,

Made my approaches, from her hand
    Unto her lip did rise,
And did already understand
    The language of her eyes;

Proceeded on with no less art—
    My tongue was engineer;
I thought to undermine the heart
    By whispering in the ear.

When this did nothing, I brought down
    Great cannon-oaths, and shot
A thousand thousand to the town;
    And still it yielded not.

I then resolved to starve the place
    By cutting off all kisses,
Praising and gazing on her face,
    And all such little blisses.

To draw her out and from her strength,
    I drew all batteries in;
And brought myself to lie at length
    As if no siege had been.

When I had done what man could do
    And thought the place mine own,
The enemy lay quiet too
    And smiled at all was done.

I sent to know from whence and where
    These hopes and this relief?
A spy informed Honour was there,
    And did command in chief.

March, march, quoth I; the word straight give;
    Let's lose no time, but leave her:
That giant upon air will live
    And hold it out for ever.

To such a place our camp remove,
    As will no siege abide:
I hate a fool that starves her love
    Only to feed her pride.

A *Ballad* upon a Wedding

I tell thee, Dick, where I have been;
Where I the rarest things have seen,
   O, things without compare!
Such sights again cannot be found
In any place on English ground,
   Be it at wake or fair.

At Charing Cross, hard by the way
Where we, thou know'st, do sell our hay,
   There is a house with stairs;
And there did I see coming down
Such folks as are not in our town,
   Forty at least in pairs.

Amongst the rest one pest'lent fine,
His beard no bigger though than thine,
   Walked on before the rest:
Our landlord looks like nothing to him:
The King, God bless him!, 'twould undo him,
   Should he go still so dressed.

At Course-a-Park without all doubt
He should have first been taken out
   By all the maids i' th' town:
Though lusty Roger there had been,
Or little George upon the Green,
   Or Vincent of the Crown.

But wot you what? the youth was going
To make an end of all his wooing;
   The parson for him staid:
Yet by his leave, for all his haste,
He did not so much wish all past,
   Perchance, as did the maid.

The maid—and thereby hangs a tale;
For such a maid no Whitson-ale
   Could ever yet produce:

No grape, that's kindly ripe, could be
So round, so plump, so soft as she,
    Nor half so full of juice.

Her finger was so small, the ring
Would not stay on, which they did bring;
    It was too wide a peck:
And to say truth, for out it must,
It looked like the great collar, just,
    About our young colt's neck.

Her feet beneath her petticoat
Like little mice stole in and out,
    As if they feared the light:
But O, she dances such a way!
No sun upon an Easter-day
    Is half so fine a sight.

He would have kissed her once or twice;
But she would not, she was so nice,
    She would not do't in sight:
And then she looked as who should say,
"I will do what I list to-day,
    And you shall do't at night."

Her cheeks so rare a white was on,
No daisy makes comparison;
    Who sees them is undone:
For streaks of red were mingled there
Such as are on a Catherine pear,
    The side that's next the sun.

Her lips were red; and one was thin
Compared to that was next her chin,
    Some bee had stung it newly:
But, Dick, her eyes so guard her face,
I durst no more upon them gaze
    Than on the sun in July.

Her mouth so small, when she does speak
Thou'dst swear her teeth her words did break
    That they might passage get;
But she so handled still the matter
They came as good as ours, or better,
    And are not spent a whit.

If wishing should be any sin,
The parson himself had guilty been,
    She looked that day so purely;
And, did the youth so oft the feat
At night, as some did in conceit,
    It would have spoiled him surely.

Just in the nick the cook knocked thrice,
And all the waiters in a trice
    His summons did obey:
Each serving-man, with dish in hand,
Marched boldly up, like our trained band,
    Presented, and away.

The business of the kitchen's great,
For it is fit that man should eat;
    Nor was it there denied—
Passion o' me, how I run on!
There's that that would be thought upon,
    I trow, besides the bride.

Now hats fly off and youths carouse,
Healths first go round and then the house:
    The bride's came thick and thick;
And, when 'twas named another's health,
Perhaps he made it hers by stealth;
    And who could help it, Dick?

O' th' sudden up they rise and dance;
Then sit again and sigh and glance;
    Then dance again and kiss:
Thus several ways the time did pass,
Whilst every woman wished her place,
    And every man wished his.

By this time all were stolen aside
To counsel and undress the bride;
   But that he must not know:
But yet 'twas thought he guessed her mind,
And did not mean to stay behind
   Above an hour or so.

When in he came, Dick, there she lay
Like new-fallen snow melting away;
   'Twas time, I trow, to part:
Kisses were now the only stay,
Which soon she gave, as one would say,
   Good-bye with all my heart.

But, just as Heavens would have, to cross it,
In came the bridesmaids with the posset;
   The bridegroom ate in spite:
For, had he left the women to't,
It would have cost two hours to do't,
   Which were too much that night.

At length the candle's out; and now
All that they had not done they do;
   What that is, who can tell?
But I believe it was no more
Than thou and I have done before
   With Bridget and with Nell.

A Poem

Out upon it! I have loved
   Three whole days together;
And am like to love three more,
   If it prove fair weather.

Time shall moult away his wings,
   Ere he shall discover
In the whole wide world again
   Such a constant lover.

But the spite on't is, no praise
    Is due at all to me;
Love with me had made no stays,
    Had it any been but she.

Had it any been but she,
    And that very face,
There had been at least ere this
    A dozen dozen in her place.

Song

I prithee send me back my heart,
    Since I cannot have thine;
For if from yours you will not part,
    Why then shouldst thou have mine?

Yet now I think on't, let it lie;
    To find it were in vain,
For th' hast a thief in either eye
    Would steal it back again.

Why should two hearts in one breast lie,
    And yet not lodge together?
O love, where is thy sympathy,
    If thus our breasts thou sever?

But love is such a mystery,
    I cannot find it out;
For when I think I'm best resolved,
    I then am most in doubt.

Then farewell care, and farewell woe,
    I will no longer pine;
For I'll believe I have her heart
    As much as she hath mine.

Song

Why so pale and wan, fond lover?
    Prithee, why so pale?
Will, when looking well can't win her,
    Looking ill prevail?
    Prithee, why so pale?

Why so dull and mute, young sinner?
    Prithee, why so mute?
Will, when speaking well can't win her,
    Saying nothing do't?
    Prithee, why so mute?

Quit, quit for shame, this will not move;
    This cannot take her.
If of herself she will not love,
    Nothing can make her;
    The devil take her!

Aglaura, 1646

WILLIAM CARTWRIGHT
(1611–1643)

To Chloe,
Who Wished Herself Young Enough for Me

Chloe, why wish you that your years
    Would backward run, till they meet mine,
That perfect likeness which endears
    Things unto things might us combine?
Our ages so in date agree
That twins do differ more than we.

There are two births; the one when light
    First strikes the new awakened sense;
The other when two souls unite;
    And we must count our life from thence.
When you loved me and I loved you,
The both of us were born anew.

Love then to us did new souls give,
   And in those souls did plant new powers;
Since when another life we live,
   The breath we breathe is his, not ours;
Love makes those young whom age doth chill,
And whom he finds young, keeps young still.

Love, like that angel that shall call
   Our bodies from the silent grave,
Unto one age doth raise us all,
   None too much, none too little have.
Nay, that the difference may be none,
He makes two not alike, but one.

And now since you and I are such,
   Tell me what's yours, and what is mine?
Our eyes, our ears, our taste, smell, touch,
   Do, like our souls, in one combine.
So by this, I as well may be
Too old for you as you for me.

JAMES GRAHAM, Marquess of Montrose
(1612–1650)

Montrose to His Mistress

My dear and only love, I pray
   This noble world of thee,
Be governed by no other sway
   But purest monarchy.
For if confusion have a part,
   Which virtuous souls abhor,
And hold a synod in thy heart,
   I'll never love thee more.

Like Alexander I will reign,
   And I will reign alone,
My thoughts shall evermore disdain
   A rival on my throne.

He either fears his fate too much,
   Or his deserts are small,
That puts it not unto the touch,
   To win or lose it all.

But I must rule, and govern still,
   And always give the law,
And have each subject at my will,
   And all to stand in awe.
But 'gainst my battery if I find
   Thou shun'st the prize so sore,
As that thou set'st me up a blind,
   I'll never love thee more.

Or in the empire of thy heart,
   Where I should solely be,
Another do pretend a part,
   And dares to vie with me,
Or if committees thou erect,
   And go on such a score,
I'll sing and laugh at thy neglect,
   And never love thee more.

But if thou wilt be constant then,
   And faithful of thy word,
I'll make thee glorious by my pen,
   And famous by my sword.
I'll serve thee in such noble ways
   Was never heard before:
I'll crown and deck thee all with bays,
   And love thee evermore.

His Metrical Vow
(ON THE DEATH OF KING CHARLES I)

Great, Good and Just, could I but rate
My grief to thy too rigid fate!
I'd weep the world in such a strain,
As it would once deluge again:

But since thy loud-tongued blood demands supplies,
More from Briareus' hands than Argus' eyes,
I'll tune thy elegies to trumpet-sounds,
And write thy epitaph in blood and wounds.

SAMUEL BUTLER

(1612–1680)

FROM *Hudibras*

1.

When civil dudgeon first grew high,
And men fell out, they knew not why;
When hard words, jealousies, and fears,
Set folks together by the ears,
And made them fight, like mad or drunk,
For Dame Religion, as for punk;
Whose honesty they all durst swear for,
Though not a man of them knew wherefore;
When Gospel-trumpeter, surrounded
With long-eared rout, to battle sounded;
And pulpit, drum ecclesiastic,
Was beat with fist instead of a stick:
Then did Sir Knight abandon dwelling,
And out he rode a-colonelling.
A wight he was whose very sight would
Entitle him Mirror of Knighthood,
That never bowed his stubborn knee
To any thing but chivalry,
Nor put up blow, but that which laid
Right Worshipful on shoulder-blade;
Chief of domestic knights and errant,
Either for chartel or for warrant;
Great on the bench, great in the saddle,
That could as well bind o'er as swaddle.
Mighty he was at both of these,
And styled of War, as well as Peace
(So some rats of amphibious nature,
Are either for the land or water):
But here our authors make a doubt
Whether he was more wise or stout:
Some hold the one, and some the other;

But, howso'er they make a pother,
The diff'rence was so small, his brain
Outweighed his rage but half a grain;
Which made some take him for a tool
That knaves do work with, called a Fool.
For 't has been held by many, that
As Montaigne, playing with his cat,
Complains she thought him but an ass,
Much more she would Sir Hudibras
(For that's the name our valiant Knight
To all his challenges did write):
But they're mistaken very much,
'Tis plain enough he was no such.
We grant, although he had much wit,
H'was very shy of using it,
As being loath to wear it out,
And therefore bore it not about,
Unless on holidays or so,
As men their best apparel do.
Beside, 'tis known he could speak Greek
As naturally as pigs squeak;
That Latin was no more difficile,
Than to a blackbird 'tis to whistle.
Being rich in both, he never scanted
His bounty unto such as wanted;
But much of either could afford
To many that had not one word.
For Hebrew roots, although they're found
To flourish most in barren ground,
He had such plenty as sufficed
To make some think him circumcised:
And truly so perhaps he was,
'Tis many a pious Christian's case.

2.

For his religion, it was fit
To match his learning and his wit:
'Twas Presbyterian true blue;
For he was of that stubborn crew
Of errant Saints, whom all men grant

To be the true Church Militant;
Such as do build their faith upon
The holy text of pike and gun;
Decide all controversies by
Infallible artillery;
And prove their doctrine orthodox
By apostolic blows and knocks;
Call fire, sword, and desolation,
A godly, thorough Reformation,
Which always must be carried on,
And still be doing, never done;
As if Religion were intended
For nothing else but to be mended:
A sect whose chief devotion lies
In odd perverse antipathies;
In falling out with that or this,
And finding somewhat still amiss:
More peevish, cross, and splenetic,
Than dog distract, or monkey sick;
That with more care kept holiday
The wrong, than others the right way;
Compound for sins they are inclined to,
By damning those they have no mind to.
Still so perverse and opposite,
As if they worshipped God for spite:
The self-same thing they will abhor
One way, and long another for.
Free-will they one way disavow,
Another, nothing else allow:
All piety consists therein
In them, in other men all sin:
Rather than fail, they will defy
That which they love most tenderly;
Quarrel with minced-pies, and disparage
Their best and dearest friend, plum-porridge;
Fat pig and goose itself oppose,
And blaspheme custard through the nose.
Th'apostles of this fierce religion,
Like Mahomet's, were ass and widgeon,
To whom our Knight, by fast instinct
Of wit and temper, was so linked,

As if hypocrisy and nonsense
Had got th'advowson of his conscience.

3.

This sturdy Squire, he had, as well
As the bold Trojan Knight, seen hell,
Not with a counterfeited pass
Of golden bough, but true gold lace:
His knowledge was not far behind
The Knight's, but of another kind,
And he another way came by't:
Some call it Gifts, and some New-Light;
A lib'ral art, that cost no pains
Of study, industry, or brains.
His wit was sent him for a token,
But in the carriage cracked and broken;
Like commendation ninepence crooked,
With—To and from my Love—it looked.
He ne'er considered it, as loath
To look a gift-horse in the mouth,
And very wisely would lay forth
No more upon it than 'twas worth;
But as he got it freely, so
He spent it frank and freely too:
For Saints themselves will sometimes be
Of gifts that cost them nothing, free.
By means of this, with hem and cough,
Prolongers to enlightened stuff,
He could deep mysteries unriddle,
As easily as thread a needle;
For as of vagabonds we say,
That they are ne'er beside their way;
Whate'er men speak by this new light,
Still they are sure to be i' th' right.
'Tis a dark lantern of the spirit,
Which none sees by but those that bear it;
A light that falls down from on high,
For spiritual trades to cozen by;
An *ignis fatuus*, that bewitches
And leads men into pools and ditches,

To make them dip themselves, and sound
For Christendom in dirty pond;
To dive, like wild-fowl, for salvation,
And fish to catch regeneration.
This light inspires and plays upon
The nose of Saint, like bagpipe drone,
And speaks through hollow empty soul,
As through a trunk, or whisp'ring hole,
Such language as no mortal ear
But spiritual eaves-droppers can hear:
So Phoebus, or some friendly Muse,
Into small poets song infuse,
Which they at second-hand rehearse,
Through reed or bagpipe, verse for verse.

RICHARD CRASHAW

(1613?–1649)

FROM *Epithalamium*

Come, virgin tapers of pure wax,
  Made in the hive of love, all white
As snow and yet as cold, where lacks
  Hymen's holy heat and light;
    Where blooming kisses
      Their beds yet keep,
    And steep their blisses
      In rosy sleep;
Where sister buds yet wanting brothers
Kiss their own lips in lieu of others;
Help me to mourn a matchless maidenhead
    That now is dead.

A fine thin negative thing it was,
  A nothing with a dainty name,
Which pruned her plumes in self-love's glass,
  Made up of fancy and fond fame;
    Within the shade
      Of its own wing

It sate and played
　　A self-crowned King;
A froward flower, whose peevish pride
Within itself itself did hide,
Flying all fingers, and even thinking much
　　　Of its own touch.

The bird indeed the phoenix was
　　Late chased by Love's revengeful arrows,
Whose wars now left the wonted pass
　　And spared the little lives of sparrows;
　　　To hunt this fool,
　　　　Whose froward pride
　　　Love's noble school
　　　　And courts denied,
And froze the fruits of fair desire
Which flourisheth in mutual fire,
'Gainst Nature, who 'mong all the webs she spun
　　　Ne'er wove a Nun.

She of Cupid's shafts afraid
　　Left her own balm-breathing East,
And in a western bosom made
　　A softer and a sweeter nest:
　　　There did she rest
　　　　In the sweet shade
　　　Of a soft breast,
　　　　Whose beauties made
Thames oft stand still and lend a glass
While in her own she saw heaven's face,
And sent him full of her fair name's report
　　　To Thetis' Court.

And now poor Love was at a stand.
　　The crystal castle which she kept
Was proof against the proudest hand;
　　There in safest hold she slept;
　　　His shafts' expence
　　　　Left there no smart,

But bounding thence
Broached his own heart;
At length a fort he did devise
Built in noble Brampston's eyes,
And aiming thence this matchless maidenhead
Was soon found dead.

Yet Love in death did wait upon her,
Granting leave she should expire
In her fumes, and have the honour
T'exhale in flames of his own fire.
Her funeral pile
The marriage bed,
In a sighed smile
She vanishéd.
So rich a dress of death ne'er famed
The cradles where her kindred flamed;
So sweet her mother phoenixes of th'East
Ne'er spiced their nest.

FROM *Wishes. To His Supposed Mistress*

Whoe'er she be,
That not impossible she
That shall command my heart and me;

Where'er she lie,
Locked up from mortal eye
In shady leaves of Destiny:

Till that ripe birth
Of studied fate stand forth,
And teach her fair steps to our earth;

Till that divine
Idea take a shrine
Of crystal flesh through which to shine:

Meet you her my wishes,
Bespeak her to me blisses,
And be ye called my absent kisses.

I wish her Beauty
That owes not all his duty
To gaudy tire or glist'ring shoe-tie.

Something more than
Taffata or tissue can,
Or rampant feather or rich fan.

More than the spoil
Of shop or silkworms' toil,
Or a bought blush or a set smile.

A Face that's best
By its own beauty drest,
And can alone commend the rest.

A Face made up
Out of no other shop
Than what Nature's white hand sets ope.

A Cheek where youth
And blood with pen of truth
Write what the reader sweetly ru'th.

A Cheek where grows
More than a morning rose,
Which to no box his being owes.

Lips, where all day
A lover's kiss may play,
Yet carry nothing thence away.

Looks that oppress
Their richest tires, but dress
And clothe their simplest nakedness.

Eyes, that displaces
The neighbour diamond, and outfaces
That sunshine by their own sweet graces.

Tresses, that wear
Jewels but to declare
How much themselves more precious are;

Whose native ray
Can tame the wanton day
Of gems, that in their bright shades play.

Each ruby there,
Or pearl that dare appear,
Be its own blush, be its own tear.

A well tamed Heart,
For whose more noble smart
Love may be long choosing a dart.

Eyes, that bestow
Full quivers on Love's bow,
Yet pay less arrows than they owe.

Smiles, that can warm
The blood, yet teach a charm
That chastity shall take no harm.

Blushes, that bin
The burnish of no sin,
Nor flames of aught too hot within.

Joys, that confess
Virtue, their mistress,
And have no other head to dress.

Fears, fond and slight,
As the coy bride's, when night
First does the longing lover right.

Tears, quickly fled,
And vain, as those are shed
For a dying maidenhead.

Days, that need borrow
No part of their good morrow
From a forespent night of sorrow.

Days, that in spite
Of darkness, by the light
Of a clear mind are day all night.

Nights, sweet as they
Made short by lovers' play,
Yet long by th'absence of the day.

Life, that dares send
A challenge to his end,
And when it comes say, Welcome friend.

I wish her store
Of worth may leave her poor
Of wishes; and I wish—no more.

A Song

Lord, when the sense of Thy sweet grace
Sends up my soul to seek Thy face,
Thy blessed eyes breed such desire
I die in love's delicious fire.
O Love, I am thy Sacrifice.
Be still triumphant, blessed eyes.
Still shine on me, fair suns! that I
Still may behold, though still I die.

Though still I die, I live again,
Still longing so to be still slain;
So gainful is such loss of breath,
I die even in desire of death.
Still live in me this loving strife
Of living Death and dying Life.
For while Thou sweetly slayest me,
Dead to myself I live in Thee.

For Hope

Dear hope! Earth's dowry and heav'n's debt!
The entity of those that are not yet.
Subtlest, but surest being! Thou by whom
Our nothing has a definition!
Substantial shade! whose sweet allay
Blends both the noons of night and day.
Fates cannot find out a capacity
Of hurting thee.
From Thee their lean dilemma with blunt horn
Shrinks, as the sick moon from the wholesome morn.
Rich hope! Love's legacy under lock
Of faith! still spending and still growing stock!
Our crown-land lies above, yet each meal brings
A seemly portion for the sons of kings.
Nor will the virgin joys we wed
Come less unbroken to our bed
Because that from the bridal cheek of bliss
Thou steal'st us down a distant kiss.
Hope's chaste stealth harms no more joy's maidenhead
Than spousal rites prejudge the marriage bed.
Fair hope! Our earlier heav'n, by thee
Young time is taster to eternity.
Thy generous wine with age grows strong, not sour.
Nor does it kill the fruit to smell the flower.
Thy golden, growing head never hangs down,
Till in the lap of love's full noon
It falls, and dies! O no, it melts away
As does the dawn into the day,
As lumps of sugar lose themselves and twine
Their supple essence with the soul of wine.
Fortune? Alas, above the world's low wars,
Hope walks, and kicks the curl'd heads of conspiring stars.
Her keel cuts not the waves where these winds stir;
Fortune's whole lottery is one blank to her.
Her shafts and she fly far above
And forage in the fields of light and love.
Sweet hope! Kind cheat! Fair fallacy! By thee
We are not Where nor What we be,

But What and Where we would be. Thus art thou
Our absent Presence and our future Now.
Faith's sister! Nurse of fair desire!
Fear's antidote! A wise and well-stay'd fire!
Temper 'twixt chill despair and torrid joy!
Queen Regent in young Love's minority!
Though the vext chymick vainly chases
His fugitive gold through all her faces,
Though Love's more fierce, more fugitive fires assay
One face more fugitive than all they,
True hope's a glorious hunter, and her chase
The God of Nature in the fields of grace.

FROM A Hymn of the Nativity

Gloomy Night embraced the place
   Where the noble Infant lay;
The Babe looked up, and shewed his face,
   In spite of darkness it was day.
It was thy day, sweet, and did rise
Not from the East, but from thy eyes.

Winter chid the world, and sent
   The angry North to wage his wars;
The North forgot his fierce intent,
   And left perfumes instead of scars;
By those sweet eyes' persuasive powers
Where he meant frosts he scattered flowers.

We see thee in thy balmy nest,
   Bright Dawn of our eternal day;
We saw thine eyes break from the East
   And chase the trembling shades away;
We saw thee (and we blessed the sight)
We saw thee by thine own sweet light.

I saw the curled drops soft and slow
   Come hovering o'er the place's head,
Off'ring their whitest sheets of snow
   To furnish the fair Infant's bed.
Forbear, (said I) be not too bold,
Your fleece is white, but 'tis too cold.

I saw th'officious angels bring
   The down that their soft breasts did strow,
For well they now can spare their wings,
   When Heaven itself lies here below.
Fair youth, (said I) be not too rough,
Thy down though soft's not soft enough.

The Babe no sooner 'gan to seek
   Where to lay his lovely head,
But straight his eyes advised his cheek
   'Twixt Mother's breasts to go to bed.
Sweet choice (said I) no way but so
Not to lie cold, yet sleep in snow.

Welcome to our wondering sight,
   Eternity shut in a span!
Summer in winter! Day in night!
   Heaven in earth! and God in man!
Great little one, whose glorious birth
Lifts earth to Heaven, stoops Heaven to earth.

FROM *The Weeper*

Hail Sister Springs!
Parents of silver-forded rills!
   Ever bubbling things!
Thawing crystal! Snowy hills!
Still spending, never spent; I mean
Thy fair eyes, sweet Magdalene.

Heavens thy fair eyes be,
Heavens of ever-falling stars;
   'Tis seed-time still with thee,
And stars thou sowest, whose harvest dares
Promise the earth to countershine
Whatever makes Heaven's forehead fine.

But we are deceived all,
Stars they are indeed too true,
   For they but seem to fall

As Heaven's other spangles do;
It is not for our earth and us
To shine in things so precious.

   Upwards thou dost weep;
Heaven's bosom drinks the gentle stream.
   Where the milky rivers meet
Thine crawls above and is the cream.
Heaven, of such fair floods as this
Heaven the crystal ocean is.

   The dew no more will weep,
The primrose's pale cheek to deck;
   The dew no more will sleep,
Nuzzled in the lily's neck.
Much rather would it tremble here,
And leave them both to be thy tear.

   Not the soft gold which
Steals from the amber-weeping tree,
   Makes Sorrow half so rich
As the drops distilled from thee.
Sorrow's best jewels lie in these
Caskets, of which Heaven keeps the keys.

   Not in the Evening's eyes
When they red with weeping are
   For the sun that dies,
Sits Sorrow with a face so fair.
Nowhere but here did ever meet
Sweetness so sad, sadness so sweet.

   Well does the May that lies
Smiling in thy cheeks, confess
   The April in thine eyes;
Mutual sweetness they express.
No April e'er lent softer showers
Nor May returnéd fairer flowers.

   Whither away so fast?
O whither? for the sluttish earth
   Your sweetness cannot taste,

Nor does the dust deserve your birth.
Whither haste ye then? O say
Why ye trip so fast away?

We go not to seek
The darlings of Aurora's bed,
  The rose's modest cheek
Nor the violet's humble head.
No such thing; we go to meet
A worthier object, Our Lord's feet.

JOHN CLEVELAND

(1613–1658)

Mark Antony

When as the nightingale chanted her vespers,
  And the wild forester couched on the ground,
Venus invited me in th'evening whispers
  Unto a fragrant field with roses crowned,
      Where she before had sent
      My wishes' compliment;
      Unto my heart's content
      Played with me on the green.
          Never Mark Antony
          Dallied more wantonly
          With the fair Egyptian Queen.

First on her cherry cheeks I mine eye feasted,
  Thence fear of surfeiting made me retire;
Next on her warmer lips, which, when I tasted,
  My duller spirits were active as fire.
      Then we began to dart,
      Each at another's heart,
      Arrows that know no smart,
      Sweet lips and smiles between.
          Never Mark Antony
          Dallied more wantonly
          With the fair Egyptian Queen.

Wanting a glass to plait her amber tresses
   Which like a bracelet rich deckéd mine arm,
Gaudier than Juno wears when as she graces
   Jove with embraces more stately than warm,
         Then did she peep in mine
         Eyes' humor crystalline;
         I in her eyes was seen
         As if we one had been.
            Never Mark Antony
            Dallied more wantonly
            With the fair Egyptian Queen.

Mystical grammar of amorous glances;
   Feeling of pulses, the physic of love;
Rhetorical courtings and musical dances;
   Numbering of kisses arithmetic prove;
         Eyes like astronomy;
         Straight-limbed geometry;
         In her art's ingeny
         Our wits were sharp and keen.
            Never Mark Antony
            Dallied more wantonly
            With the fair Egyptian Queen.

FROM *The Rebel Scot*

Come, keen iambics, with your badger's feet
And badger-like bite till your teeth do meet.
Help, ye tart satirists, to imp my rage
With all the scorpions that should whip this age.
Scots are like witches; do but whet your pen,
Scratch till the blood come, they'll not hurt you then.
Now, as the martyrs were enforced to take
The shapes of beasts, like hypocrites at stake,
I'll bait my Scot so, yet not cheat your eyes;
A Scot within a beast is no disguise.
   No more let Ireland brag her harmless nation
Fosters no venom since the Scot's plantation:
Nor can ours feigned antiquity maintain;
Since they came in, England hath wolves again.

The Scot that kept the Tower might have shown
Within the grate of his own breast alone,
The leopard and the panther, and engrossed
What all those wild collegiates had cost
The honest high-shoes in their termly fees;
First to the salvage lawyer, next to these.
Nature herself doth Scotchmen beasts confess,
Making their country such a wilderness:
A land that brings in question and suspense
God's omnipresence, but that Charles came thence,
But that Montrose and Crawford's loyal band
Atoned their sins and christened half the land.
Nor is it all the nation hath these spots;
There is a Church as well as Kirk of Scots.
As in a picture where the squinting paint
Shows fiend on this side, and on that side saint.
He, that saw Hell in's melancholy dream
And in the twilight of his fancy's theme,
Scared from his sins, repented in a fright,
Had he viewed Scotland, had turned proselyte.
A land where one may pray with cursed intent,
"Oh may they never suffer banishment!"
Had Cain been Scot, God would have changed his doom;
Not forced him wander but confined him home!

SIR JOHN DENHAM

(1615–1669)

FROM *Cooper's Hill*

My eye descending from the Hill, surveys
Where Thames amongst the wanton valleys strays.
Thames, the most loved of all the Ocean's sons,
By his old sire to his embraces runs,
Hastening to pay his tribute to the sea,
Like mortal life to meet Eternity.
Though with those streams he no resemblance hold,
Whose foam is amber and their gravel gold;
His genuine and less guilty wealth t' explore,
Search not his bottom, but survey his shore;
O'er which he kindly spreads his spacious wing

And hatches plenty for th' ensuing spring.
Nor then destroys it with too fond a stay,
Like mothers which their infants overlay.
Nor with a sudden and impetuous wave,
Like profuse kings, resumes the wealth he gave.
No unexpected inundations spoil
The mower's hopes nor mock the ploughman's toil,
But God-like his unwearied bounty flows,
First loves to do, then loves the good he does.
Nor are his blessings to his banks confined,
But free and common as the sea or wind;
When he to boast or to disperse his stores
Full of the tributes of his grateful shores,
Visits the world, and in his flying towers
Brings home to us, and makes both Indies ours;
Finds wealth where 'tis, bestows it where it wants,
Cities in deserts, woods in cities plants.
So that to us no thing, no place is strange,
While his fair bosom is the world's exchange.
Oh, could I flow like thee, and make thy stream
My great example, as it is my theme!
Though deep, yet clear, though gentle, yet not dull,
Strong without rage, without o'er-flowing full.

RICHARD LOVELACE

(1618–1658)

The Rose

Sweet serene sky-like flower,
Haste to adorn her bower:
From thy long cloudy bed
Shoot forth thy damask head.

New-startled blush of Flora!
The grief of pale Aurora,
Who will contest no more;
Haste, haste, to strew her floor.

Vermilion ball that's given
From lip to lip in Heaven;
  Love's couch's coverlet;
  Haste, haste, to make her bed.

Dear offspring of pleased Venus
And jolly, plump Silenus:
  Haste, haste to deck the hair
  Of the only, sweetly fair.

See! rosy is her bower,
Her floor is all this flower;
  Her bed a rosy nest
  By a bed of roses prest.

But early as she dresses,
Why fly you her bright tresses?
  Ah! I have found, I fear—
  Because her cheeks are near.

To Amarantha

Amarantha sweet and fair,
Ah, braid no more that shining hair!
As my curious hand or eye
Hovering round thee, let it fly!

Let it fly as unconfined
As its calm ravisher the wind,
Who hath left his darling, th' East,
To wanton o'er that spicy nest.

Every tress must be confest,
But neatly tangled at the best;
Like a clue of golden thread
Most excellently ravelléd.

Do not then wind up that light
In ribbands, and o'ercloud in night
Like the sun in's early ray;
But shake your head, and scatter day!

To Lucasta, Going beyond the Seas

If to be absent were to be
      Away from thee;
   Or that when I am gone,
   You or I were alone;
Then, my Lucasta, might I crave
Pity from blustering wind, or swallowing wave.

But I'll not sigh one blast or gale
      To swell my sail,
   Or pay a tear t' assuage
   The foaming blue god's rage;
For whether he will let me pass
Or no, I'm still as happy as I was.

Though seas and land betwixt us both,
      Our faith and troth,
   Like separated souls,
   All time and space controls;
Above the highest sphere we meet
Unseen, unknown, and greet as angels greet.

So then we do anticipate
      Our after-fate,
   And are alive i' the skies,
   If thus our lips and eyes
Can speak like spirits unconfined
In Heaven, their earthly bodies left behind.

To Althea from Prison

When Love with unconfinéd wing
      Hovers within my gates;
   And my divine Althea brings
      To whisper at the grates;
When I lie tangled in her hair,
      And fettered to her eye;
   The birds that wanton in the air
      Know no such liberty.

When flowing cups run swiftly round
   With no allaying Thames,
Our careless heads with roses bound,
   Our hearts with loyal flames;
When thirsty grief in wine we steep,
   When healths and draughts go free,
Fishes that tipple in the deep
   Know no such liberty.

When, like committed linnets, I
   With shriller voice shall sing
The sweetness, mercy, majesty
   And glories of my King;
When I shall voice aloud, how good
   He is, how great should be;
Enlargéd winds that curl the flood
   Know no such liberty.

Stone walls do not a prison make,
   Nor iron bars a cage;
Minds innocent and quiet take
   That for an Hermitage;
If I have freedom in my love,
   And in my soul am free;
Angels alone that soar above
   Enjoy such liberty.

To Lucasta, Going to the Wars

Tell me not, sweet, I am unkind
   That from the nunnery
Of thy chaste breast and quiet mind
   To wars and arms I fly.

True, a new mistress now I chase:
   The first foe in the field;
And with a stronger faith embrace
   A sword, a horse, a shield.

Yet this inconstancy is such
    As you too shall adore;
I could not love thee, dear, so much,
    Loved I not honour more.

ABRAHAM COWLEY
(1618–1667)

FROM *On the Death of Mr. William Hervey*

It was a dismal and a fearful night,
Scarce could the morn drive on th'unwilling light,
When sleep, death's image, left my troubled breast,
      By something liker death possest.
My eyes with tears did uncommanded flow,
      And on my soul hung the dull weight
      Of some intolerable Fate.
What bell was that? Ah me! Too much I know.

My sweet companion and my gentle peer,
Why hast thou left me thus unkindly here,
Thy end for ever and my life to moan?
      Oh, thou hast left me all alone!
Thy soul and body when death's agony
      Besieged around thy noble heart,
      Did not with more reluctance part
Than I, my dearest friend, do part from thee.

My dearest friend, would I had died for thee!
Life and this world henceforth will tedious be.
Nor shall I know hereafter what to do
      If once my griefs prove tedious too.
Silent and sad I walk about all day,
      As sullen ghosts stalk speechless by
      Where their hidden treasures lie;
Alas, my treasure's gone, why do I stay?

He was my friend, the truest friend on earth;
A strong and mighty influence joined our birth.
Nor did we envy the most sounding name
      By friendship given of old to fame.

None but his brethren he, and sisters knew,
      Whom the kind youth preferred to me;
      And even in that we did agree,
For much above myself I loved them too.

Say, for you saw us, ye immortal lights,
How oft unwearied have we spent the nights?
Till the Ledaean stars so famed for love
      Wondered at us from above.
We spent them not in toys, in lusts or wine;
      But search of deep philosophy,
      Wit, eloquence, and poetry,
Arts which I loved, for they, my friend, were thine.

Ye fields of Cambridge, our dear Cambridge, say
Have ye not seen us walking every day?
Was there a tree about which did not know
      The love betwixt us two?
Henceforth, ye gentle trees, for ever fade;
      Or your sad branches thicker join,
      And into darksome shades combine,
Dark as the grave wherein my friend is laid.

On the Death of Mr. Crashaw

Poet and saint! to thee alone are given
The two most sacred names of Earth and Heaven.
The hard and rarest union which can be
Next that of Godhead with humanity.
Long did the Muses banished slaves abide,
And built vain pyramids to mortal pride;
Like Moses thou, though spells and charms withstand,
Hast brought them nobly home back to their Holy Land.

Ah wretched we, poets of Earth! but thou
Wert living the same poet which thou'rt now.
Whilst angels sing to thee their airs divine,
And joy in an applause so great as thine.
Equal society with them to hold,
Thou need'st not make new songs, but say the old.

And they, kind spirits! shall all rejoice to see
How little less than they exalted man may be.
Still the old heathen gods in numbers dwell,
The heav'nliest thing on Earth still keeps up Hell.
Nor have we yet quite purged the Christian land;
Still idols here, like calves at Bethel stand.
And though Pan's death long since all oracles broke,
Yet still in rhyme the fiend Apollo spoke:
Nay, with the worst of heathen dotage we,
Vain men! the monster woman deify;
Find stars, and tie our fates there in a face,
And Paradise in them by whom we lost it place.
What different faults corrupt our Muses thus?
Wanton as girls, as old wives fabulous!

Thy spotless Muse, like Mary, did contain
The boundless Godhead; she did well disdain
That her eternal verse employed should be
On a less subject than eternity;
And for a sacred mistress scorned to take
But her whom God Himself scorned not his spouse to make.
It, in a kind, her miracle did do;
A fruitful mother was and virgin too.

How well, blest swan, did Fate contrive thy death;
And made thee render up thy tuneful breath
In thy great Mistress' arms! thou most divine
And richest offering of Loretto's shrine!
Where like some holy sacrifice t' expire,
A fever burns thee, and love lights the fire.
Angels, they say, brought the famed chapel there,
And bore the sacred load in triumph through the air.
'Tis surer much they brought thee there, and they
And thou, their charge, went singing all the way.

Pardon, my Mother Church, if I consent
That angels led him when from thee he went,
For even in error sure no danger is
When joined with so much piety as his.
Ah, mighty God, with shame I speak't and grief,
Ah, that our greatest faults were in belief!

And our weak reason were ev'n weaker yet,
Rather than thus our wills too strong for it.
His faith perhaps in some nice tenets might
Be wrong; his life, I'm sure, was in the right.
And I myself a Catholic will be,
So far at least, great saint, to pray to thee.

Hail, bard triumphant! and some care bestow
On us, the poets militant below!
Opposed by our old en'my, adverse chance,
Attacked by envy and by ignorance,
Enchained by beauty, tortured by desires,
Exposed by tyrant love to savage beasts and fires.
Thou from low earth in nobler flames didst rise,
And, like Elijah, mount alive the skies.
Elisha-like (but with a wish much less,
More fit thy greatness and my littleness)
Lo here I beg (I whom thou once didst prove
So humble to esteem, so good to love)
Not that thy spirit might on me doubled be,
I ask but half thy mighty spirit for me.
And when my Muse soars with so strong a wing,
'Twill learn of things divine, and first of thee to sing.

The Wish

Well then, I now do plainly see
This busy world and I shall ne'er agree;
The very honey of all earthly joy
Does of all meats the soonest cloy,
And they methinks deserve my pity
Who for it can endure the stings,
The crowd and buzz and murmurings
Of this great hive, the city.

Ah, yet, ere I descend to th' grave
May I a small house and large garden have!
And a few friends and many books, both true,
Both wise and both delightful too!

And since love ne'er will from me flee,
A mistress moderately fair,
And good as guardian-angels are,
Only beloved and loving me!

O fountains, when in you shall I
Myself eased of unpeaceful thoughts espy?
O fields, O woods, when, when shall I be made
The happy tenant of your shade?
Here's the spring-head of pleasure's flood;
Here's wealthy Nature's treasury,
Where all the riches lie that she
Has coined and stamped for good.

Pride and ambition here
Only in far-fetched metaphors appear;
Here nought but winds can hurtful murmurs scatter,
And nought but echo flatter.
The gods when they descended hither
From heaven did always choose their way;
And therefore we may boldly say,
That 'tis the way too thither.

How happy here should I
And one dear she live and embracing die!
She who is all the world, and can exclude
In deserts solitude.
I should have then this only fear,
Lest men, when they my pleasures see,
Should hither throng to live like me,
And so make a city here.

FROM *Essay on Solitude*

Hail, old patrician trees, so great and good!
Hail, ye plebeian underwood!
Where the poetic birds rejoice
And for their quiet nests and plenteous food,
Pay with their grateful voice.

Hail, the poor Muse's richest manor seat!
    Ye country houses and retreat,
    Which all the happy gods so love,
That for you oft they quit their bright and great
    Metropolis above.

Here Nature does a house for me erect,
    Nature, the wisest architect,
    Who those fond artists does despise
That can the fair and living trees neglect,
    Yet the dead timber prize.

Here let me careless and unthoughtful lying
    Hear the soft winds above me flying,
    With all their wanton boughs dispute,
And the more tuneful birds to both replying,
    Nor be myself too mute.

Ah wretched and too solitary he
    Who loves not his own company!
    He'll feel the weight of 't many a day
Unless he call in sin or vanity
    To help to bear 't away.

Whilst this hard truth I teach, methinks I see
    The monster London laugh at me,
    I should at thee too, foolish city,
If it were fit to laugh at misery,
    But thy estate I pity.

Let but thy wicked men from out thee go,
    And all the fools that crowd thee so,
    Even thou who dost thy millions boast,
A village less than Islington wilt grow,
    A solitude almost.

The Chronicle

Margarita first possessed,
If I remember well, my breast;
   Margarita first of all!
But when awhile the wanton maid
With my restless heart had played,
   Martha took the flying ball.

Martha soon did it resign
To the beauteous Catherine,
   Beauteous Catherine gave place
(Though loath and angry she to part
With the possession of my heart)
   To Eliza's conquering face.

Eliza to this hour might reign,
Had not she evil counsels ta'en.
   Fundamental laws she broke;
And still new favourites she chose,
Till up in arms my passions rose,
   And cast away her yoke.

Mary then and gentle Anne
Both to reign at once began.
   Alternately they swayed;
And sometimes Mary was the fair,
And sometimes Anne the crown did wear;
   And sometimes both I obeyed.

Another Mary then arose
And did the rigorous laws impose;
   A mighty tyrant she!
Long, alas, should I have been
Under that iron-sceptered queen,
   Had not Rebecca set me free.

When fair Rebecca set me free,
'Twas then a golden time with me.
   But soon these pleasures fled,

For the gracious princess died
In her youth and beauty's pride,
  And Judith reigned in her stead.

But when Isabella came,
Armed with a resistless flame
  And the artillery of her eye,
Whilst she proudly marched about
Greater conquests to find out,
  She beat out Susan by the bye.

But in her place I then obeyed
Black-eyed Bess, her viceroy maid,
  To whom ensued a vacancy.
Thousand worse passions then possessed
The interregnum of my breast;
  Bless me from such an anarchy!

Gentle Henrietta then,
And a third Mary next began;
  Then Joan and Jane and Audria,
And then a pretty Thomasine,
And then another Katherine,
  And then a long et cetera.

But should I now to you relate
The strength and riches of their state,
  The powder, patches, and the pins,
The ribands, jewels, and the rings,
The lace, the paint and warlike things
  That make up all their magazines;

If I should tell the politic arts
To take and keep men's hearts,
  The letters, embassies and spies,
The frowns, and smiles and flatteries,
The quarrels, tears, and perjuries
  Numberless, nameless, mysteries;

And all the little lime-twigs laid
By Machiavel, the waiting-maid,
  I more voluminous should grow

(Chiefly if I, like them, should tell
All change of weathers that befell)
   Than Holinshed or Stow.

But I will briefer with them be,
Since few of them were long with me.
   A higher and a nobler strain
My present Emperess doth claim:
Eleonora first o' th' name,
   Whom God grant long to reign.

ANDREW MARVELL

(1621–1678)

Bermudas

Where the remote Bermudas ride
In th' ocean's bosom unespied,
From a small boat that rowed along
The listening winds received this song:
   What should we do but sing His praise
Who led us through the watery maze,
Unto an isle so long unknown,
And yet far kinder than our own?
Where He the huge sea-monsters wracks
That lift the deep upon their backs.
He lands us on a grassy stage,
Safe from the storms and prelate's rage.
He gave us this eternal spring
Which here enamels every thing;
And sends the fowls to us in care
On daily visits through the air.
He hangs in shades the orange bright,
Like golden lamps in a green night;
And does in the pomegranates close
Jewels more rich than Ormus shows.
He makes the figs our mouths to meet,
And throws the melons at our feet;
But apples plants of such a price
No tree could ever bear them twice.

With cedars chosen by His hand
From Lebanon He stores the land;
And makes the hollow seas that roar
Proclaim the ambergris on shore.
He cast (of which we rather boast)
The gospel's pearl upon our coast,
And in these rocks for us did frame
A temple, where to sound His name.
Oh, let our voice His praise exalt
Till it arrive at Heaven's vault,
Which then perhaps rebounding may
Echo beyond the Mexique bay.
    Thus sung they in the English boat
A holy and a cheerful note,
And all the way to guide their chime
With falling oars they kept the time.

To His Coy Mistress

Had we but world enough and time,
This coyness, lady, were no crime.
We would sit down, and think which way
To walk, and pass our long love's day.
Thou by the Indian Ganges' side
Should'st rubies find; I by the tide
Of Humber would complain. I would
Love you ten years before the flood;
And you should if you please refuse
Till the conversion of the Jews.
My vegetable love should grow
Vaster than empires and more slow.
A hundred years should go to praise
Thine eyes, and on thy forehead gaze.
Two hundred to adore each breast;
But thirty thousand to the rest.
An age at least to every part,
And the last age should show your heart.
For, lady, you deserve this state,
Nor would I love at lower rate.

But at my back I always hear
Time's wingéd chariot hurrying near;
And yonder all before us lie
Deserts of vast eternity.
Thy beauty shall no more be found,
Nor in thy marble vault shall sound
My echoing song; then worms shall try
That long preserved virginity,
And your quaint honour turn to dust,
And into ashes all my lust.
The grave's a fine and private place,
But none I think do there embrace.
Now therefore while the youthful hue
Sits on thy skin like morning dew,
And while thy willing soul transpires
At every pore with instant fires,
Now let us sport us while we may;
And now like amorous birds of prey
Rather at once our time devour
Than languish in his slow-chapped power.
Let us roll all our strength and all
Our sweetness up into one ball,
And tear our pleasures with rough strife
Thorough the iron gates of life.
Thus, though we cannot make our sun
Stand still, yet we will make him run.

The Garden

How vainly men themselves amaze
To win the palm, the oak, or bays;
And their incessant labours see
Crowned from some single herb or tree,
Whose short and narrow-vergéd shade
Does prudently their toils upbraid;
While all flow'rs and all trees do close
To weave the garlands of repose.

Fair quiet, have I found thee here,
And innocence, thy sister dear!
Mistaken long, I sought you then
In busy companies of men.
Your sacred plants, if here below,
Only among the plants will grow.
Society is all but rude,
To this delicious solitude.

No white nor red was ever seen
So amorous as this lovely green.
Fond lovers, cruel as their flame,
Cut in these trees their mistress' name.
Little, alas, they know or heed
How far these beauties hers exceed!
Fair trees! wheres'e'er your barks I wound,
No name shall but your own be found.

When we have run our passions' heat,
Love hither makes his best retreat.
The gods, that mortal beauty chase,
Still in a tree did end their race.
Apollo hunted Daphne so,
Only that she might laurel grow;
And Pan did after Syrinx speed,
Not as a nymph, but for a reed.

What wond'rous life is this I lead!
Ripe apples drop about my head;
The luscious clusters of the vine
Upon my mouth do crush their wine;
The nectarine and curious peach
Into my hands themselves do reach;
Stumbling on melons as I pass,
Ensnared with flow'rs, I fall on grass.

Meanwhile the mind, from pleasure less,
Withdraws into its happiness;
The mind, that ocean where each kind
Does straight its own resemblance find;

Yet it creates, transcending these,
Far other worlds and other seas;
Annihilating all that's made
To a green thought in a green shade.

Here at the fountain's sliding foot
Or at some fruit-tree's mossy root,
Casting the body's vest aside,
My soul into the boughs does glide;
There like a bird it sits and sings,
Then whets and combs its silver wings;
And, till prepared for longer flight,
Waves in its plumes the various light.

Such was that happy garden-state,
While Man there walked without a mate.
After a place so pure and sweet,
What other help could yet be meet!
But 'twas beyond a mortal's share
To wander solitary there;
Two paradises 'twere in one
To live in Paradise alone.

How well the skilful gardener drew
Of flow'rs and herbs this dial new,
Where from above the milder sun
Does through a fragrant zodiac run;
And as it works th' industrious bee
Computes its time as well as we.
How could such sweet and wholesome hours
Be reckoned but with herbs and flowers!

FROM A Horatian Ode upon Cromwell

So restless Cromwell could not cease
In the inglorious arts of peace,
    But through adventurous war
    Urged his active star.
And, like the three-forked lightning, first
Breaking the clouds where it was nursed,

Did thorough his own side
His fiery way divide.
'Tis madness to resist or blame
The force of angry Heaven's flame;
   And if we would speak true
   Much to the man is due.
What field of all the civil wars
Where his were not the deepest scars?
   And Hampton shows what part
   He had of wiser art.
Where, twining subtle fears with hope,
He wove a net of such a scope
   That Charles himself might chase
   To Carisbrooke's narrow case.
That thence the royal actor borne,
The tragic scaffold might adorn;
   While round the arméd bands
   Did clap their bloody hands.
He nothing common did or mean
Upon that memorable scene;
   But with his keener eye
   The axe's edge did try:
Nor called the gods with vulgar spite
To vindicate his helpless right,
   But bowed his comely head
   Down as upon a bed.

FROM A Poem upon the Death of Oliver Cromwell

I saw him dead, a leaden slumber lies
And mortal sleep over those wakeful eyes;
Those gentle rays under the lids were fled,
Which through his looks that piercing sweetness shed;
That port which so majestic was and strong,
Loose and deprived of vigour, stretched along,
All withered, all discoloured, pale and wan,
How much another thing, no more that man!
O human glory vain, O death, O wings,
O worthless world, O transitory things!

Yet dwelt that greatness in his shape decayed
That still, though dead, greater than death he laid;
And in his altered face you something feign
That threatens death he yet will live again.

FROM *The Loyal Scot*

But who considers well will find indeed
'Tis Holy Island parts us, not the Tweed.
Nothing but clergy could us two seclude,
No Scotch was ever like a Bishop's feud.
All litanies in this have wanted faith;
There's no "deliver us from a Bishop's wrath."
Never shall Calvin pardoned be for sales,
Never for Burnet's sake the Lauderdales,
For Becket's sake Kent always shall have tails.
Who sermons e'er can pacify and prayers?
Or to the joint stools reconcile the chairs?
Nothing, not bogs, not sands, not seas, not alps,
Separate the world so as the Bishops' scalps.
Stretch for your Line their circingle alone,
'Twill make a more inhabitable zone.
The friendly loadstone hath not more combined
Than Bishops cramped the commerce of mankind.
A Bishop will like Mahomet tear the moon
And slip one half into his sleeve as soon.
The juggling prelate on his hocus calls,
Shows you first one, then makes that one two balls.
Instead of all the plagues, had Bishops come,
Pharaoh at first would have sent Israel home.
From church they need not censure men away,
A Bishop's self is an anathema.
Where foxes dung their earths, the badgers yield;
At Bishops' dung the foxes quit the field.
Their rank ambition all this heat hath stirred;
A Bishop's rennet makes the strongest curd.
How reverend things are Lord, lawn sleeves and ease!
How a clean laundress and no sermons please!
They wanted zeal and learning, so mistook
The Bible and grammar for the service book.

Religion has the world too long depraved,
A shorter way's to be by clergy saved.
Believe but only as the Church believes,
And learn to pin your faith upon their sleeves.
Ah! like Lot's wife they still look back and halt,
And surpliced show like pillars too of salt.
Who that is wise would pulpit toil endure?
A Bishopric is a great sinecure.
Enough for them, God knows, to count their wealth,
To excommunicate, and study health;
A higher work is to their Court annexed:
The nation they divide, their curates text.
No Bishop rather than it should be so!
No Church, no trade, no king, no people, no!
All mischiefs moulded by those state divines;
Aaron casts calves, but Moses them calcines.
The legion devil did but one man possess,
One Bishop fiend spirits a whole diocese.
That power alone can loose this spell that ties,
For only Kings can Bishops exorcise.
Will you be treated princes? Here fall to,
Fish and flesh Bishops are the ambigu;
Howe'er insipid, yet the sauce will mend 'em;
Bishops are very good when in commendum.
If wealth or vice can tempt your appetites,
These Templar Lords exceed the Templar Knights,
And in a Baron Bishop you have both
Leviathan served up and Behemoth.

HENRY VAUGHAN

(1622–1695)

A Song to Amoret

If I were dead, and in my place
   Some fresher youth designed
To warm thee with new fires, and grace
   Those arms I left behind;

Were he as faithful as the sun,
   That's wedded to the sphere;

His blood as chaste and temp'rate run,
    As April's mildest tear;

Or were he rich, and with his heaps
    And spacious share of earth,
Could make divine affection cheap,
    And court his golden birth:

For all these arts I'd not believe,
    No, though he should be thine—
The mighty amorist could not give
    So rich a heart as mine.

Fortune and beauty thou might'st find,
    And greater men than I;
But my true resolvéd mind
    They never shall come nigh.

For I not for an hour did love,
    Or for a day desire,
But with my soul had from above
    This endless, holy fire.

FROM *To His Retired Friend*

Come! leave this sullen state, and let not wine
And precious wit lie dead for want of thine.
Shall the dull market-landlord with his rout
Of sneaking tenants dirtily swill out
This harmless liquor? shall they knock and beat
For sack, only to talk of rye and wheat?
Oh, let not such prepost'rous tippling be
In our metropolis; may I ne'er see
Such tavern-sacrilege, nor lend a line
To weep the rapes and tragedy of wine!

Here lives that chymic quick fire which betrays
Fresh spirits to the blood, and warms our lays.
I have reserved 'gainst thy approach a cup
That were thy Muse stark dead, shall raise her up,
And teach her yet more charming words and skill
Than ever Celia, Chloris, Astrophil,
Or any of the threadbare names inspired
Poor rhyming lovers with a mistress fired.
Come then! and while the slow icicle hangs
At the stiff thatch, and winter's frosty pangs
Benumb the year, blithe—as of old—let us
'Midst noise and war, of peace and mirth discuss.
This portion thou wert born for; why should we
Vex at the time's ridiculous misery?
An age that thus hath fooled itself, and will
—Spite of thy teeth and mine—persist so still.
Let's sit then at this fire, and while we steal
A revel in the town, let others seal,
Purchase or cheat, and who can let them pay,
Till those black deeds bring on the darksome day.
Innocent spenders we! a better use
Shall wear out our short lease, and leave th' obtuse
Rout to their husks; they and their bags at best
Have cares in earnest; we care for a jest.

FROM *The Waterfall*

With what deep murmurs, through Time's silent stealth,
Doth thy transparent, cool and watery wealth
   Here flowing fall,
   And chide and call,
As if his liquid, loose retinue stayed
Lingering, and were of this steep place afraid,
   The common pass,
   Where clear as glass,
   All must descend
   Not to an end,
But quickened by this deep and rocky grave,
Rise to a longer course more bright and brave.

The Shower

'Twas so; I saw thy birth. That drowsy lake
  From her faint bosom breathed thee, the disease
  Of her sick waters and infectious ease.
        But now at even,
        Too gross for Heaven,
Thou fall'st in tears, and weep'st for thy mistake.

Ah! it is so with me. Oft have I pressed
  Heaven with a lazy breath, but fruitless this
  Pierced not; love only can with quick access
        Unlock the way,
        When all else stray,
The smoke and exhalations of the breast.

Yet, if as thou dost melt, and with thy train
  Of drops make soft the Earth, my eyes could weep
  O'er my hard heart, that's bound up and asleep;
        Perhaps, at last,
        Some such showers past,
My God would give a sunshine after rain.

The Morning-Watch

    O joys! infinite sweetness! with what flowers
    And shoots of glory my soul breaks and buds!
        All the long hours
        Of night and rest,
        Through the still shrouds
        Of sleep and clouds,
      This dew fell on my breast.
      Oh, how it bloods
    And spirits all my earth! hark! in what rings
    And hymning circulations the quick world
        Awakes and sings!
        The rising winds,
        And falling springs,
        Birds, beasts, all things
      Adore Him in their kinds.
      Thus all is hurled

In sacred hymns and order; the great chime
And symphony of Nature. Prayer is
>   The world in tune,
>   A spirit-voice,
>   And vocal joys,
>   Whose echo is Heaven's bliss.
>   Oh, let me climb
When I lie down! The pious soul by night
Is like a clouded star, whose beams, though said
>   To shed their light
>   Under some cloud,
>   Yet are above,
>   And shine and move
>   Beyond that misty shroud.
>   So in my bed,
That curtained grave, though sleep like ashes hide
My lamp and life, both shall in Thee abide.

The Retreat

>   Happy those early days when I
>   Shined in my angel-infancy!
>   Before I understood this place
>   Appointed for my second race,
>   Or taught my soul to fancy ought
>   But a white, celestial thought;
>   When yet I had not walked above
>   A mile, or two, from my first love,
>   And looking back (at that short space,)
>   Could see a glimpse of his bright face;
>   When on some gilded cloud or flower
>   My gazing soul would dwell an hour,
>   And in those weaker glories spy
>   Some shadows of eternity;
>   Before I taught my tongue to wound
>   My conscience with a sinful sound,
>   Or had the black art to dispense
>   A sev'ral sin to ev'ry sense;
>   But felt through all this fleshly dress
>   Bright shoots of everlastingness.

O how I long to travel back
And tread again that ancient track!
That I might once more reach that plain,
Where first I left my glorious train,
From whence th'enlightened spirit sees
That shady city of palm trees;
But (ah!) my soul with too much stay
Is drunk, and staggers in the way.
Some men a forward motion love,
But I by backward steps would move,
And when this dust falls to the urn,
In that state I came, return.

The World

I saw Eternity the other night,
Like a great ring of pure and endless light,
    All calm, as it was bright;
And round beneath it, Time in hours, days, years,
    Driven by the spheres
Like a vast shadow moved; in which the world
    And all her train were hurled.
The doting lover in his quaintest strain
    Did there complain;
Near him, his lute, his fancy, and his flights,
    Wit's sour delights;
With gloves, and knots, the silly snares of pleasure,
    Yet his dear treasure,
All scattered lay, while he his eyes did pour
    Upon a flower.

The darksome statesman, hung with weights and woe,
Like a thick midnight-fog, moved there so slow,
    He did not stay, nor go;
Condemning thoughts—like sad eclipses—scowl
    Upon his soul,
And clouds of crying witnesses without
    Pursued him with one shout.

Yet digged the mole, and lest his ways be found,
        Worked underground,
Where he did clutch his prey; but one did see
        That policy.
Churches and altars fed him; perjuries
        Were gnats and flies;
It rained about him blood and tears, but he
        Drank them as free.

The fearful miser on a heap of rust
Sat pining all his life there, did scarce trust
        His own hands with the dust,
Yet would not place one piece above, but lives
        In fear of thieves.
Thousands there were as frantic as himself,
        And hugged each one his pelf;
The downright epicure placed heav'n in sense,
        And scorned pretence;
While others, slipped into a wide excess,
        Said little less;
The weaker sort slight, trivial wares enslave,
        Who think them brave;
And poor, despiséd Truth sat counting by
    .   Their victory.

Yet some, who all this while did weep and sing,
And sing and weep, soared up into the ring;
        But most would use no wing.
Oh, fools—said I—thus to prefer dark night
        Before true light!
To live in grots and caves, and hate the day
        Because it shows the way;
The way, which from this dead and dark abode
        Leads up to God;
A way where you might tread the sun, and be
        More bright than he!
But as I did their madness so discuss,
        One whispered thus,
"This ring the Bridegroom did for none provide,
        But for His bride."

"They Are All Gone..."

They are all gone into the world of light!
    And I alone sit lingering here;
Their very memory is fair and bright,
    And my sad thoughts doth clear.

It glows and glitters in my cloudy breast,
    Like stars upon some gloomy grove,
Or those faint beams in which this hill is dressed,
    After the sun's remove.

I see them walking in an air of glory,
    Whose light doth trample on my days;
My days, which are at best but dull and hoary,
    Mere glimmering and decays.

O holy Hope! and high Humility!
    High as the heavens above!
These are your walks, and you have showed them me,
    To kindle my cold love.

Dear beauteous Death! the jewel of the just,
    Shining nowhere but in the dark;
What mysteries do lie beyond thy dust,
    Could man outlook that mark!

He that hath found some fledged bird's nest may know
    At first sight if the bird be flown;
But what fair well or grove he sings in now,
    That is to him unknown.

And yet, as angels in some brighter dreams
    Call to the soul when man doth sleep,
So some strange thoughts transcend our wonted themes,
    And into glory peep.

If a star were confined into a tomb,
    Her captive flames must needs burn there;
But when the hand that locked her up gives room,
    She'll shine through all the sphere.

O Father of eternal life, and all
    Created glories under Thee!
Resume Thy spirit from this world of thrall
    Into true liberty.

Either disperse these mists, which blot and fill
    My perspective still as they pass;
Or else remove me hence unto that hill
    Where I shall need no glass.

THOMAS STANLEY

(1625–1678)

Song

When I lie burning in thine eye,
    Or freezing in thy breast,
What martyrs, in wished flames that die,
    Are half so pleased or blest?

When thy soft accents through mine ear
    Into my soul do fly,
What angel would not quit his sphere
    To hear such harmony?

Or when the kiss thou gav'st me last
    My soul stole in its breath,
What life would sooner be embraced
    Than so desired a death?

When I commanded am by thee,
    Or by thine eye or hand,
What monarch would not prouder be
    To serve than to command?

Then think no freedom I desire,
    Or would my fetters leave,
Since Phoenix-like I from this fire
    Both life and youth receive.

Song

I prithee let my heart alone,
  Since now 'tis raised above thee,
Not all the beauty thou dost own,
  Again can make me love thee:

He that was shipwrecked once before
  By such a siren's call,
And yet neglects to shun that shore,
  Deserves his second fall.

Each flatt'ring kiss, each tempting smile,
  Thou dost in vain bestow,
Some other lovers might beguile,
  Who not thy falsehood know.

But I am proof against all art,
  No vows shall e'er persuade me
Twice to present a wounded heart
  To her that hath betrayed me.

Could I again be brought to love
  Thy form, though more divine,
I might thy scorn as justly move,
  As now thou sufferest mine.

JOHN HALL

(1627–1656)

The Call

  Romira, stay
And run not thus like a young roe away;
    No enemy
Pursues thee, foolish girl! 'tis only I:
    I'll keep off harms,
If thou'll be pleased to garrison mine arms;
    What, dost thou fear
I'll turn a traitor? may these roses here

To paleness shred,
And lilies stand disguiséd in new red,
If that I lay
A snare wherein thou wouldst not gladly stay.
See, see, the sun
Does slowly to his azure lodging run;
Come, sit but here,
And presently he'll quit our hemisphere:
So, still among
Lovers, time is too short or else too long;
Here will we spin
Legends for them that have love-martyrs been;
Here on this plain
We'll talk Narcissus to a flower again.
Come here, and choose
On which of these proud plats thou would repose;
Here may'st thou shame
The rusty violets with the crimson flame
Of either cheek,
And primroses white as thy fingers seek;
Nay, thou may'st prove
That man's most noble passion is to love.

CHARLES COTTON

(1630–1687)

FROM *To Mr. Izaak Walton*

Farewell, thou busy world, and may
We never meet again;
Here I can eat, and sleep, and pray,
And do more good in one short day,
Than he who his whole age out-wears
Upon thy most conspicuous theatres,
Where naught but vice and vanity do reign.

Good God! how sweet are all things here!
How beautiful the fields appear!
How cleanly do we feed and lie!
Lord! what good hours do we keep!

How quietly we sleep!
What peace! what unanimity!
How innocent from the lewd fashion
Is all our business, all our conversation!

Oh, how happy here's our leisure!
Oh, how innocent our pleasure!
O ye valleys, O ye mountains,
O ye groves and crystal fountains,
    How I love at liberty
By turn to come and visit ye!

O Solitude, the soul's best friend,
That man acquainted with himself dost make,
And all his Maker's wonders to intend;
    With thee I here converse at will,
    And would be glad to do so still;
For it is thou alone that keep'st the soul awake.

How calm and quiet a delight
    It is alone
To read, and meditate, and write,
By none offended, nor offending none;
To walk, ride, sit, or sleep at one's own ease,
And pleasing a man's self, none other to displease!

O my beloved nymph, fair Dove,
Princess of rivers, how I love
    Upon thy flowery banks to lie,
    And view thy silver stream
    When gilded by a summer's beam,
    And in it all thy wanton fry
        Playing at liberty,
    And with my angle upon them
        The all of treachery
I ever learned to practise and to try!

O my beloved rocks, that rise
To awe the earth and brave the skies,
From some aspiring mountain's crown

How dearly do I love,
Giddy with pleasure, to look down,
And from the vales to view the noble heights above!

Lord! would men let me alone,
What an over-happy one
Should I think myself to be,
Might I in this desert place,
Which most men by their voice disgrace,
Live but undisturbed and free!
Here in this despised recess,
Would I maugre winter's cold
And the summer's worst excess,
Try to live out to sixty full years old,
And all the while
Without an envious eye
On any thriving under Fortune's smile,
Contented live, and then contented die.

FROM *Old Tityrus to Eugenia*

Eugenia, young and fair and sweet,
The glories of the plains,
In thee alone the graces meet
To conquer all the swains;
Tall as the poplar of the grove,
Straight as the wingéd shaft of Love,
As the spring's early blossoms white,
Soft as the kisses of the light,
Serene and modest as the morn,
Ere vapours do from fens arise
To dim the glory of the skies,
Untainted, or with pride or scorn,
T' oblige the world, bright nymph, thou sure wast born.

Ode

Good night, my Love, may gentle rest
   Charm up your senses till the light,
Whilst I with care and woe opprest
   Go to inhabit endless night.

There, whilst your eyes shall grace the day,
   I must in the despairing shade,
Sigh such a woeful time away,
   As never yet poor lover had.

Yet to this endless solitude
   There is one dangerous step to pass,
To one that loves your sight, so rude,
   As flesh and blood is loath to pass.

But I will take it to express
   I worthily your favours wore,
Your merits, sweet, can claim no less,
   Who dies for you can do no more.

Sonnet

Chloris, whilst thou and I were free,
Wedded to naught but liberty,
How sweetly happy did we live,
How free to promise, free to give!

Then, monarchs of ourselves, we might
Love here or there, to change delight,
And tied to none, with all dispense,
Paying each Love its recompense.

But in that happy freedom, we
Were so improvidently free,
To give away our liberties;

And now in fruitful sorrow pine
At what we are, what might have been,
Had thou or I or both been wise.

Song

Join once again, my Celia, join
Thy rosy lips to these of mine,
   Which, though they be not such,
Are full as sensible of bliss,
That is, as soon can taste a kiss,
   As thine of softer touch.

Each kiss of thine creates desire,
Thy odorous breath inflames Love's fire,
   And wakes the sleeping coal;
Such a kiss to be I find
The conversation of the mind,
   And whisper of the soul.

Thanks, sweetest, now thou'rt perfect grown,
For by this last kiss I'm undone;
   Thou breathest silent darts;
Henceforth each little touch will prove
A dangerous stratagem in love,
   And thou wilt blow up hearts.

Laura Sleeping

Winds, whisper gently whilst she sleeps,
   And fan her with your cooling wings;
Whilst she her drops of beauty weeps
   From pure and yet unrivalled springs.

Glide over beauty's field, her face,
   To kiss her lip and cheek be bold,
But with a calm and stealing pace,
   Neither too rude nor yet too cold.

Play in her beams and crisp her hair
   With such a gale as wings soft Love,
And with so sweet, so rich an air
   As breathes from the Arabian grove.

A breath as hushed as lover's sigh,
    Or that unfolds the morning door;
Sweet as the winds that gently fly
    To sweep the spring's enamelled floor.

Murmur soft music to her dreams,
    That pure and unpolluted run,
Like to the new-born crystal streams
    Under the bright enamoured sun.

But when she waking shall display
    Her light, retire within your bar;
Her breath is life, her eyes are day,
    And all mankind her creatures are.

FROM *Ode*

Without the evening dew and showers
    The Earth would be a barren place,
Of trees and plants, or herbs and flowers,
    To crown her now enamelled face;

Nor can wit spring or fancies grow
    Unless we dew our heads in wine,
Plump autumn's wealthy overflow
    And sprightly issue of the vine.

Wine is the cure of cares and sloth
    That rust the metal of the mind,
The juice that man to man does both
    In freedom and in friendship bind.

This clears the monarch's cloudy brows
    And cheers the hearts of sullen swains,
To wearied souls repose allows,
    And makes slaves caper in their chains.

Wine, that distributes to each part
    Its heat and motion, is the spring,
The poet's head, the subject's heart,
    'Twas wine made old Anacreon sing.

Then let us quaff it, whilst the night
   Serves but to hide such guilty souls,
As fly the beauty of the light
   Or dare not pledge our loyal bowls.

JOHN DRYDEN

(1631–1700)

Song

Sylvia the fair, in the bloom of fifteen,
Felt an innocent warmth as she lay on the green;
She had heard of a pleasure, and something she guessed
By the towsing and tumbling and touching her breast;
She saw the men eager, but was at a loss
What they meant by their sighing and kissing so close;
      By their praying and whining,
      And clasping and twining,
      And panting and wishing,
      And sighing and kissing,
      And sighing and kissing so close.

Ah, she cried, ah, for a languishing maid
In a country of Christians to die without aid!
Not a Whig or a Tory or Trimmer at least,
Or a Protestant parson or Catholic priest,
To instruct a young virgin that is at a loss
What they meant by their sighing and kissing so close;
      By their praying &c.

Cupid in shape of a swain did appear;
He saw the sad wound, and in pity drew near,
Then showed her his arrow and bid her not fear,
For the pain was no more than a maiden may bear;
When the balm was infused, she was not at a loss
What they meant by their sighing and kissing so close;
      By their praying &c.

Rondelay

Chloe found Amyntas lying
   All in tears upon the plain,
Sighing to himself and crying:
   Wretched I to love in vain!
Kiss me, dear, before my dying;
   Kiss me once, and ease my pain.

Sighing to himself and crying:
   Wretched I to love in vain!
Ever scorning and denying
   To reward your faithful swain.
Kiss me, dear, before my dying;
   Kiss me once, and ease my pain!

Ever scorning and denying
   To reward your faithful swain.
Chloe, laughing at his crying,
   Told him that he loved in vain.
Kiss me, dear, before my dying;
   Kiss me once, and ease my pain!

Chloe, laughing at his crying,
   Told him that he loved in vain;
But repenting, and complying,
   When he kissed, she kissed again;
Kissed him up, before his dying;
   Kissed him up, and eased his pain.

"*Ah, Fading Joy...*"

Ah, fading joy, how quickly art thou past!
   Yet we thy ruin haste;
As if the cares of human life were few,
   We seek out new,
And follow fate that does too fast pursue

See how on ev'ry bough the birds express
　In their sweet notes their happiness.
　They all enjoy and nothing spare;
But on their mother Nature lay their care.
Why then should Man, the lord of all below,
　Such troubles choose to know,
As none of all his subjects undergo?

Hark, hark, the waters fall, fall, fall,
　And with a murmuring sound
　Dash, dash upon the ground,
　　To gentle slumbers call.

The Indian Emperor, 1665

"After the Pangs of a Desperate Lover"

After the pangs of a desperate lover,
　When day and night I have sighed all in vain;
Ah, what a pleasure it is to discover
　In her eyes pity, who causes my pain!

When with unkindness our love at a stand is,
　And both have punished ourselves with the pain,
Ah, what a pleasure the touch of her hand is,
　Ah, what a pleasure to press it again!

When the denial comes fainter and fainter,
　And her eyes give what her tongue does deny,
Ah, what a trembling I feel when I venture,
　Ah, what a trembling does usher my joy!

When with a sigh she accords me the blessing,
　And her eyes twinkle 'twixt pleasure and pain,
Ah, what a joy 'tis beyond all expressing,
　Ah, what a joy to hear: Shall we again?

An Evening's Love, 1668

"Ah, How Sweet It Is to Love"

Ah, how sweet it is to love,
Ah, how gay is young desire!
And what pleasing pains we prove
When we first approach Love's fire.
Pains of Love be sweeter far
Than all other pleasures are.

Sighs which are from lovers blown,
Do but gently heave the heart;
Ev'n the tears they shed alone
Cure like trickling balm their smart.
Lovers when they lose their breath
Bleed away in easy death.

Love and time with reverence use,
Treat them like a parting friend,
Nor the golden gifts refuse
Which in youth sincere they send;
For each year their price is more,
And they less simple than before.

Love, like spring-tides full and high,
Swells in ev'ry youthful vein;
But each tide does less supply,
Till they quite shrink in again.
If a flow in age appear,
'Tis but rain, and runs not clear.

Tyrannic Love, 1669

"Why Should a Foolish Marriage Vow"

Why should a foolish marriage vow
Which long ago was made
Oblige us to each other now,
When passion is decayed?
We loved, and we loved, as long as we could,
Till our love was loved out in us both;
But our marriage is dead when the pleasure is fled;
'Twas pleasure first made it an oath.

If I have pleasures for a friend
  And further love in store,
What wrong has he whose joys did end,
  And who could give no more?
'Tis a madness that he
Should be jealous of me,
Or that I should bar him of another;
For all we can gain is to give ourselves pain
When neither can hinder the other.

Marriage a-la-Mode, 1672

"Long betwixt Love and Fear..."

Long betwixt love and fear Phillis tormented
Shunned her own wish, yet at last she consented;
But loath that day should her blushes discover:
  Come gentle night, she said,
  Come quickly to my aid,
  And a poor shamefaced maid
  Hide from her lover.

Now cold as ice I am, now hot as fire,
I dare not tell myself my own desire,
But let day fly away and let night haste her.
  Grant, ye kind powers above,
  Slow hours to parting love,
  But when to bliss we move,
  Bid them fly faster.

How sweet it is to love when I discover
That fire which burns my heart warming my lover;
'Tis pity love so true should be mistaken.
  But if this night he be
  False or unkind to me,
  Let me die ere I see
  That I'm forsaken.

The Assignation, 1673

"Can Life Be a Blessing"

Can life be a blessing
  Or worth the possessing,
Can life be a blessing if love were away?
  Ah no! though our love all night keep us waking,
And though he torment us with cares all the day,
  Yet he sweetens, he sweetens our pains in the taking,
There's an hour at the last, there's an hour to repay.

In ev'ry possessing
  The ravishing blessing,
In ev'ry possessing the fruit of our pain,
  Poor lovers forget long ages of anguish,
Whate'er they have suffered and done to obtain;
  'Tis a pleasure, a pleasure to sigh and to languish,
When we hope, when we hope to be happy again.

Troilus and Cressida, 1679

"Farewell, Ungrateful Traitor"

Farewell, ungrateful traitor,
  Farewell, my perjured swain;
Let never injured creature
  Believe a man again.
The pleasure of possessing
Surpasses all expressing,
But 'tis too short a blessing,
  And love too long a pain.

'Tis easy to deceive us
  In pity of your pain,
But when we love you leave us
  To rail at you in vain.
Before we have described it,
There is no bliss beside it,
But she that once has tried it,
  Will never love again.

The passion you pretended
   Was only to obtain,
But when the charm is ended
   The charmer you disdain.
Your love by ours we measure
Till we have lost our treasure,
But dying is a pleasure,
   When living is a pain.

                           The Spanish Friar, 1681

"Fair Iris and Her Swain"

Thyrsis: Fair Iris and her swain
      Were in a shady bower,
Where Thyrsis long in vain
      Had sought the shepherd's hour.
At length his hand advancing upon her snowy
          breast,
      He said, Oh kiss me longer,
      And longer yet and longer,
         If you will make me blest.

Iris: An easy trusting maid
      By trusting is undone;
Our sex is oft betrayed
      By granting love too soon.
If you desire to gain me, your sufferings to redress,
      Prepare to love me longer,
      And longer yet, and longer,
        Before you shall possess.

Thyrsis: The little care you show
      Of all my sorrows past
Makes death appear too slow,
      And life too long to last.
Fair Iris, kiss me kindly, in pity of my fate;
      And kindly still, and kindly,
        Before it is too late.

Iris: You fondly court your bliss
            And no advances make;
            'Tis not for maids to kiss,
            But 'tis for men to take.
        So you may kiss me kindly, and I will not rebel;
            But kindly still, and kindly,
            But kiss me not and tell.

Chorus: Thus at the height we love and live,
            And fear not to be poor;
        We give, and give, and give, and give,
            Till we can give no more:
        But what to day will take away
            To morrow will restore.
        Thus at the height we love and live,
            And fear not to be poor.

                                    Amphitryon, 1690

"How Happy the Lover"

        How happy the lover,
            How easy his chain,
            How pleasing his pain!
        How sweet to discover
            He sighs not in vain.
        For love ev'ry creature
        Is formed by his nature;
        No joys are above
        The pleasures of love.

        In vain are our graces,
            In vain are your eyes,
            If love you despise;
        When age furrows faces,
            'Tis time to be wise.
        Then use the short blessing,
        That flies in possessing:
        No joys are above
        The pleasures of love.

                                King Arthur, 1691

"No, No, Poor Suffering Heart..."

No, no, poor suffering heart, no change endeavour;
Choose to sustain the smart rather than leave her;
My ravished eyes behold such charms about her,
I can die with her, but not live without her.
One tender sigh of hers to see me languish
Will more than pay the price of my past anguish;
Beware, O cruel fair, how you smile on me,
'Twas a kind look of yours that has undone me.

Love has in store for me one happy minute,
And she will end my pain who did begin it;
Then no day void of bliss or pleasure leaving
Ages shall slide away without perceiving:
Cupid shall guard the door the more to please us,
And keep out time and death when they would seize us;
Time and death shall depart and say in flying
Love has found out a way to live by dying.

Cleomenes, 1692

FROM *Annus Mirabilis*

Yet London, empress of the northern clime,
By an high fate thou greatly didst expire;
Great as the world's, which, at the death of time,
Must fall and rise a nobler frame by fire.

As when some dire usurper Heav'n provides
To scourge his country with a lawless sway,
His birth perhaps some petty village hides,
And sets his cradle out of Fortune's way.

Till fully ripe his swelling fate breaks out,
And hurries him to mighty mischiefs on;
His prince, surprised at first, no ill could doubt,
And wants the power to meet it when 'tis known.

Such was the rise of this prodigious fire,
Which in mean buildings first obscurely bred,
From thence did soon to open streets aspire,
And straight to palaces and temples spread.

The diligence of trades and noiseful gain,
And luxury, more late, asleep were laid;
All was the night's, and in her silent reign
No sound the rest of Nature did invade.

In this deep quiet, from what source unknown,
Those seeds of fire their fatal birth disclose;
And first, few scatt'ring sparks about were blown,
Big with the flames that to our ruin rose.

Then in some close-pent room it crept along,
And, smould'ring as it went, in silence fed;
Till th' infant monster, with devouring strong
Walked boldly upright with exalted head.

At length the crackling noise and dreadful blaze
Called up some waking lover to the sight;
And long it was ere he the rest could raise,
Whose heavy eyelids yet were full of night.

The next to danger, hot pursued by fate,
Half-clothed, half-naked, hastily retire;
And frighted mothers strike their breasts too late
For helpless infants left amidst the fire.

Their cries soon waken all the dwellers near;
Now murmuring noises rise in every street;
The more remote run stumbling with their fear,
And in the dark men justle as they meet.

A key of fire ran all along the shore,
And lightened all the river with a blaze;
The wakened tides began again to roar,
And wondering fish in shining waters gaze.

Old Father Thames raised up his reverend head,
But feared the fate of Simois would return;
Deep in his ooze he sought his sedgy bed,
And shrunk his waters back into his urn.

The Fire meantime walks in a broader gross;
To either hand his wings he opens wide;
He wades the streets, and straight he reaches cross,
And plays his longing flames on th' other side.

To every nobler portion of the town
The curling billows roll their restless tide;
In parties now they straggle up and down,
As armies unopposed for prey divide.

One mighty squadron with a side-wind sped
Through narrow lanes his cumbered fire does haste;
By powerful charms of gold and silver led,
The Lombard bankers and the Change to waste.

Another backward to the Tower would go,
And slowly eats his way against the wind;
But the main body of the marching foe
Against th' imperial palace is designed.

Those who have homes, when home they do repair,
To a last lodging call their wand'ring friends;
Their short uneasy sleeps are broke with care,
To look how near their own destruction tends.

Those who have none, sit round where once it was,
And with full eyes each wonted room require;
Haunting the yet warm ashes of the place,
As murdered men walk where they did expire.

The most in fields like herded beasts lie down,
To dews obnoxious on the grassy floor;
And while their babes in sleep their sorrows drown,
Sad parents watch the remnants of their store.

FROM *Absalom and Achitophel*

1.

Of these the false Achitophel was first,
A name to all succeeding ages curst.
For close designs and crooked counsels fit,
Sagacious, bold, and turbulent of wit,
Restless, unfixed in principles and place,
In power unpleased, impatient of disgrace;
A fiery soul, which working out its way,
Fretted the pygmy body to decay;
And o'er-informed the tenement of clay.
A daring pilot in extremity,
Pleased with the danger when the waves went high
He sought the storms; but for a calm unfit
Would steer too nigh the sands to boast his wit.
Great wits are sure to madness near allied,
And thin partitions do their bounds divide;
Else why should he, with wealth and honours blest,
Refuse his age the needful hours of rest?
And all to leave what with his toil he won
To that unfeathered two-legged thing, a son;
Got while his soul did huddled notions try,
And born a shapeless lump like anarchy.
In friendship false, implacable in hate,
Resolved to ruin or to rule the State.

2.

In the first rank of these did Zimri stand;
A man so various that he seemed to be
Not one, but all mankind's epitome.
Stiff in opinions, always in the wrong,
Was everything by starts, and nothing long,
But in the course of one revolving moon
Was chymist, fiddler, statesman and buffoon,
Then all for women, painting, rhyming, drinking,
Besides ten thousand freaks that died in thinking.
Blest madman, who could every hour employ
With something new to wish or to enjoy!
Railing and praising were his usual themes,
And both (to show his judgment) in extremes;

So over violent or over civil
That every man with him was God or Devil.
In squandering wealth was his peculiar art,
Nothing went unrewarded but desert.
Beggared by fools, whom still he found too late,
He had his jest, and they had his estate.

FROM *MacFlecknoe*

All human things are subject to decay,
And when fate summons monarchs must obey;
This Flecknoe found, who like Augustus young
Was called to empire, and had governed long,
In prose and verse was owned without dispute
Through all the realms of Nonsense absolute.
This aged prince now flourishes in peace
And blest with issue of a large increase,
Worn out with business did at length debate
To settle the succession of the State;
And pondered which of all his sons was fit
To reign and wage immortal war with wit,
Cried: 'Tis resolved, for nature pleads that he
Should only rule who most resembles me;
Shadwell alone my perfect image bears,
Mature in dullness from his tender years,
Shadwell alone of all my sons is he
Who stands confirmed in full stupidity.
The rest to some faint meaning make pretence,
But Shadwell never deviates into sense.
Some beams of wit on other souls may fall,
Strike through and make a lucid interval,
But Shadwell's genuine night admits no ray,
His rising fogs prevail upon the day;
Besides, his goodly fabric fills the eye
And seems designed for thoughtless majesty;
Thoughtless as monarch oaks that shade the plain
And, spread in solemn state, supinely reign.

FROM *Religio Laici*

Dim, as the borrowed beams of moon and stars
To lonely, weary, wandering travellers
Is Reason to the soul; and as on high
Those rolling fires discover but the sky
Not light us here; so Reason's glimmering ray
Was lent, not to assure our doubtful way,
But guide us upward to a better day.
And as those nightly tapers disappear
When day's bright lord ascends our hemisphere;
So pale grows Reason at Religion's sight,
So dies, and so dissolves in supernatural light.
Some few whose lamp shone brighter have been led
From cause to cause to Nature's secret head;
And found that one first principle must be.
But what or who that universal He,
Whether some soul encompassing this ball,
Unmade, unmoved, yet making, moving all;
Or various atoms' interfering dance
Leapt into form (the noble work of chance)
Or this great All was from eternity;
Not ev'n the Stagirite himself could see,
And Epicurus guessed as well as he.

To the Memory of Mr. Oldham

Farewell, too little and too lately known,
Whom I began to think and call my own;
For sure our souls were near allied, and thine
Cast in the same poetic mould with mine.
One common note on either lyre did strike,
And knaves and fools we both abhorred alike.
To the same goal did both our studies drive,
The last set out the soonest did arrive.
Thus Nisus fell upon the slippery place,
Whilst his young friend performed and won the race.
Oh, early ripe! to thy abundant store
What could advancing age have added more?

It might (what Nature never gives the young)
Have taught the numbers of thy native tongue.
But satire needs not those, and wit will shine
Through the harsh cadence of a rugged line.
A noble error, and but seldom made,
When poets are by too much force betrayed.
Thy generous fruits, though gathered ere their prime,
Still shewed a quickness; and maturing time
But mellows what we write to the dull sweets of rhyme.
Once more, hail and farewell! farewell, thou young,
But ah! too short, Marcellus of our tongue!
Thy brow's with ivy and with laurels bound;
But fate and gloomy night encompass thee around.

FROM *Tyrannic Love*, 1669

PROLOGUE

Self-love (which never rightly understood)
Makes poets still conclude their plays are good,
And malice in all critics reigns so high,
That for small errors, they whole plays decry;
So that to see this fondness, and that spite,
You'd think that none but madmen judge or write.
Therefore our Poet, as he thinks not fit
T'impose upon you what he writes for wit
So hopes that, leaving you your censures free,
You equal judges of the whole will be:
They judge but half, who only faults will see.
Poets, like lovers, should be bold and dare,
They spoil their business with an over-care;
And he, who servilely creeps after sense,
Is safe, but ne'er will reach an excellence.
Hence 'tis, our Poet, in his conjuring,
Allow'd his fancy the full scope and swing.
But when a tyrant for his theme he had,
He loos'd the reins, and bid his Muse run mad;
And though he stumbles in a full career,
Yet rashness is a better fault than fear.

He saw his way; but in so swift a pace,
To choose the ground might be to lose the race.
They then, who of each trip th' advantage take,
Find but those faults, which they want wit to make.

EPILOGUE

*Spoken by Mrs. Ellen [i.e., Nell Gwynn] when she was to be
carried off by the Bearers*

To the Bearer:

Hold! are you mad? you damned, confounded dog!
I am to rise, and speak the epilogue.

To the Audience:

I come, kind gentlemen, strange news to tell ye;
I am the ghost of poor departed Nelly.
Sweet ladies, be not frightened; I'll be civil;
I'm what I was, a little harmless devil.
For, after death, we sprites have just such natures,
We had, for all the world, when human creatures;
And, therefore, I, that was an actress here,
Play all my tricks in Hell, a goblin there.
Gallants, look to 't, you say there are no sprites;
But I'll come dance about your beds at nights;
And faith you'll be in a sweet kind of taking,
When I surprise you between sleep and waking.
To tell you true, I walk, because I die
Out of my calling, in a tragedy.
O poet, damned dull poet, who could prove
So senseless, to make Nelly die for love!
Nay, what's yet worse, to kill me in the prime
Of Easter-term, in tart and cheese-cake time!
I'll fit the fop; for I'll not one word say,
T' excuse his godly, out of fashion play;
A play, which, if you dare but twice sit out,
You'll all be slandered, and be thought devout.
But farewell, gentlemen, make haste to me,
I'm sure ere long to have your company.
As for my epitaph when I am gone,
I'll trust no poet, but will write my own:
"Here Nelly lies, who, though she lived a slater'n,
Yet died a princess, acting in S. Cathar'n.

FROM *The Secular Masque*

CHORUS

All, all of a piece throughout:
   Thy chase had a beast in view;
Thy wars brought nothing about;
   Thy lovers were all untrue.
'Tis well an old age is out,
   And time to begin a new.

KATHERINE PHILIPS
(1631–1664)

Friendship's Mystery
(TO MY DEAREST LUCASIA)

Come, my Lucasia, since we see
   That miracles men's faith do move,
By wonder and by prodigy
   To the dull angry world let's prove
   There's a religion in our love.

For though we were designed t' agree,
   That Fate no liberty destroys,
But our election is as free
   As angels', who with greedy choice
   Are yet determined to their joys.

Our hearts are doubled by the loss;
   Here mixture is addition grown;
We both diffuse, and both engross:
   And we whose minds are so much one,
   Never, yet ever are alone.

We court our own captivity
   Than thrones more great and innocent:
'Twere banishment to be set free,
   Since we wear fetters whose intent
   Not bondage is but ornament.

Divided joys are tedious found,
　　And griefs united easier grow:
We are ourselves but by rebound,
　　And all our titles shuffled so,
　　Both princes, and both subjects too.

Our hearts are mutual victims laid,
　　While they (such power in friendship lies)
Are altars, priests and off'rings made:
　　And each heart which thus kindly dies,
　　Grows deathless by the sacrifice.

SIR GEORGE ETHEREGE

(1635?–1691)

Song

Ye happy swains, whose hearts are free
　　From love's imperial chain,
Take warning and be taught by me,
　　T' avoid th' enchanting pain.
Fatal the wolves to trembling flocks,
　　Fierce winds to blossoms prove,
To careless seamen hidden rocks,
　　To human quiet love.

Fly the fair sex, if bliss you prize;
　　The snake's beneath the flower:
Whoever gazed on beauteous eyes
　　That tasted quiet more?
How faithless is the lover's joy!
　　How constant is their care,
The kind with falsehood to destroy,
　　The cruel with despair!

Upon the Downs...

Upon the downs when shall I breathe at ease,
Have nothing else to do but what I please?
In a fresh cooling shade upon the brink
Of Arden's spring have time to read and think.

And stretch, and sleep, when all my care shall be
For health, and pleasure my philosophy?
When shall I rest from business, noise, and strife,
Lay down the soldier's and the courtier's life,
And in a little melancholy seat
Begin at last to live and to forget
The nonsense and the farce of what the fools call great?

To a Lady, Asking Him How Long He Would Love Her

It is not, Celia, in our power
To say how long our love will last;
It may be we within this hour
May lose those joys we now do taste;
The blessed, that immortal be,
From change in love are only free.

Then, since we mortal lovers are,
Ask not how long our love will last;
But while it does, let us take care
Each minute be with pleasure passed:
Were it not madness to deny
To live because we're sure to die?

To a Very Young Lady

Sweetest bud of beauty, may
No untimely frost decay
Th' early glories which we trace
Blooming in thy matchless face!
But kindly opening like the rose
Fresh beauties every day disclose,
Such as by nature are not shown
In all the blossoms she has blown.
And then what conquests shall you make
Who hearts already daily take!

Scorched in the morning with thy beams,
How shall he bear those sad extremes,
Which must attend thy threatening eyes
When thou shalt to thy noon arise!

SIR CHARLES SEDLEY

(1639–1701)

Song

Not, Celia, that I juster am,
  Or better than the rest,
For I would change each hour like them,
  Were not my heart at rest.

But I am tied to very thee
  By every thought I have,
Thy face I only care to see,
  Thy heart I only crave.

All that in Woman is adored
  In thy dear self I find,
For the whole sex can but afford
  The handsome and the kind.

Why then should I seek farther store,
  And still make love anew?
When change itself can give no more,
  'Tis easy to be true.

Song

Love still has something of the sea
  From whence his mother rose;
No time his slaves from doubt can free,
  Nor give their thoughts repose.

They are becalmed in clearest days,
  And in rough weather tost;
They wither under cold delays,
  Or are in tempests lost.

One while they seem to touch the port,
    Then straight into the main,
Some angry wind in cruel sport
    The vessel drives again.

At first disdain and pride they fear,
    Which if they chance to 'scape,
Rivals and falsehood soon appear
    In a more dreadful shape.

By such degrees to joy they come,
    And are so long withstood,
So slowly they receive the sum,
    It hardly does them good.

'Tis cruel to prolong a pain,
    And to defer a joy,
Believe me, gentle Celimene,
    Offends the wingéd boy.

An hundred thousand oaths your fears
    Perhaps would not remove;
And if I gazed a thousand years
    I could no deeper love.

Song

Ah Chloris! that I now could sit
    As unconcerned, as when
Your infant beauty could beget
    No pleasure nor no pain.

When I the dawn used to admire,
    And praised the coming day;
I little thought the growing fire
    Must take my rest away.

Your charms in harmless childhood lay,
    Like metals in the mine,
Age from no face took more away
    Than youth concealed in thine.

But as your charms insensibly
    To their perfections prest,
Fond Love as unperceived did fly
    And in my bosom rest.

My passion with your beauty grew,
    And Cupid in my heart
Still as his mother favoured you
    Threw a new flaming dart.

Each gloried in their wanton part;
    To make a lover he
Employed the utmost of his art,
    To make a beauty she.

Though now I slowly bend to love
    Uncertain of my fate,
If your fair self my chains approve
    I shall my freedom hate.

Lovers, like dying men, may well
    At first disordered be,
Since none alive can truly tell
    What fortune they must see.

The Mulberry Garden, 1668

APHRA BEHN

(1640–1689)

The Coquet

Melinda, who had never been
Esteemed a beauty at fifteen,
Always amorous was and kind;
    To every swain she lent an ear,
Free as air but false as wind;
    Yet none complained she was severe.
She eased more than she made complain,
Was always singing, pert, and vain.

Where-e'er the throng was, she was seen,
And swept the youths along the green;
With equal grace she flattered all;
    And fondly proud of all address,
Her smiles invite, her eyes do call,
    And her vain heart her looks confess.
She rallies this, to that she bowed,
Was talking ever, laughing loud.

On every side she makes advance,
And everywhere a confidence;
She tells for secrets all she knows,
    And all to know she does pretend.
Beauty in maids she treats as foes,
    But every handsome youth as friend.
Scandal still passes off for truth,
And noise and nonsense, wit and youth.

Coquet all o'er and every part,
Yet wanting beauty even of art,
Herds with the ugly and the old,
    And plays the critic on the rest;
Of men the bashful and the bold
    Either and all by turns likes best;
Even now, though youth be languished, she
Sets up for love and gallantry.

The Willing Mistress

Amyntas led me to a grove
    Where all the trees did shade us;
The sun itself though it had strove
    It could not have betrayed us.
The place secured from human eyes
    No other fear allows,
But when the winds that gently rise
    Do kiss the yielding boughs.

Down there we sat upon the moss,
    And did begin to play
A thousand amorous tricks, to pass
    The heat of all the day.
A many kisses he did give,
    And I returned the same,
Which made me willing to receive
    That which I dare not name.

His charming eyes no aid required
    To tell their softening tale;
On her that was already fired
    'Twas easy to prevail.
He did but kiss and clasp me round,
    Whilst those his thoughts exprest;
And laid me gently on the ground:
    Ah, who can guess the rest?

Song

Love in fantastic triumph sate
    Whilst bleeding hearts around him flow'd,
For whom fresh pains he did create
    And strange tyrannic power he show'd:
From thy bright eyes he took his fires,
    Which round about in sport he hurl'd;
But 'twas from mine he took desires
    Enough t' undo the amorous world.

From me he took his sighs and tears,
    From thee his pride and cruelty;
From me his languishments and fears,
    And every killing dart from thee.
Thus thou and I the god have arm'd
    And set him up a deity;
But my poor heart alone is harm'd,
    Whilst thine the victor is, and free!

                                    Abdelazer, 1676

THOMAS SHADWELL

(1642?–1692)

Song

The fringéd vallance of your eyes advance,
Shake off your canopied and downy trance;
Phoebus already quaffs the morning dew,
Each does his daily lease of life renew.

He darts his beams on the lark's mossy house,
And from his quiet tenement does rouse
The little charming and harmonious fowl,
Which sings its lump of body to a soul;
Swiftly it clambers up in the steep air
With warbling throat, and makes each note a stair.

This the solicitous lover straight alarms,
Who too long slumbered in his Celia's arms.
And now the swelling spunges of the night
With aching heads stagger from their delight;
Slovenly tailors to their needles haste;
Already now the moving shops are placed
By those who crop the treasures of the fields,
And all those gems the ripening summer yields.

JOHN WILMOT, Earl of Rochester

(1647–1680)

from *The Mistress*

An age in her embraces past
    Would seem a winter's day,
Where life and light with envious haste
    Are torn and snatched away.

But oh! how slowly minutes roll
    When absent from her eyes;
That fed my love, which is my soul,
    It languishes and dies.

For then no more a soul, but shade,
   It mournfully does move,
And haunts my breast by absence made
   The living tomb of love.

A Song

Absent from thee I languish still;
   Then ask me not, when I return?
The straying fool 'twill plainly kill
   To wish all day, all night to mourn.

Dear, from thine arms then let me fly,
   That my fantastic mind may prove
The torments it deserves to try,
   That tears my fixed heart from my love.

When wearied with a world of woe,
   To thy safe bosom I retire,
Where love and peace and truth do flow,
   May I contented there expire.

Lest once more wandering from that heaven
   I fall on some base heart unblest,
Faithless to thee, false, unforgiven,
   And lose my everlasting rest.

Love and Life

All my past life is mine no more,
   The flying hours are gone;
Like transitory dreams given o'er,
Whose images are kept in store
   By memory alone.

The time that is to come is not;
   How can it then be mine?
The present moment's all my lot,
And that as fast as it is got,
   Phyllis, is only thine.

Then talk not of inconstancy,
   False hearts and broken vows;
If I by miracle can be
This live-long minute true to thee,
   'Tis all that Heaven allows.

Upon His Leaving His Mistress

'Tis not that I am weary grown
Of being yours, and yours alone,
But with what face can I incline
To damn you to be only mine?
You, whom some kinder power did fashion
By merit and by inclination
The joy at least of a whole nation.

Let meaner spirits of your sex
With humble aims their thoughts perplex,
And boast if by their arts they can
Contrive to make one happy man;
While moved by an impartial sense
Favours, like Nature, you dispense
With universal influence.

See the kind seed-receiving earth
To every grain affords a birth:
On her no showers unwelcome fall,
Her willing womb retains 'em all,
And shall my Cælia be confined?
No, live up to thy mighty mind,
And be the mistress of Mankind!

Upon Nothing

Nothing! Thou elder brother ev'n to shade,
Thou hadst a being ere the world was made,
And well-fixed art alone of ending not afraid.

Ere time and place were, time and place were not,
With primitive Nothing something straight begot,
Then all proceeded from the great united—what?

Something, the general attribute of all,
Severed from thee, its sole original,
Into thy boundless self must undistinguished fall.

Yet something did thy mighty power command,
And from thy fruitful emptiness's hand
Snatched men, beasts, birds, fire, air and land.

Matter, the wicked'st offspring of thy race,
By Form assisted flew from thy embrace,
And rebel Light obscured thy reverend dusky face.

With Form and Matter, Time and Place did join,
Body, thy foe, with thee did leagues combine,
To spoil thy peaceful realm, and ruin all thy line.

But turn-coat Time assists the foe in vain,
And bribed by thee assists thy short-lived reign,
And to thy hungry womb drives back thy slaves again.

Though mysteries are barred from laic eyes,
And the divine alone with warrant pries
Into thy bosom, where the truth in private lies;

Yet this of thee the wise may freely say,
Thou from the virtuous nothing tak'st away,
And to be part with thee the wicked wisely pray.

Great Negative, how vainly would the wise
Enquire, define, distinguish, teach, devise,
Didst thou not stand to point their dull philosophies!

Is or is not, the two great ends of Fate,
And, true or false, the subject of debate,
That perfect or destroy the vast designs of Fate,

When they have racked the politician's breast
Within thy bosom most securely rest,
And when reduced to thee are least unsafe and best.

But, Nothing, why does Something still permit
That sacred monarchs should at council sit,
With persons highly thought at best for nothing fit?

Whilst weighty something modestly abstains
From princes' coffers and from statesmen's brains,
And nothing there like stately Nothing reigns?

Nothing, who dwell'st with fools in grave disguise,
For whom they reverend shapes and forms devise,
Lawn sleeves and furs and gowns, when they like thee look
       wise.

French truth, Dutch prowess, British policy,
Hibernian learning, Scotch civility,
Spaniards' despatch, Danes' wit, are mainly seen in thee.

The great man's gratitude to his best friend,
Kings' promises, whores' vows towards thee they bend,
Flow swiftly into thee, and in thee ever end.

King Charles II

Here lies our sovereign lord the King,
     Whose word no man relies on,
Who never said a foolish thing
     And never did a wise one.

THOMAS OTWAY

(1652–1685)

The Enchantment

I did but look and love awhile,
     'Twas but for one half-hour;
Then to resist I had no will,
     And now I have no power.

To sigh and wish is all my ease;
   Sighs which do heat impart
Enough to melt the coldest ice
   Yet cannot warm your heart.

O would your pity give my heart
   One corner of your breast,
'Twould learn of yours the winning art
   And quickly steal the rest.

JOHN OLDHAM

(1653–1683)

FROM A Satire

(The ghost of Spenser speaks)

But, grant thy poetry should find success,
And, which is rare, the squeamish critics please;
Admit it read, and praised, and courted be
By this nice age and all posterity;
If thou expectest aught but empty fame,
Condemn thy hopes and labours to the flame.
The rich have now learned only to admire;
He, who to greater favours does aspire,
Is mercenary thought, and writes for hire.

"Bless me! how great his genius! how each line
Is big with sense! how glorious a design
Does through the whole and each proportion shine!
How lofty all his thoughts and how inspired!
Pity, such wondrous thoughts are not preferred,"
Cries a gay wealthy sot, who would not bail
For bare five pounds the author out of jail
Should he starve there and rot; who if a brief
Came out the needy poets to relieve
To the whole tribe would scarce a tester give.

But fifty guineas for a punk—good hap!
The peer's well used, and comes off wondrous cheap;
A poet would be dear, and out o' th' way,
Should he expect above a coachman's pay.
For this will any dedicate, and lie,
And daub the gaudy ass with flattery?
For this will any prostitute his sense
To coxcombs void of bounty as of brains?
Yet such is the hard fate of writers now,
They're forced for alms to each great name to bow;
Fawn, like her lap-dog, on her tawdry Grace,
Commend her beauty, and belie her glass,
By which she every morning primes her face;
Sneak to his Honour, call him witty, brave,
And just, though a known coward, fool or knave;
And praise his lineage and nobility
Whose arms at first came from the Company.

'Tis so, 'twas ever so, since heretofore
The blind old bard, with dog and bell before
Was fain to sing for bread from door to door;
The needy Muses all turned gipsies then,
And of the begging trade e'er since have been.

My own hard usage here I need not press,
Where you have every day before your face
Plenty of fresh resembling instances.
Great Cowley's muse the same ill treatment had,
Whose verse shall live for ever to upbraid
The ungrateful world that left such worth unpaid.
Waller himself may thank inheritance
For what he else had never got by sense.
On Butler who can think without just rage,
The glory and the scandal of the age?
Fair stood his hopes when first he came to town,
Met everywhere with welcomes of renown,
Courted, and loved by all, with wonder read,
And promises of princely favour fed;
But what reward for all had he at last,
After a life in dull expectance passed?

The wretch at summing up his misspent days
Found nothing left but poverty and praise;
Of all his gains by verse he could not save
Enough to purchase flannel and a grave;
Reduced to want, he in due time fell sick,
Was fain to die, and be interred on tick;
And well might bless the fever that was sent
To rid him hence, and his worse fate prevent.

All trades and all professions here abound,
And yet encouragement for all is found;
Here a vile empiric, who by license kills,
Who every week helps to increase the bills,
Wears velvet, keeps his coach, and jade beside,
For what less villains must to Tyburn ride.
There a dull trading sot, in wealth o'ergrown
By thriving knavery, can call his own
A dozen manors, and, if fate still bless,
Expects as many counties to possess.
Punks, panders, bawds, all their due pensions gain,
And every day the great men's bounty drain;
Lavish expense on wit, has never yet
Been taxed among the grievances of state.

Then be advised, the slighted Muse forsake,
And Coke and Dalton for thy study take;
For fees each term sweat in the crowded hall,
And there for charters and cracked titles bawl;
Or else to orders and the church betake
Thyself, and that thy future refuge make;
There fawn on some proud patron to engage
The advowson of cast punk and parsonage.
Or soothe the Court, and preach up kingly right,
To gain a prebend or a mitre by 't.
In fine, turn pettifogger, canonist,
Civilian, pedant, mountebank or priest,
Soldier or merchant, fiddler, painter, fencer,
Jack-pudding, juggler, player or rope-dancer;
Preach, plead, cure, fight, game, pimp, beg, cheat or thieve;
Be all but poet, and there's way to live.

ANNE FINCH, COUNTESS OF WINCHELSEA

(1661?–1720)

A Song

If for a woman I would die,
   It should for Gloriana be;
But lovers, you that talk so high,
Inform, whilst in the grave I lie,
   What reward shall reach to me?

If I my freedom would resign,
   That freedom she alone should have;
But tell me, you that can define,
If I by marriage make her mine
   Which may be called the greater slave?

Then Gloriana, since 'tis plain,
   Love with these two can ne'er agree,
Since death and marriage are his bane,
Those melancholy thoughts we'll flee,
   And cheerful lovers always be.

RICHARD BENTLEY

(1662–1742)

Verses

Who strives to mount Parnassus hill
   And thence poetic laurels bring,
Must first acquire due force and skill,
   Must fly with swan's or eagle's wing.

Who Nature's treasures would explore,
   Her mysteries and arcana know,
Must high as lofty Newton soar,
   Must stoop as searching Woodward low.

Who studies ancient laws and rites,
   Tongues, arts, and arms, all history,
Must drudge like Selden days and nights,
   And in the endless labour die.

Who travels in religious jars,
    (Truth mixed with errors, shade with rays),
Like Whiston, wanting Pyx and stars
    In ocean wide or sinks, or stays.

But grant our hero's hopes long toil
    And comprehensive genius crown;
All sciences, all arts, his spoil,
    Yet what reward or what renown?

Envy, innate in vulgar souls,
    Envy steps in and stops his rise;
Envy with poisoned tarnish fouls
    His lustre, and his worth decries.

Inglorious, or by wants enthralled,
    To College and old books confined,
A pedant for his learning called,
    Dunces advanced, he's left behind;
Yet left content, a genuine Stoic he,
Great without patron, rich without South-Sea.

WILLIAM WALSH

(1663–1708)

Song

Of all the torments, all the cares,
    With which our lives are cursed;
Of all the plagues a lover bears,
    Sure rivals are the worst!
By partners, in each other kind,
    Afflictions easier grow;
In love alone we hate to find
    Companions of our woe.

Sylvia, for all the pangs you see
    Are labouring in my breast;
I beg not you would favour me,
    Would you but slight the rest!

How great so e'er your rigours are,
    With them alone I'll cope;
I can endure my own despair,
    But not another's hope.

Sonnet on Death

What has this bugbear Death that's worth our care?
After a life in pain and sorrow past,
After deluding hope and dire despair,
Death only gives us quiet at the last.
How strangely are our love and hate misplaced!
Freedom we seek, and yet from freedom flee;
Courting those tyrant-sins that chain us fast,
And shunning Death that only sets us free.
'Tis not a foolish fear of future pains—
Why should they fear who keep their souls from stains?—
That makes me dread thy terrors, Death, to see;
'Tis not the loss of riches or of fame,
Or the vain toys the vulgar pleasures name:
'Tis nothing, Celia, but the losing thee.

MATTHEW PRIOR

(1664–1721)

An Ode

The merchant, to secure his treasure,
    Conveys it in a borrowed name;
Euphelia serves to grace my measure,
    But Cloe is my real flame.

My softest verse, my darling lyre,
    Upon Euphelia's toilet lay;
When Cloe noted her desire,
    That I should sing, that I should play.

My lyre I tune, my voice I raise;
  But with the numbers mix my sighs;
And whilst I sing Euphelia's praise,
  I fix my soul on Cloe's eyes.

Fair Cloe blushed; Euphelia frowned;
  I sung and gazed, I played and trembled;
And Venus to the Loves around
  Remarked, how ill we all dissembled.

Cupid's Mistaken

As after noon, one summer's day,
  Venus stood bathing in a river,
Cupid a-shooting went that way,
  New strung his bow, new filled his quiver.

With skill he chose his sharpest dart,
  With all his might his bow he drew;
Swift to his beauteous parent's heart
  The too well-guided arrow flew.

I faint! I die! the goddess cried,
  O cruel, couldst thou find none other
To wreck thy spleen on? Parricide!
  Like Nero, thou hast slain thy mother.

Poor Cupid sobbing scarce could speak;
  Indeed, mamma, I did not know ye;
Alas! how easy my mistake,
  I took you for your likeness, Cloe.

The Lady Who Offers Her Looking Glass

Venus, take my votive glass,
Since I am not what I was;
What from this day I shall be,
Venus, let me never see.

                    From the Greek of PLATO

To Cloe Jealous, a Better Answer

Dear Cloe, how blubber'd is that pretty face;
  Thy cheek all on fire, and thy hair all uncurl'd:
Prythee quit this caprice; and (as old Falstaff says)
  Let us e'en talk a little like folks of this world.

How canst thou presume, thou hast leave to destroy
  The beauties, which Venus but lent to thy keeping?
Those looks were design'd to inspire love and joy:
  More ord'nary eyes may serve people for weeping.

To be vex'd at a trifle or two that I writ,
  Your judgment at once, and my passion you wrong:
You take that for fact, which will scarce be found wit:
  Odds life! must one swear to the truth of a song?

What I speak, my fair Cloe, and what I write, shows
  The difference there is betwixt nature and art:
I court others in verse; but I love thee in prose:
  And they have my whimsies, but thou hast my heart.

The god of us verse-men (you know, child) the sun,
  How after his journeys he sets up his rest:
If at morning o'er earth 'tis his fancy to run;
  At night he declines on his Thetis's breast.

So when I am wearied with wandering all day,
  To thee, my delight, in the evening I come:
No matter what beauties I saw in my way;
  They were all but my visits, but thou art my home.

Then finish, dear Cloe, this pastoral war;
  And let us, like Horace and Lydia, agree:
For thou art a girl as much brighter than her,
  As he was a poet sublimer than me.

JONATHAN SWIFT
(1667–1745)

A Description of the Morning

Now hardly here and there a hackney coach
Appearing, showed the ruddy morn's approach.
Now Betty from her master's bed had flown,
And softly stole to discompose her own;
The slip-shod 'prentice from his master's door
Had pared the dirt and sprinkled round the floor.
Now Moll had whirled her mop with dext'rous airs,
Prepared to scrub the entry and the stairs.
The youth with broomy stumps began to trace
The kennel's edge, where wheels had worn the place.
The small-coal man was heard with cadence deep,
Till drowned in shriller notes of chimney-sweep:
Duns at his lordship's gate began to meet;
And brickdust Moll had screamed through half the street.
The turnkey now his flock returning sees,
Duly let out a-nights to steal for fees:
The watchful bailiffs take their silent stands,
And schoolboys lag with satchels in their hands.

FROM A Description of a City Shower

Ah! where must needy poet seek for aid,
When dust and rain at once his coat invade?
Sole coat! where dust cemented by the rain
Erects the nap, and leaves a cloudy stain!
Now in contiguous drops the flood comes down,
Threatening with deluge this *devoted* town.
To shops in crowds the daggled females fly,
Pretend to cheapen goods, but nothing buy.
The Templar spruce, while every spout's abroach,
Stays till 'tis fair, yet seems to call a coach.
The tucked-up sempstress walks with hasty strides,
While streams run down her oiled umbrella's sides.
Here various kinds, by various fortunes led,
Commence acquaintance underneath a shed.

Triumphant Tories and desponding Whigs
Forget their feuds, and join to save their wigs.
Boxed in a chair the beau impatient sits,
While spouts run clattering o'er the roof by fits,
And ever and anon with frightful din
The leather sounds; he trembles from within.

FROM On the Death of Doctor Swift

1.

The time is not remote when I
Must by the course of nature die;
When I foresee, my special friends
Will try to find their private ends:
And, though 'tis hardly understood
Which way my death can do them good,
Yet thus, methinks, I hear them speak:
"See, how the dean begins to break!
Poor gentleman, he droops apace!
You plainly find it in his face.
That old vertigo in his head
Will never leave him till he's dead.
Besides, his memory decays;
He recollects not what he says;
He cannot call his friends to mind;
Forgets the place where last he dined;
Plies you with stories o'er and o'er,
He told them fifty times before.
How does he fancy we can sit
To hear his out-of-fashion wit?
But he takes up with younger folks,
Who for his wine will bear his jokes.
Faith! he must make his stories shorter,
Or change his comrades once a quarter;
In half the time he talks them round,
There must another set be found.
For poetry he's past his prime;
He takes an hour to find a rhyme;
His fire is out, his wit decayed,
His fancy sunk, his Muse a jade.

I'd have them throw away his pen—
But there's no talking to some men."
And then their tenderness appears
By adding largely to my years:
"He's older than he would be reckoned,
And well remembers Charles the Second.
He hardly drinks a pint of wine;
And that, I doubt, is no good sign.
His stomach too begins to fail;
Last year we thought him strong and hale;
But now he's quite another thing;
I wish he may hold out till spring!"
They hug themselves, and reason thus:
"It is not yet so bad with us!"

2.

Behold the fatal day arrive!
"How is the dean?" "He's just alive."
Now the departing prayer is read.
"He hardly breathes." "The dean is dead."
Before the passing bell begun,
The news through half the town is run.
"O! may we all for death prepare!
What has he left? and who's his heir?"
"I know no more than what the news is;
'Tis all bequeathed to public uses."
"To public uses! There's a whim!
What had the public done for him?
Mere envy, avarice, and pride;
He gave it all—but first he died.
And had the dean in all the nation
No worthy friend, no poor relation?
So ready to do strangers good,
Forgetting his own flesh and blood!"

3.

From Dublin soon to London spread,
'Tis told at Court, "the dean is dead."
And Lady Suffolk, in the spleen,
Runs laughing up to tell the Queen.

The Queen, so gracious, mild, and good,
Cries: "Is he gone? 'Tis time he should.
He's dead, you say; then let him rot;
I'm glad the medals were forgot.
I promised him, I own; but when?
I only was the Princess then;
But now, as consort of the King,
You know 'tis quite another thing."
Now Chartres, at Sir Robert's levee,
Tells with a sneer the tidings heavy:
"Why, if he died without his shoes,"
Cries Bob, "I'm sorry for the news;
Oh, were the wretch but living still,
And in his place my good friend Will!
Or had a mitre on his head,
Provided Bolingbroke were dead!"
Now Curll his shop from rubbish drains;
Three genuine tomes of Swift's remains!
And then to make them pass the glibber,
Revised by Tibbalds, Moore, and Cibber.
He'll treat me as he does my betters,
Publish my will, my life, my letters;
Revive the libels born to die;
Which Pope must bear as well as I.

4.

My female friends, whose tender hearts
Have better learned to act their parts,
Receive the news in doleful dumps:
"The dean is dead—pray what is trumps?—
The Lord have mercy on his soul!
—Ladies, I'll venture for the vole.—
Six deans, they say, must bear the pall—
I wish I knew what king to call.—
Madam, your husband will attend
The funeral of so good a friend?
No, madam, 'tis a shocking sight,
And he's engaged to-morrow night;
My Lady Club will take it ill
If he should fail her at quadrille.

He loved the dean—I lead a heart—
But dearest friends, they say, must part.
His time was come, he ran his race;
We hope he's in a better place."

5.

"He gave the little wealth he had
To build a house for fools and mad;
And showed by one satiric touch
No nation wanted it so much.
That kingdom he had left his debtor,
I wish it soon may have a better."

WILLIAM CONGREVE
(1670–1729)

Song

False though she be to me and love,
    I'll ne'er pursue revenge;
For still the charmer I approve,
    Though I deplore her change.

In hours of bliss we oft have met;
    They could not always last;
And though the present I regret,
    I'm grateful for the past.

Amoret

Fair Amoret is gone astray;
    Pursue and seek her, every lover;
I'll tell the signs by which you may
    The wandering shepherdess discover.

Coquet and coy at once her air,
    Both studied, though both seem neglected;
Careless she is with artful care,
    Affecting to seem unaffected.

With skill her eyes dart every glance,
 Yet change so soon you'd ne'er suspect them;
For she'd persuade they wound by chance,
 Though certain aim and art direct them.

She likes herself, yet others hates
 For that which in herself she prizes;
And, while she laughs at them, forgets
 She is the thing that she despises.

FROM *The Mourning Bride*, 1697

Almeria: Music has charms to soothe a savage breast,
 To soften rocks, or bend a knotted oak.
 I've read that things inanimate have moved,
 And, as with living souls, have been informed,
 By magic numbers and persuasive sound.
 What then am I? O force of constant woe!
 'Tis not in harmony to calm my griefs . . .
 Why do I live to say you are no more?

SIR RICHARD STEELE

(1672–1729)

Song

Why, lovely charmer, tell me why,
So very kind, so very shy?
Why does that cold forbidding air
Give damps of sorrow and despair?
Or why that smile my soul subdue,
And kindle up my flames anew?

In vain you strive with all your art,
By turns to freeze and fire my heart:
When I behold a face so fair,
So sweet a look, so soft an air,
My ravished soul is charmed all o'er,
I cannot love thee less nor more.

The Tender Husband, 1705

ABEL EVANS
(1679–1737)

Epitaph on Sir John Vanbrugh

Under this stone, reader, survey
Dead Sir John Vanbrugh's house of clay.
Lie heavy on him, Earth! for he
Laid many heavy loads on thee!

EDWARD YOUNG
(1683–1765)

Extempore to Voltaire Criticising Milton

You are so witty, profligate and thin,
At once we think you Milton, death, and sin.

GEORGE BERKELEY
(1685–1753)

Verses on the Prospect of Planting Arts and Learning in America

The Muse, disgusted at an age and clime
    Barren of every glorious theme,
In distant lands now waits a better time,
    Producing subjects worthy fame:

In happy climes, where from the genial sun
    And virgin earth such scenes ensue,
The force of art by nature seems outdone,
    And fancied beauties by the true:

In happy climes, the seat of innocence,
    Where nature guides and virtue rules,
Where men shall not impose for truth and sense
    The pedantry of courts and schools:

There shall be sung another golden age,
    The rise of empire and of arts,
The good and great inspiring epic rage,
    The wisest heads, and noblest hearts.

Not such as Europe breeds in her decay;
    Such as she bred when fresh and young,
When heavenly flame did animate her clay,
    By future poets shall be sung.

Westward the course of empire takes its way;
    The first four acts already past,
A fifth shall close the drama with the day;
    Time's noblest offspring is the last.

JOHN GAY

(1685–1732)

Ballad

'Twas when the seas were roaring
    With hollow blasts of wind;
A damsel lay deploring,
    All on a rock reclined.
Wide o'er the rolling billows
    She cast a wistful look;
Her head was crowned with willows
    That tremble o'er the brook.

Twelve months are gone and over,
    And nine long tedious days.
Why didst thou, vent'rous lover,
    Why didst thou trust the seas?
Cease, cease, thou cruel ocean,
    And let my lover rest;
Ah! what's thy troubled motion
    To that within my breast?

The merchant robbed of pleasure
  Sees tempests in despair;
But what's the loss of treasure
  To losing of my dear?
Should you some coast be laid on
  Where gold and di'monds grow,
You'd find a richer maiden,
  But none that loves you so.

How can they say that nature
  Has nothing made in vain,
Why then beneath the water
  Should hideous rocks remain?
No eyes the rocks discover,
  That lurk beneath the deep,
To wreck the wand'ring lover,
  And leave the maid to weep.

All melancholy lying,
  Thus wailed she for her dear;
Repaid each blast with sighing,
  Each billow with a tear;
When, o'er the white wave stooping,
  His floating corpse she spied;
Then like a lily drooping,
  She bowed her head, and died.

The What D'ye Call It, 1715

Love in Her Eyes Sits Playing

Love in her eyes sits playing,
  And sheds delicious death;
Love in her lips sits straying,
  And warbling in her breath.
Love on her breast sits panting,
  And swells with soft desire;
No grace, no charm is wanting
  To set the heart on fire.

Acis and Galatea, 1732

O Ruddier Than the Cherry

O ruddier than the cherry,
O sweeter than the berry,
O Nymph more bright
Than moonshine night,
Like kidlings blithe and merry.
Ripe as the melting cluster,
No lily has such lustre,
Yet hard to tame
As raging flame,
And fierce as storms that bluster.

Acis and Galatea, 1732

Air XXXV

How happy could I be with either,
Were t'other dear charmer away!
But while you thus tease me together,
To neither a word will I say:
But tol de rol.

The Beggar's Opera, 1728

Air XXIII

Sleep, O sleep,
With thy rod of incantation,
Charm my imagination.
Then, only then, I cease to weep.
By thy power,
The virgin, by time o'ertaken,
For years forlorn, forsaken,
Enjoys the happy hour.
What's to sleep?
'Tis a visionary blessing;
A dream that's past expressing;
Our utmost wish possessing;
So may I always keep.

Polly, 1729

FROM *The Fan*

Rise, happy youth, this bright machine survey,
Whose rattling sticks my busy fingers sway,
This present shall thy cruel charmer move,
And in her fickle bosom kindle love.
The fan shall flutter in all female hands,
And various fashions learn from various lands.
For this shall elephants their ivory shed,
And polished sticks the waving engine spread;
His clouded mail the tortoise shall resign,
And round the rivet pearly circles shine.
On this shall Indians all their art employ,
And with bright colours stain the gaudy toy;
Their paint shall here in wildest fancies flow,
Their dress, their customs, their religion show,
So shall the British fair their minds improve,
And on the fan to distant climates rove.
Here China's ladies shall their pride display,
And silver figures gild their loose array;
This boasts her little feet and winking eyes;
That tunes the fife, or tinkling cymbal plies;
Here cross-legged nobles in rich state shall dine,
There in bright mail distorted heroes shine.
The peeping fan in modern times shall rise
Through which unseen the female ogle flies;
This shall in temples the sly maid conceal,
And shelter love beneath devotion's veil.
Gay France shall make the fan her artist's care,
And with the costly trinket arm the fair.
As learned orators that touch the heart,
With various actions raise their soothing art,
Both head and hand affect the listening throng,
And humour each expression of the tongue.
So shall each passion by the fan be seen,
From noisy anger to the sullen spleen.

His Own Epitaph

Life is a jest, and all things show it;
I thought so once, and now I know it.

ALLAN RAMSAY

(1686–1758)

FROM "An Thou Were My Ain Thing"

An thou were my ain thing,
I wou'd love thee, I wou'd love thee;
An thou were my ain thing,
   How dearly wou'd I love thee!

Like bees that suck the morning dew,
Frae flow'rs of sweetest scent and hue,
Sae would I dwell upon thy mow,
   And gar the gods envy me.

Sae lang's I had the use of light
I'd on thy beauties feast my sight,
Syne in saft whispers through the night
   I'd tell how much I love thee.

Time's on the wing and will not stay,
In shining youth let's make our hay;
Since love admits of no delay,
   O, let nae scorn undo thee.

An thou were my ain thing,
I wou'd love thee, I wou'd love thee;
And thou were my ain thing,
   How dearly wou'd I love thee.

Peggy

My Peggy is a young thing,
   Just entered in her teens,
Fair as the day, and sweet as May,
Fair as the day, and always gay.

Mow, mouth. Gar, make.

My Peggy is a young thing,
  And I'm not very auld,
Yet well I like to meet her at
  The wauking of the fauld.

My Peggy speaks sae sweetly,
  Whene'er we meet alane,
I wish nae mair to lay my care,
I wish nae mair of a' that's rare.
  My Peggy speaks sae sweetly,
    To a' the lave I'm cauld;
  But she gars a' my spirits glow
    At wauking of the fauld.

My Peggy smiles sae kindly,
  Whene'er I whisper love,
That I look doun on a' the toun,
That I look doun upon a croun.
  My Peggy smiles sae kindly,
    It makes me blythe and bauld,
  And naething gi'es me sic delight
    As wauking of the fauld.

My Peggy sings sae saftly,
  When on my pipe I play;
By a' the rest it is confessed,
By a' the rest, that she sings best.
  My Peggy sings sae saftly,
    And in her sangs are tald,
  With innocence, the wale of sense,
    At wauking of the fauld.

HENRY CAREY

(1687–1743)

Sally in Our Alley

Of all the girls that are so smart
  There's none like pretty Sally;
She is the darling of my heart,
  And she lives in our alley.

Wauking, *watching*. The lave, *the rest*. Bauld, *bold*. Wale, *pick*.

There's ne'er a lady in the land
　　That's half so sweet as Sally;
She is the darling of my heart,
　　And she lives in our alley.

Her father he makes cabbage-nets,
　　And thro' the street does cry 'em;
Her mother she sells laces long
　　To such as please to buy 'em;
But sure such folks could ne'er beget
　　So sweet a girl as Sally;
She is the darling of my heart,
　　And she lives in our alley.

When she is by I leave my work,
　　I love her so sincerely:
My master comes like any Turk
　　And bangs me most severely;
But let him bang his bellyful,
　　I'll bear it all for Sally;
She is the darling of my heart,
　　And she lives in our alley.

Of all the days that's in the week
　　I dearly love but one day,
And that's the day that comes betwixt
　　A Saturday and Monday,
For then I'm dressed in all my best
　　To walk abroad with Sally;
She is the darling of my heart,
　　And she lives in our alley.

My master carries me to church,
　　And often am I blamed
Because I leave him in the lurch
　　As soon as text is named;
I leave the church in sermon time
　　And slink away to Sally;
She is the darling of my heart,
　　And she lives in our alley.

When Christmas comes about again,
   O, then I shall have money;
I'll hoard it up, and box and all,
   I'll give it to my honey;
And would it were ten thousand pounds,
   I'd give it all to Sally;
She is the darling of my heart,
   And she lives in our alley.

My master and the neighbours all
   Make game of me and Sally,
And, but for her, I'd better be
   A slave, and row a galley;
But when my seven long years are out,
   O, then I'll marry Sally;
O, then we'll wed, and then we'll bed,
   But not in our alley.

ALEXANDER POPE

(1688–1744)

Ode on Solitude

Happy the man whose wish and care
   A few paternal acres bound,
Content to breath his native air,
     In his own ground.

Whose herds with milk, whose fields with bread,
   Whose flocks supply him with attire,
Whose trees in summer yield him shade,
     In winter fire.

Blest, who can unconcern'dly find
   Hours, days, and years slide soft away,
In health of body, peace of mind,
     Quiet by day,

Sound sleep by night; study and ease,
   Together mixt; sweet recreation;
And Innocence, which most does please
     With meditation.

Thus let me live, unseen, unknown,
Thus unlamented, let me die,
Steal from the world, and not a stone
Tell where I lie.

FROM An Essay on Criticism

'Tis with our judgments as our watches, none
Go just alike, yet each believes his own.
In poets as true genius is but rare,
True taste as seldom is the critic's share;
Both must alike from Heav'n derive their light,
These born to judge, as well as those to write.
Let such teach others who themselves excel,
And censure freely who have written well.
Authors are partial to their wit, 'tis true,
But are not critics to their judgment too?

Yet if we look more closely, we shall find
Most have the seeds of judgment in their mind:
Nature affords at least a glimm'ring light;
The lines, though touched but faintly, are drawn right.
But as the slightest sketch, if justly traced,
Is by ill-colouring but the more disgraced,
So by false learning is good sense defaced:
Some are bewildered in the maze of schools,
And some made coxcombs Nature meant but fools.
In search of wit these lose their common sense,
And then turn critics in their own defence:
Each burns alike, who can, or cannot write,
Or with a rival's, or an eunuch's spite.
All fools have still an itching to deride,
And fain would be upon the laughing side.
If Maevius scribble in Apollo's spite,
There are who judge still worse than he can write.

Some have at first for wits, then poets past,
Turned critics next, and proved plain fools at last.
Some neither can for wits nor critics pass,
As heavy mules are neither horse nor ass.

Those half-learn'd witlings, num'rous in our isle,
As half-formed insects on the banks of Nile;
Unfinished things, one knows not what to call,
Their generation's so equivocal:
To tell 'em, would a hundred tongues require,
Or one vain wit's, that might a hundred tire.

FROM *The Rape of the Lock*

Not with more glories, in th'etherial plain,
The Sun first rises o'er the purpled main,
Than, issuing forth, the rival of his beams
Launched on the bosom of the silver Thames.
Fair nymphs and well-drest youths around her shone
But ev'ry eye was fixed on her alone.
On her white breast a sparkling cross she wore,
Which Jews might kiss, and infidels adore.
Her lively looks a sprightly mind disclose,
Quick as her eyes, and as unfixed as those:
Favours to none, to all she smiles extends;
Oft she rejects, but never once offends.
Bright as the sun, her eyes the gazers strike,
And, like the sun, they shine on all alike.
Yet graceful ease, and sweetness void of pride,
Might hide her faults, if belles had faults to hide:
If to her share some female errors fall,
Look on her face, and you'll forget 'em all.

This Nymph, to the destruction of mankind,
Nourished two locks, which graceful hung behind
In equal curls, and well conspired to deck
With shining ringlets the smooth iv'ry neck.
Love in these labyrinths his slaves detains,
And mighty hearts are held in slender chains.
With hairy springes we the birds betray,
Slight lines of hair surprise the finny prey,
Fair tresses man's imperial race ensnare,
And beauty draws us with a single hair.

2.

Ye Sylphs and Sylphids, to your chief give ear!
Fays, Fairies, Genii, Elves, and Daemons, hear!
Ye know the spheres and various tasks assigned
By laws eternal to th'aërial kind.
Some in the fields of purest aether play,
And bask and whiten in the blaze of day.
Some guide the course of wand'ring orbs on high,
Or roll the planets through the boundless sky.
Some less refined, beneath the moon's pale light
Pursue the stars that shoot athwart the night,
Or suck the mists in grosser air below,
Or dip their pinions in the painted bow,
Or brew fierce tempests on the wintry main,
Or o'er the glebe distil the kindly rain.
Others on earth o'er human race preside,
Watch all their ways, and all their actions guide:
Of these the chief the care of Nations own,
And guard with Arms divine the British Throne.

Our humbler province is to tend the Fair,
Not a less pleasing, though less glorious care;
To save the powder from too rude a gale,
Nor let th'imprisoned essences exhale;
To draw fresh colours from the vernal flowers;
To steal from rainbows ere they drop in showers
A brighter wash; to curl their waving hairs,
Assist their blushes, and inspire their airs;
Nay oft, in dreams, invention we bestow,
To change a Flounce, or add a Furbelow.

This day, black Omens threat the brightest Fair,
That ere deserved a watchful spirit's care;
Some dire disaster, or by force, or sleight;
But what, or where, the fates have wrapped in night.
Whether the nymph shall break Diana's law,
Or some frail China jar receive a flaw;
Or stain her honour or her new brocade;
Forget her pray'rs, or miss a masquerade;
Or lose her heart, or necklace, at a ball;
Or whether Heav'n has doomed that Shock must fall.

Haste, then, ye spirits! to your charge repair:
The flutt'ring fan be Zephyretta's care;
The drops to thee, Brillante, we consign;
And, Momentilla, let the watch be thine;
Do thou, Crispissa, tend her fav'rite lock;
Ariel himself shall be the guard of Shock.

To fifty chosen Sylphs, of special note,
We trust th'important charge, the Petticoat:
Oft have we known that seven-fold fence to fail,
Though stiff with hoops, and armed with ribs of whale;
Form a strong line about the silver bound,
And guard the wide circumference around.

Whatever spirit, careless of his charge,
His post neglects, or leaves the fair at large,
Shall feel sharp vengeance soon o'ertake his sins,
Be stopped in vials, or transfixed with pins;
Or plunged in lakes of bitter washes lie,
Or wedged whole ages in a bodkin's eye:
Gums and Pomatums shall his flight restrain,
While clogged he beats his silken wings in vain;
Or Alum styptics with contracting power
Shrink his thin essence like a rivel'd flower:
Or, as Ixion fixed, the wretch shall feel
The giddy motion of the whirling Mill,
In fumes of burning Chocolate shall glow,
And tremble at the sea that froths below!

3.

For lo! the board with cups and spoons is crowned,
The berries crackle, and the mill turns round;
On shining altars of Japan they raise
The silver lamp; the fiery spirits blaze:
From silver spouts the grateful liquors glide,
While China's earth receives the smoking tide:
At once they gratify their scent and taste,
And frequent cups prolong the rich repast.
Straight hover round the Fair her airy band;
Some, as she sipped, the fuming liquor fanned,

Some o'er her lap their careful plumes displayed,
Trembling, and conscious of the rich brocade.
Coffee (which makes the politician wise,
And see through all things with his half-shut eyes)
Sent up in vapours to the Baron's brain
New stratagems the radiant Lock to gain.
Ah cease, rash youth! desist ere 'tis too late,
Fear the just Gods, and think of Scylla's fate!
Changed to a bird, and sent to flit in air,
She dearly pays for Nisus' injured hair!

But when to mischief mortals bend their will,
How soon they find fit instruments of ill!
Just then, Clarissa drew with tempting grace
A two-edged weapon from her shining case:
So ladies in Romance assist their knight,
Present the spear, and arm him for the fight.
He takes the gift with rev'rence, and extends
The little engine on his fingers' ends;
This just behind Belinda's neck he spread,
As o'er the fragrant steams she bends her head.
Swift to the Lock a thousand sprites repair,
A thousand wings, by turns, blow back the hair;
And thrice they twitched the diamond in her ear;
Thrice she looked back, and thrice the foe drew near.
Just in that instant, anxious Ariel sought
The close recesses of the Virgin's thought;
As on the nosegay in her breast reclined,
He watched th'Ideas rising in her mind,
Sudden he viewed, in spite of all her art,
An earthly Lover lurking at her heart.
Amazed, confused, he found his pow'r expired,
Resigned to fate, and with a sigh retired.

The Peer now spreads the glitt'ring forfex wide,
T'enclose the Lock; now joins it, to divide.
Ev'n then, before the fatal engine closed,
A wretched Sylph too fondly interposed;
Fate urged the shears, and cut the Sylph in twain,
(But airy substance soon unites again)

The meeting points the sacred hair dissever
From the fair head, for ever and for ever!
Then flashed the living lightning from her eyes,
And screams of horror rend th'affrighted skies.
Not louder shrieks to pitying heav'n are cast,
When husbands, or when lapdogs breathe their last;
Or when rich China vessels fall'n from high,
In glitt'ring dust and painted fragments lie!

FROM *Eloisa to Abelard*

How oft, when pressed to marriage, have I said,
Curse on all laws but those which love has made?
Love, free as air, at sight of human ties,
Spreads his light wings, and in a moment flies.
Let wealth, let honour, wait the wedded dame,
August her deed, and sacred be her fame;
Before true passion all those views remove,
Fame, wealth, and honour! what are you to Love?
The jealous God, when we profane his fires,
Those restless passions in revenge inspires,
And bids them make mistaken mortals groan,
Who seek in love for aught but love alone.
Should at my feet the world's great master fall,
Himself, his throne, his world, I'd scorn 'em all:
Not Caesar's empress would I deign to prove;
No, make me mistress to the man I love;
If there be yet another name more free,
More fond than mistress, make me that to thee!
Oh! happy state! when souls each other draw,
When love is liberty, and nature law:
All then is full, possessing, and possessed,
No craving void left aching in the breast:
Ev'n thought meets thought, ere from the lips it part,
And each warm wish springs mutual from the heart,
This sure is bliss (if bliss on earth there be)
And once the lot of Abelard and me.

FROM *Essay on Man*

1.

Heav'n from all creatures hides the book of Fate,
All but the page prescribed, their present state:
From brutes what men, from men what spirits know:
Or who could suffer Being here below?
The lamb thy riot dooms to bleed to-day,
Had he thy Reason, would he skip and play?
Pleased to the last, he crops the flow'ry food,
And licks the hand just raised to shed his blood.
Oh blindness to the future! kindly giv'n,
That each may fill the circle marked by Heav'n:
Who sees with equal eye, as God by all,
A hero perish, or a sparrow fall,
Atoms or systems into ruin hurled,
And now a bubble burst and now a world.

Hope humbly then; with trembling pinions soar;
Wait the great teacher Death; and God adore.
What future bliss, He gives not thee to know,
But gives that Hope to be thy blessing now.
Hope springs eternal in the human breast:
Man never Is, but always To be blest:
The soul, uneasy and confined from home,
Rests and expatiates in a life to come.

2.

Know then thyself, presume not God to scan;
The proper study of Mankind is Man.
Placed on this isthmus of a middle state,
A Being darkly wise, and rudely great:
With too much knowledge for the Sceptic side,
With too much weakness for the Stoic's pride,
He hangs between; in doubt to act, or rest;
In doubt to deem himself a God, or Beast;
In doubt his Mind or Body to prefer;
Born but to die, and reas'ning but to err;
Alike in ignorance, his reason such,
Whether he thinks too little, or too much:

Chaos of Thought and Passion, all confused;
Still by himself abused, or disabused;
Created half to rise, and half to fall;
Great lord of all things, yet a prey to all;
Sole judge of Truth, in endless Error hurled:
The glory, jest, and riddle of the world!

3.

For Forms of Government let fools contest;
Whate'er is best administered is best:
For Modes of Faith let graceless zealots fight;
He can't be wrong whose life is in the right:
In Faith and Hope the world will disagree,
But all Mankind's concern is Charity;
All must be false that thwart this One great End;
And all of God, that bless Mankind or mend.

4.

What's Fame? a fancied life in others' breath,
A thing beyond us, ev'n before our death.
Just what you hear, you have, and what's unknown
The same (my Lord) if Tully's, or your own.
All that we feel of it begins and ends
In the small circle of our foes or friends;
To all beside as much an empty shade
As Eugene living, as a Caesar dead;
Alike or when, or where, they shone, or shine,
Or on the Rubicon, or on the Rhine.
A Wit's a feather, and a Chief a rod;
An honest Man's the noblest work of God.
Fame but from death a villain's name can save,
As Justice tears his body from the grave;
When what t'oblivion better were resigned,
Is hung on high, to poison half mankind.
All fame is foreign, but of true desert;
Plays round the head, but comes not to the heart:
One self-approving hour whole years out-weighs
Of stupid starers, and of loud huzzas;
And more true joy Marcellus exiled feels,
Than Caesar with a senate at his heels.

In Parts superior what advantage lies?
Tell (for You can) what is it to be wise?
'Tis but to know how little can be known;
To see all others' faults, and feel our own:
Condemned in business or in arts to drudge,
Without a second, or without a judge:
Truths would you teach, or save a sinking land,
All fear, none aid you, and few understand.
Painful pre-eminence! yourself to view
Above life's weakness, and its comforts too.

Bring then these blessings to a strict account;
Make fair deductions; see to what they mount:
How much of other each is sure to cost;
How each for other oft is wholly lost;
How inconsistent greater goods with these;
How sometimes life is risked, and always ease:
Think, and if still the things thy envy call,
Say, would'st thou be the Man to whom they fall?
To sigh for ribbands if thou art so silly,
Mark how they grace Lord Umbra, or Sir Billy:
Is yellow dirt the passion of thy life?
Look but on Gripus, or on Gripus' wife:
If Parts allure thee, think how Bacon shined,
The wisest, brightest, meanest of mankind:
Or ravished with the whistling of a name,
See Cromwell damned to everlasting fame!

5.

Search then the Ruling Passion: there, alone,
The Wild are constant, and the Cunning known;
The Fool consistent, and the False sincere;
Priests, Princes, Women, no dissemblers here.
This clue once found, unravels all the rest,
The prospect clears, and Wharton stands confest.
Wharton, the scorn and wonder of our days,
Whose ruling passion was the lust of praise:
Born with whate'er could win it from the wise,
Women and fools must like him or he dies;
Though wond'ring Senates hung on all he spoke,

The Club must hail him master of the joke.
Shall parts so various aim at nothing new?
He'll shine a Tully and a Wilmot too.
Then turns repentant, and his God adores
With the same spirit that he drinks and whores;
Enough if all around him but admire,
And now the Punk applaud, and now the Friar.
Thus with each gift of nature and of art,
And wanting nothing but an honest heart;
Grown all to all, from no one vice exempt;
And most contemptible, to shun contempt:
His passion still, to covet gen'ral praise,
His life, to forfeit it a thousand ways;
A constant bounty which no friend has made;
An angel tongue, which no man can persuade;
A fool with more of wit than half mankind,
Too rash for thought, for action too refined:
A tyrant to the wife his heart approves;
A rebel to the very king he loves;
He dies, sad outcast of each church and state,
And harder still! flagitious, yet not great.
Ask you why Wharton broke through ev'ry rule?
'Twas all for fear the knaves should call him Fool.

FROM *Epistle to Dr. Arbuthnot*

1.

Why did I write? what sin to me unknown
Dipt me in ink, my parents', or my own?
As yet a child, not yet a fool to fame,
I lisped in numbers, for the numbers came.
I left no calling for this idle trade,
No duty broke, no father disobeyed.
The Muse but served to ease some friend, not wife,
To help me through this long disease, my life . . .

2.

Peace to all such! but were there One whose fires
True genius kindles, and fair fame inspires;
Blest with each talent and each art to please,
And born to write, converse, and live with ease:

Should such a man, too fond to rule alone,
Bear, like the Turk, no brother near the throne;
View him with scornful, yet with jealous eyes,
And hate for arts that caused himself to rise;
Damn with faint praise, assent with civil leer,
And without sneering, teach the rest to sneer;
Willing to wound, and yet afraid to strike,
Just hint a fault, and hesitate dislike;
Alike reserved to blame, or to commend,
A tim'rous foe, and a suspicious friend;
Dreading ev'n fools, by flatterers besieged,
And so obliging, that he ne'er obliged;
Like Cato, give his little Senate laws,
And sit attentive to his own applause;
While wits and Templars ev'ry sentence raise,
And wonder with a foolish face of praise—
Who but must laugh, if such a man there be?
Who would not weep, if Atticus were he?

Let Sporus tremble—*A.* What? that thing of silk,
Sporus, that mere white curd of ass's milk?
Satire or sense, alas! can Sporus feel?
Who breaks a butterfly upon a wheel?
P. Yet let me flap this bug with gilded wings,
This painted child of dirt, that stinks and stings;
Whose buzz the witty and the fair annoys,
Yet wit ne'er tastes, and beauty ne'er enjoys:
So well-bred spaniels civilly delight
In mumbling of the game they dare not bite.
Eternal smiles his emptiness betray,
As shallow streams run dimpling all the way.
Whether in florid impotence he speaks,
And, as the prompter breathes, the puppet squeaks;
Or at the ear of Eve, familiar Toad,
Half froth, half venom, spits himself abroad,
In puns, or politics, or tales, or lies,
Or spite, or smut, or rhymes, or blasphemies.
His wit all see-saw, between *that* and *this*,
Now high, now low, now master up, now miss,
And he himself one vile Antithesis.

Amphibious thing! that acting either part,
The trifling head or the corrupted heart,
Fop at the toilet, flatt'rer at the board,
Now trips a Lady, and now struts a Lord.
Eve's tempter thus the rabbins have exprest,
A cherub's face, a reptile all the rest;
Beauty that shocks you, parts that none will trust;
Wit that can creep, and pride that licks the dust.

FROM *The Dunciad*

In vain, in vain—the all-composing hour
Resistless falls: the Muse obeys the Power.
She comes! she comes! the sable throne behold
Of Night primaeval and of Chaos old!
Before her, Fancy's gilded clouds decay,
And all its varying rainbows die away.
Wit shoots in vain its momentary fires,
The meteor drops, and in a flash expires.
As one by one, at dread Medea's strain,
The sickening stars fade off th'ethereal plain;
As Argus' eyes by Hermes' wand opprest,
Closed one by one to everlasting rest;
Thus at her felt approach, and secret might,
Art after Art goes out, and all is Night.
See skulking Truth to her old cavern fled,
Mountains of Casuistry heaped o'er her head!
Philosophy, that leaned on Heav'n before,
Shrinks to her second cause, and is no more.
Physic of Metaphysic begs defence,
And Metaphysic calls for aid on Sense!
See Mystery to Mathematics fly!
In vain! they gaze, turn giddy, rave, and die.
Religion blushing veils her sacred fires,
And unaware Morality expires.
Nor public flame, nor private, dares to shine;
Nor human spark is left, nor glimpse divine!
Lo! thy dread empire, Chaos, is restored;
Light dies before thy uncreating word;
Thy hand, great Anarch! lets the curtain fall,
And universal darkness buries all.

Epitaph on Sir Isaac Newton

Nature and Nature's laws lay hid in night;
God said: "Let Newton be", and all was light.

THOMAS WARTON THE ELDER
(1688–1745)

FROM Retirement, an Ode

Joy, rose-lipped dryad, loves to dwell
In sunny field or mossy cell,
Delights on echoing hills to hear
The reaper's song or lowing steer;
Or view with tenfold plenty spread
The crowded cornfield, blooming mead;
While beauty, health, and innocence
Transport the eye, the soul, the sense.

Nymphs of the grove in green arrayed,
Conduct me to your thickest shade,
Deep in the bosom of the vale,
Where haunts the lonesome nightingale;
Where Contemplation, maid divine,
Leans against some aged pine,
Wrapped in steadfast thought profound,
Her eyes fixed steadfast on the ground.

O Virtue's nurse! retired Queen,
By saints alone and virtues seen,
Beyond vain mortals' wishes wise,
Teach me St. James's to despise;
For what are courts, but schools
For fops, or hospitals for fools?
Where slaves and madmen, young and old,
Meet to adore some Calf of Gold.

JOHN BYROM
(1692–1763)

A Toast

God bless the King!—I mean the Faith's defender;
God bless—no harm in blessing—the Pretender!
But who Pretender is, or who is King—
God bless us all! that's quite another thing.

WILLIAM OLDYS
(1696–1761)

On a Fly Drinking Out of His Cup

Busy, curious, thirsty fly!
Drink with me and drink as I:
Freely welcome to my cup,
Couldst thou sip and sip it up:
Make the most of life you may,
Life is short and wears away.

Just alike, both mine and thine,
Hasten quick to their decline:
Thine's a summer, mine no more,
Though repeated to three-score.
Three-score summers, when they're gone,
Will appear as short as one!

ROBERT BLAIR
(1699–1746)

FROM The Grave

See yonder hallowed fane, the pious work
Of names once famed, now dubious or forgot,
And buried midst the wreck of things which were:
There lie interred the more illustrious dead.
The wind is up: hark how it howls! Methinks
Till now I never heard a sound so dreary.
Doors creak, and windows clap, and night's foul bird,

Rooked in the spire, screams loud. The gloomy aisles,
Black-plaistered, and hung round with shreds of 'scutcheons
And tattered coats of arms, send back the sound,
Laden with heavier airs, from the low vaults,
The mansions of the dead. Roused from their slumbers,
In grim array the grisly spectres rise,
Grin horribly, and obstinately sullen
Pass and repass, hushed as the foot of night.
Again the screech owl shrieks—ungracious sound.
I'll hear no more; it makes one's blood run chill.
Quite round the pile, a row of reverend elms,
Co-eval near with that, all ragged show,
Long lashed by the rude winds; some rift half down
Their branchless trunks, others so thin atop
That scarce two crows could lodge in the same tree.
Strange things, the neighbours say, have happened here.
Wild shrieks have issued from the hollow tombs;
Dead men have come again, and walked about;
And the great bell has tolled unrung, untouched.
Such tales their cheer, at wake or gossiping,
When it draws near the witching time of night.

JOHN DYER

(1700?–1758)

FROM Grongar Hill

Old castles on the cliff arise,
Proudly towering in the skies.
Rushing from the woods, the spires
Seem from hence ascending fires.

Below me, trees unnumbered rise,
Beautiful in various dyes:
The gloomy pine, the poplar blue,
The yellow beech, the sable yew,
The slender fir that taper grows,
The sturdy oak with broad-spread boughs.
And beyond the purple grove,
Haunt of Phyllis, queen of love,

Gaudy as the opening dawn,
Lies a long and level lawn,
On which a dark hill, steep and high,
Holds and charms the wandering eye.
Deep are his feet in Towy's flood,
His sides are clothed with waving wood,
And ancient towers crown his brow,
That cast an aweful look below;
Whose ragged walls the ivy creeps,
And with her arms from falling keeps.

Yet time has seen that lifts the low,
And level lays the lofty brow,
Has seen this broken pile complete,
Big with the vanity of state.
But transient is the smile of fate;
A little rule, a little sway,
A sunbeam in a winter's day,
Is all the proud and mighty have
Between the cradle and the grave.

JAMES THOMSON THE ELDER
(1700–1748)

FROM *The Castle of Indolence*

I.

In lowly dale, fast by a river's side,
With woody hill o'er hill encompassed round,
A most enchanting wizard did abide,
Than whom a fiend more fell is nowhere found.
It was, I ween, a lovely spot of ground;
And there a season atween June and May,
Half prankt with spring, with summer half imbrowned,
A listless climate made, where, sooth to say,
No living wight could work, ne caréd even for play.

Was nought around but images of rest:
Sleep-soothing groves, and quiet lawns between;
And flowery beds that slumbrous influence kest,
From poppies breathed; and beds of pleasant green,
Where never yet was creeping creature seen.

Meantime unnumbered glittering streamlets played,
And hurléd everywhere their waters sheen;
That, as they bickered through the sunny glade,
Though restless still themselves, a lulling murmur made.

Joined to the prattle of the purling rills,
Were heard the lowing herds along the vale,
And flocks loud-bleating from the distant hills,
And vacant shepherds piping in the dale:
And now and then sweet Philomel would wail,
Or stock-droves plain amid the forest deep,
That drowsy rustled to the sighing gale;
And still a coil the grasshopper did keep:
Yet all these sounds yblent inclinéd all to sleep.

Full in the passage of the vale, above,
A sable, silent, solemn forest stood;
Where nought but shadowy forms were seen to move,
As Idless fancied in her dreaming mood.
And up the hills, on either side, a wood
Of blackening pines, ay waving to and fro,
Sent forth a sleepy horror through the blood;
And where this valley winded out, below,
The murmuring main was heard, and scarcely heard, to flow

A pleasing land of drowsyhed it was:
Of dreams that wave before the half-shut eye;
And of gay castles in the clouds that pass,
For ever flushing round a summer sky:
There eke the soft delights, that witchingly
Instil a wanton sweetness through the breast,
And the calm pleasures always hovered nigh;
But whate'er smacked of noyance, or unrest,
Was far far off expelled from this delicious nest.

The landskip such, inspiring perfect ease;
Where Indolence (for so the wizard hight)
Close-hid his castle mid embowering trees,
That half shut out the beams of Phoebus bright,
And made a kind of checkered day and night.

2.

The doors that knew no shrill alarming bell,
Ne curséd knocker plied by villain's hand,
Self-opened into halls, where, who can tell
What elegance and grandeur wide expand
The pride of Turkey and of Persia land?
Soft quilts on quilts, on carpets carpets spread,
And couches stretched around in seemly band;
And endless pillows rise to prop the head;
So that each spacious room was one full-swelling bed.

And everywhere huge covered tables stood,
With wines high-flavoured and rich viands crowned;
Whatever sprightly juice or tasteful food
On the green bosom of this Earth are found,
And all old Ocean genders in his round—
Some hand unseen these silently displayed,
Even undemanded by a sign or sound;
You need but wish, and instantly obeyed,
Fair-ranged the dishes rose, and thick the glasses played.

Here freedom reigned without the least alloy;
Nor gossip's tale, nor ancient maiden's gall,
Nor saintly spleen durst murmur at our joy,
And with envenomed tongues our pleasures pall.
For why? there was but one great rule for all;
To wit, that each should work his own desire,
And eat, drink, study, sleep, as it may fall,
Or melt the time in love, or wake the lyre,
And carol what, unbid, the Muses might inspire.

The rooms with costly tapestry were hung,
Where was inwoven many a gentle tale,
Such as of old the rural poets sung
Or of Arcadian or Sicilian vale:
Reclining lovers, in the lonely dale,
Poured forth at large the sweetly tortured heart;
Or, looking tender passion, swelled the gale,
And taught charmed echo to resound their smart;
While flocks, woods, streams around, repose and peace impart.

Those pleased the most, where, by a cunning hand,
Depeinten was the patriarchal age;
What time Dan Abraham left the Chaldee land,
And pastured on from verdant stage to stage,
Where fields and fountains fresh could best engage.
Toil was not then. Of nothing took they heed,
But with wild beasts the sylvan war to wage,
And o'er vast plains their herds and flocks to feed:
Blest sons of nature they! true golden age indeed!

Sometimes the pencil, in cool airy halls,
Bade the gay bloom of vernal landskips rise,
Or Autumn's varied shades imbrown the walls:
Now the black tempest strikes the astonished eyes;
Now down the steep the flashing torrent flies;
The trembling sun now plays o'er ocean blue,
And now rude mountains frown amid the skies;
Whate'er Lorrain light-touched with softening hue,
Or savage Rosa dashed, or learnéd Poussin drew.

Each sound too here to languishment inclined,
Lulled the weak bosom, and inducéd ease.
Aërial music in the warbling wind,
At distance rising oft, by small degrees,
Nearer and nearer came, till o'er the trees
It hung, and breathed such soul-dissolving airs
As did, alas! with soft perdition please:
Entangled deep in its enchanting snares,
The listening heart forgot all duties and all cares.

A certain music, never known before,
Here soothed the pensive melancholy mind;
Full easily obtained. Behoves no more,
But sidelong to the gently-waving wind
To lay the well-tuned instrument reclined;
From which, with airy flying fingers light,
Beyond each mortal touch the most refined,
The god of winds drew sounds of deep delight:
Whence, with just cause, the Harp of Æolus it hight.

Ah me! what hand can touch the strings so fine?
Who up the lofty diapason roll
Such sweet, such sad, such solemn airs divine,
Then let them down again into the soul?
Now rising love they fanned; now pleasing dole
They breathed, in tender musings, through the heart;
And now a graver sacred strain they stole,
As when seraphic hands an hymn impart:
Wild warbling Nature all, above the reach of Art!

FROM *Spring*

At length the finished garden to the view
Its vistas opens and its alleys green.
Snatched through the verdant maze, the hurried eye
Distracted wanders; now the bowery walk
Of covert close, where scarce a speck of day
Falls on the lengthened gloom, protracted sweeps;
Now meets the bending sky, the river now
Dimpling along, the breezy ruffled lake,
The forest darkening round, the glittering spire,
The ethereal mountain, and the distant main.
But why so far excursive? when at hand,
Along these blushing borders bright with dew,
And in yon mingled wilderness of flowers,
Fair-handed Spring unbosoms every grace—
Throws out the snow-drop and the crocus first,
The daisy, primrose, violet darkly blue,
And polyanthus of unnumbered dyes;
The yellow wall-flower, stained with iron brown,
And lavish stock, that scents the garden round:
From the soft wing of vernal breezes shed,
Anemones, auriculas, enriched
With shining meal o'er all their velvet leaves;
And full ranunculus of glowing red.
Then comes the tulip-race, where beauty plays
Her idle freaks: from family diffused
To family, as flies the father-dust,
The varied colours run; and, while they break,
On the charmed eye, the exulting florist marks

With secret pride the wonders of his hand.
No gradual bloom is wanting—from the bud
First-born of Spring to Summer's musky tribes;
Nor hyacinths, of purest virgin white,
Low bent and blushing inward; nor jonquils,
Of potent fragrance; nor narcissus fair,
As o'er the fabled fountain hanging still;
Nor broad carnations, nor gay-spotted pinks;
Nor, showered from every bush, the damask-rose:
Infinite numbers, delicacies, smells.
With hues on hues expression cannot paint,
The breath of Nature, and her endless bloom.

FROM Winter

The keener tempests come: and, fuming dun
From all the livid east or piercing north,
Thick clouds ascend, in whose capacious womb
A vapoury deluge lies, to snow congealed.
Heavy they roll their fleecy world along,
And the sky saddens with the gathered storm.
Through the hushed air the whitening shower descends,
At first thin-wavering; till at last the flakes
Fall broad and wide and fast, dimming the day
With a continual flow. The cherished fields
Put on their winter-robe of purest white.
'Tis brightness all; save where the new snow melts
Along the mazy current. Low the woods
Bow their hoar head; and, ere the languid sun
Faint from the west emits his evening ray,
Earth's universal face, deep-hid and chill,
Is one wild dazzling waste, that buries wide
The works of man. Drooping, the labourer-ox
Stands covered o'er with snow, and then demands
The fruit of all his toil. The fowls of heaven,
Tamed by the cruel season, crowd around
The winnowing store, and claim the little boon
Which Providence assigns them. One alone,
The redbreast, sacred to the household gods,
Wisely regardful of the embroiling sky,

In joyless fields and thorny thickets leaves
His shivering mates, and pays to trusted man
His annual visit. Half afraid, he first
Against the window beats; then brisk alights
On the warm hearth; then, hopping o'er the floor,
Eyes all the smiling family askance,
And pecks, and starts, and wonders where he is—
Till, more familiar grown, the table-crumbs
Attract his slender feet. The foodless wilds
Pour forth their brown inhabitants. The hare,
Though timorous of heart, and hard beset
By death in various forms, dark snares, and dogs,
And more unpitying men, the garden seeks,
Urged on by fearless want. The bleating kind
Eye the bleak heaven, and next the glistening earth,
With looks of dumb despair; then, sad-dispersed,
Dig for the withered herb through heaps of snow.

HENRY FIELDING

(1707-1754)

"A-Hunting We Will Go"

The dusky night rides down the sky,
   And ushers in the morn;
The hounds all join in glorious cry;
   The huntsman winds his horn.
   And a-hunting we will go.

The wife around her husband throws
   Her arms, and begs his stay;
"My dear, it rains, and hails, and snows!
   You will not hunt to-day!"
   But a-hunting we will go!

A brushing fox in yonder wood,
   Secure to find we seek;
For why, I carried sound and good,
   A cartload there last week!
   And a-hunting we will go!

Away he goes! He flies the rout!
   Their steeds all spur and switch!
Some are thrown in, and some thrown out,
   And some thrown in the ditch!
   But a-hunting we will go!

At length, his strength to faintness worn,
   Poor Reynard ceases flight,
Then hungry homeward we return,
   To feast away the night.
   Then a-drinking we will go!

SAMUEL JOHNSON

(1709-1784)

FROM *The Vanity of Human Wishes*

On what foundations stands the warrior's pride,
How just his hopes, let Swedish Charles decide.
A frame of adamant, a soul of fire,
No dangers fright him, and no labours tire;
O'er love, o'er fear, extends his wide domain,
Unconquered lord of pleasure and of pain;
No joys to him pacific sceptres yield,
War sounds the trump, he rushes to the field.
Behold surrounding kings their powers combine,
And one capitulate, and one resign:
Peace courts his hand, but spreads her charms in vain;
"Think nothing gained," he cries, "till nought remain,
On Moscow's walls till Gothic standards fly,
And all be mine beneath the polar sky."
The march begins, in military state,
And nations on his eye suspended wait;
Stern Famine guards the solitary coast,
And Winter barricades the realms of Frost;
He comes, nor want nor cold his course delay!—
Hide, blushing glory, hide Pultowa's day:
The vanquished hero leaves his broken bands,
And shows his miseries in distant lands;
Condemned a needy suppliant to wait,
While ladies interpose, and slaves debate.

But did not Chance at length her error mend?
Did no subverted empire mark his end?
Did rival monarchs give the fatal wound?
Or hostile millions press him to the ground?
His fall was destined to a barren strand,
A petty fortress, and a dubious hand;
He left the name at which the world grew pale,
To point a moral, or adorn a tale.

FROM *London*

By numbers here from shame or censure free,
All crimes are safe, but hated poverty.
This, only this the rigid law pursues,
This, only this provokes the snarling muse.
The sober trader at a tattered cloak
Wakes from his dream, and labours for a joke;
With brisker air the silken courtiers gaze,
And turn the varied taunt a thousand ways.
Of all the griefs that harass the distressed,
Sure the most bitter is a scornful jest;
Fate never wounds more deep the generous heart,
Than when a blockhead's insult points the dart.
Has Heaven reserved, in pity to the poor,
No pathless waste, or undiscovered shore?
No secret island in the boundless main?
No peaceful desert yet unclaimed by Spain?
Quick, let us rise, the happy seats explore,
And bear oppression's insolence no more.
This mournful truth is everywhere confest:
Slow rises worth by poverty depressed.

FROM *On the Death of Mr. Robert Levet, a Practiser in Physic*

In Misery's darkest cavern known,
  His useful care was ever nigh,
Where hopeless Anguish poured his groan,
  And lonely Want retired to die.

No summons mocked by chill delay,
   No petty gain disdained by pride,
The modest wants of every day
   The toil of every day supplied.

His virtues walked their narrow round,
   Nor made a pause, nor left a void;
And sure th' Eternal Master found
   The single talent well employed.

FROM *On the Coming of Age of a Rich Extravagant Young Man*

Wealth, my lad, was made to wander,
   Let it wander as it will;
Call the jockey, call the pander,
   Bid them come and take their fill.

When the bonny blade carouses,
   Pockets full, and spirits high—
What are acres? what are houses?
   Only dirt, or wet or dry.

Should the guardian friend or mother
   Tell the woes of wilful waste;
Scorn their counsel, scorn their pother—
   You can hang or drown at last.

"Hermit Hoar..."

Hermit hoar, in solemn cell,
   Wearing out life's evening gray,
Smite thy bosom, sage, and tell,
   What is bliss? and which the way?

Thus I spoke; and speaking sighed;
   Scarce repressed the starting tear;
When the smiling sage replied:
   "Come, my lad, and drink some beer."

Boswell's Life of Johnson

WILLIAM THOMPSON

(1712?–1766?)

FROM The Happy Life

A book, a friend, a song, a glass,
A chaste, yet laughter-loving lass,
To mortals various joys impart,
Inform the sense, and warm the heart.

Thrice happy they, who careless laid
Beneath a kind-embowering shade,
With rosy wreaths their temples crown,
In rosy wine their sorrow drown.

Begone, ambition, riches, toys,
And splendid cares, and guilty joys—
Give me a book, a friend, a glass,
And a chaste, laughter-loving lass.

RICHARD GLOVER

(1712–1785)

Admiral Hosier's Ghost

As near Porto-Bello lying
  On the gently swelling flood,
At midnight with streamers flying,
  Our triumphant navy rode:
There while Vernon sat all-glorious
  From the Spaniards' late defeat;
And his crews, with shouts victorious,
  Drank success to England's fleet:

On a sudden shrilly sounding,
  Hideous yells and shrieks were heard;
Then each heart with fear confounding,
  A sad troop of ghosts appeared,

All in dreary hammocks shrouded,
　　Which for winding-sheets they wore,
And with looks by sorrow clouded,
　　Frowning on that hostile shore.

On them gleamed the moon's wan lustre,
　　When the shade of Hosier brave
His pale bands was seen to muster,
　　Rising from their watery grave:
O'er the glimmering wave he hied him,
　　Where the Burford reared her sail,
With three thousand ghosts beside him,
　　And in groans did Vernon hail:

"Heed, O heed, our fatal story,
　　I am Hosier's injured ghost,
You, who now have purchased glory
　　At this place where I was lost;
Though in Porto-Bello's ruin
　　You now triumph free from fears,
When you think on our undoing,
　　You will mix your joy with tears.

"See these mournful spectres, sweeping
　　Ghastly o'er this hated wave,
Whose wan cheeks are stained with weeping;
　　These were England's captains brave:
Mark those numbers pale and horrid,
　　Those were once my sailors bold,
Lo! each hangs his drooping forehead,
　　While his dismal tale is told.

"I, by twenty sail attended,
　　Did this Spanish town affright:
Nothing then its wealth defended
　　But my orders not to fight:
Oh! that in this rolling ocean
　　I had cast them with disdain,
And obeyed my heart's warm motion,
　　To have quelled the pride of Spain.

"For resistance I could fear none,
    But with twenty ships had done
What thou, brave and happy Vernon,
    Hast achieved with six alone.
Then the Bastimentos never
    Had our foul dishonour seen,
Nor the sea the sad receiver
    Of this gallant train had been.

"Thus, like thee, proud Spain dismaying,
    And her galleons leading home,
Though condemned for disobeying,
    I had met a traitor's doom;
To have fallen, my country crying,
    He has played an English part,
Had been better far than dying
    Of a grieved and broken heart.

"Unrepining at thy glory,
    Thy successful arms we hail;
But remember our sad story,
    And let Hosier's wrongs prevail.
Sent in this foul clime to languish,
    Think what thousands fell in vain,
Wasted with disease and anguish,
    Not in glorious battle slain.

"Hence, with all my train attending
    From their oozy tombs below,
Through the hoary foam ascending,
    Here I feed my constant woe:
Here the Bastimentos viewing,
    We recall our shameful doom,
And our plaintive cries renewing,
    Wander through the midnight gloom.

"O'er these waves for ever mourning
    Shall we roam deprived of rest,
If to Britain's shores returning,
    You neglect my just request.

After this proud foe subduing,
    When your patriot friends you see,
Think on vengeance for my ruin,
    And for England shamed in me."

WILLIAM SHENSTONE

(1714–1763)

Written at an Inn at Henley

To thee, fair freedom, I retire
    From flattery, cards, and dice, and din;
Nor art thou found in mansions higher
    Than the low cot, or humble inn.

'Tis here with boundless power I reign;
    And every health which I begin,
Converts dull port to bright champagne;
    Such freedom crowns it at an inn.

I fly from pomp, I fly from plate,
    I fly from falsehood's specious grin!
Freedom I love, and form I hate,
    And choose my lodgings at an inn.

Here, waiter, take my sordid ore,
    Which lackeys else might hope to win;
It buys, what courts have not in store;
    It buys me freedom at an inn.

Whoe'er has travelled life's dull round,
    Where'er his stages may have been,
May sigh to think he still has found
    The warmest welcome at an inn.

THOMAS GRAY

(1716–1771)

Elegy Written in a Country Churchyard

The curfew tolls the knell of parting day,
  The lowing herd winds slowly o'er the lea,
The ploughman homeward plods his weary way,
  And leaves the world to darkness and to me.

Now fades the glimmering landscape on the sight,
  And all the air a solemn stillness holds,
Save where the beetle wheels his droning flight,
  And drowsy tinklings lull the distant folds.

Save that from yonder ivy-mantled tower,
  The moping owl does to the moon complain
Of such as, wandering near her secret bower,
  Molest her ancient solitary reign.

Beneath these rugged elms, that yew-tree's shade,
  Where heaves the turf in many a mould'ring heap,
Each in his narrow cell for ever laid,
  The rude forefathers of the hamlet sleep.

The breezy call of incense-breathing morn,
  The swallow twittering from the straw-built shed,
The cock's shrill clarion, or the echoing horn,
  No more shall rouse them from their lowly bed.

For them no more the blazing hearth shall burn,
  Or busy housewife ply her evening-care;
No children run to lisp their sire's return,
  Or climb his knees the envied kiss to share.

Oft did the harvest to their sickle yield,
  Their furrow oft the stubborn glebe has broke:
How jocund did they drive their team afield!
  How bowed the woods beneath their sturdy stroke!

Let not Ambition mock their useful toil,
  Their homely joys and destiny obscure;
Nor Grandeur hear with a disdainful smile,
  The short and simple annals of the poor.

The boast of heraldry, the pomp of power,
  And all that beauty, all that wealth e'er gave,
Awaits alike th' inevitable hour.
  The paths of glory lead but to the grave.

Nor you, ye proud, impute to these the fault,
  If Memory o'er their tomb no trophies raise,
Where through the long-drawn aisle, and fretted vault,
  The pealing anthem swells the note of praise.

Can storied urn, or animated bust,
  Back to its mansion call the fleeting breath?
Can Honour's voice provoke the silent dust,
  Or flattery soothe the dull cold ear of Death?

Perhaps in this neglected spot is laid
  Some heart once pregnant with celestial fire;
Hands, that the rod of empire might have swayed,
  Or waked to ecstasy the living lyre.

But Knowledge to their eyes her ample page,
  Rich with the spoils of Time, did ne'er unroll;
Chill penury repressed their noble rage,
  And froze the genial current of the soul.

Full many a gem of purest ray serene
  The dark unfathomed caves of ocean bear;
Full many a flower is born to blush unseen,
  And waste its sweetness on the desert air.

Some village Hampden, that with dauntless breast
  The little tyrant of his fields withstood,
Some mute inglorious Milton here may rest,
  Some Cromwell, guiltless of his country's blood.

Th' applause of listening senates to command,
　The threats of pain and ruin to despise,
To scatter plenty o'er a smiling land,
　And read their history in a nation's eyes,

Their lot forbade: nor circumscribed alone
　Their growing virtues, but their crimes confined;
Forbade to wade through slaughter to a throne,
　And shut the gates of Mercy on mankind,

The struggling pangs of conscious truth to hide,
　To quench the blushes of ingenuous shame,
Or heap the shrine of luxury and pride
　With incense kindled at the Muse's flame.

Far from the madding crowd's ignoble strife,
　Their sober wishes never learned to stray;
Along the cool sequestered vale of life
　They kept the noiseless tenor of their way.

Yet ev'n these bones from insult to protect
　Some frail memorial still erected nigh,
With uncouth rhymes and shapeless sculpture decked,
　Implores the passing tribute of a sigh.

Their name, their years, spelt by th' unlettered Muse,
　The place of fame and elegy supply:
And many a holy text around she strews,
　That teach the rustic moralist to die.

For who, to dumb Forgetfulness a prey,
　This pleasing anxious being e'er resigned,
Left the warm precincts of the cheerful day,
　Nor cast one longing, ling'ring look behind?

On some fond breast the parting soul relies,
　Some pious drops the closing eye requires;
Ev'n from the tomb the voice of Nature cries,
　Ev'n in our ashes live their wonted fires.

For thee, who, mindful of th' unhonoured dead,
 Dost in these lines their artless tale relate;
If chance, by lonely Contemplation led,
 Some kindred spirit shall inquire thy fate,—

Haply some hoary-headed swain may say,
 "Oft have we seen him at the peep of dawn
Brushing with hasty steps the dews away,
 To meet the sun upon the upland lawn;

"There at the foot of yonder nodding beech,
 That wreathes its old fantastic roots so high,
His listless length at noon-tide would he stretch,
 And pore upon the brook that babbles by.

"Hard by yon wood, now smiling as in scorn,
 Mutt'ring his wayward fancies would he rove;
Now drooping, woeful-wan, like one forlorn,
 Or crazed with care, or crossed in hopeless love.

"One morn I missed him from the customed hill,
 Along the heath, and near his fav'rite tree;
Another came; nor yet beside the rill,
 Nor up the lawn, nor at the wood was he;

"The next, with dirges due in sad array
 Slow through the church-way path we saw him borne,—
Approach and read, for thou canst read, the lay
 Graved on the stone beneath yon agéd thorn."

THE EPITAPH

Here rests his head upon the lap of earth
 A youth to Fortune and to Fame unknown:
Fair Science frowned not on his humble birth,
 And Melancholy marked him for her own.

Large was his bounty, and his soul sincere,
 Heaven did a recompense as largely send:
He gave to Misery (all he had) a tear,
 He gained from Heaven ('twas all he wished) a friend.

No farther seek his merits to disclose,
    Or draw his frailties from their dread abode,
(There they alike in trembling hope repose,)
    The bosom of his Father and his God.

Stanzas Cancelled from the Elegy

Hark! how the sacred calm that breathes around,
    Bids every fierce tumultuous passion cease;
In still small accents whispering from the ground,
    A grateful earnest of eternal peace.

Him have we seen the greenwood-side along,
    While o'er the heath we hied, our labour done,
What time the wood-lark piped her farewell song,
    With wistful eyes pursue the setting sun.

There scattered oft, the earliest of the year,
    By hands unseen are showers of violets found;
The red-breast loves to build and warble there,
    And little footsteps lightly print the ground.

Ode on a Distant Prospect of Eton College

Ye distant spires, ye antique towers,
    That crown the wat'ry glade,
Where grateful Science still adores
    Her Henry's holy shade;
And ye, that from the stately brow
Of Windsor's heights th' expanse below
    Of grove, of lawn, of mead survey,
Whose turf, whose shade, whose flowers among
Wanders the hoary Thames along
    His silver-winding way:

Ah, happy hills! ah, pleasing shade!
    Ah, fields beloved in vain!
Where once my careless childhood strayed,
    A stranger yet to pain!

I feel the gales that from ye blow
A momentary bliss bestow,
   As, waving fresh their gladsome wing,
My weary soul they seem to soothe,
And, redolent of joy and youth,
   To breathe a second spring.

Say, Father Thames, for thou hast seen
   Full many a sprightly race
Disporting on thy margent green
   The paths of pleasure trace;
Who foremost now delight to cleave,
With pliant arm, thy glassy wave?
   The captive linnet which enthrall?
What idle progeny succeed
To chase the rolling circle's speed,
   Or urge the flying ball?

While some, on earnest business bent,
   Their murm'ring labours ply
'Gainst graver hours, that bring constraint
   To sweeten liberty:
Some bold adventurers disdain
The limits of their little reign,
   And unknown regions dare descry:
Still as they run they look behind,
They hear a voice in every wind,
   And snatch a fearful joy.

Gay hope is theirs, by Fancy fed,
   Less pleasing when possest;
The tear forgot as soon as shed,
   The sunshine of the breast:
Their buxom health of rosy hue,
Wild wit, invention ever new,
   And lively cheer of vigour born;
The thoughtless day, the easy night,
The spirits pure, the slumbers light,
   That fly th'approach of morn.

Alas! regardless of their doom,
　　The little victims play!
No sense have they of ills to come,
　　Nor care beyond to-day:
Yet see, how all around them wait
The ministers of human fate,
　　And black Misfortune's baleful train!
Ah, show them where in ambush stand,
To seize their prey, the murd'rous band!
　　Ah, tell them, they are men!

These shall the fury Passions tear,
　　The vultures of the mind,
Disdainful Anger, pallid Fear,
　　And Shame that skulks behind;
Or pining Love shall waste their youth,
Or Jealousy, with rankling tooth,
　　That inly gnaws the secret heart;
And Envy wan, and faded Care,
Grim-visaged comfortless Despair,
　　And Sorrow's piercing dart.

Ambition this shall tempt to rise,
　　Then whirl the wretch from high,
To bitter Scorn a sacrifice,
　　And grinning Infamy.
The strings of Falsehood those shall try,
And hard Unkindness' altered eye,
　　That mocks the tear it forced to flow;
And keen Remorse with blood defiled,
And moody Madness laughing wild,
　　Amid severest woe.

Lo! in the vale of years beneath
　· A grisly troop are seen,
The painful family of Death,
　　More hideous than their Queen:
This racks the joints, this fires the veins,
That every labouring sinew strains,
　　Those in the deeper vitals rage:

Lo! Poverty, to fill the band,
That numbs the soul with icy hand,
 And slow-consuming Age.

To each his sufferings: all are men,
 Condemned alike to groan;
The tender for another's pain,
 Th' unfeeling for his own.
Yet, ah! why should they know their fate,
Since sorrow never comes too late,
 And happiness too swiftly flies.
Thought would destroy their paradise.
No more—where ignorance is bliss,
 'Tis folly to be wise.

The Progress of Poesy

Awake, Æolian lyre, awake,
And give to rapture all thy trembling strings.
From Helicon's harmonious springs
 A thousand rills their mazy progress take:
The laughing flowers, that round them blow,
Drink life and fragrance as they flow.
Now the rich stream of Music winds along,
Deep, majestic, smooth, and strong,
Through verdant vales, and Ceres' golden reign;
Now rolling down the steep amain,
Headlong, impetuous, see it pour;
The rocks and nodding groves re-bellow to the roar.

Oh! Sovereign of the willing soul,
Parent of sweet and solemn-breathing airs,
Enchanting shell! the sullen Cares
 And frantic Passions hear thy soft control.
On Thracia's hills the Lord of War
Has curbed the fury of his car,
And dropt his thirsty lance at thy command.
Perching on the sceptred hand

Of Jove, thy magic lulls the feathered king
With ruffled plumes and flagging wing:
Quenched in dark clouds of slumber lie
The terror of his beak, and lightnings of his eye.

Thee, the voice, the dance, obey,
Tempered to thy warbled lay.
O'er Idalia's velvet-green
The rosy-crownéd Loves are seen
On Cytherea's day
With antic Sports and blue-eyed Pleasures.
Frisking light in frolic measures;
Now pursuing, now retreating,
    Now in circling troops they meet:
To brisk notes in cadence beating,
    Glance their many-twinkling feet.
Slow melting strains their Queen's approach declare:
    Where'er she turns, the Graces homage pay.
With arms sublime, that float upon the air,
    In gliding state she wins her easy way:
O'er her warm cheek and rising bosom move
The bloom of young Desire and purple light of Love.

    Man's feeble race what ills await!
Labour and Penury, the racks of Pain,
Disease, and Sorrow's weeping train,
    And Death, sad refuge from the storms of Fate!
The fond complaint, my song, disprove,
And justify the laws of Jove.
Say, has he given in vain the heavenly Muse?
Night and all her sickly dews,
Her spectres wan, and birds of boding cry,
He gives to range the dreary sky:
Till down the eastern cliffs afar
Hyperion's march they spy, and glittering shafts of war.

    In climes beyond the solar road,
Where shaggy forms o'er ice-built mountains roam,
The Muse has broke the twilight-gloom
    To cheer the shivering native's dull abode.
And oft, beneath the odorous shade
Of Chili's boundless forests laid,

She deigns to hear the savage youth repeat,
In loose numbers wildly sweet,
Their feather-cinctured chief and dusky loves.
Her track, where'er the goddess roves,
Glory pursue and generous Shame,
Th' unconquerable Mind, and Freedom's holy flame.

Woods, that wave o'er Delphi's steep,
Isles, that crown th'Ægean deep,
    Fields, that cool Ilissus laves,
    Or where Maeander's amber waves
In lingering lab'rinths creep,
    How do your tuneful Echoes languish,
    Mute, but to the voice of Anguish!
Where each old poetic mountain
    Inspiration breathed around;
Ev'ry shade and hallowed fountain
    Murmured deep a solemn sound:
Till the sad Nine, in Greece's evil hour,
    Left their Parnassus for the Latin plains.
Alike they scorn the pomp of tyrant Power,
    And coward Vice, that revels in her chains.
When Latium had her lofty spirit lost,
They sought, oh Albion! next thy sea-encircled coast.

Far from the sun and summer-gale,
In thy green lap was Nature's darling laid,
What time, where lucid Avon strayed,
    To him the mighty mother did unveil
Her awful face: the dauntless child
Stretched forth his little arms and smiled.
"This pencil take (she said), whose colours clear
Richly paint the vernal year:
Thine too these golden keys, immortal Boy!
This can unlock the gates of Joy;
Of Horror that, and thrilling Fears,
Or ope the sacred source of sympathetic tears."

Nor second he, that rode sublime
Upon the seraph-wings of ecstasy,
The secrets of th'abyss to spy.
    He passed the flaming bounds of place and time:

The living throne, the sapphire-blaze,
Where angels tremble while they gaze,
He saw; but, blasted with excess of light,
Closed his eyes in endless night.
Behold, where Dryden's less presumptuous car,
Wide o'er the fields of glory bear
Two coursers of ethereal race,
With necks in thunder clothed, and long-resounding pace.

Hark, his hands the lyre explore!
Bright-eyed Fancy, hovering o'er,
Scatters from her pictured urn
Thoughts that breathe, and words that burn.
But ah! 'tis heard no more—
    Oh! Lyre divine, what daring Spirit
    Wakes thee now? Though he inherit
Nor the pride, nor ample pinion
    That the Theban eagle bear,
Sailing with supreme dominion
    Through the azure deep of air:
Yet oft before his infant eyes would run
    Such forms as glitter in the Muse's ray,
With orient hues, unborrowed of the sun:
    Yet shall he mount, and keep his distant way
Beyond the limits of a vulgar fate,
Beneath the Good how far—but far above the Great

Sonnet on the Death of Mr. Richard West

In vain to me the smiling mornings shine,
And redd'ning Phoebus lifts his golden fire:
The birds in vain their amorous descant join;
Or cheerful fields resume their green attire:
These ears, alas! for other notes repine,
A different object do these eyes require:
My lonely anguish melts no heart but mine;
And in my breast the imperfect joys expire.
Yet morning smiles the busy race to cheer,
And new-born pleasure brings to happier men:

The fields to all their wonted tribute bear:
To warm their little loves the birds complain:
I fruitless mourn to him that cannot hear,
And weep the more, because I weep in vain.

FRANCIS FAWKES

(1720-1777)

The Brown Jug

Dear Tom, this brown jug that now foams with mild ale,
(In which I will drink to sweet Nan of the Vale,)
Was once Toby Fillpot, a thirsty old soul
As e'er drank a bottle, or fathomed a bowl;
In boosing about 'twas his praise to excel,
And among jolly topers he bore off the bell.

In chanced as in dog-days he sat at his ease
In his flower-woven arbour as gay as you please,
With a friend and a pipe puffing sorrows away,
And with honest old stingo was soaking his clay,
His breath-doors of life on a sudden were shut,
And he died full as big as a Dorchester butt.

His body, when long in the ground it had lain,
And time into clay had resolved it again,
A potter found out in its covert so snug,
And with part of fat Toby he formed this brown jug,
Now sacred to friendship, and mirth, and mild ale;
So here's to my lovely sweet Nan of the Vale.

From the Latin of AMALTHEUS

JAMES GRAINGER

(1721-1767)

FROM *Ode to Solitude*

O solitude, romantic maid!
Whether by nodding towers you tread,
Or hunt the desert's trackless gloom,
Or hover o'er the yawning tomb,

Or climb the Andes' clifted side,
Or by the Nile's coy source abide,
Or starting from your half-year's sleep
From Hecla view the thawing deep,
Or, at the purple dawn of day,
Tadmor's marble wastes survey,
You, recluse, again I woo,
And again your steps pursue.

With you roses brighter bloom,
Sweeter every sweet perfume,
Purer every fountain flows,
Stronger every wilding grows.
Let those toil for gold who please,
Or for fame renounce their ease.
What is fame? an empty bubble.
Gold? a transient shining trouble.
Let them for their country bleed,
What was Sidney's, Raleigh's meed?
Man's not worth a moment's pain,
Base, ungrateful, fickle, vain.
Then let me, sequestered fair,
To your sibyl grot repair;
On yon hanging cliff it stands,
Scooped by nature's savage hands,
Bosomed in the gloomy shade
Of cypress not with age decayed.
Where the owl still-hooting sits,
Where the bat incessant flits,
There in loftier strains I'll sing
Whence the changing seasons spring,
Tell how storms deform the skies,
Whence the waves subside and rise,
Trace the comet's blazing tail,
Weigh the planets in a scale;
Bend, great God, before thy shrine,
The bournless macrocosm's thine.

WILLIAM COLLINS

(1721–1759)

Ode

How sleep the brave, who sink to rest
By all their country's wishes blessed!
When Spring with dewy fingers cold
Returns to deck their hallowed mould,
She there shall dress a sweeter sod
Than Fancy's feet have ever trod.

By fairy hands their knell is rung;
By forms unseen their dirge is sung;
There Honour comes, a pilgrim gray,
To bless the turf that wraps their clay;
And Freedom shall awhile repair,
To dwell a weeping hermit there.

Ode to Evening

If aught of oaten stop, or pastoral song,
May hope, chaste Eve, to soothe thy modest ear,
  Like thy own brawling springs,
  Thy springs, and dying gales;

O Nymph reserved, while now the bright-haired sun
Sits in yon western tent, whose cloudy skirts,
  With brede ethereal wove,
  O'erhang his wavy bed:

Now air is hushed, save where the weak-eyed bat
With short shrill shriek flits by on leathern wing;
  Or where the beetle winds
  His small but sullen horn,

As oft he rises midst the twilight path,
Against the pilgrim borne in heedless hum:
  Now teach me, maid composed,
  To breathe some softened strain,

Whose numbers, stealing through thy darkening vale,
May not unseemly with its stillness suit;
   As, musing slow, I hail
   Thy genial loved return.

For when thy folding-star arising shows
His paly circlet, at his warning lamp
   The fragrant Hours, and Elves
   Who slept in buds the day,

And many a Nymph who wreathes her brows with sedge,
And sheds the freshening dew, and, lovelier still,
   The pensive Pleasures sweet,
   Prepare thy shadowy car;

Then let me rove some wild and heathy scene;
Or find some ruin, midst its dreary dells,
   Whose walls more awful nod
   By thy religious gleams.

Or, if chill blustering winds, or driving rain,
Prevent my willing feet, be mine the hut,
   That, from the mountain's side,
   Views wilds, and swelling floods,

And hamlets brown, and dim-discovered spires;
And hears their simple bell, and marks o'er all
   Thy dewy fingers draw
   The gradual dusky veil.

While Spring shall pour his showers, as oft he wont,
And bathe thy breathing tresses, meekest Eve!
   While Summer loves to sport
   Beneath thy lingering light;

While sallow Autumn fills thy lap with leaves;
Or Winter, yelling through the troublous air,
   Affrights thy shrinking train,
   And rudely rends thy robes;

So long, regardful of thy quiet rule,
Shall Fancy, Friendship, Science, smiling Peace,
   Thy gentlest influence own,
   And love thy favourite name!

Dirge in Cymbeline

To fair Fidele's grassy tomb
   Soft maids and village hinds shall bring
Each opening sweet of earliest bloom,
   And rifle all the breathing spring.

No wailing ghost shall dare appear
   To vex with shrieks this quiet grove;
But shepherd lads assemble here,
   And melting virgins own their love.

No withered witch shall here be seen;
   No goblins lead their nightly crew:
The female fays shall haunt the green,
   And dress thy grave with pearly dew.

The redbreast oft, at evening hours,
   Shall kindly lend his little aid,
With hoary moss, and gathered flowers,
   To deck the ground where thou art laid.

When howling winds, and beating rain,
   In tempests shake the sylvan cell;
Or midst the chase, on every plain,
   The tender thought on thee shall dwell;

Each lonely scene shall thee restore;
   For thee the tear be duly shed;
Beloved till life can charm no more,
   And mourned till Pity's self be dead.

CHRISTOPHER SMART

(1722–1771)

FROM *Song to David*

O servant of God's holiest charge,
The minister of praise at large,
   Which thou mayst now receive;
From thy blest mansion hail and hear,
From topmost eminence appear
   To this the wreath I weave.

His muse, bright angel of his verse,
Gives balm for all the thorns that pierce,
   For all the pangs that rage;
Blest light, still gaining on the gloom,
The more than Michal of his bloom,
   The Abishag of his age.

He sang of God—the mighty source
Of all things—the stupendous force
   On which all strength depends;
From whose right arm, beneath whose eyes,
All period, power and enterprise
   Commences, reigns and ends.

The world—the clustering spheres he made,
The glorious light, the soothing shade,
   Dale, champaign, grove, and hill;
The multitudinous abyss,
Whose secrecy remains in bliss,
   And wisdom hides her skill.

Trees, plants and flowers—of virtuous root;
Gem yielding blossom, yielding fruit,
   Choice gums and precious balm;
Bless ye the nosegay in the vale,
And with the sweetness of the gale
   Enrich the thankful psalm.

Of fowl—even every beak and wing
Which cheer the winter, hail the spring,
    That live in peace, or prey;
They that make music, or that mock,
The quail, the brave domestic cock,
    The raven, swan, and jay.

Of beasts—the beaver plods his task;
While the sleek tigers roll and bask,
    Nor yet the shades arouse;
Her cave the mining coney scoops;
Where o'er the mead the mountain stoops,
    The kids exult and browse.

Of gems—their virtue and their price,
Which, hid in earth from man's device,
    Their darts of lustre sheath;
The jasper of the master's stamp,
The topaz blazing like a lamp,
    Among the mines beneath.

The pillars of the Lord are seven,
Which stand from earth to topmost heaven;
    His wisdom drew the plan;
His word accomplished the design,
From brightest gem to deepest mine,
    From Christ enthroned to man.

Alpha, the cause of causes, first
In station, fountain, whence the burst
    Of light and blaze of day;
Whence bold attempt, and brave advance,
Have motion, life and ordinance,
    And heaven itself its stay.

Gamma supports the glorious arch
On which angelic legions march,
    And is with sapphires paved;
Thence the fleet clouds are sent adrift,
And thence the painted folds that lift
    The crimson veil, are waved.

Eta with living sculpture breathes,
With verdant carvings, flowery wreathes
   Of never-wasting bloom;
In strong relief his goodly base
All instruments of labour grace,
   The trowel, spade, and loom.

Next Theta stands to the supreme—
Who formed in number, sign and scheme,
   The illustrious lights that are;
And one addressed his saffron robe,
And one, clad in a silver globe,
   Held rule with every star.

Iota's tuned to choral hymns
Of those that fly, while he that swims
   In thankful safety lurks;
And foot, and chapiter, and niche,
The various histories enrich
   Of God's recorded works.

Sigma presents the social droves
With him that solitary roves,
   And man of all the chief;
Fair on whose face, and stately frame,
Did God impress his hallowed name,
   For ocular belief.

Omega! greatest and the best,
Stands sacred to the day of rest,
   For gratitude and thought;
Which blessed the world upon his pole,
And gave the universe his goal,
   And closed the infernal draught.

O David, scholar of the Lord!
Such is thy science, whence reward,
   And infinite degree;
O strength, O sweetness, lasting ripe!
God's harp thy symbol, and thy type
   The lion and the bee!

For Adoration all the ranks
Of angels yield eternal thanks,
   And David in the midst;
With God's good poor, which, last and least,
In man's esteem, thou to thy feast,
   O blessed bridegroom, bidst.

For Adoration seasons change,
And order, truth, and beauty range,
   Adjust, attract, and fill:
The grass the polyanthus checks;
And polished porphyry reflects,
   By the descending rill.

Rich almonds colour to the prime
For Adoration; tendrils climb,
   And fruit-trees pledge their gems;
And Ivis, with her gorgeous vest,
Builds for her eggs her cunning nest,
   And bell-flowers bow their stems.

The spotted ounce and playsome cubs
Run rustling 'mongst the flowering shrubs,
   And lizards feed the moss;
For Adoration beasts embark,
While waves upholding halcyon's ark
   No longer roar and toss.

While Israel sits beneath his fig,
With coral root and amber sprig
   The weaned adventurer sports;
Where to the palm the jasmine cleaves,
For Adoration 'mong the leaves
   The gale his peace reports.

The wealthy crop of whitening rice
'Mongst thyine woods and groves of spice,
   For Adoration grow;
And, marshalled in the fencéd land,
The peaches and pomegranates stand,
   Where wild carnations blow.

The laurels with the winter strive;
The crocus burnishes alive
  Upon the snow-clad earth;
For Adoration myrtles stay
To keep the garden from dismay,
  And bless the sight from dearth.

The pheasant shows his pompous neck;
And ermine, jealous of a speck,
  With fear eludes offence;
The sable, with his glossy pride,
For Adoration is descried,
  Where frosts and waves condense.

For Adoration, beyond match,
The scholar bullfinch aims to catch
  The soft flute's ivory touch;
And careless, on the hazel spray
The daring redbreast keeps at bay
  The damsel's greedy clutch.

For Adoration, in the skies,
The Lord's philosopher espies
  The dog, the ram, the rose;
The planets' ring, Orion's sword;
Nor is his greatness less adored
  In the vile worm that glows.

For Adoration, on the strings
The western breezes work their wings,
  The captive ear to soothe—
Hark! 'tis a voice—how still, and small—
That makes the cataracts to fall,
  Or bids the sea be smooth!

For Adoration, incense comes
From bezoar, and Arabian gums,
  And from the civet's fur;
But as for prayer, or e'er it faints,
Far better is the breath of saints
  Than galbanum or myrrh.

For Adoration, in the dome
Of Christ, the sparrows find a home,
    And on his olives perch:
The swallow also dwells with thee,
O man of God's humility,
    Within his Saviour's church.

Sweet is the dew that falls betimes,
And drops upon the leafy limes;
    Sweet Hermon's fragrant air:
Sweet is the lily's silver bell,
And sweet the wakeful tapers' smell
    That watch for early prayer.

Sweet the young Nurse, with love intense,
Which smiles o'er sleeping innocence;
    Sweet when the lost arrive:
Sweet the musician's ardour beats,
While his vague mind's in quest of sweets,
    The choicest flowers to hive.

Sweeter, in all the strains of love,
The language of thy turtle-dove,
    Paired to thy swelling chord;
Sweeter, with every grace endued,
The glory of thy gratitude,
    Respired unto the Lord.

Strong is the horse upon his speed;
Strong in pursuit the rapid glede,
    Which makes at once his game:
Strong the tall ostrich on the ground;
Strong through the turbulent profound
    Shoots xiphias to his aim.

Strong is the lion—like a coal
His eyeball—like a bastion's mole
    His chest against the foes:
Strong the gier-eagle on his sail,
Strong against tide the enormous whale
    Emerges as he goes.

But stronger still in earth and air,
And in the sea the man of prayer,
  And far beneath the tide:
And in the seat to faith assigned,
Where ask is have, where seek is find,
  Where knock is open wide.

Beauteous the fleet before the gale;
Beauteous the multitudes in mail,
  Ranked arms, and crested heads;
Beauteous the garden's umbrage mild,
Walk, water, meditated wild,
  And all the bloomy beds.

Beauteous the moon full on the lawn;
And beauteous when the veil's withdrawn,
  The virgin to her spouse:
Beauteous the temple, decked and filled,
When to the heaven of heavens they build
  Their heart-directed vows.

Beauteous, yea beauteous more than these,
The Shepherd King upon his knees,
  For his momentous trust;
With wish of infinite conceit,
For man, beast, mute, the small and great,
  And prostrate dust to dust.

Precious, the bounteous widow's mite;
And precious, for extreme delight,
  The largess from the churl:
Precious the ruby's blushing blaze,
And alba's blest imperial rays,
  And pure cerulean pearl.

Precious the penitential tear;
And precious is the sigh sincere;
  Acceptable to God:
And precious are the winning flowers,
In gladsome Israel's feast of bowers,
  Bound on the hallowed sod.

More precious that diviner part
Of David, even the Lord's own heart,
　Great, beautiful, and new:
In all things, where it was intent,
In all extremes, in each event,
　Proof—answering true to true.

Glorious the sun in mid career;
Glorious the assembled fires appear;
　Glorious the comet's train:
Glorious the trumpet and alarm;
Glorious the Almighty's stretched-out arm;
　Glorious the enraptured main:

Glorious the northern lights astream;
Glorious the song, when God's the theme;
　Glorious the thunder's roar:
Glorious hosannah from the den;
Glorious the catholic amen;
　Glorious the martyr's gore:

Glorious—more glorious is the crown
Of Him that brought salvation down,
　By meekness called thy Son;
Thou that stupendous truth believed,
And now the matchless deed's achieved,
　Determined, Dared, and Done.

JANE ELLIOT

(1727–1805)

Lament for Flodden

I've heard them lilting at our ewe-milking,
　Lasses a-lilting before dawn o' day;
But now they are moaning on ilka green loaning:
　The flowers of the forest are a' wede away.

Lilting, *singing.* Ilka, *every.* Loaning, *field-track.* Wede, *weeded.*

At bughts, in the morning, nae blythe lads are scorning,
  Lassies are lonely and dowie and wae;
Nae daffing, nae gabbing, but sighing and sabbing,
  Ilk ane lifts her leglin and hies her away.

In hairst, at the shearing, nae youths now are jeering,
  Bandsters are lyart, and runkled, and gray;
At fair or at preaching, nae wooing, nae fleeching:
  The flowers of the forest are a' wede away.

At e'en, in the gloaming, nae swankies are roaming
  'Bout stacks wi' the lasses at bogle to play;
But ilk ane sits eerie, lamenting her dearie:
  The flowers of the forest are a' wede away.

Dool and wae for the order sent our lads to the Border!
  The English, for ance, by guile wan the day;
The flowers of the forest, that fought aye the foremost,
  The prime of our land, lie cauld in the clay.

We'll hear nae mair lilting at our ewe-milking;
  Women and bairns are heartless and wae;
Sighing and moaning on ilka green loaning:
  The flowers of the forest are a' wede away.

THOMAS WARTON THE YOUNGER

(1728–1790)

Sonnet, to the River Loddon

Ah! what a weary race my feet have run,
Since first I trod thy banks with alders crowned,
And thought my way was all through fairy ground,
Beneath thy azure sky and golden sun,
Where first my Muse to lisp her notes begun.
While pensive memory traces back the round,
Which fills the varied interval between,
Much pleasure, more of sorrow, mark the scene.
Sweet native stream, those skies and suns so pure

Bughts, *sheepfolds.* Dowie, *low-spirited.* Wae, *woe.* Daffing, *joking.* Gabbing, *prattling.* Leglin, *milk-pail.* Hairst, *harvest.* Shearing, *reaping.* Bandsters, *binders.* Lyart, *grizzled.* Runkled, *wrinkled.* Fleeching, *coaxing.* Swankies, *lusty lads.* Bogle, *hide-and-seek.* Dool, *mourning.*

No more return to cheer my evening road.
Yet still one joy remains; that not obscure
Nor useless all my vacant days have flowed,
From youth's gay dawn to manhood's prime mature,
Nor with the Muse's laurel unbestowed.

OLIVER GOLDSMITH

(1728?–1774)

FROM *The Traveller*

Remote, unfriended, melancholy, slow,
Or by the lazy Scheldt or wandering Po;
Or onward where the rude Carinthian boor
Against the homeless stranger shuts the door;
Or where Campania's plain forsaken lies,
A weary waste expanding to the skies;
Where'er I roam, whatever realms to see,
My heart untravelled fondly turns to thee;
Still to my brother turns, with ceaseless pain,
And drags at each remove a lengthening chain.
Eternal blessings crown my earliest friend,
And round his dwelling guardian saints attend;
Blessed be that spot, where cheerful guests retire
To pause from toil, and trim their evening fire;
Blessed that abode where want and pain repair,
And every stranger finds a ready chair;
Blessed be those feasts with simple plenty crowned,
Where all the ruddy family around
Laugh at the jests or pranks that never fail,
Or sigh with pity at some mournful tale;
Or press the bashful stranger to his food,
And learn the luxury of doing good.
But me, not destined such delights to share,
My prime of life in wandering spent and care;
Impelled with steps unceasing to pursue
Some fleeting good, that mocks me with the view;
That, like the circle bounding earth and skies,
Allures from far, yet as I follow flies;
My fortune leads to traverse realms alone,
And find no spot of all the world my own.

FROM *The Deserted Village*

Sweet Auburn! loveliest village of the plain,
Where health and plenty cheered the labouring swain,
Where smiling spring its earliest visit paid,
And parting summer's lingering blooms delayed;
Dear lovely bowers of innocence and ease.
Seats of my youth, when every sport could please!
How often have I loitered o'er thy green,
Where humble happiness endeared each scene!
How often have I paused on every charm,
The sheltered cot, the cultivated farm,
The never-failing brook, the busy mill,
The decent church that topped the neighbouring hill,
The hawthorn bush with seats beneath the shade,
For talking age and whispering lovers made!
How often have I blessed the coming day,
When toil remitting lent its turn to play,
And all the village train, from labour free,
Led up their sports beneath the spreading tree;
While many a pastime circled in the shade,
The young contending as the old surveyed;
And many a gambol frolicked o'er the ground,
And sleights of art and feats of strength went round;
And still, as each repeated pleasure tired,
Succeeding sports the mirthful band inspired;
The dancing pair that simply sought renown,
By holding out, to tire each other down;
The swain mistrustless of his smutted face,
While secret laughter tittered round the place;
The bashful virgin's sidelong looks of love,
The matron's glance that would those looks reprove:
These were thy charms, sweet village! sports like these,
With sweet succession, taught e'en toil to please;
These round thy bowers their cheerful influence shed,
These were thy charms—but all these charms are fled.

Sweet smiling village, loveliest of the lawn!
Thy sports are fled, and all thy charms withdrawn;
Amidst thy bowers the tyrant's hand is seen,

And desolation saddens all thy green.
One only master grasps thy whole domain,
And half a tillage stints thy smiling plain;
No more thy glassy brook reflects the day,
But choked with sedges works its weedy way;
Along thy glades, a solitary guest,
The hollow-sounding bittern guards its nest;
Amidst thy desert-walks the lapwing flies,
And tires their echoes with unvaried cries.
Sunk are thy bowers in shapeless ruin all,
And the long grass o'ertops the mouldering wall;
And, trembling, shrinking from the spoiler's hand,
Far, far away thy children leave the land.

Ill fares the land, to hastening ills a prey,
Where wealth accumulates, and men decay.
Princes and lords may flourish or may fade;
A breath can make them, as a breath has made;
But a bold peasantry, their country's pride,
When once destroyed, can never be supplied.

Song

When lovely woman stoops to folly,
    And finds too late that men betray,
What charm can soothe her melancholy?
    What art can wash her guilt away?

The only art her guilt to cover,
    To hide her shame from every eye,
To give repentance to her lover,
    And wring his bosom, is—to die.

The Vicar of Wakefield, 1765

Song

O memory! thou fond deceiver,
    Still importunate and vain;
To former joys recurring ever,
    And turning all the past to pain;

Thou, like the world, the oppressed oppressing,
　Thy smiles increase the wretch's woe!
And he who wants each other blessing,
　In thee must ever find a foe.

Song

Let schoolmasters puzzle their brains
　With grammar and nonsense and learning;
Good liquor, I stoutly maintain,
　Gives genius a better discerning.
Let them brag of their heathenish gods,
　Their Lethes, their Styxes and Stygians;
Their quis and their quaes and their quods,
　They're all but a parcel of pigeons.
　　　　Toroddle, toroddle, toroll.

When methodist preachers come down,
　A-preaching that drinking is sinful,
I wager the rascals a crown,
　They always preach best with a skinful.
But when you come down with your pence
　For a slice of their scurvy religion,
I'll leave it to all men of sense,
　But you, my good friend, are the pigeon.
　　　　Toroddle, toroddle, toroll.

Then come, put the jorum about,
　And let us be merry and clever;
Our hearts and our liquors are stout;
　Here's the Three Jolly Pigeons for ever.
Let some cry up woodcock or hare,
　Your bustards, your ducks, and your widgeons;
But of all the birds in the air,
　Here's a health to the Three Jolly Pigeons.
　　　　Toroddle, toroddle, toroll.

She Stoops to Conquer, 1773

JOHN SCOTT OF AMWELL

(1730–1783)

The Drum

I hate that drum's discordant sound,
Parading round, and round, and round:
To thoughtless youth it pleasure yields,
And lures from cities and from fields,
To sell their liberty for charms
Of tawdry lace, and glittering arms;
And when ambition's voice commands,
To march, to fight, and fall in foreign lands.

I hate that drum's discordant sound,
Parading round, and round, and round;
To me it talks of ravaged plains,
And burning towns, and ruined swains,
And mangled limbs, and dying groans,
And widow's tears, and orphan's moans,
And all that Misery's hand bestows,
To fill the catalogue of human woes.

WILLIAM COWPER

(1731–1800)

John Gilpin

John Gilpin was a citizen
    Of credit and renown,
A train-band captain eke was he
    Of famous London town.

John Gilpin's spouse said to her dear:
    "Though wedded we have been
These twice ten tedious years, yet we
    No holiday have seen.

"To-morrow is our wedding-day,
    And we will then repair
Unto the Bell at Edmonton
    All in a chaise and pair.

"My sister, and my sister's child,
  Myself, and children three,
Will fill the chaise; so you must ride
  On horseback after we."

He soon replied: "I do admire
  Of womankind but one,
And you are she, my dearest dear,
  Therefore it shall be done.

"I am a linen-draper bold,
  As all the world doth know,
And my good friend the calender
  Will lend his horse to go."

Quoth Mrs. Gilpin: "That's well said;
  And, for that wine is dear,
We will be furnished with our own,
  Which is both bright and clear."

John Gilpin kissed his loving wife;
  O'erjoyed was he to find
That, though on pleasure she was bent,
  She had a frugal mind.

The morning came, the chaise was brought,
  But yet was not allowed
To drive up to the door, lest all
  Should say that she was proud.

So three doors off the chaise was stayed,
  Where they did all get in;
Six precious souls, and all agog
  To dash through thick and thin!

Smack went the whip, round went the wheels,
  Were never folk so glad,
The stones did rattle underneath,
  As if Cheapside were mad.

John Gilpin at his horse's side
　Seized fast the flowing mane,
And up he got, in haste to ride,
　But soon came down again;

For saddle-tree scarce reached had he,
　His journey to begin,
When, turning round his head, he saw
　Three customers come in.

So down he came; for loss of time,
　Although it grieved him sore,
Yet loss of pence, full well he knew,
　Would trouble him much more.

'Twas long before his customers
　Were suited to their mind,
When Betty screaming came downstairs:
　"The wine is left behind!"

"Good lack!" quoth he, "yet bring it me,
　My leathern belt likewise,
In which I bear my trusty sword
　When I do exercise."

Now mistress Gilpin (careful soul!)
　Had two stone bottles found,
To hold the liquor that she loved,
　And keep it safe and sound.

Each bottle had a curling ear,
　Through which the belt he drew,
And hung a bottle on each side,
　To make his balance true.

Then, over all, that he might be
　Equipped from top to toe,
His long red cloak, well brushed and neat,
　He manfully did throw.

Now see him mounted once again
 Upon his nimble steed,
Full slowly pacing o'er the stones,
 With caution and good heed!

But, finding soon a smoother road
 Beneath his well-shod feet,
The snorting beast began to trot,
 Which galled him in his seat.

So, "Fair and softly," John he cried,
 But John he cried in vain;
The trot became a gallop soon,
 In spite of curb and rein.

So stooping down, as needs he must
 Who cannot sit upright,
He grasped the mane with both his hands,
 And eke with all his might.

His horse, who never in that sort
 Had handled been before,
What thing upon his back had got
 Did wonder more and more.

Away went Gilpin, neck or nought;
 Away went hat and wig!
He little dreamt, when he set out,
 Of running such a rig!

The wind did blow, the cloak did fly,
 Like streamer long and gay,
Till, loop and button failing both,
 At last it flew away.

Then might all people well discern
 The bottles he had slung;
A bottle swinging at each side,
 As hath been said or sung.

The dogs did bark, the children screamed,
 Up flew the windows all;
And every soul cried out: "Well done!"
 As loud as he could bawl.

Away went Gilpin—Who but he?
 His fame soon spread around—
"He carries weight!" "He rides a race!"
 " 'Tis for a thousand pound!"

And still, as fast as he drew near,
 'Twas wonderful to view
How in a trice the turnpike men
 Their gates wide open threw.

And now, as he went bowing down
 His reeking head full low,
The bottles twain behind his back
 Were shattered at a blow.

Down ran the wine into the road,
 Most piteous to be seen,
Which made his horse's flanks to smoke
 As they had basted been.

But still he seemed to carry weight,
 With leathern girdle braced;
For all might see the bottle-necks
 Still dangling at his waist.

Thus all through merry Islington
 These gambols he did play,
And till he came unto the Wash
 Of Edmonton so gay.

And there he threw the wash about
 On both sides of the way,
Just like unto a trundling mop,
 Or a wild goose at play.

At Edmonton his loving wife
  From the balcóny spied
Her tender husband, wond'ring much
  To see how he did ride.

"Stop, stop, John Gilpin! Here's the house!"
  They all at once did cry;
"The dinner waits, and we are tired."
  Said Gilpin: "So am I!"

But yet his horse was not a whit
  Inclined to tarry there;
For why?—his owner had a house
  Full ten miles off, at Ware.

So like an arrow swift he flew,
  Shot by an archer strong;
So did he fly—which brings me to
  The middle of my song.

Away went Gilpin, out of breath,
  And sore against his will,
Till at his friend the calender's
  His horse at last stood still.

The calender, amazed to see
  His neighbour in such trim,
Laid down his pipe, flew to the gate,
  And thus accosted him:

"What news? what news? your tidings tell;
  Tell me you must and shall—
Say why bare-headed you are come,
  Or why you come at all?"

Now Gilpin had a pleasant wit,
  And loved a timely joke;
And thus unto the calender
  In merry guise he spoke:

"I came because your horse would come;
　　And, if I well forebode,
My hat and wig will soon be here—
　　They are upon the road."

The calender, right glad to find
　　His friend in merry pin,
Returned him not a single word,
　　But to the house went in;

Whence straight he came with hat and wig;
　　A wig that flowed behind,
A hat not much the worse for wear,
　　Each comely in its kind.

He held them up, and, in his turn,
　　Thus showed his ready wit:
"My head is twice as big as yours,
　　They therefore needs must fit.

"But let me scrape the dirt away
　　That hangs upon your face;
And stop and eat, for well you may
　　Be in a hungry case."

Said John: "It is my wedding-day,
　　And all the world would stare,
If wife should dine at Edmonton
　　And I should dine at Ware!"

So, turning to his horse, he said:
　　"I am in haste to dine;
'Twas for your pleasure you came here,
　　You shall go back for mine."

Ah, luckless speech, and bootless boast!
　　For which he paid full dear;
For, while he spake, a braying ass
　　Did sing most loud and clear;

Whereat his horse did snort, as he
    Had heard a lion roar,
And galloped ·off with all his might,
    As he had done before.

Away went Gilpin, and away
    Went Gilpin's hat and wig!
He lost them sooner than at first—
    For why?—they were too big!

Now, mistress Gilpin, when she saw
    Her husband posting down
Into the country far away,
    She pulled out half a crown;

And thus unto the youth she said
    That drove them to the Bell—
"This shall be yours when you bring back
    My husband safe and well."

The youth did ride, and soon did meet
    John coming back amain;
Whom in a trice he tried to stop
    By catching at the rein;

But, not performing what he meant,
    And gladly would have done,
The frightened steed he frighted more,
    And made him faster run.

Away went Gilpin, and away
    Went post-boy at his heels!
The post-boy's horse right glad to miss
    The lumb'ring of the wheels.

Six gentlemen upon the road,
    Thus seeing Gilpin fly,
With post-boy scamp'ring in the rear,
    They raised the hue and cry:

"Stop thief, stop thief!—a highwayman!"
    Not one of them was mute;
And all and each that passed that way
    Did join in the pursuit.

And now the turnpike gates again
    Flew open in short space;
The toll-men thinking, as before,
    That Gilpin rode a race.

And so he did—and won it too!
    For he got first to town;
Nor stopped till where he had got up
    He did again get down.

Now let us sing Long live the King,
    And Gilpin long live he;
And, when he next doth ride abroad,
    May I be there to see!

SAMUEL BISHOP

(1731–1795)

To His Wife on the Fourteenth Anniversary of Her Wedding-Day, with a Ring

"Thee, Mary, with this ring I wed,"
So fourteen years ago I said.
Behold another ring! "For what?"
To wed thee o'er again—why not?

With the first ring I married youth,
Grace, beauty, innocence, and truth;
Taste long admired, sense long revered,
And all my Molly then appeared.

If she, by merit since disclosed,
Prove twice the woman I supposed,
I plead that double merit now,
To justify a double vow.

Here then, to-day, with faith as sure,
With ardour as intense and pure,
As when amidst the rites divine
I took thy troth, and plighted mine,
To thee, sweet girl, my second ring,
A token and a pledge I bring;
With this I wed, till death us part,
Thy riper virtues to my heart;
Those virtues which, before untried,
The wife has added to the bride—
Those virtues, whose progressive claim,
Endearing wedlock's very name,
My soul enjoys, my song approves,
For conscience' sake as well as love's.

For why? They show me every hour
Honour's high thought, affection's power,
Discretion's deed, sound judgment's sentence,
And teach me all things—but repentance.

SIR BROOKE BOOTHBY

(1734–1824)

Sonnet on Life

What art thou, Life? The shadow of a dream:
The past and future dwell in thought alone;
The present, ere we note its flight, is gone;
And all ideal, vain, fantastic, seem.
Whence is thy source? And whither dost thou tend?
So short thy period, and thy form so frail;
Poor prisoner! pent in Death's surrounding vale,
Born but to breathe, to suffer, and to end.
Why, Shadow, bring'st thou on thy raven wing
Dark trains of grief and visions of the night,
Rather than graces robed in purple light,
Elysian flowers and love's unclouded spring,
Since sad or gay, whatever be thy theme,
Death surely ends at once the dreamer and the dream?

JAMES BEATTIE

(1735–1803)

FROM *The Minstrel*

But who the melodies of morn can tell?
The wild brook babbling down the mountain side;
The lowing herd; the sheepfold's simple bell;
The pipe of early shepherd dim descried
In the lone valley; echoing far and wide
The clamorous horn along the cliffs above;
The hollow murmur of the ocean-tide;
The hum of bees, the linnet's lay of love,
And the full choir that wakes the universal grove.

The cottage curs at early pilgrim bark;
Crowned with her pail the tripping milkmaid sings;
The whistling ploughman stalks afield; and hark!
Down the rough slope the ponderous wagon rings;
Through rustling corn the hare astonished springs;
Slow tolls the village clock the drowsy hour;
The partridge bursts away on whirring wings;
Deep mourns the turtle in sequestered bower,
And shrill lark carols clear from her aërial tower.

ISAAC BICKERSTAFFE

(1735?–1812?)

FROM *Love in a Village*

There was a jolly miller once,
    Lived on the river Dee;
He worked and sung, from morn till night,
    No lark more blithe than he.
And this the burthen of his song
    For ever used to be:
"I care for nobody, not I,
    If no one cares for me."

WILLIAM JULIUS MICKLE

(1735–1788)

FROM *Cumnor Hall*

The dews of summer night did fall,
  The moon, sweet regent of the sky,
Silvered the walls of Cumnor Hall,
  And many an oak that grew thereby.

Now nought was heard beneath the skies,
  The sounds of busy life were still,
Save an unhappy lady's sighs,
  That issued from that lonely pile.

Thus sore and sad that lady grieved
  In Cumnor Hall so lone and drear;
And many a heartfelt sigh she heaved,
  And let fall many a bitter tear.

And ere the dawn of day appeared,
  In Cumnor Hall, so lone and drear,
Full many a piercing scream was heard,
  And many a cry of mortal fear.

The death-bell thrice was heard to ring,
  An aërial voice was heard to call,
And thrice the raven flapped his wings
  Around the towers of Cumnor Hall.

The mastiff howled at village door,
  The oaks were shattered on the green;
Woe was the hour, for never more
  That hapless Countess e'er was seen.

And in that manor, now no more
  Is cheerful feast or sprightly ball;
For ever since that dreary hour
  Have spirits haunted Cumnor Hall.

The village maids, with fearful glance,
Avoid the ancient moss-grown wall;
Nor ever lead the merry dance
  Among the groves of Cumnor Hall.

Full many a traveller has sighed,
  And pensive wept the Countess' fall,
As wandering onwards they've espied
  The haunted towers of Cumnor Hall.

The Mariner's Wife

But are ye sure the news is true?
  And are ye sure he's weel?
Is this a time to think o' wark?
  Ye jauds, fling by your wheel.
    For there's nae luck about the house,
    There's nae luck at a',
    There's nae luck about the house,
    When our gudeman's awa.

Is this a time to think o' wark,
  When Colin's at the door?
Rax down my cloak—I'll to the quay,
  And see him come ashore.

Rise up and make a clean fireside,
  Put on the mickle pot;
Gie little Kate her cotton goun,
  And Jock his Sunday's coat.

And mak their shoon as black as slaes,
  Their stockins white as snaw;
It's a' to pleasure our gudeman—
  He likes to see them braw.

Jauds, jades. Rax, take. Braw, handsome.

There are twa hens into the crib,
    Hae fed this month and mair;
Mak haste and thraw their necks about,
    That Colin weel may fare.

My Turkey slippers I'll put on,
    My stockins pearl blue—
It's a' to pleasure our gudeman,
    For he's baith leal and true.

Sae sweet his voice, sae smooth his tongue;
    His breath's like caller air;
His very fit has music in't,
    As he comes up the stair.

And will I see his face again?
    And will I hear him speak?
I'm downright dizzy wi' the thought:
    In troth I'm like to greet.
      For there's nae luck about the house,
        There's nae luck at a',
      There's nae luck about the house,
        When our gudeman's awa.

MICHAEL BRUCE

(1746–1767)

To the Cuckoo

Hail, beauteous stranger of the grove!
    Thou messenger of Spring!
Now Heaven repairs thy rural seat,
    And woods thy welcome ring.

What time the daisy decks the green,
    Thy certain voice we hear:
Hast thou a star to guide thy path,
    Or mark the rolling year?

Thraw, *twist.* Caller, *fresh.* Fit, *foot.* Greet, *weep.*

Delightful visitant! with thee
  I hail the time of flowers,
And hear the sound of music sweet
  From birds among the bowers.

The schoolboy, wand'ring through the wood,
  To pull the primrose gay,
Starts, the new voice of Spring to hear,
  And imitates thy lay.

What time the pea puts on the bloom,
  Thou fly'st thy vocal vale,
An annual guest in other lands,
  Another Spring to hail.

Sweet bird! thy bower is ever green,
  Thy sky is ever clear;
Thou hast no sorrow in thy song,
  No winter in thy year.

O could I fly, I'd fly with thee!
  We'd make, with joyful wing,
Our annual visit o'er the globe,
  Companions of the Spring.

CHARLOTTE SMITH

(1749–1806)

The Gossamer

O'er faded heath-flowers spun or thorny furze,
The filmy gossamer is lightly spread;
Waving in every sighing air that stirs,
As fairy fingers had entwined the thread:
A thousand trembling orbs of lucid dew
Spangle the texture of the fairy loom,
As if soft Sylphs, lamenting as they flew,
Had wept departed summer's transient bloom:
But the wind rises, and the turf receives
The glittering web: so, evanescent, fade

Bright views that youth with sanguine heart believes;
So vanish schemes of bliss by Fancy made;
Which, fragile as the fleeting dreams of morn,
Leave but the withered heath and barren thorn.

LADY ANNE LINDSAY
(1750–1825)

Auld Robin Gray

When the sheep are in the fauld, and the kye at hame,
And a' the warld to rest are gane,
The waes o' my heart fa' in showers frae my e'e,
While my gudeman lies sound by me.

Young Jamie lo'ed me weel, and sought me for his bride;
But saving a croun he had naething else beside:
To make the croun a pund, young Jamie gaed to sea;
And the croun and the pund were baith for me.

He hadna been awa' a week but only twa,
When my father brak his arm, and the cow was stown awa';
My mother she fell sick—and my Jamie at the sea—
And auld Robin Gray came a-courtin' me.

My father couldna work, and my mother couldna spin;
I toiled night and day, but their bread I couldna win;
Auld Rob maintained them baith, and wi' tears in his e'e
Said, "Jennie, for their sakes, O, marry me!"

My heart it said nay; I looked for Jamie back;
But the wind it blew high, and the ship it was a wrack;
His ship it was a wrack—why didna Jamie dee?
Or why do I live to cry, Wae's me!

My father urged me sair; my mother didna speak;
But she looked in my face till my heart was like to break;
They gi'ed him my hand, though my heart was in the sea;
Sae auld Robin Gray he was gudeman to me.

Fauld, *fold*. Kye, *cows*. Waes, *woes*. Stown, *stolen*.

I hadna been a wife a week but only four,
When mournfu' as I sat on the stane at the door,
I saw my Jamie's wraith—for I couldna think it he,
Till he said, "I'm come hame to marry thee."

O sair, sair did we greet, and muckle did we say;
We took but ae kiss, and we tore ourselves away;
I wish that I were dead, but I'm no like to dee;
And why was I born to say, Wae's me!

I gang like a ghaist, and I carena to spin;
I daurna think of Jamie, for that wad be a sin;
But I'll do my best a gude wife to be,
For auld Robin Gray he is kind unto me.

JOHN PHILPOT CURRAN

(1750–1817)

The Deserter

If sadly thinking
With spirits sinking,
Could more than drinking
    My cares compose,
A cure for sorrow
From sighs I'd borrow,
And hope to-morrow
    Would end my woes.
But as in wailing
There's nought availing,
And Death unfailing
    Will strike the blow,
Then for that reason,
And for a season,
Let us be merry
    Before we go.
To joy a stranger,
A way-worn ranger,

Greet, weep.

In every danger
　　My course I've run;
Now hope all ending,
And Death befriending,
His last aid lending,
　　My cares are done:
No more a rover,
Or hapless lover,
My griefs are over,
　　My glass runs low;
Then for that reason,
And for a season,
Let us be merry
　　Before we go!

RICHARD BRINSLEY SHERIDAN
(1751–1816)

Song

Here's to the maiden of bashful fifteen!
　　Here's to the widow of fifty!
Here's to the flaunting extravagant quean;
　　And here's to the housewife that's thrifty!
　　　　Let the toast pass,
　　　　Drink to the lass!
　　　　I'll warrant she'll prove an excuse for the glass!

Here's to the charmer, whose dimples we prize!
　　Now to the maid who has none, sir!
Here's to the girl with a pair of blue eyes;
　　And here's to the nymph with but one, sir!
　　　　Let the toast pass, &c.

Here's to the maid with a bosom of snow!
　　Now to her that's as brown as a berry!
Here's to the wife with a face full of woe,
　　And now to the girl that is merry!
　　　　Let the toast pass, &c.

For let them be clumsy, or let them be slim,
   Young or ancient, I care not a feather!
So fill a pint bumper, quite up to the brim,
   And let us e'en toast them together!
      Let the toast pass,
      Drink to the lass!
   I'll warrant she'll prove an excuse for the glass!

The School for Scandal, 1777

PHILIP FRENEAU

(1752–1832)

Song of Thyrsis

The turtle on yon withered bough,
That lately mourned her murdered mate,
Has found another comrade now—
Such changes all await!
Again her drooping plume is drest,
Again she's willing to be blest
And takes her lover to her nest.
If nature has decreed it so
With all above, and all below,
Let us like them forget our woe,
   And not be killed with sorrow.
If I should quit your arms to-night
And chanced to die before 'twas light—
I would advise you—and you might—
   Love again to-morrow.

THOMAS CHATTERTON

(1752–1770)

FROM Aella

The budding floweret blushes at the light,
The meads are sprinkled with the yellow hue;
In daisied mantles is the mountain dight,
The nesh young cowslip bendeth with the dew;
The trees enleaféd, unto heaven straught,
When gentle winds do blow, to whistling din are brought.

Nesh, tender. Straught, extended?

The evening comes, and brings the dew along:
The ruddy welkin shineth to the eyne;
Around the ale-stake minstrels sing the song,
Young ivy round the doorpost doth entwine;
    I lay me on the grass; yet, to my will,
Albeit all is fair, there lacketh something still.

So Adam thought when once, in Paradise,
All heaven and earth did homage to his mind;
In woman only man's chief solace lies,
As instruments of joy are those of kind.
    Go, take a wife unto thine arms, and see
Winter and barren hills will have a charm for thee.

When Autumn sere and sunburnt doth appear,
With his gold hand gilding the falling leaf,
Bringing up Winter to fulfil the year,
Bearing upon his back the ripened sheaf,
    When all the hills with woody seed are white,
When lightning-fires and gleams do meet from far the sight;

When the fair apples, red as evening sky,
Do bend the tree unto the fruitful ground,
When juicy pears, and berries of black dye,
Do dance in air, and call the eyes around;
    Then, be the evening foul, or be it fair,
Methinks my heart's delight is mingled with some care.

Angels are wrought to be of neither kind,
Angels alone from hot desire are free;
There is a somewhat ever in the mind,
That, without woman, cannot stilléd be;
    No saint in cell but having blood and tere
Doth find the spright to joy in sight of woman fair.

Kind, *nature*. Tere, *muscle*.

ANONYMOUS

(18TH CENTURY)

The Vicar of Bray

In good King Charles's golden days,
When loyalty no harm meant;
A furious High-Church man was I,
And so I got preferment.
Unto my flock I daily preached
Kings are by God appointed,
And damned are those who dare resist
Or touch the Lord's anointed.
   And this is law, I will maintain
   Unto my dying day, Sir,
   That whatsoever king shall reign,
   I will be Vicar of Bray, Sir.

When royal James possessed the crown,
And Popery came in fashion;
The penal laws I hooted down,
And read the Declaration:
The Church of Rome, I found, would fit
Full well my constitution,
And I had been a Jesuit
But for the Revolution.
   And this is law, I will maintain
   Unto my dying day, Sir,
   That whatsoever king shall reign,
   I will be Vicar of Bray, Sir.

When William our deliverer came,
To heal the nation's grievance,
I turned the Cat in Pan again,
And swore to him allegiance:
Old principles I did revoke,
Set conscience at a distance,
Passive obedience is a joke,
A jest is non-resistance.
   And this is law, I will maintain,
   Unto my dying day, Sir,
   That whatsoever king shall reign,
   I will be Vicar of Bray, Sir.

When glorious Anne became our Queen,
The Church of England's glory,
Another face of things was seen,
And I became a Tory:
Occasional-Conformists base
I damned, and moderation,
And thought the Church in danger was
From such prevarication.
    And this is law, I will maintain,
    Unto my dying day, Sir,
    That whatsoever king shall reign,
    I will be Vicar of Bray, Sir.

When George in pudding-time came o'er,
And mod'rate men looked big, Sir,
My principles I changed once more,
And I became a Whig, Sir:
And thus preferment I procured
From our faith's great Defender,
And almost every day abjured
The Pope and the Pretender.
    And this is law, I will maintain,
    Unto my dying day, Sir,
    That whatsoever king shall reign,
    I will be Vicar of Bray, Sir.

Th' illustrious house of Hanover
And Protestant succession,
To these I lustily will swear
While they can keep possession:
For in my faith and loyalty
I never once will falter,
But George my lawful king shall be
Except the times shall alter.
    And this is law, I will maintain,
    Unto my dying day, Sir,
    That whatsoever king shall reign,
    I will be Vicar of Bray, Sir.

ANONYMOUS

(18TH CENTURY)

Verses Copied from the Window of an Obscure Lodging-House, in the Neighbourhood of London

Stranger! whoe'er thou art, whose restless mind,
Like me within these walls is cribbed, confined;
Learn how each want that heaves our mutual sigh
A woman's soft solicitudes supply.
From her white breast retreat all rude alarms,
Or fly the magic circle of her arms;
While souls exchanged alternate grace acquire,
And passions catch from passion's glorious fire:
What though to deck this roof no arts combine,
Such forms as rival every fair but mine;
No nodding plumes, our humble couch above,
Proclaim each triumph of unbounded love;
No silver lamp with sculptured Cupids gay,
O'er yielding beauty pours its midnight ray;
Yet Fanny's charms could Time's slow flight beguile,
Soothe every care, and make each dungeon smile:
In her, what kings, what saints have wished, is given,
Her heart is empire, and her love is heaven.

WILLIAM BLAKE

(1757-1827)

Song

How sweet I roam'd from field to field
And tasted all the summer's pride,
Till I the Prince of Love beheld
Who in the sunny beams did glide!

He show'd me lilies for my hair,
And blushing roses for my brow;
He led me through his gardens fair
Where all his golden pleasures grow.

With sweet May dews my wings were wet,
And Phoebus fir'd my vocal rage;
He caught me in his silken net,
And shut me in his golden cage.

He loves to sit and hear me sing,
Then, laughing, sports and plays with me;
Then stretches out my golden wing,
And mocks my loss of liberty.

To the Muses

Whether on Ida's shady brow
  Or in the chambers of the East,
The chambers of the sun, that now
  From ancient melody have ceas'd;

Whether in Heav'n ye wander fair,
  Or the green corners of the earth,
Or the blue regions of the air,
  Where the melodious winds have birth;

Whether on crystal rocks ye rove,
  Beneath the bosom of the sea
Wand'ring in many a coral grove,
  Fair Nine, forsaking Poetry!

How have you left the ancient love
  That bards of old enjoy'd in you!
The languid strings do scarcely move!
  The sound is forc'd, the notes are few!

Introduction to Songs of Innocence

Piping down the valleys wild,
Piping songs of pleasant glee,
On a cloud I saw a child,
And he laughing said to me:

"Pipe a song about a Lamb!"
So I piped with merry cheer.
"Piper, pipe that song again;"
So I piped: he wept to hear.

"Drop thy pipe, thy happy pipe;
Sing thy songs of happy cheer:"
So I sang the same again,
While he wept with joy to hear.

"Piper, sit thee down and write
In a book, that all may read."
So he vanish'd from my sight,
And I pluck'd a hollow reed,

And I made a rural pen,
And I stain'd the water clear,
And I wrote my happy songs
Every child may joy to hear.

A Cradle Song

Sweet dreams, form a shade
O'er my lovely infant's head;
Sweet dreams of pleasant streams
By happy, silent, moony beams.

Sweet sleep, with soft down
Weave thy brows and infant crown.
Sweet sleep, Angel mild,
Hover o'er my happy child.

Sweet smiles, in the night
Hover over my delight;
Sweet smiles, mother's smiles,
All the livelong night beguiles.

Sweet moans, dovelike sighs,
Chase not slumber from thy eyes.
Sweet moans, sweeter smiles,
All the dovelike moans beguiles.

Sleep, sleep, happy child,
All creation slept and smil'd;
Sleep, sleep, happy sleep,
While o'er thee thy mother weep.

Sweet babe, in thy face
Holy image I can trace.
Sweet babe, once like thee,
Thy Maker lay and wept for me,

Wept for me, for thee, for all,
When He was an infant small.
Thou His image ever see,
Heavenly face that smiles on thee,

Smiles on thee, on me, on all;
Who became an infant small.
Infant smiles are His own smiles;
Heaven and earth to peace beguiles.

The Divine Image

To Mercy, Pity, Peace, and Love
All pray in their distress;
And to these virtues of delight
Return their thankfulness.

For Mercy, Pity, Peace, and Love
Is God, our Father dear,
And Mercy, Pity, Peace, and Love
Is man, His child and care.

For Mercy has a human heart,
Pity a human face,
And Love, the human form divine,
And Peace, the human dress.

Then every man, of every clime,
That prays in his distress,
Prays to the human form divine,
Love, Mercy, Pity, Peace.

And all must love the human form,
In heathen, Turk, or Jew;
Where Mercy, Love, and Pity dwell
There God is dwelling too.

Infant Joy

"I have no name:
"I am but two days old."
What shall I call thee?
"I happy am,
"Joy is my name."
Sweet joy befall thee!

Pretty joy!
Sweet joy but two days old,
Sweet joy I call thee:
Thou dost smile,
I sing the while,
Sweet joy befall thee!

On Another's Sorrow

Can I see another's woe,
And not be in sorrow too?
Can I see another's grief,
And not seek for kind relief?

Can I see a falling tear,
And not feel my sorrow's share?
Can a father see his child
Weep, nor be with sorrow fill'd?

Can a mother sit and hear
An infant groan an infant fear?
No, no! never can it be!
Never, never can it be!

And can he who smiles on all
Hear the wren with sorrows small,
Hear the small bird's grief and care,
Hear the woes that infants bear,

And not sit beside the nest,
Pouring pity in their breast;
And not sit the cradle near,
Weeping tear on infant's tear;

And not sit both night and day,
Wiping all our tears away?
O, no! never can it be!
Never, never can it be!

He doth give his joy to all;
He becomes an infant small;
He becomes a man of woe;
He doth feel the sorrow too.

Think not thou canst sigh a sigh
And thy maker is not by;
Think not thou canst weep a tear
And thy maker is not near.

O! he gives to us his joy
That our grief he may destroy;
Till our grief is fled and gone
He doth sit by us and moan.

The Clod and the Pebble

"Love seeketh not Itself to please,
"Nor for itself hath any care,
"But for another gives its ease,
"And builds a Heaven in Hell's despair."

So sung a little Clod of Clay
Trodden with the cattle's feet,
But a Pebble of the brook
Warbled out these metres meet:

"Love seeketh only Self to please,
"To bind another to Its delight,
"Joys in another's loss of ease,
"And builds a hell in Heaven's despite."

The Tiger

Tiger! Tiger! burning bright
In the forests of the night,
What immortal hand or eye
Could frame thy fearful symmetry?

In what distant deeps or skies
Burnt the fire of thine eyes?
On what wings dare he aspire?
What the hand dare seize the fire?

And what shoulder, and what art,
Could twist the sinews of thy heart?
And when thy heart began to beat,
What dread hand? and what dread feet?

What the hammer? what the chain?
In what furnace was thy brain?
What the anvil? what dread grasp
Dare its deadly terrors clasp?

When the stars threw down their spears,
And water'd heaven with their tears,
Did he smile his work to see?
Did he who made the Lamb make thee?

Tiger! Tiger! burning bright
In the forests of the night,
What immortal hand or eye,
Dare frame thy fearful symmetry?

The Sick Rose

O Rose, thou art sick!
The invisible worm,
That flies in the night,
In the howling storm,

Has found out thy bed
Of crimson joy;
And his dark secret love
Does thy life destroy.

"Ah! Sun-Flower!..."

Ah! Sun-flower! weary of time,
Who countest the steps of the sun;
Seeking after that sweet golden clime,
Where the traveller's journey is done;

Where the Youth pined away with desire,
And the pale Virgin shrouded in snow,
Arise from their graves, and aspire
Where my Sun-flower wishes to go.

The Garden of Love

I went to the Garden of Love
And I saw what I never had seen:
A Chapel was built in the midst,
Where I used to play on the green.

And the gates of this Chapel were shut,
And "Thou shalt not" writ over the door;
So I turn'd to the Garden of Love
That so many sweet flowers bore;

And I saw it was filled with graves,
And tomb-stones where flowers should be;
And Priests in black gowns were walking their rounds,
And binding with briars my joys and desires.

London

I wander thro' each charter'd street,
Near where the charter'd Thames doth flow,
And mark in every face I meet
Marks of weakness, marks of woe.

In ev'ry cry of every Man,
In ev'ry Infant's cry of fear,
In every voice, in every ban,
The mind-forg'd manacles I hear.

How the Chimney-sweeper's cry
Every black'ning Church appalls;
And the hapless Soldier's sigh
Runs in blood down Palace walls.

But most thro' midnight streets I hear
How the youthful Harlot's curse
Blasts the new born Infant's tear
And blights with plagues the Marriage hearse.

A Little Boy Lost

"Nought loves another as itself,
"Nor venerates another so,
"Nor is it possible to thought
"A greater than itself to know:

"And Father, how can I love you
"Or any of my brothers more?
"I love you like the little bird
"That picks up crumbs around the door."

The Priest sat by and heard the child,
In trembling zeal he seiz'd his hair:
He led him by his little coat,
And all admir'd the Priestly care.

And standing on the altar high,
"Lo! what a fiend is here!" said he,
"One who sets reason up for judge
"Of our most holy Mystery."

The weeping child could not be heard,
The weeping parents wept in vain;
They strip'd him to his little shirt,
And bound him in an iron chain;

And burn'd him in a holy place,
Where many had been burn'd before:
The weeping parents wept in vain.
Are such things done on Albion's shore?

FROM *Poems from MSS.*

1.

Never seek to tell thy love
Love that never told can be;
For the gentle wind does move
Silently, invisibly.

I told my love, I told my love,
I told her all my heart,
Trembling, cold, in ghastly fears—
Ah, she doth depart.

Soon as she was gone from me
A traveller came by
Silently, invisibly—
O, was no deny.

2.

I laid me down upon a bank
Where love lay sleeping.
I heard among the rushes dank
Weeping, Weeping.

3.

> I asked a thief to steal me a peach:
> He turn'd up his eyes.
> I ask'd a lithe lady to lie her down:
> Holy and meek she cries.
>
> As soon as I went an angel came:
> He wink'd at the thief
> And smil'd at the dame,
> And without one word spoke
> Had a peach from the tree,
> And 'twixt earnest and joke
> Enjoy'd the Lady.

4.

> Love to faults is always blind,
> Always is to joy inclin'd,
> Lawless, wing'd, and unconfin'd,
> And breaks all chains from every mind.
>
> Deceit to secresy confin'd,
> Lawful, cautious, and refin'd;
> To every thing but interest blind,
> And forges fetters for the mind.

5.

> Abstinence sows sand all over
> The ruddy limbs and flaming hair,
> But Desire Gratified
> Plants fruits of life and beauty there.

The Question Answer'd

> What is it men in women do require?
> The lineaments of Gratified Desire.
> What is it women do in men require?
> The lineaments of Gratified Desire.

FROM *Auguries of Innocence*

To see a World in a Grain of Sand
And a Heaven in a Wild Flower,
Hold Infinity in the palm of your hand
And Eternity in an hour.

FROM *Visions of the Daughters of Albion*

"Father of Jealousy, be thou accursed from the earth!
Why hast thou taught my Theotormon this accursed thing?
Till beauty fades from off my shoulders, darken'd and cast out,
A solitary shadow wailing on the margin of non-entity.

"I cry: Love! Love! Love! happy happy Love! free as the
        mountain wind!
Can that be Love that drinks another as a sponge drinks water,
That clouds with jealousy his nights, with weeping all the day,
To spin a web of age around him, grey and hoary, dark,
Till his eyes sicken at the fruit that hangs before his sight?
Such is self-love that envies all, a creeping skeleton
With lamplike eyes watching around the frozen marriage bed."

FROM *Vala, or the Four Zoas*

1.

The Cities send to one another saying: "My sons are Mad
With wine of cruelty. Let us plait a scourge, O Sister City."
Children are nourish'd for the Slaughter; once the Child was
        fed
With Milk, but wherefore now are Children fed with blood?

The Horse is of more value than the Man. The Tiger fierce
Laughs at the Human form; the Lion mocks and thirsts for
        blood.
They cry, "O Spider, spread thy web! Enlarge thy bones and,
        fill'd
With marrow, sinews and flesh, Exalt thyself, attain a voice.

"Call to thy dark arm'd hosts; for all the sons of Men muster
    together
To desolate their cities! Man shall be no more! Awake, O
    Hosts!"

2.

O Lord, wilt thou not look upon our sore afflictions
Amongst these flames incessant labouring? our hard masters
    laugh
At all our sorrow. We are made to turn the wheel for water,
To carry the heavy basket on our scorched shoulders, to sift
The sand and ashes, and to mix the clay with tears and re-
    pentance.
The times are now return'd upon us; we have given ourselves
To scorn, and now are scorned by the slaves of our enemies.
Our beauty is cover'd over with clay and ashes, and our backs
Furrow'd with whips, and our flesh bruised with the heavy
    basket.
Forgive us, O thou piteous one whom we have offended!
    forgive
The weak remaining shadow of Vala that returns in sorrow
    to thee.

FROM *Milton*

And did those feet in ancient time
Walk upon England's mountains green?
And was the Holy Lamb of God
On England's pleasant pastures seen?

And did the Countenance Divine
Shine forth upon our clouded hills?
And was Jerusalem builded here
Among these dark Satanic Mills?

Bring me my Bow of burning gold:
Bring me my Arrows of desire:
Bring me my Spear: O clouds unfold!
Bring me my Chariot of fire.

I will not cease from Mental Fight,
Nor shall my Sword sleep in my hand
Till we have built Jerusalem
In England's green and pleasant Land.

FROM *Jerusalem*

The Rhine was red with human blood,
The Danube roll'd a purple tide,
    On the Euphrates Satan stood,
And over Asia stretch'd his pride.

He wither'd up sweet Zion's Hill
From every Nation of the Earth;
    He wither'd up Jerusalem's Gates
And in a dark Land gave her birth.

He wither'd up the Human Form
By laws of sacrifice for sin,
    Till it became a Mortal Worm,
But O! translucent all within.

The Divine Vision still was seen,
Still was the Human Form Divine,
    Weeping in weak and mortal clay,
O Jesus, still the Form was thine.

And thine the Human Face, and thine
The Human Hands and Feet and Breath,
    Entering thro' the Gates of Birth
And passing thro' the Gates of Death.

And O thou Lamb of God, whom I
Slew in my dark self-righteous pride,
    Art thou return'd to Albion's Land?
And is Jerusalem thy Bride?

Come to my arms and never more
Depart but dwell for ever here:
    Create my Spirit to thy Love:
Subdue my Spectre to thy Fear.

Spectre of Albion! warlike Fiend!
In clouds of blood and ruin roll'd,
I here reclaim thee as my own,
My Selfhood! Satan! arm'd in gold.

Is this thy soft Family-Love,
Thy cruel Patriarchal pride,
Planting thy Family alone,
Destroying all the World beside?

A man's worst enemies are those
Of his own house and family;
And he who makes his law a curse,
By his own law shall surely die.

In my Exchanges every Land
Shall walk, and mine in every Land,
Mutual shall build Jerusalem,
Both heart in heart and hand in hand.

To the Accuser Who Is the God of This World

Truly, my Satan, thou art but a Dunce,
And dost not know the Garment from the Man.
Every Harlot was a Virgin once,
Nor canst thou ever change Kate into Nan.

Tho' thou art Worship'd by the Names Divine
Of Jesus and Jehovah, thou art still
The Son of Morn in weary Night's decline,
The lost Traveller's Dream under the Hill.

ROBERT BURNS

(1759–1796)

A Poet's Welcome to His Love-Begotten Daughter

Thou's welcome, wean; mishanter fa' me,
If thoughts o' thee, or yet thy mammie,
Shall ever daunton me or awe me,
  My sweet wee lady,
Or if I blush when thou shalt ca' me
  Tyta or daddie.

Tho' now they ca' me fornicator,
An' tease my name wi' countra clatter,
The mair they talk, I'm kend the better,
  E'en let them clash;
An auld wife's tongue's a feckless matter
  To gie ane fash.

Welcome! my bonie, sweet, wee dochter,
Tho' ye come here a wee unsought for,
And tho' your comin' I hae fought for,
  Baith kirk and queir;
Yet, by my faith, ye're no unwrought for,
  That I shall swear!

Sweet fruit o' monie a merry dint,
My funny toil is no a' tint,
Tho' thou cam to the warl' asklent,
  Which fools may scoff at;
In my last plack thy part's be in't
  The better ha'f o't.

Tho' I should be the waur bestead,
Thou's be as braw and bienly clad,
And thy young years as nicely bred
  Wi' education,
As onie brat o' wedlock's bed,
  In a' thy station.

Mishanter, *mishap*. Clash, *gossip*. Fash, *trouble*. Tint, *lost*. Plack, *a coin*.
Bienly, *comfortably*.

Wee image o' my bonie Betty,
As fatherly I kiss and daut thee,
As dear and near my heart I set thee
  Wi' as gude will
As a' the priests had seen me get thee
  That's out o' hell.

Lord grant that thou may aye inherit
Thy mither's person, grace, an' merit,
An' thy poor, worthless daddy's spirit,
  Without his failins,
'Twill please me more to see thee heir it,
  Than stockit mailens.

For if thou be what I wad hae thee,
And tak the counsel I shall gie thee,
I'll never rue my trouble wi' thee—
  The cost nor shame o't,
But be a loving father to thee,
  And brag the name o't.

Holy Willie's Prayer

And send the godly in a pet to pray.—POPE

O Thou, that in the heavens dost dwell,
Wha, as it pleases best Thysel',
Sends ane to heaven an ten to hell,
  A' for Thy glory,
And no for onie guid or ill
  They've done afore Thee!

I bless and praise Thy matchless might,
When thousands Thou hast left in night,
That I am here afore Thy sight,
  For gifts an' grace
A burning and a shining light
  To a' this place.

Daut, *pet*. Mailens, *farms*.

What was I, or my generation,
That I should get sic exaltation,
I wha deserv'd most just damnation
      For broken laws,
Sax thousand years ere my creation,
      Thro' Adam's cause.

When from my mither's womb I fell,
Thou might hae plung'd me deep in hell,
To gnash my gooms, and weep and wail,
      In burnin lakes,
Where damnéd devils roar and yell,
      Chain'd to their stakes.

Yet I am here a chosen sample,
To show Thy grace is great and ample;
I'm here a pillar o' Thy temple,
      Strong as a rock,
A guide, a buckler, and example,
      To a' Thy flock.

O Lord, Thou kens what zeal I bear,
When drinkers drink, an' swearers swear,
An' singing here, an' dancing there,
      Wi' great and sma';
For I am keepit by Thy fear
      Free frae them a'.

But yet, O Lord! confess I must,
At times I'm fash'd wi' fleshly lust:
An' sometimes, too, in warldly trust,
      Vile self gets in;
But Thou remembers we are dust,
      Defil'd wi' sin.

O Lord! yestreen, Thou kens, wi' Meg—
Thy pardon I sincerely beg;
O! may't ne'er be a livin plague
      To my dishonour,
An' I'll ne'er lift a lawless leg
      Again upon her.

Besides, I farther maun allow,
Wi' Leezie's lass, three times I trow—
But Lord, that Friday I was fou,
      When I cam near her;
Or else, Thou kens, Thy servant true
      Wad never steer her.

Maybe Thou lets this fleshly thorn
Buffet Thy servant e'en and morn,
Lest owre proud and high shou'd turn,
      That he's sae gifted:
If sae, Thy han' maun e'en be borne,
      Until Thou lift it.

Lord, bless Thy chosen in this place,
For here Thou has a chosen race:
But God confound their stubborn face
      An' blast their name,
Wha bring Thy elders to disgrace
      An' public shame.

Lord, mind Gaw'n Hamilton's deserts;
He drinks, an' swears, an' plays at cartes,
Yet has sae mony takin arts,
      Wi' great and sma',
Frae God's ain priest the people's hearts
      He steals awa.

An' when we chasten'd him therefor,
Thou kens how he bred sic a splore,
An' set the warld in a roar
      O' laughing at us;—
Curse Thou his basket and his store,
      Kail an' potatoes.

Lord, hear my earnest cry and pray'r,
Against that Presbyt'ry o' Ayr;
Thy strong right hand, Lord, make it bare
      Upo' their heads;
Lord, visit them, an' dinna spare,
      For their misdeeds.

Fou, drunk. Steer, *stir.* Splore, uproar. Kail, *broth.*

O Lord, my God! that glib-tongu'd Aiken,
My vera heart and flesh are quakin,
To think how we stood sweatin, shakin,
    An' p——'d wi' dread,
While he, wi' hingin lip an' snakin,
    Held up his head.

Lord, in Thy day o' vengeance try him,
Lord, visit them wha did employ him,
And pass not in Thy mercy by them,
    Nor hear their pray'r,
But for Thy people's sake destroy them,
    An' dinna spare.

But, Lord, remember me an' mine
Wi' mercies temporal and divine,
That I for grace and gear may shine,
    Excell'd by nane,
And a' the glory shall be Thine,
    Amen, Amen!

To a Louse on Seeing One on a Lady's Bonnet at Church

Ha! whaur ye gaun, ye crowlin ferlie?
Your impudence protects you sairly;
I canna say but ye strunt rarely,
    Owre gauze and lace;
Tho', faith! I fear ye dine but sparely
    On sic a place.

Ye ugly, creepin, blastit wonner,
Detested, shunn'd by saunt an' sinner,
How daur ye set your fit upon her—
    Sae fine a lady?
Gae somewhere else and seek your dinner
    On some poor body.

Snakin, *sneering.* Gear, *money.*

Crowlin ferlie, *crawling wonder.* Strunt, *strut.* Fit, *feet.*

Swith! in some beggar's haffet squattle;
There ye may creep, and sprawl, and sprattle,
Wi' ither kindred, jumping cattle,
          In shoals and nations;
Whaur horn nor bane ne'er daur unsettle
          Your thick plantations.

Now haud you there, ye're out o' sight,
Below the fatt'rels, snug and tight;
Na, faith ye yet; ye'll no be right,
          Till ye've got on it—
The verra tapmost, tow'rin height
          O' Miss's bonnet.

My sooth! right bauld ye set your nose out,
As plump and grey as ony groset:
O for some rank, mercurial rozet,
          Or fell, red smeddum,
I'd gie you sic a hearty dose o't,
          Wad dress your droddum.

I wad na be surpris'd to spy
You on an auld wife's flainen toy;
Or aiblins some bit duddie boy,
          On's wyliecoat;
But Miss's fine Lunardi! fye!
          How daur ye do't?

O Jeany, dinna toss your head,
An' set your beauties a' abread!
Ye little ken what cursed speed
          The blastie's makin:
Thae winks an' finger-ends, I dread,
          Are notice takin.

Haffet, *temple*. Squattle, *sprawl*. Sprattle, *struggle*. Fatt'rels, *trimmings*.
Bauld, *bold*. Groset, *gooseberry*. Rozet, ? . Smeddum, *powder*. Drod-
dum, *breech*. Flainen, *flannel*. Aiblins, *perhaps*. Duddie, *ragged*. Wyliecoat,
vest. Lunardi, *balloon-bonnet*. Abread, *abroad*.

O wad some Power the giftie gie us
To see oursels as ithers see us!
It wad frae mony a blunder free us,
    An' foolish notion:
What airs in dress an' gait wad lea'e us,
    An' ev'n devotion!

Address to the Unco Guid or the Rigidly Righteous

O ye wha are sae guid yoursel',
    Sae pious and sae holy,
Ye've nought to do but mark and tell
    Your neibours' fauts and folly!
Whase life is like a weel-gaun mill,
    Supplied wi' store o' water;
The heapéd happer's ebbing still,
    An' still the clap plays clatter.

Hear me, ye venerable core,
    As counsel for poor mortals
That frequent pass douce Wisdom's door
    For glaikit Folly's portals:
I, for their thoughtless, careless sakes,
    Would here propone defences—
Their donsie tricks, their black mistakes,
    Their failings and mischances.

Ye see your state wi' theirs compared,
    And shudder at the niffer;
But cast a moment's fair regard,
    What makes the mighty differ?
Discount what scant occasion gave,
    That purity ye pride in;
And (what's aft mair than a' the lave)
    Your better art o' hidin.

Happer, hopper. Clap, clapper. Douce, sedate. Glaikit, giddy. Donsie,
vicious. Niffer, exchange. Lave, rest.

Think, when your castigated pulse
    Gies now and then a wallop,
What ragings must his veins convulse,
    That still eternal gallop!
Wi' wind and tide fair i' your tail,
    Right on ye scud your sea-way;
But in the teeth o' baith to sail,
    It makes an unco lee-way.

See Social Life and Glee sit down,
    All joyous and unthinking,
Till quite transmugrified, they're grown
    Debauchery and Drinking:
O would they stay to calculate
    Th' eternal consequences;
Or your more dreaded hell to state,
    Damnation of expenses!

Ye high, exalted, virtuous dames,
    Tied up in godly laces,
Before ye gie poor Frailty names,
    Suppose a change o' cases;
A dear-lov'd lad, convenience snug,
    A treach'rous inclination—
But let me whisper i' your lug,
    Ye're aiblins no temptation.

Then gently scan your brother man,
    Still gentler sister woman;
Tho' they may gang a kennin wrang,
    To step aside is human;
One point must still be greatly dark—
    The moving *Why* they do it;
And just as lamely can ye mark
    How far perhaps they rue it.

Who made the heart, 'tis He alone
    Decidely can try us;
He knows each chord, its various tone,
    Each spring, its various bias:

Lug, ear. Aiblins, perhaps. Kennin, a very little.

Then at the balance let's be mute,
  We never can adjust it;
What's done we partly may compute,
  But know not what's resisted.

Address to a Haggis

Fair fa' your honest, sonsie face,
Great chieftain o' the pudding-race!
Aboon them a' ye take your place,
    Painch, tripe, or thairm:
Weel are ye wordy o' a grace
    As lang's my arm.

The groaning trenchers there ye fill,
Your hurdies like a distant hill,
Your pin wad help to mend a mill
    In time o' need,
While thro' your pores the dews distil
    Like amber bead.

His knife see rustic Labour dight,
An' cut you up wi' ready sleight,
Trenching your gushing entrails bright,
    Like ony ditch;
And then, O what a glorious sight,
    Warm-reekin, rich!

Then, horn for horn, they stretch an strive:
Deil tak the hindmost! on they drive,
Till a' their weel-swall'd kytes belyve,
    Are bent lyke drums;
Then auld Guidman, maist like to rive,
    "Bethankit!" hums.

Sonsie, *jolly*. Painch, *paunch*. Thairm, *gut*. Hurdies, *buttocks*. Weel-swall'd kytes belyve, *well-swollen bellies soon*. Rive, *burst*.

Is there that owre his French *ragout*
Or *olio* that wad staw a sow,
Or fricassee wad mak her spew
      Wi' perfect sconner,
Looks down wi' sneering, scornfu' view
      On sic a dinner?

Poor devil! see him owre his trash,
As feckless as a wither'd rash,
His spindle shank, a guid whip-lash,
      His nieve a nit;
Thro' bloody flood or field to dash,
      O how unfit!

But mark the Rustic, haggis fed,
The trembling earth resounds his tread.
Clap in his walie nieve a blade,
      He'll mak it whissle;
An' legs an' arms, an' heads will send,
      Like taps o' thrissle.

Ye Pow'rs wha mak mankind your care,
And dish them out their bill o' fare,
Auld Scotland wants nae skinking ware
      That jaups in luggies;
But, if ye wish her gratefu' prayer,
      Gie her a haggis!

Tam o' Shanter
(A TALE)

When chapman billies leave the street,
And drouthy neibors neibors meet;
As market days are wearing late,
And folk begin to tak the gate,

Staw, *surfeit*. Sconner, *disgust*. Rash, *rush*. Nieve, *fist*. Nit, *nut*. Walie, *stout*. Taps o' thrissle, *thistle tops*. Skinking, *watery*. Jaups, *splashes*. Luggies, *wooden bowls*.

Chapman billies, *fellow pedlars*. Drouthy, *thirsty*. Gate, *way*.

While we sit bousing at the nappy,
An' getting fou and unco happy,
We think na on the lang Scots miles,
The mosses, waters, slaps and stiles,
That lie between us and our hame,
Where sits our sulky, sullen dame,
Gathering her brows like gathering storm,
Nursing her wrath to keep it warm.

This truth fand honest TAM O' SHANTER,
As he frae Ayr ae night did canter:
(Auld Ayr, wham ne'er a town surpasses,
For honest men and bonie lasses).

O Tam! had'st thou but been sae wise,
As taen thy ain wife Kate's advice!
She tauld thee weel thou was a skellum,
A blethering, blustering, drunken blellum;
That frae November till October,
Ae market-day thou was na sober;
That ilka melder wi' the Miller,
Thou sat as lang as thou had siller;
That ev'ry naig was ca'd a shoe on
The Smith and thee gat roarin fou on;
That at the Lord's house, ev'n on Sunday,
Thou drank wi' Kirkton Jean till Monday;
She prophesied that late or soon,
Thou wad be found, deep drown'd in Doon,
Or catch'd wi' warlocks in the mirk,
By Alloway's auld, haunted kirk.

Ah, gentle dames! it gars me greet,
To think how mony counsels sweet,
How mony lengthen'd, sage advices,
The husband frae the wife despises!

Bousing at the nappy, *drinking ale.* Fou, *drunk.* Slaps, *hedge gaps.* Skellum, *rascal.* Blellum, *babbler.* Melder, *grinding of corn.* Naig, *nag.* Shoe on, *appetiser.* Warlocks, *wizards.* Gars me greet, *makes me cry.*

But to our tale:—Ae market night,
Tam had got planted unco right,
Fast by an ingle, bleezing finely,
Wi' reaming swats that drank divinely;
And at his elbow, Souter Johnie,
His ancient, trusty, drouthy crony:
Tam lo'ed him like a very brither;
They had been fou for weeks thegither.
The night drave on wi' sangs an' clatter;
And aye the ale was growing better:
The Landlady and Tam grew gracious,
Wi' favours secret, sweet and precious:
The Souter tauld his queerest stories;
The Landlord's laugh was ready chorus:
The storm without might rair and rustle,
Tam did na mind the storm a whistle.

Care, mad to see a man sae happy,
E'en drowned himsel among the nappy.
As bees flee hame wi' lades o' treasure,
The minutes wing'd their way wi' pleasure:
Kings may be blest, but Tam was glorious,
O'er a' the ills o' life victorious!

But pleasures are like poppies spread,
You seize the flow'r, its bloom is shed;
Or like the snow falls in the river,
A moment white—then melts for ever;
Or like the Borealis race,
That flit ere you can point their place;
Or like the Rainbow's lovely form
Evanishing amid the storm.—
Nae man can tether Time nor Tide,
The hour approaches Tam maun ride;
That hour, o' night's black arch the key-stane,
That dreary hour he mounts his beast in;
And sic a night he taks the road in,
As ne'er poor sinner was abroad in.

Reaming swats, *frothing ale.* Souter, *cobbler.* Rair, *roar.* Lades, *loads.*

The wind blew as 'twad blawn its last;
The rattling showers rose on the blast;
The speedy gleams the darkness swallow'd;
Loud, deep, and lang the thunder bellow'd:
That night, a child might understand,
The deil had business on his hand.

Weel-mounted on his grey mare Meg,
A better never lifted leg.
Tam skelpit on thro' dub and mire,
Despising wind, and rain, and fire;
Whiles holding fast his gude blue bonnet,
Whiles crooning o'er some auld Scots sonnet,
Whiles glow'rin round wi' prudent cares,
Lest bogles catch him unawares;
Kirk-Alloway was drawing nigh,
Where ghaists and houlets nightly cry.

By this time he was cross the ford,
Where in the snaw the chapman smoor'd;
And past the birks and meikle stane,
Where drunken Charlie brak's neck-bane;
And thro' the whins, and by the cairn,
Where hunters fand the murder'd bairn;
And near the thorn, aboon the well,
Where Mungo's mither hang'd hersel'.
Before him Doon pours all his floods,
The doubling storm roars thro' the woods,
The lightnings flash from pole to pole,
Near and more near the thunders roll,
When, glimmering thro' the groaning trees,
Kirk-Alloway seem'd in a bleeze,
Thro' ilka bore the beams were glancing,
And loud resounded mirth and dancing.

Skelpit, *hurried.* Dub, *puddle.* Bogles, *hobgoblins.* Houlets, *owls.* Smoor'd,
smothered. Birks, *birch trees.* Meikle, *big.* Whins, *gorse.* Bore, *chink.*

Inspiring bold John Barleycorn!
What dangers thou canst make us scorn!
Wi' tipenny, we fear nae evil;
Wi' usquabae, we'll face the devil!
The swats sae ream'd in Tammie's noddle,
Fair play, he car'd na deils a boddle,
But Maggie stood, right sair astonish'd,
Till, by the heel and hand admonish'd,
She ventur'd forward on the light;
And, wow! Tam saw an unco sight!

Warlocks and witches in a dance:
Nae cotillon, brent new frae France,
But hornpipes, jigs, strathspeys, and reels,
Put life and mettle in their heels.
A winnock-bunker in the east,
There sat auld Nick, in shape o' beast;
A tousie tyke, black, grim, and large,
To gie them music was his charge:
He screw'd the pipes, and gart them skirl,
Till roof and rafters a' did dirl.—
Coffins stood round, like open presses,
That shaw's the Dead in their last dresses;
And (by some devilish cantraip sleight)
Each in its cauld hand held a light.
By which heroic Tam was able
To note upon the haly table,
A murderer's banes, in gibbet-airns;
Two span-lang, wee, unchristened bairns;
A thief, new-cutted frae a rape,
Wi' his last gasp his gab did gape;
Five tomahawks, wi' blude red-rusted;
Five scimitars, wi' murder crusted;
A garter which a babe had strangled;
A knife, a father's throat had mangled,
Whom his ain son of life bereft,
The grey hairs yet stack to the heft;
Wi' mair of horrible and awfu',
Which even to name wad be unlawfu'.

Tipenny, *twopenny ale.* Boddle, *twopence Scots.* Winnock-bunker, *window seat.* Tousie tyke, *shaggy dog.* Gart, *made.* Skirl, *squeal.* Dirl, *rattle.* Cantraip, *magic.* Haly table, *altar.*

As Tammie glowr'd, amaz'd and curious,
The mirth and fun grew fast and furious;
The piper loud and louder blew,
The dancers quick and quicker flew,
They reel'd, they set, they cross'd, they cleekit,
Till ilka carlin swat and reekit,
And coost her duddies to the wark,
And linkit at it in her sark!

Now Tam, O Tam! had they been queans,
A' plump and strapping in their teens!
Their sarks, instead of creeshie flainen,
Been snaw-white seventeen-hunder linen!—
Thir breeks o' mine, my only pair,
That aince were plush, o' guid blue hair,
I wad hae gien them off my hurdies,
For ae blink o' the bonie burdies!
But wither'd beldams, auld and droll,
Rigwoodie hags wad spean a foal,
Louping an' flinging on a crummock,
I wonder did na turn thy stomach.

But Tam kent what was what fu' brawlie:
There was ae winsome wench and waulie
That night enlisted in the core,
Lang after ken'd on Carrick shore
(For mony a beast to dead she shot,
And perish'd mony a bonie boat,
And shook baith meikle corn and bear,
And kept the country-side in fear);
Her cutty sark, o' Paisley harn,
That while a lassie she had worn,
In longitude tho' sorely scanty,
It was her best, and she was vauntie.

Cleekit, joined hands. Ilka carlin, each old woman. Reekit, smoked. Coost,
cast. Duddies, clothes. Wark, work. Linkit, tripped. Sark, chemise. Queans,
girls. Creeshie flainen, greasy flannel. Hurdies, buttocks. Blink, glimpse.
Burdies, girls. Rigwoodie, bony. Spean, wean. Louping an' flinging, leaping
and kicking out. Crummock, staff. Brawlie, very well. Waulie, jolly. Bear,
barley. Cutty, short. Harn, coarse cloth. Vauntie, proud.

Ah! little ken'd thy reverend grannie,
That sark she coft for her wee Nannie,
Wi' twa pund Scots ('twas a' her riches),
Wad ever grac'd a dance of witches!

But here my Muse her wing maun cour,
Sic flights are far beyond her power;
To sing how Nannie lap and flang
(A souple jade she was and strang),
And how Tam stood, like ane bewitch'd,
And thought his very een enrich'd:
Even Satan glowr'd, and fidg'd fu' fain,
And hotch'd and blew wi' might and main:
Till first ae caper, syne anither,
Tam tint his reason a' thegither,
And roars out, "Weel done, Cutty-Sark!"
And in an instant all was dark:
And scarcely had he Maggie rallied,
When out the hellish legion sallied.

As bees bizz out wi' angry fyke,
When plundering herds assail their byke ;
As open pussie's mortal foes,
When, pop! she starts before their nose;
As eager runs the market-crowd,
When "Catch the thief!" resounds aloud;
So Maggie runs, the witches follow,
Wi' mony an eldritch skreich and hollo.

Ah, Tam! Ah, Tam! thou'll get thy fairin!
In hell they'll roast thee like a herrin!
In vain thy Kate awaits thy comin!
Kate soon will be a woefu' woman!
Now, do thy speedy utmost, Meg,
And win the key-stane o' the brig;
There, at them thou thy tail may toss,
A running stream they dare na cross,

Coft, bought. Lap and flang, leaped and kicked. Fidg'd, wriggled. Hotch'd,
jerked. Fyke, bustle. Byke, hive. Pussie, hare. Eldritch, unearthly. Fairin,
reward. Brig, bridge.

But ere the key-stane she could make,
The fient a tail she had to shake!
For Nannie, far before the rest,
Hard upon noble Maggie prest,
And flew at Tam wi' furious ettle;
But little wist she Maggie's mettle!
Ae spring brought off her master hale,
But left behind her ain grey tail:
The carlin claught her by the rump,
And left poor Maggie scarce a stump.

Now, wha this tale o' truth shall read,
Ilk man, and mother's son, take heed:
Whene'er to Drink you are inclin'd,
Or Cutty-Sarks rin in your mind,
Think ye may buy the joys o'er dear;
Remember Tam o' Shanter's mare.

The Rigs o' Barley

It was upon a Lammas night,
  When corn rigs are bonie,
Beneath the moon's unclouded light,
  I held awa to Annie;
The time flew by, wi' tentless heed,
  Till, 'tween the late and early,
Wi' sma' persuasion she agreed
  To see me thro' the barley.

Corn rigs, an' barley rigs,
  An' corn rigs are bonie:
I'll ne'er forget that happy night
  Amang the rigs wi' Annie.

Fient a, not a. Ettle, *intent.* Claught, *clutched.*

Rig, *a ridge of land.* Tentless, *careless.*

The sky was blue, the wind was still,
    The moon was shining clearly;
I set her down, wi' right good will,
    Amang the rigs o' barley:
I ken't her heart was a' my ain;
    I lov'd her most sincerely;
I kiss'd her owre and owre again,
    Amang the rigs o' barley.
              Corn rigs, an' barley rigs, etc.

I lock'd her in my fond embrace;
    Her heart was beating rarely:
My blessings on that happy place,
    Amang the rigs o' barley!
But by the moon and stars so bright,
    That shone that hour so clearly!
She aye shall bless that happy night
    Amang the rigs o' barley.
              Corn rigs, an' barley rigs, etc.

I hae been blythe wi' comrades dear;
    I hae been merry drinking;
I hae been joyfu' gath'rin gear;
    I hae been happy thinking;
But a' the pleasures e'er I saw,
    Tho' three times doubl'd fairly,
That happy night was worth them a'
    Amang the rigs o' barley.
              Corn rigs, an' barley rigs, etc.

Green Grow the Rashes

Green grow the rashes, O;
    Green grow the rashes, O;
The sweetest hours that e'er I spend,
    Are spent amang the lasses, O.

Rashes, *rushes.*

There's nought but care on ev'ry han',
    In ev'ry hour that passes, O:
What signifies the life o' man,
    An 'twere na for the lasses, O.
        Green grow, etc.

The war'ly race may riches chase,
    An' riches still may fly them, O;
An' tho' at last they catch them fast,
    Their hearts can ne'er enjoy them, O
        Green grow, etc.

But gie me a cannie hour at e'en,
    My arms about my dearie, O;
An' war'ly cares, an' war'ly men,
    May a' gang tapsalteerie, O!
        Green grow, etc.

For you sae douce, ye sneer at this;
    Ye're nought but senseless asses, O:
The wisest man that warl' e'er saw,
    He dearly lov'd the lasses, O.
        Green grow, etc.

Auld Nature swears, the lovely dears
    Her noblest work she classes, O;
Her prentice han' she try'd on man,
    An' then she made the lasses, O.
        Green grow, etc.

The Birks of Aberfeldy

Bonie lassie, will ye go,
Will ye go, will ye go,
Bonie lassie, will ye go
    To the birks of Aberfeldy!

War'ly, *worldly.* Cannie, *gentle.* Tapsalteerie, *topsy-turvy.* Douce, *sober.*

Birks, *birch trees.*

Now Simmer blinks on flowery braes,
And o'er the crystal streamlets plays;
Come let us spend the lightsome days
    In the birks of Aberfeldy.
        Bonie lassie, etc.

The little birdies blythely sing,
While o'er their heads the hazels hing,
Or lightly flit on wanton wing
    In the birks of Aberfeldy.
        Bonie lassie, etc.

The braes ascend like lofty wa's,
The foamy stream deep-roaring fa's,
O'erhung wi' fragrant spreading shaws—
    The birks o' Aberfeldy.
        Bonie lassie, etc.

The hoary cliffs are crown'd wi' flowers,
White o'er the linns the burnie pours,
And rising, weets wi' misty showers
    The birks o' Aberfeldy.
        Bonie lassie, etc.

Let Fortune's gifts at random flee,
They ne'er shall draw a wish frae me;
Supremely blest wi' love and thee,
    In the birks o' Aberfeldy.
        Bonie lassie, etc.

I'm O'er Young to Marry Yet

I'm o'er young, I'm o'er young,
    I'm o'er young to marry yet;
I'm o'er young, 'twad be a sin
    To tak me frae my mammy yet.

Blinks, beams. Braes, slopes. Shaws, woods. Linns, waterfalls. Burnie, stream.

I am my mammy's ae bairn,
 Wi' unco folk I weary, sir;
And lying in a man's bed,
 I'm fley'd it mak me eerie, sir.
  I'm o'er young, etc.

Hallowmass is come and gane,
 The nights are lang in winter, sir,
And you and I in ae bed,—
 In trowth, I dare na venture, sir.
  I'm o'er young, etc.

Fu' loud an' shill the frosty wind
 Blaws thro' the leafless timmer, sir;
But if ye come this gate again,
 I'll aulder be gin simmer, sir.
  I'm o'er young, etc.

Of A' the Airts the Wind Can Blaw

Of a' the airts the wind can blaw,
 I dearly like the west,
For there the bonie lassie lives,
 The lassie I lo'e best;
There's wild-woods grow, and rivers row,
 And mony a hill between:
But day and night my fancy's flight
 Is ever wi' my Jean.

I see her in the dewy flowers,
 I see her sweet and fair:
I hear her in the tunefu' birds,
 I hear her charm the air:
There's not a bonie flower that springs,
 By fountain, shaw, or green;
There's not a bonie bird that sings,
 But minds me o' my Jean.

Unco, strange. Fley'd, scared. Eerie, frightened. Shill, shrill. Simmer, summer.

Airts, directions. Row, flow. Shaw, wood.

My Bonie Mary

Go, fetch to me a pint o' wine,
  And fill it in a silver tassie;
That I may drink before I go
  A service to my bonie lassie.
The boat rocks at the pier o' Leith;
  Fu' loud the wind blaws frae the Ferry;
The ship rides by the Berwick-law,
  And I maun leave my bonie Mary.

The trumpets sound, the banners fly,
  The glittering spears are rankéd ready;
The shouts o' war are heard afar,
  The battle closes deep and bloody;
It's not the roar o' sea or shore,
  Wad mak me langer wish to tarry,
Nor shouts o' war that's heard afar—
  It's leaving thee, my bonie Mary!

John Anderson, My Jo

John Anderson, my jo, John,
  When we were first acquent,
Your locks were like the raven,
  Your bonie brow was brent;
But now your brow is beld, John,
  Your locks are like the snow;
But blessings on your frosty pow,
  John Anderson, my jo.

John Anderson, my jo, John,
  We clamb the hill thegither;
And mony a cantie day, John,
  We've had wi' ane anither:
Now we maun totter down, John,
  And hand in hand we'll go,
And sleep thegither at the foot,
  John Anderson, my jo.

Tassie, goblet.

Jo, sweetheart. Brent, smooth. Beld, bald. Pow, head. Cantie, merry.

My Love, She's but a Lassie Yet

My love, she's but a lassie yet,
My love, she's but a lassie yet;
We'll let her stand a year or twa,
She'll no be half sae saucy yet.

I rue the day I sought her O!
I rue the day I sought her O!
Wha gets her needs na say he's woo'd,
But he may say he has bought her O.

Come draw a drap o' the best o't yet,
Come draw a drap o' the best o't yet,
Gae seek for pleasure whare you will,
But here I never miss'd it yet.

We're a' dry wi' drinkin o't,
We're a' dry wi' drinkin o't;
The minister kiss'd the fiddler's wife ;
He could na preach for thinkin o't.

Willie Brew'd a Peck o' Maut

O Willie brew'd a peck o' maut,
And Rob and Allen cam to see;
Three blyther hearts, that lee-lang night,
Ye wadna found in Christendie.

We are na fou, we're nae that fou,
But just a drappie in our ee;
The cock may craw, the day may daw,
And aye we'll taste the barley bree.

Here are we met, three merry boys,
Three merry boys I trow are we;
And mony a night we've merry been,
And mony may we hope to be!
We are na fou, etc.

Maut, malt. Fou, drunk. Drappie, drop. Bree, juice. Lift, sky.

It is the moon, I ken her horn,
    That's blinkin' in the lift sae hie;
She shines sae bright to wile us hame,
    But, by my sooth, she'll wait a weel
        We are na fou, etc.

Wha first shall rise to gang awa,
    A cuckold, cowardly loun is he!
Wha first beside his chair shall fa',
    He is the King amang us three.
        We are na fou, etc.

The Banks o' Doon

Ye banks and braes o' bonie Doon,
    How can ye bloom sae fresh and fair?
How can ye chant, ye little birds,
    And I sae weary fu' o' care!
Thou'll break my heart, thou warbling bird,
    That wantons thro' the flowering thorn:
Thou minds me o' departed joys,
    Departed never to return.

Aft hae I rov'd by Bonie Doon,
    To see the rose and woodbine twine:
And ilka bird sang o' its luve,
    And fondly sae did I o' mine.
Wi' lightsome heart I pu'd a rose,
    Fu' sweet upon its thorny tree!
And my fause luver staw my rose,
    But ah! he left the thorn wi' me.

Ae Fond Kiss, and Then We Sever

Ae fond kiss, and then we sever;
Ae fareweel, and then for ever!
Deep in heart-wrung tears I'll pledge thee,
Warring sighs and groans I'll wage thee.

Loun, *fellow.*

Who shall say that Fortune grieves him,
While the star of hope she leaves him?
Me, nae cheerful twinkle lights me;
Dark despair around benights me.

I'll ne'er blame my partial fancy,
Naething could resist my Nancy:
But to see her was to love her;
Love but her, and love for ever.
Had we never lov'd sae kindly,
Had we never lov'd sae blindly,
Never met—or never parted,
We had ne'er been broken-hearted.

Fare-thee-weel, thou first and fairest!
Fare-thee-weel, thou best and dearest!
Thine be ilka joy and treasure,
Peace, Enjoyment, Love and Pleasure.
Ae fond kiss, and then we sever!
Ae fareweel, alas, for ever!
Deep in heart-wrung tears I'll pledge thee,
Warring sighs and groans I'll wage thee.

The Deil's Awa wi' the Exciseman

The deil cam fiddlin thro' the town,
　　And danc'd awa wi' th' Exciseman,
And ilka wife cries, "Auld Mahoun,
　　I wish you luck o' the prize, man."

　　The deil's awa, the deil's awa,
　　　　The deil's awa wi' the Exciseman,
　　He's danced awa, he's danced awa,
　　　　He's danced awa wi' the Exciseman.

We'll mak our maut, and we'll brew our drink,
　　We'll laugh, sing, and rejoice, man,
And mony braw thanks to the meikle black deil,
　　That's danced awa wi' the Exciseman,
　　　　The deil's awa, etc.

There's threesome reels, there's foursome reels.
There's hornpipes and strathspeys, man,
But the ae best dance ere came to the land
Was "The deil's awa wi' th' Exciseman."
The deil's awa, etc.

Highland Mary

Ye banks and braes and streams around
   The castle o' Montgomery!
Green be your woods, and fair your flowers,
   Your waters never drumlie:
There Simmer first unfald her robes,
   And there the langest tarry;
For there I took the last fareweel
   O' my sweet Highland Mary.

How sweetly bloom'd the gay, green birk,
   How rich the hawthorn's blossom,
As underneath their fragrant shade,
   I clasp'd her to my bosom!
The golden hours on angel wings,
   Flew o'er me and my dearie;
For dear to me, as light and life,
   Was my sweet Highland Mary.

Wi' mony a vow, and lock'd embrace,
   Our parting was fu' tender;
And, pledging aft to meet again,
   We tore oursels asunder;
But, O, fell Death's untimely frost,
   That nipt my flower sae early!
Now green's the sod, and cauld's the clay
   That wraps my Highland Mary!

O pale, pale now, those rosy lips,
   I aft hae kiss'd sae fondly!
And clos'd for aye, the sparkling glance
   That dwelt on me sae kindly!

Drumlie, *turbid.*

And mouldering now in silent dust,
That heart that lo'ed me dearly!
But still within my bosom's core
Shall live my Highland Mary.

Whistle an' I'll Come to Ye, My Lad

O whistle an' I'll come to ye, my lad,
O whistle and I'll come to ye, my lad,
Tho' father an' mother an' a' should gae mad,
O whistle an' I'll come to ye, my lad.

But warily tent when ye come to court me,
And come nae unless the back-yett be a-jee;
Syne up the back-stile, and let naebody see,
And come as ye were na comin to me,
And come as ye were na comin to me.
   O whistle an' I'll come, etc.

At kirk, or at market, whene'er ye meet me,
Gang by me as tho' that ye car'd not a flie;
But steal me a blink o' your bonie black e'e,
Yet look as ye were na lookin to me,
Yet look as ye were na lookin to me.
   O whistle an' I'll come, etc.

Aye vow and protest that ye care na for me,
And whiles ye may lightly my beauty a-wee;
But court na anither, tho' jokin ye be,
For fear that she wile your fancy frae me,
For fear that she wile your fancy frae me.
   O whistle an' I'll come, etc.

A Red, Red Rose

O my luve is like a red, red rose,
 That's newly sprung in June:
O my luve is like the melodie,
 That's sweetly play'd in tune.

Tent, take care. Back-yett, back-gate.

H

As fair art thou, my bonie lass,
   So deep in luve am I;
And I will luve thee still, my dear,
   Till a' the seas gang dry.

Till a' the seas gang dry, my dear,
   And the rocks melt wi' the sun;
And I will love thee still, my dear,
   While the sands o' life shall run.

And fare-thee-weel, my only luve!
   And fare-thee-weel a while!
And I will come again, my luve,
   Though it were ten thousand mile.

Charlie, He's My Darling

'Twas on a Monday morning,
   Right early in the year,
That Charlie came to our town,
   The young Chevalier.

     An' Charlie, he's my darling,
     My darling, my darling,
     Charlie, he's my darling,
       The young Chevalier.

As he was walking up the street,
   The city for to view,
O there he spied a bonie lass
   The window looking through.
       An' Charlie, etc.

Sae light's he jumped up the stair,
   And tirl'd at the pin;
And wha sae ready as hersel'
   To let the laddie in.
       An' Charlie, etc.

He sets his Jenny on his knee,
　　All in his Highland dress;
For brawlie wéel he ken'd the way
　　To please a bonie lass.
　　　　　An' Charlie, etc.

It's up yon heathery mountain,
　　An' down yon scroggie glen,
We daur na gang a milking,
　　For Charlie and his men.
　　　　　An' Charlie, etc.

A Man's a Man for A' That

Is there for honest poverty
　　That hings his head, an' a' that;
The coward slave—we pass him by,
　　We dare be poor for a' that!
For a' that, an' a' that,
　　Our toils obscure an' a' that,
The rank is but the guinea's stamp,
　　The man's the gowd for a' that.

What though on hamely fare we dine,
　　Wear hoddin grey, an' a' that?
Gie fools their silks, and knaves their wine,
　　A man's a man for a' that.
For a' that, an' a' that,
　　Their tinsel show an' a' that,
The honest man, tho' e'er sae poor,
　　Is king o' men for a' that.

Ye see yon birkie ca'd a lord,
　　Wha struts, an' stares, an' a' that;
Tho' hundreds worship at his word,
　　He's but a coof for a' that.
For a' that, an' a' that,
　　His ribband, star, an' a' that,
The man o' independent mind
　　He looks an' laughs at a' that.

Birkie, *fellow.* Coof, *fool.*

A prince can mak a belted knight,
   A marquis, duke, an' a' that;
But an honest man's aboon his might,
   Gude faith, he maunna fa' that!
For a' that, an' a' that,
   Their dignities an' a' that,
The pith o' sense, an' pride o' worth,
   Are higher rank than a' that.

Then let us pray that come it may,
   (As come it will for a' that,)
That Sense and Worth, o'er a' the earth,
   Shall bear the gree, an' a' that.
For a' that, an' a' that,
   It's coming yet for a' that,
That man to man, the world o'er,
   Shall brithers be for a' that.

WILLIAM LISLE BOWLES

(1762–1850)

At Dover Cliffs, July 20, 1787

On these white cliffs, that calm above the flood
Uplift their shadowing heads, and, at their feet,
Scarce hear the surge that has for ages beat,
Sure many a lonely wanderer has stood;
And, whilst the lifted murmur met his ear,
And o'er the distant billows the still Eve
Sailed slow, has thought of all his heart must leave
To-morrow; of the friends he loved most dear;
Of social scenes, from which he wept to part;
But if, like me, he knew how fruitless all
The thoughts that would full fain the past recall,
Soon would he quell the risings of his heart,
And brave the wild winds and unhearing tide,
The world his country, and his God his guide.

Fa', deserve. Gree, prize.